BEITRÄGE ZUR
GESCHICHTE DER BIBLISCHEN EXEGESE

Herausgegeben von

OSCAR CULLMANN, BASEL/PARIS · NILS A. DAHL, NEW HAVEN
ERNST KÄSEMANN, TÜBINGEN · HANS-JOACHIM KRAUS, GÖTTINGEN
HEIKO A. OBERMAN, TÜBINGEN · HARALD RIESENFELD, UPPSALA
KARL HERMANN SCHELKLE, TÜBINGEN

26

Independence and Exegesis

The Study of Early Christianity in the Work
of Alfred Loisy (1857–1940), Charles Guignebert (1857–1939)
and Maurice Goguel (1880–1955)

by

ALAN H. JONES

1983

J.C.B. MOHR (PAUL SIEBECK) TÜBINGEN

CIP-Kurztitelaufnahme der Deutschen Bibliothek

Jones, Alan H.:
Independence and exegesis: the study of early christianity in the work of Alfred Loisy
(1857–1940), Charles Guignebert (1857–1939), and Maurice Goguel (1880–1955) /
by Alan H. Jones. – Tübingen: Mohr, 1983.
  (Beiträge zur Geschichte der biblischen Exegese; 26)
  ISBN 3-16-144451-5

NE: GT

© Alan H. Jones / J. C. B. Mohr (Paul Siebeck) Tübingen 1983.
Alle Rechte vorbehalten. Ohne ausdrückliche Genehmigung des Verlags ist es auch nicht
gestattet, das Buch oder Teile daraus auf photomechanischem Wege (Photokopie, Mikro-
kopie) zu vervielfältigen.
Printed in Germany. Offsetdruck: Gulde-Druck GmbH, Tübingen. Einband: Heinrich
Koch, Großbuchbinderei, Tübingen.

CONTENTS

1. THE SETTING

2. LOISY'S WORK ON EARLY CHRISTIANITY 1909–1927

3. GUIGNEBERT'S WORK ON EARLY CHRISTIANITY
1906–1933

INTRODUCTION

This study is intended as a contribution to the history of the interpretation of Christian origins. The application of historico-critical
methods to the early Christian documents occupies a special place in
modern European thought, since the very foundations of Christianity,
as traditionally conceived, were thereby brought into question as
never before. The repercussions upon Christian theology and upon
institutional Christianity were far-reaching, and their shock-waves
may still be felt. The story of interpretation has frequently been
told, but with a concentration upon the German contribution, and
upon the special problem of the historical Jesus. This is understandable: the magnitude, depth and radicality of German scholarship, and
the absolute centrality of the question of Jesus in Christian thought,
justify repeated attempts to assess the debate in those quarters.

But other areas of criticism may rightly claim our attention. If we
turn to nineteenth-century France, we find a religious situation, an
ideological climate and an academic system very different from those
across the Rhine. We find the field of Christian origins dominated by
one name, that of Ernest Renan; unlike many German critics, he had
decisively abdicated his earlier Christian allegiance. We also find, in
the face of the majority Catholic tradition, persistent attempts to
establish the study of the history of religions on independent, non-
confessional lines. It is true that Renan is chiefly remembered for his
Vie de Jésus; but this was only the first of seven volumes on Christian origins. Overall, these created a tradition of independent French-
speaking scholarship which was taken up in various ways by Loisy,
Guignebert and Goguel. Like Renan, each of them considered that
early Christianity was a religious phenomenon to be investigated with
all the resources of history, unaided by theology. They too were
concerned with the problem of Jesus, but two of them (Loisy and
Guignebert) concluded that very little could be known about the
historical person of Jesus, and that the Gospels yielded up information
principally about the early Church.

It is therefore proposed to leave aside for the most part their treatments of the question of Jesus and to concentrate upon their reconstruction of the Christian religion as it arose upon the basis of resurrection faith, and as it developed over the first hundred years or so of its history. We are therefore concerned very largely with questions of New Testament interpretation. Our three selected critics did not of course ascribe any special status to 'the New Testament' as sacred Scripture, although the state of documentation meant that they were largely preoccupied with the canonical literature. But as self-proclaimed historians, they were bound to reject such an ecclesiastical concept as that of the Canon. Indeed, this rejection may be taken as a sign of their 'independence', for the independence they claimed in their work was a consciously held alternative to much that was proposed by ecclesiastical tradition.

It is therefore the theme of 'independence' which provides a guiding thread throughout this study, not however as a fixed position, but as a stance continually to be redefined according to religious and academic circumstances. If the term is understood in this dynamic way, it seems permissible to refer not infrequently to the dialectic between 'independent' and 'confessional'. This is not to imply that the independent critic is a hero merely by virtue of his swimming against the confessional tide. He will indeed be found to have his own prejudices, which are not always justifiable upon strictly objective grounds. But this dialectic undoubtedly corresponds to much in the circumstances and intentions of the critical activity to be investigated below.

Alfred Loisy is the best-known among the three. This is on account of his role in the Modernist crisis within Catholicism. Since much has been written about him in that role, he will here be considered in the thirty years of intensive critical activity which followed his excommunication. Many of his critical positions were both well established and well known before his departure from the Church: indeed, they made that departure inevitable. But in spite of this continuity between the 'abbé Loisy' and the 'professeur Loisy', he himself believed that independent critical work within Catholicism had become a lost cause, and therefore saw himself free to devote his subsequent career to non-confessional researches, which themselves underwent several significant stages of development.

The period of interpretation surveyed below is lengthy: a century spans the statement of Renan's intent in *L'Avenir de la Science* (1847) and Goguel's concluding volume *L'Eglise Primitive* (1947).

But Renan is here treated as a forerunner of the later critics, with no attempt to do full justice to his achievement. Further 'background' considerations belong mainly to the religiously turbulent years c.1890—1910. The bulk of the study takes a significant period of each critic's activity, with a considerable chronological overlap between the three, and finally attempts to estimate the views which they reached at the end of their careers. It will be maintained that together they constituted a distinctive phase of French criticism and that their achievement can only be fully understood against the background of French intellectual and ecclesiastical life.

It would of course have been possible to extend the study still further and to show how the French tradition of disinterested research into Christian origins has been continued by subsequent scholars, for instance by Oscar Cullmann who succeeded Maurice Goguel in his 'secular' posts at the Sorbonne and at the Ecole Pratique des Hautes Etudes. But the continuing story of French independent scholarship is deserving of separate treatment, especially with the emergence of new factors, such as the discoveries at Qumran and Nag Hammadi, the increasing emancipation of Catholic Biblical scholarship and a recognition that a theological appreciation of the early documents need not be in fundamental conflict with the legitimate demands of the historian. Such factors have led to an increased 'scientific' understanding of the deep religious impulses at work in early Christianity, which could only have been welcomed by earlier critics. But any history of exegesis has to be held within bounds and therefore a chronological decision (rather than any ideological judgement) governed the choice of three roughly contemporaneous critics over the stated period. Each of them may well be deserving of separate monograph treatment. But our understanding of them is enhanced when they are seen in relation to each other and against their national, academic and religious background. This procedure may also be seen as corresponding to the significance of the debate on Christian origins within the wider context of European thought.

It remains for me to mention that an important study of Loisy's exegesis appeared at the same time as the presentation of my own thesis. I refer to *Alfred Loisy als Historiker des Urchristentums* by Dr. Peter Klein (Bonn 1977). Dr. Klein surveys the whole of Loisy's historical work on early Christianity, and his study is therefore chronologically wider in scope then my own Chapter II. In particular, it pays close attention to Loisy's larger commentaries on books of the New

Testament, especially the Gospels. I believe that Dr. Klein is right to assert a fundamental unity of purpose running through Loisy's whole academic career, both ecclesiastical and secular, although I would claim that there was a real sense in which he achieved a new 'independence' through his excommunication. Dr. Klein also identifies some of the constant presuppositions which informed Loisy's writing, notably his evolutionary schemes of thought and his quest for synthesis. He underlines correctly the French critic's lifelong preoccupation with the early Christian period. He refers more thoroughly and consistently than I myself have done to Loisy's early debts in exegesis to German Protestant scholarship, though at each turn he rightly rescues Loisy from any charge of slavish imitation. The third part of Dr. Klein's study corresponds most closely to my own work, as it covers Loisy's output from 1911/12 to *La Naissance du christianisme* (1933). His global treatment leads to some glossing over of significant shifts in Loisy's opinions (though he rightly defends the French critic's underlying consistency against the strictures of Sartiaux) and it fails to do justice to some of Loisy's individual contributions to exegesis, notably the commentary on Acts of 1920. But, in general, I am very happy to concur with Dr. Klein's positive assessment of Loisy's achievement (pp.190–3). I remain however convinced that alongside the 'inner logic' which informed that achievement, one must take full account of the specifically French circumstances which formed the counterpoint to Loisy's views as they underwent their own evolution.

ACKNOWLEDGMENTS

In the first place, I wish to express my thanks to my research supervisor, the Reverend Robert Morgan of the University of Oxford, for his careful and patient scrutiny of work in progress; his very exact knowledge of the history of interpretation has saved me from many a blunder. Next, I must thank the authorities of S. Martin's College, Lancaster for granting me study-leave during the academic year 1975—6, which was invaluable for the completion of my researches. I am greatly indebted to conversations in France with the following: in Paris, the late Professor Henri-Irénée Marrou of the Department of the History of Religions at the Sorbonne, and M. Raymond de Boyer de Sainte-Suzanne; in Strasbourg, the late Mgr. Maurice Nédoncelle, Dean of the Catholic Faculty, and M. Emile Goichot of the Institute of French Literature. All were most generous with their advice and encouragement. The staff of the following libraries in Paris were helpful: Bibliothèque Nationale (Département des Manuscrits), the Bibliothèque de l'Histoire des Religions, and the Bibliothèque de la Faculté Protestante. Then, I am extremely grateful to Mme. A. Louis-David of Paris, to the Reverend Dr. A.R. Vidler of Rye, Sussex, and to M. Goichot for allowing me to consult unpublished material in their possession. I would also like to thank Mrs. D.M. Callis for rendering a complicated manuscript into typescript. But my greatest expression of gratitude must go to Professor Marcel Simon, Head of the Institute of the History of Religions in the University of Strasbourg. He encouraged me in the choice of my research area, he allowed me access to the papers of his own teacher Charles Guignebert and he gave me much valuable information about the study of religion in France. His personal kindness and interest have been an unfailing stimulus in my work.

Finally, I feel greatly honoured that Professor Oscar Cullmann and Professor Ernst Käsemann have accepted my work for inclusion in the series which they jointly edit.

ABBREVIATIONS

AmHistR	American Historical Review
AnnEPHE	Annuaire de l'Ecole Pratique des Hautes Etudes
AnnUnivP	Annales de l'Université de Paris
ARW	Archiv für Religionswissenschaft
ASR	Archives de Sociologie des Religions
BLE	Bulletin de Littérature Ecclésiastique
BN n.a.f.	Bibliothèque Nationale: nouvelles acquisitions françaises
ConNT	Coniectanea Neotestamentica
ConstQ	Constructive Quarterly
CQ	Church Quarterly
DACL	Dictionnaire d'Archéologie Chrétienne et de Liturgie
DB (Suppl)	Dictionnaire de la Bible (Supplément)
DHGE	Dictionnaire d'Histoire et de Géographie Ecclésiastiques
DR	Downside Review
DTC	Dictionnaire de Théologie Catholique
EglTh	Eglise et Théologie
EPHE	Ecole Pratique des Hautes Etudes
ERE	Encyclopaedia of Religion and Ethics
ET	English translation
FF	Faith and Freedom
FrHistSt	French Historical Studies
HJ	Hibbert Journal
HTR	Harvard Theological Review
JBL	Journal of Biblical Literature
JEH	Journal of Ecclesiastical History
JPs	Journal de Psychologie
JTS	Journal of Theological Studies
MEFRM	Mélanges de l'Ecole Française de Rome: Moyen Age — Temps Modernes
MémI	A. Loisy, Mémoires Vol. I (1930)
Mém II	A. Loisy, Mémoires Vol. II (1930)
Mém III	A. Loisy, Mémoires Vol. III (1931)

ModCh	*Modern Churchman*
OC	*Oeuvres Complètes*
RScR	*Recherches de Science Religieuse*
RB	*Revue Biblique*
RC	*Revue Critique*
RChr	*Revue Chrétienne*
RCF	*Revue du Clergé Français*
RH	*Revue Historique*
RHD	*Revue d'Histoire Diplomatique*
RHLR	*Revue d'Histoire et de Littérature Religieuses*
RHPR	*Revue d'Histoire et de Philosophie Religieuses*
RHR	*Revue d'Histoire des Religions*
RMI	*Revue Moderniste Internationale*
RMM	*Revue de Métaphysique et de Morale*
RSH	*Revue de Synthèse Historique*
RUnivB	*Revue de l'Université de Bruxelles*
ThB	*Theologische Blätter*
ThR	*Theologische Rundschau*
VerbC	*Verbum Caro*
ZNW	*Zeitschrift für die Neutestamentliche Wissenschaft*

1. THE SETTING

1.1 THE LEGACY OF ERNEST RENAN

1.1.1 The Achievement of Renan

In his youthful programmatic work, *L'Avenir de la Science,* written in 1849 at the age of twenty-six, but not finally published until 1890, Ernest Renan expressed the opinion that the most import-ant work to be written in the nineteenth century would be 'l'histoire critique des origines du christianisme'[1]. He hoped to be able to undertake the task himself[2]. Whether or not he foresaw the storm that would greet the first volume of this enterprise, *La Vie de Jésus* (1863), he did not allow himself to be deflected from his early ambi-tion and over the following twenty years successive volumes appeared, seven in all[3]. Even more was to follow and another ten years elapsed before the completion of *L'Histoire du peuple d'Israël* in five volumes, which Renan saw as providing further understanding of the emergence of Christianity[4]. Thus a period of some forty years was devoted to this major French language contribution to the whole nineteenth century concern to reconstruct historically the beginnings of the European religious tradition.

In Renan's approach to his task, there are two sides to be disting-uished. On the one hand he wished to be analytical. Although in *L'Avenir de la Science* he criticised Auguste Comte for his 'geome-

---

1 *Op. cit.* XV; *Oeuvres Complètes* III p950.
2 A letter to Ste-Beuve in 1860 confirms this intention: 'Une histoire critique des origines du christianisme, faite avec toutes les ressources de l'érudition moderne, en dehors et bien au-dessus de toute intention de polémique comme d'apologétique, a toujours été le rêve que j'ai caressé' . (Quoted in A. Albalat, *La Vie de Jésus d'Ernest Renan* (1933) p26).
3 *Les Apôtres* (1866); *Saint Paul* (1869); *L'Antéchrist* (1873); *Les Evangiles,* (1877); *L'Eglise Chrétienne* (1879); *Marc-Aurèle* (1882). The general title of the work is *Histoire des origines du christianisme,* reprinted in Vols IV and V of the *Oeuvres Complètes* (hereafter abbreviated *OC*).
4 Published 1887–1893 (the last volume posthumously, after Renan's death in 1892); reprinted in *OC* Vol VI.

trical' approach to the history of humanity[5], Renan had his own
scheme for the development of humanity, comprising three phases:
primitive syncretism, the age of analysis and the spiritual reunifi-
cation of mankind[6]. Just as Renan himself had left the Church to
pursue an academic career, so too the nineteenth century had entered upon the age of analysis, heartbroken at giving up cherished
beliefs, but inspired by the possibilities now offered by science for a
new synthesis[7]. Nineteenth century men were workers for the
future and France in particular would go down in history as the
home of analysis[8].

On the other hand, scientific history was to be creative. The new
resources of 'philologie' were to be used to investigate the products
of the human mind[9]. By adopting an 'esprit de finesse'[10], the historian
can re-experience and recreate the thoughts of previous generations,
including those of 'prophets, apostles and founders of religions'.
For Renan, the fascination of the period of Christian origins is that
the state of the documentation demands an almost Godlike intervention on the part of the historian in order to present a coherent
narrative, summoning up all his creative powers[11]. Renan is quite
explicit about this in the Introduction to the first edition of the
Vie de Jésus:

> Dans un tel effort pour fair revivre les hautes âmes du passé, une part de divination et de
> conjecture doit être permise . . . Il faut qu'un sentiment profond embrasse l'ensemble et
> en fasse l'unité. . . Dans les histoires du genre de celle-ci, le grand signe que l'on tient le
> vrai est d'avoir réussi à combiner les textes d'une façon qui constitue un récit logique,
> vraisemblable, où rien ne détonne . . . ce qu'il s'agit de retrouver . . . c'est l'âme de
> l'histoire'[12]

---

5 Ch.VIII; *OC* III pp848—9. The contrast between the 'esprit de géométrie' and the 'esprit
   de finesse' used by Renan in this work goes back, of course, to Pascal; cf. *Pensées et
   Opuscules* ed. Brunschvicg pp317ff.
6 Ch.XVI; *OC* III p968. In his Preface of 1890, the world-weary Renan warns his readers:
   'On y trouve également enraciné un vieux reste de catholicisme, l'idée qu'on reverra
   des âges de foi' (*OC* III p721).
7 Ch.V; *OC* III pp802—3.
8 Ch.XVI; *OC* III p981.
9 Renan had a very wide understanding of 'philologie' which he defines in *L'Avenir
   de la Science* VIII as 'la science des produits de l'esprit humain' (*OC* III p839). For a
   detailed exposition of this understanding v. D.G. Charlton, *Positivist Thought in France
   during the Second Empire 1852—1870* (1959) ch.VI.
10 Cf. above n.5
11 Cf. his remark: 'Il me semble que parfois j'ai réussi à reproduire en moi par la réflexion les
   faits psychologiques qui doivent se poser naïvement dans ces grandes âmes'.(ie. the prophets, apostles and founders of religion) (*op.cit.* V; *OC* III p814).
12 *OC* IV p81.

Renan reiterated this point in Introductions and Prefaces to later volumes of his history[13] and, in presenting the final volume, he remarked that the nineteenth century had made possible the psychological delicacy which this kind of imaginative reconstruction calls for[14].

Renan has often been criticised for the subjective element in his work, for allowing the 'esprit de finesse' to predominate over the task of analysis. It is not difficult to show how personal and political concerns of his day coloured his reconstruction of early Christianity[15]. But his History of the Origins of Christianity nevertheless stands as a major historical achievement and our present very limited purpose is to draw attention to certain features of Renan's presentation which are of interest to those who have attempted to cover the same ground; these comments will not of course do justice to Renan's literary, historical, philosophical and scientific achievements which have been fully evaluated elsewhere[16].

The work was originally planned to be in six volumes, but Renan found towards the end of the series that a seventh was required to do full justice to the close of the period of origins. Following on *La Vie de Jésus, Les Apôtres* covers the early community in Jerusalem, the founding of the Church of Antioch and the first Christian missions (A.D. 33–45). *Saint Paul* follows the outline of the apostle's career as found in Acts and analyses the epistles. *L'Antéchrist* takes the story from Paul's arrival in Rome to the end of the Jewish revolution (A.D. 61–73) and, as Renan dated Revelation under Nero, he included in this volume most of the other New Testament documents, except the Gospels. The composition of the Synoptics is described in *Les Evangiles*, which also covers Jewish Christianity

---

13 *OC* IV pp436–7 (the legendary nature of the documents makes hypotheses indispensable); *OC* V p13 ('les lignes générales' and 'les grands faits résultants' are more important than the details); *OC* V pp380–1 (obscurities require 'des hypothèses ou des divinations hardies ... L'embryogénie est par son essence même la plus intéressante des sciences; c'est par elle qu'on pénètre le secret de la nature').
14 *OC* V p739.
15 For details, v. the very convincing study by H.W. Wardman: *Ernest Renan – A Critical Biography* (1964).
16 For Renan's work as literature v. R.M. Chadbourne, *Ernest Renan* (1968); for his scholarly work v. R. Dussaud, *L'oeuvre scientifique d'Ernest Renan* (1951); for his place in historiography v. E. Wilson, *To the Finland Station* (1940); for his religious ideas, v. J. Pommier, *La Pensée religieuse de Renan* (1925).

and some of the Apostolic Fathers, notably I Clement and the
Ignatian epistles, down to the time of Trajan's death. *L'Eglise Chrétienne*, devoted to the years A.D. 117—160, takes in the other Apostolic Fathers, the Johannine writings, Gnosticism, the formation of
the Canon and Justin Martyr. *Marc-Aurèle* (A.D. 161—180), as well
as describing the life and reign of the Emperor himself, includes
Montanism, events in Lyon and the work of the second-century
apologists.

There are many virtues in this general disposition of the materials.
Not being limited by Protestant over-concentration upon the New
Testament documents, Renan used the canonical writings, including
the stages of their composition and their final canonisation, to
supply a framework, but also wove into his narrative, at what he
considered to be the appropriate dates, the extracanonical literature.
There is a good balance between the inward and exterior aspects of
Christianity: the first three volumes show an increasing amount of
contact between the Church and 'the world' and *L'Antéchrist* is
specifically devoted to this theme. The next two volumes are more
ecclesiastical in emphasis but the final volume moves outward again,
leaving the reader prepared for the triumph of Christianity in the
Roman Empire. This creates the overall impression of growth both
by internal logic and by response to external stimuli.

Certain themes are vigorously pursued throughout the entire work.
Christianity is seen as essentially a Jewish product, whose founder
was Jesus and not, as some might claim, Paul[17]. If, for example,
the historical Jesus had appeared in Greece rather than Palestine,
the Greeks would never have accepted his deep seriousness and his
plain goodness[18]. It has always been the legend of Jesus which has
won converts, not the theology of Paul: *haggada* exercises greater
magnetism than *halakah*[19]. Jesus as a perfect embodiment of the
human spirit must finally triumph over the dangerous paradoxes of
Paul[20].

---

17 *OC* IV pp434—5.
18 *OC* IV p871.
19 *OC* IV p789; V pp94, 156, 540.
20 *OC* IV p1180; cf *OC* IV p1089: 'Paul voit, de nos jours, finir son règne; Jésus, au contraire, est plus vivant que jamais. Ce n'est plus l'Epître aux Romains qui est le résumé
du christianisme, c'est le Discours sur la montagne'. Paul must be classed lower than
Jesus, St. Francis and the author of the *Imitatio Christi*.

The gospel legend was the product of Jewish rather than Hellenistic Christianity[21]. Nevertheless the new religion had to adapt itself to Greco-Roman culture. For this to happen, the dual contribution of Peter and Paul was required[22]; Peter's Jewish Christianity provided a conservative element, a solid basis; Paul's Hellenism represented the onward march of progress and ensured that Christianity did not remain a formalist, ritualist sect, but that it emerged as a universal spiritual religion[23]. The Church of Rome, as a Judaeo-Christian foundation, had a marked ascetic and sacerdotal strain from the start and Peter may be seen as its true representative. As it was taken over by the political and hierarchical spirit of old pagan Rome, it inherited the authoritarian role at first exercised by the Church of Jerusalem, under James. Paul, however, was always waiting to be rediscovered at subsequent times during the history of Christianity, notably by Luther[24].

Renan's views on the future of religion, expressed at the end of *Marc-Aurèle*, help to make explicit certain assumptions running through his account of the early Church. Christianity, he says, is the most striking of all mankind's attempts to realise an ideal of enlightenment and justice; but contemporary orthodox Catholicism and Protestantism are fossilized and one can only hope for an alliance of liberal Protestantism[25], enlightened Judaism and idealist philosophy[26] in order to advance towards pure religion 'in spirit and in truth'. The place of Jesus will always be immense, for he founded Christianity, which remains the riverbed of all religion. The ideals

---

21 *OC* V p85.

22 *OC* IV pp1143ff; 1244.

23 *OC* IV p793. Renan attributes to Paul the main initiative in breaking with Judaism (just as later, his influence was to cause the split between Catholicism and Protestantism) (*OC* IV p1038).

24 *OC* IV pp817–19; for the idea that Rome inherited the harsh, orthodox spirit of Jerusalem, cf Renan's treatment of the Fall of Jerusalem *OC* IV pp1443ff; and his judgement in *OC* V pp800–801: 'Ce que Rome fonda, ce n'est pas le dogme . . . Ce que Rome fit, c'est la discipline, c'est le catholicisme'.

25 Renan had already written, during his treatment of Paul, of the rift within modern Protestantism: 'deux partis opposés, l'un voulant avant tout la conservation des vieux symboles, l'autre capable de gagner au protestantisme un monde d'adhérents nouveaux'. (*OC* IV p920).

26 Cf. the statement in *OC* IV p1089 that, whereas Paul is the father of the subtle theologians, Jesus is the father of the idealists.

expressed by the Kingdom of God concept, the Sermon on the Mount, the devotion of the martyr; the psychological insight which Christianity has acquired through the difficult and dangerous art of spiritual direction; the permanent need of a spiritual society over against the nation and the family — all of these are the contributions of Christianity to mankind[27].

Further insight into Renan's assumptions is to be gained from his frequently reiterated reasons for concluding his story of origins with Marcus Aurelius. In introducing several volumes, he informs the reader of the ultimate goal of the series and already in the Introduction to *Saint Paul* he is using the metaphor of the embryo:

> Une fois le dernier écrit du Nouveau Testament rédigé, une fois l'autorité de l'Eglise constituée et armée d'une sorte de pierre de touche pour discerner l'erreur de la vérité, une fois que les petites confréries démocratiques du premier âge apostolique ont abdiqué leurs pouvoirs entre les mains de l'evêque, le christianisme est complet. L'enfant grandira encore; mais il a tous ses membres; ce n'est plus un embryon; il n'acquerra plus d'organe essentiel.[28]

At the same time the Church has broken away from Judaism; 'elle n'a plus pour sa mère que de l'aversion'. Two volumes later, in the Introduction to *Les Evangiles,* Renan mentions these developments again, adding that Christianity is now widespread and a matter of public debate. He intends to conclude his work c.160 A.D. because what follows belongs to history and is comparatively easy to relate[29]. He thought that the next volume, *L'Eglise Chrétienne*, would be the last, but in writing it, he realised that another would be required in order to cover the Montanist reaction and Marcus Aurelius as the highest non-Christian example of striving after virtue. As further signs of the completeness of Christianity, he gives this list: the new religion has all its sacred books, all its great legends, the germ of all its dogmas, the essential parts of its liturgy[30]. 'L'histoire ecclésiastique va commercer. L'intérêt n'est pas moindre; mais tout se passe en plein jour'[31]. The hypotheses and guesswork de-

---

27 *OC* V pp1147—8. On the question of the 'spiritual society', Renan believed, on the one hand, that true Christianity could only be realised under monastic conditions; but, equally, he saw that all utopian communities were doomed to corruption and failure (cf *OC* IV pp549, 560; *OC* V pp892—4).

28 *OC* IV p751.

29 *OC* V pp12—13.

30 *OC* V p377.

31 *OC* V p381. Cf., however, for Renan's low view of church history as traditionally prac

manded by the period of 'embryogeny' are no longer called for[32]. The same points are repeated in the 'Preface' to *Marc-Aurèle*, although the actual date of the significant shift is now moved forward to the Emperor's death in 180 A.D., which, we are told, marks the end of the Ancient World. The 'Judaeo-Syrian' principle is to triumph over the 'Hellenico-Roman' principle and although another century has to elapse before the triumph is made explicit, the third century A.D. saw the death-throes of classical culture[33].

In retrospect, Renan's judgements may be seen as a combination of sound historical insight and of over-personal speculation. Even if modern scholarship cannot always agree with his assessments about the dating and historicity of the early Christian documents, he gave a much needed impulse in the French-speaking world towards the use of these writings as historical sources. He had a sound grasp of certain early Christian developments, such as the growth of 'Scripture' and the emergence of ecclesiastical structures in the second century; and also a vivid sense of the Ancient World, based upon a wide knowledge of the literature and his own travels in the Near East. He modified the more extreme views of the Tübingen school by allowing an equally important place to both Petrine and Pauline Christianity and by disallowing any serious fundamental rift between them[34]. One must also mention his sociological awareness of early Christianity as a movement to be found among the cosmopolitan artisan class in the great cities of the Roman Empire[35]; he was surely not entirely mistaken in urging the German critics to turn their gaze towards nineteenth century examples of sectarian religion, in order to acquire a more realistic 'feel' of nascent Christianity[36].

---

tised: 'Luc est le fondateur de cette éternelle fiction qu'on appelle l'histoire ecclésiastique, avec sa fadeur, son habitude d'adoucir tous les angles, ses tours niaisement béats. Le dogme à priori d'une Eglise toujours sage, toujours modérée, est la base de son récit.' (*OC* V p299).

32 *OC* V p380.

33 *OC* V p737–8.

34 Cf. *OC* IV p800: that the quarrel between Peter and Paul at Antioch did not provoke a permanent schism is 'le trait le plus admirable de l'histoire des origines du christianisme'; more details in *OC* IV pp922ff.

35 Cf. Renan's judgement on the apostles: 'Les apôtres ressemblaient bien plus à des ouvriers socialistes, répandant leurs idées de cabaret en cabaret, qu'aux missionnaires des temps modernes'. (*OC* IV p784).

36 *OC* IV p1097; Renan considers that F.C. Baur and his school have tried to turn Jesus,

Renan's limitations, on the other hand, have often been rehearsed. Apart from certain conservative aspects of his New Testament scholarship, there is, for example, the pervading aestheticism: purple passages about great men or great cities, his obsession with feminine languor as a permanent element in the appeal of Christianity, his willingness to enter equally into the states of mind of a Nero and a Marcus Aurelius, his over-nuanced judgements reflecting a basic indecision. More serious, however, is his comparative neglect of the doctrinal content of early Christianity. This can of course be explained as a reaction against Catholic theology, or as falling outside the province of the historian; or one can say that Renan was deliberately replacing beliefs with psychology. He does supply summaries of the doctrines contained in the Pauline epistles and in the heretical writings of the second century, but these are sometimes perfunctory and he is particularly weak in the area of Christology[37]. His loose manner of writing might lead one to suppose that the apostles, including Paul and his companions, simply continued to preach Galilean morality rather than a 'kerygma' about the Jesus of history who had become the Christ of faith. It is true that he represents Paul preaching in Pisidian Antioch 'le mystère de Jésus, sa mort et sa résurrection'[38], but a few pages later he sums up Paul's impact with the words 'la belle morale de Paul ravissait les bons Lycaoniens'[39]. It is precisely in the context of the missionary preaching that he makes the claim, already mentioned, that the *haggada* of the Jesus legend rather than the narrow *halakah* of orthodoxy won the hearts of the converts. He admits that in the Pauline churches, the parables of Jesus were not very well known, but he seems to regard them as

---

Peter and Paul into German Protestant theologians. NB his important statement on the Germans in *Souvenirs d'Enfance et de Jeunesse* (1883): 'Dans mes *Origines du Christianisme* (ma) réserve m'a bien guidé; car, dans ce travail, je me suis trouvé en présence d'une école exagérée, celle des protestants de Tubingue, esprits sans tact littéraire et sans mesure, auxquels, par la faute des catholiques, les études sur Jésus et l'âge apostolique se sont presque exclusivement abandonnées. Quand la réaction viendra contre cette école, on trouvera peut-être que ma critique, d'origine catholique et successivement émancipée de la tradition, m'a fait bien voir certaines choses et m'a préservé de plus d'une erreur'. (*OC* II p893).

37 E.g. in a survey of the beliefs and practices of early Christianity in *OC* IV pp891–914, only one page (912) is devoted to beliefs about Christ.

38 *OC* IV p772.

39 *OC* IV p775.

an exception to the rule.

Thus dissatisfaction with Renan's version of the rise of Christianity can be expressed, with some justification, by New Testament and patristic scholars and by historians who feel there is too much 'literature' and not enough solidly reconstructed fact. He may certainly be seen to have failed in his hopes that 'philologie' would act as the key to ancient cultures through the investigation and reinterpretation of religious myths and symbols. But his work remains a great monument of nineteenth century historical writing and, in the French context, a major breakthrough of 'independent' scholarship in the face of the predominant Catholic tradition.

1.1.2 *The Influence of Renan*

Renan's influence upon the subsequent study of early Christianity in France has to be seen against the dual background of intellectual success and ecclesiastical disapproval. As a historian, scholar and man of letters, Renan took his place during his lifetime with the great Frenchmen of the nineteenth century. But for the Catholics he remained a stumbling-block and a notorious apostate, and his study of Christian orgins, in spite of all his denials, could only be seen by them as an onslaught upon the Church. Occasional Catholic voices were raised on his behalf[1], but in general Renan was to remain for many years a target of almost myth-like proportions for Catholic theologians and apologists[2].

On the other hand — and this could only increase the hostility of Catholics — Renan was often championed by Liberal Protestants. His affinities with Liberal Protestants have already been noted above[3] and there were even hopes at one stage that he would himself join

---

1 Cf. the article written upon Renan's death by Mgr. d'Hulst, Rector of the Catholic Institute of Paris (*Le Correspondent* 25 Oct. 1892), in which Renan is praised for having worked independently of German criticism and of having helped to bring the German critics back to a more 'conservative' view of the New Testament documents. For information on the composition of this article v. A. Baudrillart, *Vie de Mgr. d'Hulst* Vol.II (1914) Ch.XXI and A. Loisy, *Mémoires* I pp232—4.

2 E.g. among many, the popular preacher and voluminous apologist Georges Frémont (1852—1912) was quite convinced of Renan's rationalism and scepticism: many references in A. Siegfried, *L'Abbé Frémont* 2 vols (1932); the distinguished Jesuit scholar Léonce de Grandmaison (1868—1927) felt it his duty to return regularly to the refutation of Renan: J. Lebreton, *Le Père Léonce de Grandmaison* (1935) p80.

3 V. also 'Athanase Coquerel Fils et le protestantisme libéral', article in *Le Journal des*

them[4]. Among those who spoke approvingly of Renan were Albert Réville[5], Auguste Sabatier[6], Gabriel Monod[7], and Paul Sabatier[8], and it is through such Liberal Protestants that something of his more positive influence can be traced. Jean Pommier has documented the correspondence which Renan maintained with Eduard Reuss, Albert Réville and others connected with the Strasbourg *Revue de Théologie*[9]. When the State Faculties of Theology were abolished in 1885 and the Catholics were building up their Institutes, it was felt necessary to continue within the State system the intellectual tradition represented by Renan's *Vie de Jésus* and in 1885 the Section des Sciences Religieuses was set up within the Ecole Pratique des Hautes Etudes, with Albert Réville as its first director[11].

Of particular importance for the present study are the statements made by Alfred Loisy about Renan's influence upon Catholic Modernists and upon himself in particular. Loisy claimed that in matters of Biblical criticism and Christian origins, Renan was 'the

---

Débats 23 Sept. 1876, in *OC* VIII pp1136–1144. Renan says that if all French Protestants had moved in a liberal direction early in the nineteenth century they would have recruited thousands of intellectuals. 'Au lieu d'être une chapelle libre, il devenait vraiment une église' (p1141).

4 Cf. J.R. Beard (ed) *The Progress of Religious Thought* (1861), a volume of essays in English translation by French Liberal Protestants, in which A. Réville says of Renan 'it would be going too far to consider E. Renan altogether one of our Church, but he is continually coming near to us. (pii).

5 He was in close correspondence with Renan over the years; v. Pommier's study cited below, n.9

6 His 1897 lecture *Religion and Modern Culture* (ET 1904 p187) mentions the 'science' of Renan as fatally hostile to Catholic tradition.

7 V. *Renan, Taine, Michelet* (1894): 'Aucun cerveau n'a été plus universel, plus compréhensif, que celui de Renan'. (p48).

8 In *L'Orientation religieuse de la France actuelle* (1911) p171, Paul Sabatier speaks of Renan's 'serenity' and 'independence'.

9 In *Renan et Strasbourg* (1926). Renan did not accept all the critical positions of the Strasbourg group e.g. he maintained, against them, the historicity of the Fourth Gospel. But A. Réville was appreciative of successive volumes of the *Histoire des origines du christianisme* (v. letters of 11 mai 1866 and 19 novembre 1879 reproduced by Pommier pp193 and 195), and thanked Renan for influencing him in the direction of comparative religion (letter of 19 mai 1879, reproduced in J. Marty, *Albert Réville* (1912) p136).

11 For details, v. the publications of the Section esp. *Etudes de Critique et d'Histoire* (1889) with a policy statement by A. Réville; *Problèmes et Méthodes d'Histoire des Religions* (1968) with much historical material. Hereafter the Ecole is abbreviated EPHE. The career of A. Réville is considered below, 1.3.

great master of the French modernists'[12]. Loisy attended Renan's classes on the textual criticism of the Hebrew Bible at the Collège de France[13] and when describing those classes at the Renan centenary in 1923, he maintained that Renan represented an independent French tradition in Biblical scholarship going back to Richard Simon[14]. He admitted some philosophical influence by Renan in *L'Evangile et l'Eglise* and when, after his excommunication, he was elected himself to the Collège de France, he saw himself entering that institution under the patronage of Renan[16].

It may be that in these views Loisy was overreacting against Catholic critics who continually accused him of having been led astray by 'the Germans'[17]; he may even have cast himself in the role of a twentieth century Renan, as alleged by Sartiaux, although the evidence for this is not entirely convincing[18]. It is true however that Loisy inherited the ability of Renan to transpose into a French context the results of radical criticism which were still anathema in Catholic France. In order to do so, he forsook Renan's rhetoric and amplitude for a more trenchant and ironic tone, itself suited to the more 'scientific' appearance of Biblical studies at the end of the nineteenth century and also of course intended to contrast with the writings of theologians, apologists and metaphysicians[19].

Renan's metaphysics lingered on in attenuated forms. Liberal Protestants were happy to continue the tradition of nondogmatic religion and of reverence for the historical Jesus. The fusion of

---

12 'Renan a été, en critique biblique et en histoire des origines chrétiennes, le premier maître des modernistes français . . . Ils peuvent se tracer à partir d'Erasme, en passant par Descartes et Richard Simon pour aboutir à Lamennais et à Renan, une généalogie où Luther ne saurait à aucun titre figurer'. (Loisy in *RHLR* 1910 pp584—6).

13 From December 1882; v. *Mém* I p117.

14 'Le Cours de Renan au Collège de France' *JPs* 1923 pp325—330: Renan only consulted the German authorities after looking up the views of Houbigant. Loisy concludes: 'C'est ainsi que Renan a été mon maître en critique biblique'. (p330).

15 V. *Mém* II pp560—1.

16 V. below 2.2.

17 Cf. his remarks in reply to L. de Grandmaison: *Mém* I pp153—5.

18 Cf. allegations of A. Houtin and F. Sartiaux in *Alfred Loisy: Sa Vie — Son Oeuvre* pp183, 289, 298—9.

19 Cf. H.G. Wood, 'Ernest Renan and Alfred Loisy' in *Studies in French Language, Literature and History presented to R.L. Graeme Ritchie* (1949) pp239—247: 'One is tempted to say that Loisy picked up Renan's mantle, but if so, he wore it with a difference'. (p239).

Hegel and Comte which led the early Renan to envisage a transfigured humanity in the future leaves its traces in Loisy's more general writings on religion[20];but the 'religion of humanity' of which Loisy speaks is more moralistic than anything contemplated by either Comte or Renan, with the added ingredient of a diffused mysticism. The rediscovery of the apocalyptic Christ at the end of the nineteenth century and the relocation of 'essential' Christianity in the message about Christ rather than the teaching of Jesus conspired to cancel out Renan's portrait of Jesus whose main influence upon humanity was transmitted through his personal 'charm', both during his lifetime and in the Gospel 'legend'. However, if by 'charm', Renan meant 'charisma' rather than sentimental appeal, it must be noted that the critics whom we shall consider in detail allowed for such a personal influence by Jesus upon the earliest disciples and did not consider that resurrection faith was a *creatio ex nihilo*.

Renan, through his scholarly work in Semitic languages and his history of early Christianity, may be said more than any other man to have brought the Biblical question into prominence in France[21]. He is sometimes blamed for having obscured the more solid critical achievements of the Strasbourg group through his literary brilliance[22]. But their numbers were so small, that it probably needed the volcanic action of Renan to bring the Biblical question before a wider public, even at the risk of hardening Catholic opinion and of supplying fuel to the anticlericals. He is frequently criticised for his ambiguous and basically non-serious attitude towards religion, but it should be recollected that such criticism tends to emanate from confessional writers and circles. For example, J. Boulenger has

---

20 E.g. *La Religion* (1917); *La Morale Humaine* (1923)..

21 Cf. a judgement to this effect in A. Fawkes, *Studies in Modernism* (1913) p52. H.W. Paul in 'In Quest of Kerygma: Catholic Intellectual Life in Nineteenth Century France' *Am Hist R* December 1969 Vol.LXXV pp387—423 argues that Catholic thought was not a stagnant pool of orthodoxy and that 'Catholic scholars, such as Le Hir, Bargès and Crelier . . . more or less in the tradition of (Richard) Simon, more than held their own in the new science of religions. This tradition produced Renan and would produce the great flowering of Catholic scholarship of the Modernist epoch of Loisy and Duchesne' (p420). But this completely overlooks the problems which the Catholic scholar was likely to encounter with ecclesiastical authority in the Biblical field; cf. Duchesne's prudence in steering clear of New Testament exegesis.

22 V. e.g. A. Schweitzer, *The Quest of the Historical Jesus* (*ET* 1910) pp189—190; M. Goguel, 'L'Orientation de la Science du Nouveau Testament' *RHR* XCVI 1927 p318 (discussed below 4.4).

defended Renan against such Catholic opponents as Jacques Maritain and Henri Massis[23]. He reasonably claims that Renan possessed firm critical principles and that in his historical work he deliberately took up more than one point of view, so as to miss nothing and convey a more complete picture[24]. But even if one admits the dilettante aspects of Renan's work, there is no doubt that he helped to create a more favourable climate in France for the serious study of religions outside the usual confessional structures[25]. More especially, this applies to the study of early Christianity, where he was treading almost entirely new ground, for most of his German contemporaries, however radical, retained some ecclesiastical allegiance. He is therefore the indispensable forerunner of the independent critics we are to consider in detail, however much they may have differed from him on matters of history and interpretation; and he therefore fulfilled his stated intention, in the youthful work *L'Avenir de la Science*, of placing the origins of Christianity in the more general framework of the history of religions[27].

1.2 *THE CATHOLIC SECTOR*[1]

The Catholic Church in France at the beginning of the twentieth century had many preoccupations. Under the unexpectedly long

23 In *Renan et ses critiques* (1925).
24 *Op.cit.* p25.
25 Cf. the remarks of Maurice Barrès, quoted in A. Albalat, *La Vie de Jésus d'Ernest Renan* pp126–7: 'Il nous a appris à traiter le problème religieux avec gravité at avec amour . . . Si aujourd'hui vous trouvez chez les incroyants un sentiment de l'Eglise qui va jusqu'à la tendresse, je sais que M. Renan est pour quelque chose dans cette évolution qui aurait paru bien extraordinaire à nos pères.' (Discours à la Sorbonne ler mars 1923).
26 M. Simon in 'Histoire des Religions, Histoire du Christianisme, Histoire de l'Eglise: Réflexions Méthodologiques', *Liber Amicorum* (Bleeker Festschrift 1969) insists upon the important initial impulse supplied by Renan, A. and J. Réville and Loisy towards the non-confessional study of Christianity (p196).
27 Chapter XV of *L'Avenir de la Science*, in which Renan spoke of his projected History of Christian Origins as the most important work of the nineteenth century, is devoted to the establishment of the history of religions upon a firm scientific and philosophical basis.

1 Among general works on French Catholicism during this period may be mentioned: A. Dansette, *Histoire religieuse de la France contemporaine* (2 vols. 1948–1951); J. Brugerette, *Le Prêtre français et la société contemporaine* Vols. 2 and 3 (1935–1938); E. Lecanuet, *La Vie de l'Eglise sous Léon XIII* (1930); A. Mellor, *Histoire de l'anticléricalisme français* (1966); J. McManners, *Church and State in France 1870–1914* (1972); M. Larkin, *Church and State after the Dreyfus Affair — The Separation Issue in France*

pontificate of Leo VIII (1878–1903), internal questions of organisation, theology and ministry interacted with matters of Church and
State. Secularist administrations under the Third Republic repeatedly
placed difficulties in the Church's way, especially by directing mea-
sures against the religious orders and by introducing education laws
to undermine the Catholic sector. Faced with this republican anti-
clericalism, many French Catholics were monarchists, but their hopes
of a Restoration were dashed by Leo's policy during the 1890s of
urging them to rally to the Republic. Many, too, were convinced of
the guilt of Dreyfus, in an Affaire which greatly exacerbated the
ideological gulf splitting the nation. All these events were finally to
reach a head in the Separation of Church and State in 1905.

Internally, there were signs of a Catholic 'revival'. Popular piety
thrived upon pilgrimages[2] and was suitably impressed by vast
edifices[3]. Concern for social problems led to the formation of
Catholic associations[4]. Congresses were held at diocesan and national
level to discuss social and intellectual issues[5]. Catholic newspapers
and journals proliferated, representing many shades of theological
and political opinion[6]. Many attempts were made to improve clergy
education and the setting up of the Catholic Institutes gave a new
impetus to Catholic scholarship[7]. Towards the end of the nineteenth
century, apologists were encouraged by a new sympathy for religion
among intellectuals, some of whom were turning away from positivism and scientism in a search for spiritual values[8]. This initial sym-

---

(1974); G. Fonsegrive, *De Taine à Péguy* (1920); E. Magnin, *Un demi-siècle de pensée catholique* (1937). Much is to be learned from biography and autobiography belonging to the period; see also the literature on Modernism referred to below. Immensely in-structive is the *instrument de travail* produced by a team under the leadership of J.–M. Mayeur: *L'Histoire religieuse de la France 19e–20e siècle; problemes et méthodes* (1975).

2 E.g. Lourdes (1862ff); Paray-le-Monial (1873ff).

3 E.g. Le Sacré-Coeur de Paris (cons. 1891); La Major de Marseille (cons. 1893); Notre-Dame de Fourvière de Lyon (cons. 1896).

4 V. Dansette *op.cit.* ET Vol.II Ch.VII; Lecanuet *op.cit.* Ch.XIII; McManners *op.cit.* Ch.10; A. Vidler, *A Century of Social Catholicism* (1964) Ch.6.

5 V. Lecanuet *op.cit.* Ch.VI and XIII; A. Baudrillart, *Vie de Mgr. d'Hulst*, t.I (1912) Ch.XVII.

6 For surveys of the Catholic press v. Lecanuet *op.cit.* Ch.V; Brugerette *op.cit.* Vol.III Ch.VIII (on the progressive journals); many references in Fonsegrive and Magnin, *op.cit.;* for the Catholic press in a wider context v. G. Baldensperger, *L'Avant-guerre dans la littérature française* (1919) pp34ff.

7 These Institutes were founded, in Paris, Lille, Angers, Lyon and Toulouse, in 1875, after the suppression of the State Faculties of Theology.

8 The most frequently quoted key symptoms of this change of outlook are: Paul Bourget's

pathy was to be followed in the early years of the twentieth century by a 'Catholic revival' in literature and philosophy, which was however deliberately reactionary in politics and traditionalist in doctrine[9].

Some of the more 'progressive' trends towards Catholic reform were judged by the authorities to have gone too far. Catholic liberalism[10] and democracy, as exemplified by the Church in America, was popularised in France by Félix Klein, but such ideas were condemned under the name of 'Americanism' in 1899[11]. The 'Sillon' movement, founded by Marc Sangnier and devoted to the principles of social democracy, was condemned in 1910[12]. But, within Catholicism, the greatest intellectual threats were felt by Rome and by most French bishops to come from Biblical criticism and from philosophy. Various 'progressive' tendencies under these headings were finally lumped together by the Roman authorities under the name of 'Modernism' and condemned in 1907[13].

In fact, Modernism was never the unitary movement which the intervention of the authorities implied; there were many differences of emphasis and even of conviction among those who sought the intellectual reform of Catholicism. No Modernist Congresses were held; some of the main protagonists never even met; ideas were communicated in journals (quite often with the use of pseudonyms) and in private correspondence; and the number of sympathisers can never be estimated, because the official condemnation of Modernism, and the imposition of the anti-Modernist oath upon the clergy effectively

---

novel *Le Disciple* (1889); the founding of *L'Union pour l'Action Morale* by Paul Desjardins in 1892; the article 'Après ma visite au Vatican' by the editor of *La Revue des Deux Mondes*, Ferdinand Brunetière, in 1895, proclaiming the 'bankruptcy of science'.

9 For details v. R. Griffiths, *The Reactionary Revolution* (1966) on the literary aspects; F.C. Copleston, *From Maine de Biran to Sartre* (1975) Ch.XII for the neo-Thomist movement in philosophy.

10 'Libéralisme' in the French context usually refers to political attitudes; but, as pointed out by G. Weill, *Histoire du catholicisme libéral en France 1828–1908* (1909) p258, there was a considerable overlap of aspirations between would-be Catholic reformers in politics and in exegesis.

11 V. A. Houtin, *L'Américanisme* (1904); T.T. McAvoy, *The Great Crisis in American Catholic History 1895–1900* (1957) (reissued as *The Americanist Heresy in Roman Catholic History 1895–1900* (1963)).

12 V. a convenient short recent account in A. Vidler, *A Variety of Catholic Modernists* (1970) Ch.8, with ample bibliographical indications.

13 In the decree *Lamentabili* (4th July) and the Encyclical *Pascendi* (8th September); these were reinforced by the anti-Modernist oath, required of the clergy, in 1910.

repressed the ferment[14]. This is why there is no commonly accepted picture of the movement[15]; only since the pioneering work of Emile Poulat and the change of atmosphere produced by the Second Vatican Council has it become possible to look with some objectivity at the persons, ideas and events involved[16]. At the same time the availability of unpublished papers and correspondence has added to our sources of information and this mass of material, still not all published, will need several decades of evaluation[17].

Although Modernism was an international movement, Poulat rightly sees France as its 'chosen land'. He suggests a sociological distribution of the Frenchmen involved: Loisy as 'personnage éponyme', Duchesne as 'précurseur', Archbishop Mignot as 'modérateur' etc[18]. He also detects three major trends among the would-be reformers: 'progressives' (those like P. Batiffol and M.–J. Lagrange who, in spite of occasional trouble with the authorities, remained within the ecclesiastical system); 'modernists' proper (eg. Loisy and the philosopher Edouard Le Roy whose ideas were bound to bring them into permanent conflict with orthodoxy); and 'rationalists' (eg. J. Turmel and A. Houtin, priests who became strongly anti-Christian)[19]. This

---

14 Brugerette *op.cit.* Vol.III Pt.I Ch.12 attempts to estimate the numerical strength of Modernism in France, but concludes that the task is impossible.

15 A. Houtin, *Histoire du Modernisme Catholique* (1913) is often misleading because Houtin was too close, personally and in time, to what he described; J. Rivière, *Le Modernisme dans l'Eglise* (1929) is informative but orthodox; A. Vidler, *The Modernist Movement in the Roman Church* (1934) was an important first attempt at objectivity.

16 Poulat edited the (hostile) life of Loisy by A. Houtin and F. Sartiaux: *Alfred Loisy, Sa Vie – Son Oeuvre* (1960) and then published his doctoral thesis, *Histoire, dogme et critique dans la crise moderniste* (1962). Each is indispensable for further research. Also immensely useful is A. Vidler, *A Variety of Catholic Modernists* (1970). But the literature on Modernism has reached such vast proportions over recent years, that it would be invidious to quote any further titles at this stage.

17 Cf. comments to this effect by E. Poulat in *Monseigneur Duchesne et son temps* (1975) p373; he refers both to the complex interplay of personalities and to the failure of the characters involved to understand each other at the time. For the correspondence so far published, v. Bibliography, under A.4.

18 *Histoire, dogme et critique* p19.

19 'Panorama internazionale della crisi modernista', *Storia Contemporanea* (1971) No.2 pp673–683. Another typology was suggested at the *soutenance de thèse* for Poulat's doctorate by G. Le Bras, the eminent sociologist: 'destructeurs' (Loisy, Turmel), 'diplomates, conciliateurs' (Hébert, Mignot), 'arrivistes' (unnamed men with clerical ambitions), 'reconstructeurs' (Batiffol) *RH* CCXXX (1963) pp262–267. (But Loisy was not animated by the same destructive motives as Turmel). A further classification offered by Poulat

latter scheme, as Poulat admits, does not satisfactorily place figures like Loisy's associates Duchesne, Henri Bremond and Archbishop Mignot and the philosophers Maurice Blondel and Lucien Laberthonnière. But attempted classifications like these serve to show in the first place the variety and ferment of opinion which went to make up Modernism and, secondly, the enigmatic status of many of the principal characters involved, not to say the 'lesser lights and fellow travellers'[20]. This is notorious in the case of Loisy himself[21] and although the many studies devoted to him in recent years have begun to disperse the mists, other protagonists still await comparable treatment. Only in 1975, for example, have volumes appeared on Duchesne and Bremond which offer fresh light on two men close to Loisy at various stages of his career and upon whom widely differing interpretations have been cast[22]. No satisfactory biography exists of Archbishop Mignot[23]. Pierre Batiffol remains 'opaque' to our gaze[24].

It is usual to subdivide Modernism into the Biblical question, where certain Catholic scholars tried to gain acceptance for the methods and findings of historico-critical analysis within the Church; and philosophical Modernism, where, for the purposes of apologetics, Catholic thinkers adopted notions of evolution and of immanence and found themselves in opposition with official Thomism. Recent writers have stressed one or the other of these[25], or have pointed

---

is according to their choice of favourite spiritual ancestors among eg. Richard Simon, Fénelon, Newman, and Galileo (*Entretiens sur Henri Bremond* (1967) p78).

20 The title of Ch.7 in Vidler, *A Variety of Catholic Modernists.*

21 Cf. the two chapters in Vidler, *op.cit.* on 'The Enigma of Abbé Loisy' and 'The Enigma Resolved?'.

22 *Monseigneur Duchesne et son temps* (Ecole Française de Rome 1975); A. Blanchet, *Henri Bremond 1865–1904* (1975).

23 L. de Lacger, *Monseigneur Mignot* (1933) was an attempt to repudiate the presentation of Mignot in the *Mémoires* of Loisy; for the circumstances of its composition, v. M. Bécamel, '*Mgr. Mignot et Alfred Loisy*' *BLE* 1969 pp267–286.

24 Cf. the remark of E. Poulat in *Monseigneur Duchesne et son temps* p373.

25 Eg. B.M.G. Reardon in 'Newman and the Catholic Modernist Movement' *Church Quarterly* Vol.4 No.1 July 1971 pp50–60: 'Modernism was principally a *critical* movement . . . Philosophy played its part, but what really moved the thinkers was the gulf between traditional views of the Bible and Christian origins and those — substantially beyond question, as it seemed — of modern Protestant scholarship'. L.F. Barmann, *Baron Friedrich von Hügel and the Modernist Crisis in England* (1972) p156: 'The old medieval concept of a world embracing Christendom was very much alive in the closed world of

out, with some justice, that in such a diverse movement, there can be no hard and fast lines and that the main trends could cut across the Biblical and philosophical areas[26]. Certainly, in France, the two areas cannot be kept entirely separate. Loisy, the Biblical scholar, produced a work of apologetics, *L'Evangile et L'Eglise* (1902) which became a modernist manifesto. Philosophers discussed Biblical questions: Maurice Blondel in *Histoire et dogme* (1903), Lucien Laberthonnière in *Le Réalisme chrétien et l'idéalisme grec* (1904) and Edouard Le Roy in *Dogme et critique* (1905) each touched upon questions of Biblical interpretation[27]. Nevertheless, there is a profound difference of spirit between Loisy and his philosophical contemporaries: the latter simply did not possess Loisy's expertise in the Biblical languages and his familiarity with Protestant Biblical scholarship; while Loisy was averse, not only to scholastic theology but also to philosophical speculation without a historical basis. The correspondence between Loisy and Blondel, which culminated in the publication of the latter's *Histoire et dogme*, further brings out this incompatibility[28]. It is therefore possible to consider 'the Biblical question' in France separately from the accompanying philosophical debate, while recognising that the critical examination of, for example, Genesis and the Gospels was bound to raise questions, theological as well as historical.

The story of the Biblical question in France was told with humour

---

Roman theology and ecclesiastical and clerical life . . . an acceptance of a 'Copernican revolution' was basically what the Modernist crisis was all about'.

26 Cf. E. Poulat, 'Critique historique et théologie dans la crise moderniste' *RScR* 58, 1970, pp535—550 which in the case of Loisy draws attention to his anti-Protestantism, his counter-rationalism and his neo-Catholicism. The same author, speaking at the Cerisy-la-Salle Colloquium on Bremond, distinguished two 'questions-choc' in Modernism: first, that of exegesis, the history of dogma and the Church, leading to philosophical debate; and second 'le procès de l'intelligence' i.e. anti-intellectualism with a stress upon religious experience, especially mysticism: v. *Entretiens sur Henri Bremond* (1967) p215.

27 It should not be thought that these three philosophers formed a recognisable 'school' except in their attempts to offer alternatives to Thomism. Blondel (1861—1949) came to be a vigorous opponent of Modernism; Le Roy (1870—1954), another layman, remained a pragmatist and evolutionist (although respectfully submitting to ecclesiastical condemnation); Père Laberthonnière (1860—1932) was silenced in 1913, but exercised a wide personal influence; many of his writings were published posthumously.

28 For texts and discussion v. Loisy, *Mém* II (1931) pp228—231; R.Marlé, *Au coeur de la crise moderniste* (1960) Ch.III; Poulat, *Histoire dogme et critique* (1962) Sixième Partie, I; H. Bernard-Maitre, 'Un Episode significatif du modernisme' *RScR* 57, 1969, pp49—64.

and asperity by Albert Houtin in his two volumes[29]. These must however, be used with caution, as he was closely involved with the persons and events described and brought to his task an increasingly rationalist outlook[30]. It is not necessary to summarise the story here, if only because there were so few Catholic Biblical scholars of distinction in the latter part of the nineteenth century[31]. Antipathy towards Renan had made Catholics extremely cautious; discussions about Biblical inspiration, or about the problems of creation and Christology thrown up by the critical study of Genesis and the Gospels, were mostly conducted in very general, scholastic, terms[32]. Loisy was warned by his mentor and colleague at the Institut Catholique, Louis Duchesne, to steer clear of the historical criticism of the New Testament[33]; Duchesne as an early Church historian, always himself tried to avoid matters of scriptural exegesis. But as Loisy's *Mémoires* amply illustrate, it was the study of the Bible which was the mainspring of his own academic development, before and after his excommunication[34]; he stayed in the Church many years after his private beliefs had become quite heterodox, in order to win a place

---

Briefly, Loisy rejected Blondel's attempt to mediate between the 'extrinsécisme' of the orthodox theologians and the 'historicisme' of the Modernists and claimed that historical work should be practised without any hindrance from theorists. He denied Blondel's contention that the autonomy of history is a doctrine in itself, rather than a method.

29 *La Question biblique chez les catholiques au XIXe siècle* (1902); *La Question biblique au XXe siècle* (1906).

30 Loisy assisted with these volumes, but disagreed with Houtin's idea that certain important questions (e.g. the Resurrection) could be decided by a simple historical 'yes' or 'no'.

31 This judgement is not only based on Loisy's (generally very crushing) verdicts upon his teachers and contemporaries, but upon a Catholic consensus; eg. L. de Grandmaison in *La Vie Catholique dans la France contemporaine* (1918) mentions 1875–1893 as a 'Période d'Eveil', giving the names of Vigouroux, Brucker, Fillion, Crampon, Fouard, Le Camus, Didon (*op.cit.* pp263–8). None of these is likely to figure in a general history of interpretation. For M.–J. Lagrange v. below.

32 One is struck, for instance, in looking at the Biblical articles in the Jesuit journal *Etudes* of the period, by the comparative lack of any reference to the text of the Bible itself. For one aspect of Biblical debate at the time, v. J.T. Burtchaell, *Catholic Theories of Biblical Inspiration since 1810* (1969).

33 Although in 1881 Duchesne had written to Loisy: 'Je vois que vos lectures vous ont conduit assez sur cette voie; n'ayez peur d'y marcher'. (*Mém* I p98), in 1889 he advised against Loisy's acceptance of a post lecturing on the Bible, stressing 'l'impossibilité morale d'une évolution scientifique sur le terrain de la Bible dans l'Eglise romaine'. (*Mém* I p164).

34 'En somme, la Bible a été la cause première et principale de mon évolution intellectuelle; c'est pour l'avoir lue sérieusement que je suis devenu son critique'. (*Mém* I p155).

for the kind of Biblical investigation which had long been current in Protestantism. He first came before the general public in his 'free' lectures at the EPHE on Biblical topics (1901–1904)[35]. Even *L' Evangile et l'Eglise* and its companion volume *Autour d'un petit livre* (1903) may be seen, not only as a defence of Catholicism in the modern world, but also as a justification of his own kind of scholarly activity within Catholicism. They were in any case only 'small red books' in his estimation, not in the same academic category as his serious commentaries on the Gospels written during the same period[36]. Loisy, of course, fully recognised the wider theological debate, but it was Biblical modernism, rather than philosophical modernism which he embodied in his work and ambitions as a Catholic[37].

---

35 'Free' in the sense of Loisy not holding a permanent appointment at EPHE. For details of how he acquired the post, his lecture topics and his resignation, v. *Mém* II Ch.XX and XXXI. Among reactions to these lectures may be cited: that of the rationalist historian A. Aulard, who helped to fix the legend of Loisy's 'smile': 'c'est le sourire d'un homme raisonnable qui exerce sa raison, et qui l'exerce pour le plaisir de l'exercer' (cited in A. Houtin, *La Question Biblique au XXe siècle* (1906) p139); that of the philosopher Paul Desjardins: Loisy's lectures 'furent pendant deux ans, avec ceux de M. Bergson au Collège de France, la plus complète satisfaction que pussent se procurer, à Paris, les amateurs de l'intelligence pure' (*Catholicisme et Critique* (1905) pp27–8); that of Henri Bremond: 'Il n'est aucune de ces conférences dont je ne sois sorti plus croyant, et toute la jeunesse qui était là partageait cette impression' (Letter to von Hügel cited in A. Blanchet, *Henri Bremond 1865–1904* (1975) p164). But Brugerette, *op.cit.* Vol.III p200 says that th crowds were attracted to these lectures by the spectacle of 'un prêtre qui commence à sentir le fagot'.

36 Loisy produced fourteen 'small red books' on general religious topics during his life. In large format were *Le Quatrième Evangile* (1903) and *Les Evangiles Synoptiques* (1907–8).

37 A brief outline of Loisy's early career may be convenient at this point:

1857	Birth of Loisy at Ambrières (Marne).
1874–8	Seminary training at Châlons-sur-Marne.
1878–9	Student at the Institut Catholique, Paris.
1879–81	Ordination and curacies.
1881–4	Further studies at the Institut Catholique, including Hebrew and Assyriology. First teaching duties (Hebrew and O.T.). Theses on Biblical Inspiration and Annals of Sargon.
1885–90	'Loss of faith'. Period of illhealth. Regular lectures on O.T. and Assyriology. Doctoral thesis on O.T. Canon.
1890–93	First publications. Founding of *L'Enseignement Biblique.* Lectures on Bible generally, inc. N.T. Dismissal from Institut Catholique (Dec 1893).
1894–99	Chaplain of Dominican convent at Neuilly. Preparation of works on apologetics. Founding of *RHLR*.

The Biblical question in French Catholicism came to a head in 1893. In January there appeared an article by Loisy's superior at the Institut Catholique, Mgr. d'Hulst, designed to win acceptance for a moderately critical approach[38]; however, it rebounded upon his own head, and he had to explain himself in Rome. At the end of the year appeared the Encyclical *Providentissimus*, discouraging any radical criticism. In between the two, Loisy lost his post at the Institut[39]. This was the beginning of the end for Loisy as a Catholic, although another fifteen years were to elapse before his excommuniction. In the mean time, however, another figure had come upon the Biblical scene, the Dominican M.–J. Lagrange; in the French-speaking Catholic world he was Loisy's only peer in Biblical studies[40]. In 1890 Lagrange had founded the *Ecole Biblique* in Jerusalem, and in 1892 he launched *La Revue Biblique*. In spite of occasional trouble with the authorities, Lagrange remained a faithful son of the Church, and he is generally credited with having introduced, gradually and patiently, more liberal criticism into the Catholic sector and to have been the inspiration behind the important Encyclical on Biblical studies of 1943, *Divino Afflante Spiritu*.

Loisy and Lagrange were never close. Neither was it physical distance alone which separated them (Lagrange spending most of his time in Jerusalem). As a Dominican, Lagrange stood happily within a Thomist tradition which for Loisy represented all that he detested

---

1899–1908 Loisy in private retirement at Bellevue, Garnay and Ceffonds. EPHE lectures (1901–4), mainly on N.T. Excommunication (March 1908).

38 'La Question biblique', *Le Correspondent* 25 January 1893.

39 These events are described in great detail in *Mém* I Ch.VIII–XII; v. also A. Baudrillart, *La Vie de Mgr. d'Hulst* Vol.I (1914), Ch.XV.

40 Albert Lagrange (in religion, Marie-Joseph) 1855–1938, was almost the exact contemporary of Loisy (1857–1940). After a doctorate in law, he undertook Biblical studies in Austria. In his own *Revue Biblique* he published over 200 articles and over 1500 reviews. Among his 30 published volumes were general works, esp. *La Méthode historique* (1903), *Le messianisme chez les Juifs* (1909), *Le sens du christianisme d'après l'exégèse allemande* (1918), *Le Judaïsme avant Jésus-Christ* (1931) and three volumes of an *Introduction à l'étude du Nouveau Testament* (1933–1937); and commentaries on *Judges* (1903), *Mark* (1911), *Romans* (1916), *Galatians* (1918), *Luke* (1921), *Matthew* (1923), *John* (1925). For accounts and assessments of his work v. *L'Oeuvre exégétique et historique du Père Lagrange* (various authors 1935); F.M. Braun, *L'Oeuvre du Père Lagrange* (1943, with bibliography; ET 1963); R. Murphy (ed) *Lagrange and Biblical Renewal* (1966); *Le Père Lagrange au service de la Bible* (1967; his posthumously assembled diaries and memoirs).

in theology[41]. Lagrange therefore wrote on the question of Inspiration and on the use of the historical method in order to reconcile the new scriptural sciences with the Church's orthodoxy[42]. Loisy, however much he guarded his modes of expression, always betrayed his dissatisfaction with orthodox formulations and from the point of view of the theologians, his writings became more and more suspect. The two men respected each other's erudition, but the running battle between them lasted a lifetime. When in 1892 Loisy began his modest review *L'Enseignement Biblique*[43], he made it clear that he was not intending to compete with Lagrange's recently founded *Revue Biblique*. He even contributed some reviews to the *Revue Biblique* but when a study of his own, 'L'Apocalypse synoptique', appeared in that journal in 1896[44], the second part was accompanied by a disclaimer from the editors[45]. Lagrange maintained Catholic orthodoxy in the pages of his *Revue* by exonerating the Biblical writers of any *deliberate* error or falsification and by a rigorous scrutiny of German Protestant criticism[46]; at the same period Loisy was contributing reviews to the secular *Revue Critique* in which he tended to welcome much that was produced by the Protestants and to deal slightingly with Catholic contributions[47]. At the turn of the century, the Jesuits were mounting a general attack on all Biblical critics of progressive tendencies[48] and it was embarrassing for Lagrange to find himself placed in the same category as Loisy. Loisy replied to the Jesuit onslaught under the name of 'Isidore Després'

---

41 Loisy always claimed that the mystical faith of his adolescence was destroyed by 'the theologians', (v. *Mém* I Ch.II) and he never had a kind word for Thomism.

42 V. Burtchaell, *op.cit.* Ch.IV, which summarises articles by Lagrange on Inspiration appearing in the *Revue Biblique* between 1895 and 1900; in 1902, Lagrange published *La Méthode historique*.

43 This consisted mainly of his own lectures delivered at the Institut Catholique.

44 *RB* 1896 pp173—198, 335—359.

45 Batiffol had acted on Lagrange's behalf on securing this study from Loisy, but after the incident of the disclaimer did not wish to have any more to do with Loisy.

46 *An service de la Bible* pp95—98.

47 Loisy began his collaboration with the *Revue Critique* in 1890, which continued uninterrupted until 1927. His industry was untiring: for example, in 1905 he reviewed some 70 titles. For Loisy's boldness, irony and 'campaigns' in these reviews, as seen by a Catholic, v. an unpublished note of L. de Grandmaison reproduced in J. Lebreton, *Le Père Léonce de Grandmaison* (1935) p104.

48 In their journal *Etudes;* for details, v. Loisy *Mém* I pp505—6; Lagrange, *Au service de la Bible* pp92—3, 101—2.

and in the course of his article he mildly criticised both von Hügel and
Lagrange for their work on the Pentateuch[49]. He had forewarned von
Hügel of this and had promised him not to be too severe upon Lagrange. But he cast Lagrange in the role of a mediator between blind
orthodoxy and current fashions in criticism. Lagrange now felt obliged
to reply to this article and to adverse remarks contained in *La Revue
d'Histoire et de Littérature Religieuses,* which Loisy had helped to
found in 1896[50]. He spoke of 'the adventurous and over-affirmative
quality of Loisy's conjectures' and thereafter was to be found among
Loisy's most consistent critics. Five days in quarantine in Alexandria
gave him time to write a twenty-page review of *L'Evangile et l'Eglise*[51].
He was one of a Toulouse trio (with Batiffol and Portalié) who
attacked *Autour d'un petit livre*[52]. Loisy was accused of an implicit
philosophy of 'immanence' and of placing the demands of a
fluctuating criticism above those of ecclesiastical authority. On his
side, Loisy accused Lagrange of not speaking all his mind and of
taking shelter behind his own extreme views as a means of advancing
more moderate opinions and at the same time avoiding ecclesiastical
reprisals[53].

The story of this disagreement could be continued over another
thirty years[54] but these glimpses at the Biblical question in France

---

49 'Opinions catholiques sur l'origine du Pentateuque' *RCF* 15 février 1899; cf. *Mém* I
pp509–511.

50 V. *Au service de la Bible* p112.

51 *RB* 1903 pp292–313; cf. *Au service de la Bible* p120.

52 *BLE* January 1904; Lagrange's contribution, on 'Jésus et la Critique des Evangiles'
was reprinted as an Appendix to the second edition of his *Méthode historique.*

53 No doubt Loisy exaggerated Lagrange's caution, but it is noteworthy that the latter did
not publish any major work on the New Testament until 1911; his 1902 lectures on the
historical method are subtitled 'surtout à propos de l'Ancien Testament'. They were however hotly contested; v. *Au service de la Bible* pp138–146. For the idea that Lagrange
sheltered behind Loisy cf. a letter of Tyrrell to von Hügel of 3 Oct. 1907 (quoted in
French translation in *Lettres de George Tyrrell à Henri Bremond,* ed. A. Louis-David
(1971) pp268–9).

54 NB Loisy's many references to Lagrange in his *Mémoires* (1930–1), which prompted
Lagrange to write *M. Loisy et le modernisme* (1932), in which he concluded that Loisy
did not open up any new critical paths, but merely transposed German ideas into a
French setting (*op.cit.* p237). There is much mutual refutation in their respective com-
mentaries, so much so that the Catholic historian R. Aubert remarks that in the *Etudes
Bibliques* edited by Lagrange and in much other Catholic Biblical scholarship, 'on
étudiait moins la Bible pour elle-même que pour réfuter Wellhausen, Harnack ou Loisy'.
(*La Théologie Catholique au milieu du XXe siècle* (1954) p20).

between 1890 and 1910 will have shown why there was little original work on Christian origins emanating from the Catholic sector. Tight ecclesiastical control discouraged anything but the most conservative estimate of the New Testament documents. What Loisy offered in his *Etudes Bibliques* ([1]1894, [2]1901, [3]1903), his *Etudes Evangéliques* (1902), his two small red books of 1902—3 and in his large commentaries on the Gospels, was so untypical and so unacceptable to his superiors that it cannot really be credited to the Catholic sector at all, even though Loisy was a Catholic priest at the time of writing. To ascribe as he did, much of the Gospel material to the early Church; to deny that the Resurrection could be historically verified; to view early Christology and sacramental practice in evolutionary terms; to see Catholicism as a product of the vicissitudes of history: all of this was bound to incur the series of condemnations which befell Loisy between 1900 and 1908[55].

The phrase 'Christian origins' can however refer, as with its use by Renan, to a period beyond that of the New Testament. Some reference should therefore be made to two Catholic writers who were active at this period, and who, like Lagrange, represent more 'progressive' Catholic tendencies: Louis Duchesne[56] and Pierre Batiffol[57]. Each of them wrote about the early Church, Duchesne, as already

---

55 For a recent convenient account of Loisy's involvement in the Biblical Question during his Catholic period v. B.M.G. Reardon, *Liberalism and Tradition — Aspects of Catholic Thought in Nineteenth-Century France* (1975) Ch.12.

56 Mgr. Louis Duchesne (1843—1922) taught at the Institut Catholique in Paris from 1876—1895; he had to be 'retired' on two separate occasions for his historical treatment of French ecclesiastical legends. The second time, he held a post at EPHE and in 1895 he received the State appointment of Director of the Ecole Française de Rome, a post which he held until his death. The Italian translation of his *Histoire ancienne de l'Eglise* was placed on the Index in 1912; he submitted immediately to the decree. On Duchesne v. H. Leclercq in *DACL* t. IV Pt. 2 col. 2680—2735; P. d'Espezel in *DHGE* fasc. 81 col. 965—984; F. Cabrol, 'Mgr. L. Duchesne, son oeuvre historique' *JTS* 24 (1922—3) pp253—281; and, most importantly, the symposium *Mgr. Duchesne et son temps* (1975), drawing upon much previously unpublished material.

57 Mgr. Pierre Batiffol (1861—1929) a pupil of Duchesne, was from 1898 to 1907 Rector of the Catholic Institute of Toulouse. In spite of his proclaimed orthodoxy and opposition to Loisy, his book *L'Eucharistie* (1905) was placed on the Index in 1907 and local pressure brought about his retirement from the Institute. As a chaplain in Paris, he continued to publish extensively, including an acceptable revision of the condemned book, and he took part in the Malines Conversations of 1921—6. On Batiffol v. J. Rivière, *Monseigneur Batiffol* (1929); P. Fernessole, *Témoins de la pensée catholique* (1940) pp187—281; J. Calvet, *Mémoires* (1967).

noted, avoiding New Testament problems; Batiffol was more prepared to use the New Testament documents as historical evidence.
To survey the whole of their work is beyond the scope of this study,
so a brief account will be given of the works most relevant to our
enquiry, namely Duchesne's *Histoire ancienne de l'Eglise* (3 vols
1906—1910) and Batiffol's *L'Eglise naissante et le catholicisme*
(1909).

As Duchesne explains in his Introduction, his book was intended
to replace a set of lithographed lecture notes, dating from his time at
the Institut Catholique nearly thirty years before [58]. These notes were
widely circulated and much appreciated among the clergy and in
the seminaries as a Catholic response to Renan[59]. Some Catholic
critics claim that they are superior in quality and freshness to the
more durable volumes of 1906—1910 although this may be due to
their more strongly confessional flavour[60]. But Duchesne, as he himself explained later at the time of the condemnation of the Italian
translation, allowed himself to be persuaded to put them into a more
permanent form[61]. He believed that his 'tâche modeste, d'exposition
et de vulgarisation' was justified by the progress of scientific research[62]. The three volumes covered the period down to Gregory
the Great and a continuation, *L'Eglise au sixième siècle,* was published
posthumously in 1925. Here, of course, we are only concerned with
what Duchesne had to say on the period of origins, in his first
volume. He recognised that he might well have expanded his lecture
notes for a more thorough treatment of the earliest period, but considered that a few extra chapters would not have been the answer:
'Il eût fallu de bien plus grands développements'[63]. His short chapters of lecture length, do not therefore enter into New Testament
problems, but present Christian origins in broad strokes. After a
chapter on the Roman Empire, 'patrie du christianisme', the chapters

---

58 *Op. cit.* pX.

59 Cf. d'Espezel *op.cit.* col.970.

60 Cf. remarks to this effect by Leclercq *op.cit.* col.2707; Cabrol *op.cit.* p265 and a description of the lecture notes in *Mgr. Duchesne et son temps* pp407—8, by M. Maccarrone.

61 'Lettre à un ami à propos de l'histoire ancienne de l'Eglise', *Revue Moderniste Internationale* 1912 pp24—32; 64—76. Further details about this 'Lettre' are in *Mgr. Duchesne
et son temps* pp343, 381, 458ff. Duchesne does not name the person who did most to
persuade him, but according to Loisy, *Mém* I 433, it was von Hügel.

63 'Lettre . . . ' pp26—7.

on the Jerusalem community and on Antioch and Paul's missions, follow the outline of Acts; 'the Christian in the apostolic age' is a very general account of beliefs and practices; 'the origins of the Church of Rome' makes the most of the scarce material; 'the first heresies' surveys the false teaching denounced in the Epistles, Revelation and Ignatius; and chapters follow on 'the episcopate', 'Christianity and the law', 'the end of Jewish Christianity', 'the Christian books', taking us into the second century. It is possible to see this treatment either as deliberately avoiding the key issue of the relationship between Jesus and the early Church[64]; or it can be assessed as a vital piece of Christian apologetics, in establishing a secure historical line between the Christianity of Cyprian and Origen and that of the first disciples of Jesus Christ[65]. Duchesne's declared intention of producing a purely historical work, based only upon evidence, and excluding theological, apologetical, rhetorical and mystical considerations, make such varying interpretations possible[66].

It is perhaps the tone of Duchesne's work which most offended his contemporaries. He was the first 'modern' ecclesiastical historian of note to emerge in the French speaking world. His training in historical method in the French secular system and his further studies under De Rossi in Rome, had determined his style of presentation, which deliberately excluded those confessional elements just noted. This objectivity contrasted with the writing of his predecessors[67], and led to charges of scepticism and insincerity. His brief outline of the first Christian group and its beliefs could, said Loisy, have been countersigned by a rationalist[68]. There was undoubtedly a

---

64 Cf. C. Guignebert in his obituary of Duchesne in *RH* 141 pp307—314: 'il avait . . . bâti un mur autour de la vie de Jésus et l'établissement de l'Eglise, et il ne souffrait pas qu'on en approchât'.(p313).

65 Cf. J. Lebreton, quoted by d'Espezel *op.cit.* col.976: 'Le but est de vérifer les titres du christianisme tel qu'il était connu et pratiqué au temps de S. Cyprien et d'Origène . . . '

66 Cf. 'Lettre . . . ' p27 'C'est l'oeuvre d'un homme de foi, qui entend bien travailler pour l'Eglise et la vérité religieuse dont elle est l'organe, mais qui, dans son travail, s'attache aux seuls procédés d'investigation propres à la discipline historique'.

67 E.g. with Dom Guéranger (1805—1875); this contrast is made by H.—I. Marrou in *Mgr. Duchesne et son temps* p13. Marrou characterises Duchesne's conception of history writing as 'événementielle': if he had written a 'history of Christianity' instead of a 'Church history' he would have said more about the everyday life and worship of the 'people of God' — and more about theology.

68 *Histoire ancienne de l'Eglise* I 13—14; quoted and commented by Loisy in *George Tyrrell et Henri Bremond* (1936) p81.

sceptical streak in Duchesne (probably no more than in most professional historians) and this, coupled with his mordant wit, has led Catholics to excuse his 'worldliness' and accentuate his piety; and others to deny that Duchesne was an orthodox believer at heart[69]. The exact state of Duchesne's personal beliefs may never be known[70], but in *Histoire ancienne de l'Eglise* he tried as in his scholarly activity generally, to reconcile the demands of ecclesiastical loyalty and secular history-writing. In the eyes of the Catholic censors of the time, he learned too far towards the latter by adopting a detached tone instead of the reverential voice customarily expected in such an area of scholarship[71].

Duchesne never wished to leave the Church and submitted 'filially' to the condemnation of his *Histoire*; neither was he a Modernist (even if he is sometimes quoted as a precursor) because he came to believe that the Church was incapable of intellectual reform and because he did not see how those who had forsaken the basic beliefs of the Creed could remain in the Church[72]. Institutionally, he belonged to both Church and State and undoubtedly his professional reputation in the secular sphere, although it enhanced the standing of Catholic scholarship, also helped discredit him in ecclesiastical circles and thus to undermine his influence[73]. This is why his *Histoire*

---

69 Cf. the discussion between Loisy and von Hügel about this, reported in *Mém* III pp422–9; Guignebert, *art.cit.* stressed Duchesne's scepticism.

70 Loisy refused to pronounce finally on Duchesne's faith and Poulat agrees that this is still the case (*Mgr. Duchesne et son temps* p372 for documentation and comment).

71 On the condemnation of *Histoire ancienne de l'Eglise* v. Loisy, *Mém* III pp234–41; and for the essential, M. Maccarrone 'Monsignor Duchesne e la curia romana' in *Mgr. Duchesne et son temps* pp401–494: in spite of Maccarrone's pro-curial apologetic, it now seems clear that the condemnation was engineered by Duchesne's enemies in Rome, incensed at his successful candidature for the Académie Française in the face of the 'official' Catholic candidates.

72 v. Loisy, *Mém* e.g. I 106: 'Quoi qu'on ait pu dire, il n'a jamais été ni apologiste de l'Eglise ni novateur moderniste. Il fut Duchesne, un grand savant qui n'a pas été un grand croyant de l'Eglise ni de l'humanité'; B. Neveu, 'Lettres de Monseigneur Duchesne, Directeur de l'Ecole Française de Rome, à Alfred Loisy et à Friedrich von Hügel', *Mélanges de l'Ecole Française de Rome — Moyen Age, Temps Modernes*, Tome 84 1972, 2, pp283–307, 559–599; E. Poulat, 'Mgr. Duchesne et la crise moderniste', *Mgr. Duchesne et son temps* pp353–373.

73 On these two aspects of Duchesne's career v. the contributions in *Mgr. Duchesne et son temps* of P. Poupard, 'Mgr. Duchesne, professeur à l'Institut Catholique de Paris' (disappointing); and of J.–M Mayeur, 'Mgr. Duchesne et l'Université' (very informative and stimulating: Mayeur points out Duchesne's contribution to the renewal of higher educa-

ancienne de l'Eglise stands out as a distinguished but isolated specimen of Catholic work on early Christianity.

In 1913 Duchesne's pupil Pierre Batiffol wrote an article on 'The
French School of Early Church History' which contrasted the period
around 1880 with that of c.1900[74]. In 1880 it was Duchesne's
'grand and beneficent role' to challenge the intellectual hegemony
of Renan; it was necessary to attack the latter's 'romanticism' with
the weapons of 'empiricism' and Duchesne, following the lead of
Mommsen, made a great contribution to the eclipse of Renan's work.
But Duchesne's historical method reflected in the pages of the *Bulletin Critique* which he edited, 'hardly seemed to escape the reproach
of indifference and naturalism'[75] and in 1900 a more resolutely
theological stance was called for. Between 1880 and 1900, Duchesne's
pupils had separated into a 'left' (Loisy and his colleagues of *RHLR*)
and a 'right' (Batiffol himself and, eg. Tixeront, Vacant, de Grandmaison)[76]. Batiffol admits that in a letter of 1898 Duchesne had
rejected his analysis of the 'left' and the 'right'[77]; but he no doubt
felt by 1913 that the condemnation of Modernism had vindicated
such an analysis (as well as helping to restore his own slightly dented
orthodoxy). To demonstrate his own conception of early Church
history he had in the mean time produced his volume: *L'Eglise
naissante et le catholicisme* (1909)[78].

This work is in great contrast with that of Duchesne. Instead of

---

tion in the Third Republic and raises the question of how far Duchesne was influenced
by the University mentality).

74 In *The Constructive Quarterly* 1913 pp240—259. The article only considers Catholic
scholarship; it should be remembered that, unlike Duchesne, Batiffol spent his whole
academic life in Church institutions.

75 Duchesne's stated policy in the first number of his *Bulletin Critique* was that it should
be 'absolument orthodoxe et inexorablement scientifique': the phrase reflects a separation of faith and history which Batiffol came to regret.

76 Loisy, *Mém* I p243 n.1 mentions a similar description in an article of Batiffol written
in 1922. Loisy comments: 'Prophétie rétrospective, dont nous saisissons l'avantage'.
(c.1890, Batiffol gave no sign of being a 'right-winger').

77 'Why all this talk of left and right? Is it not evident that on the one side the directions of
the Church ought to be respected above everything and that on the other side science is
not made with extra scientific processes? On this we are all agreed'. (Letter of 22 Feb.
1898; *art.cit.* p254). Batiffol does *not* quote a letter he received the same month in
which his former teacher accused him of 'orthodoxie agressive' and of being both an
'accusator fratrum' and a 'pharisien malfaisant': quoted in *Mgr. Duchesne et son temps*
pp368—9.

78 ET *Primitive Catholicism* (1911).

the detached, magisterial survey, we have the deployment of extensive erudition for confessional purposes. The short incisive chapters of Duchesne are replaced by major sections, flanked by introductions and appendices which take up hotly debated critical questions of the day. The volume goes down as far as Cyprian, because according to Batiffol he admirably rounds off the knowledge which we have of the first two hundred and fifty years of Christianity[79].The early period is covered by three chapters. The first, entitled 'Dispersion et chrétienté', shows how the Judaism of the Dispersion provided an environment favourable to the expansion of Christianity; significant subsections are headed: 'Que le christianisme n'est pas un pur mouvement spirituel', 'Que le christianisme n'est pas seulement une fraternité d'amour et d'assistance'. There are similar headings in the second chapter on 'L'Eglise naissante': 'L'apostolat n'est pas un charisme', 'Que l'apostolat est un principe d'unité et d'autorité posé par le Christ en personne', 'Le christianisme n'est pas une "sagesse", mais une catéchèse'. The third chapter draws upon the ecclesiology of the Captivity Epistles, the Didache, the Fourth Gospel, I Clement and the Ignatian epistles to reach the conclusion: 'L'Eglise naissante est catholique'. Excursuses are devoted to Matthew 16, 18—19 in recent scholarship and to an 'Examen des théories protestantes de la formation du catholicisme', with reference to A. Sabatier, Harnack, Sohm, and others. But there are, in any case, many references throughout the text to Protestant scholarship, and the most recent developments were reported and commented in the Introduction to the fifth edition in 1911[80].

Batiffol's standpoint was therefore that of enlightened orthodoxy, and his insistence on the corporate and organisational aspects of early Christianity over against the Liberal Protestants of his day was to win some assent from later Protestant critics[81]. His detailed knowledge of and serious attention to, German and English scholarship, gives his work a 'modern' tone compared with most of his

---

79 Cf. Introduction to the 5th edition (1911) pIX.
80 This Introduction reproduces Harnack's review of Batiffol's first edition, and discusses Harnack's *Kirchenverfassung* (1910) in reply to Sohm. Batiffol possibly saw himself as a French Harnack: he often sought common ground with the German critic, agreeing with him in some matters against Loisy.
81 For the 'consensus' between Catholic and Protestant scholars in this area, v. F.M. Braun, *Aspects nouveaux du problème de l'Eglise* (1941) Ch.3.

Catholic contemproaries[82]. But his quick, wide-ranging mind was
devoted to ecclesiastical rather than purely academic interests and
the apologist often seems to predominate over the historian. He
made no special contribution to Biblical studies and is remembered
as a patristic scholar and early Church historian for whom the
historical method was always to be subservient to the control of the
Church[83].

Batiffol and Lagrange are undoubtedly the two scholars from the
Catholic sector who, although necessarily very cautious in their conclusions, made it possible for critical work on early Christianity to
be carried forward in future generations by Catholic scholars[84].
We have seen how the circumstances of French Catholicism between
1890 and 1910 led to the varying reactions of those who found
themselves at odds with orthodoxy: Loisy broke, slowly and pain-
fully, with the whole Catholic system; Duchesne's skilful diplomacy
hardly ever failed him; Batiffol and Lagrange submitted to ecclesiastical demands more or less willingly, while developing areas of specialism (eg. patristics and archaeology) which were less sensitive than
the direct study of the New Testament and the earliest period of
Christian origins. It is significant that both these critics worked
entirely within confessional structures, whereas Duchesne and Loisy
moved into the State system. Although Duchesne through his
personal eminence maintained his position in both spheres, Loisy
had to give up his successful lectures at EPHE in order to win a few
more years of uneasy existence as a Catholic[85]. So this consideration
takes us back to those matters of Church and State mentioned above:

---

82 In a lengthy Preface to a new edition of *L'Eglise naissante* ... (1971 ppi–lvi), J. Daniélou champions the abiding worth of Batiffol's work: he may now appear dated in some
   of his New Testament work and he may have lacked a theology of the history of dogma
   but his historical case for Catholic continuity remains valid against the views of Modernists and Protestants (including, more recently, W. Bauer).

83 For the formulation and rigid application of this principle at the time of the condemnation of Modernism v. L da Veiga Coutinho, *Tradition et Histoire dans la controverse
   moderniste (1898–1910)* (1954); and for Batiffol's assent to the principle v. the quotations assembled by Fernessole *op.cit.* pp270–278, summarised in the words: 'à la méthode rigoureusement scientifique de l'histoire et de la philologie, il a su joindre le con-
   trôle théologique dont les clartés viennent de plus haut que nos pauvres connaissances
   humaines'. (p273).

84 The two men first met at Issy, the seminary of St.–Sulpice, in 1878 and remained close
   friends throughout their lives.

85 For further details, v. below 1.3.

there could be no fundamental accord between the secular rationalism of the Third Republic and the guardians of Catholic faith and
morality — the hierarchy, the Catholic press, the religious orders and
a traditionalist laity. Just as the philosophers were expected to resist
secular trends and rally to the eternal truths of Thomism, so too a
picture of the early Church was required which would answer that of
Renan and of Protestant critics. But historical research had already
made untenable the static and unitary view favoured by orthodoxy
and this is why the question of Christian origins was at the heart of
the Modernist crisis. More flexible treatments were to become possible
later, but what we have described shows that this was an area where
the confessionalism of the Catholic sector, in spite of all the internal
debates and controversies, was perhaps the most important single
cultural factor affecting academic research. Whatever the tensions
between Church and State, however vociferous the rationalists and
the anticlericals, France could still be considered a Catholic country
and any contributions made by Protestant or independent critics to
the problems of Christian origins were inevitably influenced by this
majority tradition[86].

1.3 *THE PROTESTANT SECTOR*[1]

It might be thought that the minority status of French Protestantism made it comparatively simple to describe the work on early
Christianity undertaken in this sector[2]. But the problems of doing so
are almost as intricate as those encountered in the case of Catholicism. In the first place, religious minorities are not always mono-
chrome and ghetto-like: French Protestants in the nineteenth century

---

86 Jean Guitton, the Catholic lay philosopher, in his memoirs, *Ecrire comme on se souvient*
  (1974) considers that it was not until about 1930 that French Catholicism really took
  cognizance of the fact of secularisation (p205).

1 General works on French Protestantism include: M. Boegner et al., *Protestantisme français* (1945); E.G. Léonard, *Le Protestant français* (1953) (with excellent bibliographies).
  A useful introduction to the nineteenth century background is supplied by G. Weill,
  'Le Protestantisme francais au XIXe siècle', *Revue de Synthese Historique* XXIII (1911)
  pp210—239. V. also the many indications in J.—M. Mayeur (ed) *L'Histoire religieuse de
  la France 19e-20e siècle — Problèmes et méthodes* (1975).

2 Léonard *op.cit.* pp22 and 80 mentions a figure of 650,000 Protestants for the beginning
  of the 20th century; it should be remembered that at that time, Alsace-Lorraine formed
  part of Germany.

covered a whole spectrum of theological opinion[3], and in the
absence of the authoritarian structures of Catholicism, it was easier
for Protestantism to shade away into varying degrees of heterodoxy[4].
Secondly, Protestant theologians and exegetes were faced with the
same Biblical problems as those debated in Germany throughout the
nineteenth century. By contrast with Germany, academic facilities
were extremely limited and largely without State support[5]; numbers
were small and it was therefore left to a mere handful of scholars,
notably the Strasbourg group associated with the *Revue de Théologie*,
to disseminate the new ideas[6]. Basically, of course, they were caught
up in the intellectual toil which all heirs of the Reformation faced
when their supreme authority, the Bible, was laid open to the historico-critical approach. We are here concerned with those in France
who, broadly speaking, welcomed the new ideas and approach and
who can therefore be called 'liberal', by contrast with a large number of French Protestants who remained orthodox and certainly
conservative in their Biblical interpretation. The pietistic 'Réveil'
movement of the early nineteenth century helped to sustain the con-
servatives, although not all those who underwent its religious influence were automatically resistant to Liberal views[7].

Before turning, however, to questions of exegesis and early Church
history, one must note the strong influence, out of all proportion to

---

3 For the diversity and pluralism of French Protestantism, v. Léonard, *op.cit.* Pt. II Ch.1
   and 2; one should note the confessional differences as between Lutherans and Calvinists,
   as well as the liberal-conservative spectrum in theology.

4 For some examples of this, v. the final chapter of D.G. Charlton, *Secular Religions in
   France 1815—1870* (1963) where he outlines a number of reactions to the question
   posed by the Protestant E. Schérer in 1860: can religion become more rational without
   ceasing to be religion?

5 Before 1870 there were two Protestant faculties, that of Montauban (Calvinist and
   conservative) and that of Strasbourg (Lutheran and liberal); after the loss of Alsace-
   Lorraine, the Strasbourg faculty was reassembled in Paris in 1877.

6 The most important names associated with this group were: F. Reuss (1804—1891), E.
   Schérer (1815—1889), T. Colani (1824—1888) and A. Réville (1826—1906). *La Revue
   de Théologie et de la Philosophie Chrétienne* was founded in 1850, later changing its
   name to *La Nouvelle Revue de Théologie*. A number of contributions to the journal
   were translated into English as *The Progress of Religious Thought as illustrated in the
   Protestant Church of France* ed. J.R. Beard (1861). For bibliographical details v. E.G.
   Léonard *op.cit.* p285, to which should be added, for our purposes, J. Pommier, *Renan et
   Strasbourg* (1926).

7 For example, Auguste Sabatier, whose views will be considered below, was greatly influenced by the 'Réveil' in his youth.

their numbers, of Protestants and ex-Protestants upon national life, especially through the educational system. Critics of the Third Republic sometimes remarked sourly that it was a 'république des professeurs' and that many of the University trained politicians and administrators turned out to have a Protestant background, even if they no longer professed or practised their religion[8]. And it was generally recognised that whereas the Catholic who 'lost his faith' or in any way broke with the Catholic system thereby placed himself outside it, often nursing strongly anti-Catholic or anti-religious sentiments, the Protestant, even when he had shed the last scraps of orthodoxy, somehow remained a Protestant in spirit[9]. He was more likely than the ex-Catholic to retain favourable attitudes towards religion and, in particular, he tended to inherit a tradition of social Christianity, hardly perhaps to be distinguished from bourgeois 'good works' but which easily allied itself with the ideology of the Third Republic[10]. Such men, when they found themselves in positions of government or of educational influence, helped to carry through anti-clerical legislation and were firm supporters of the Separation of Church and State[11]. In Catholic eyes, Protestants were therefore barely to be distinguished from Jews, Freemasons and rationalists, who together constituted the enemy within the gates[12].

Having noted this diffused Protestant influence in French society, we may return to our central theme by tracing the study of early

---

8 Cf. A. Thibaudet, *La République des Professeurs* (1927) who complained that Protestant philosophy teachers were the 'priests' of the Third Republic, and created the national educational system in the years 1885—1905. Cf. the expression attributed to A. Aulard, 'La Sorbonne huguenote'. A brief outline of the part played by Protestants under the Third Republic, with some useful statistics, is given in Léonard *op.cit.* pp225—231.

9 Cf. the remark attributed to C. Guignebert: 'Quand on n'est plus catholique, on ne l'est plus; quand on n'est plus protestant, on l'est encore' (related by Prof. M. Simon in conversation). According to André Gide, 'Même quand la foi change ou disparaît, chez un protestant, il reste quelque chose de sa première formation. Chez le catholique, quand la foi cède, tout disparaît'. (J. Green, *Journal* Vol. 4 (1949) p242).

10 For social Christianity and its Protestant theological background, v. Léonard *op.cit.* Pt.II Ch.IV.

11 Cf. the careers of Edmond de Pressensé (1824—1891) and Francis de Pressensé (1853—1914), father and son. The older man was a Protestant pastor and a historian of early Christianity in *L'Histoire de l'Eglise aux trois premiers siècles* (1858—61); he entered politics and became a senator. His son played a significant role in the Separation legislation, as described in M. Larkin, *Church and State after the Dreyfus Affair: The Separation Issue in France* (1974) (v. esp. pp108—113).

12 Cf. the views of Dom Besse, outlined below in 1.4.

Christianity through the career of Albert Réville, a member of the Strasbourg group and, more especially in the writings of Auguste Sabatier, who was the outstanding theorist of Liberal Protestantism in France in the late nineteenth century. We shall attach particular interest to the widening perspectives which for theological and institutional reasons came to be employed by Protestants in their examination of Christian origins, noting especially the new context provided by the history of religions. There will be obvious parallels with the work of Renan, described above, but we are here concerned with the ideas and the work of confessional writers who, whatever claims they made to be 'independent', obviously spoke from Protestant presuppositions.

Writing of the Strasbourg group, P. Chazel remarks that they not only introduced into France the most revolutionary German ideas, 'from Schleiermacher to Strauss' but also, in the study of the Bible, inaugurated methods borrowed from the most recent disciplines: psychology, ethnography, the history of religions, philology; even if they were over-confident in the application of these tools, their experiment was not wasted[13]. The subsequent career of one of the group, Albert Réville, bears out this trend[14]. We have already seen how he and other Protestants were in communication with Renan, for whom early Christianity was the highest point in the general religious development of mankind. Réville worked as a pastor, at first in Calais, then in Holland[15]; he wrote a doctoral thesis on the Synoptic Gospels but simultaneously developed his interest in comparative religion and became a contributor to leading French periodicals[16]. One of his most successful works was *Histoire du dogme de la divinité de Jésus-Christ* (1869 and many subsequent editions)[17].

---

13 *Protestantisme français* p95.
14 On Réville, v. J. Marty, *Albert Réville – Sa vie – son oeuvre* (1912).
15 In *The Progress of Religious Thought* he records his relief at not having secured a teaching post at the conservative seminary of Montauban: 'I should have stifled in such a stove' (pVIII).
16 Eg. *La Revue des Deux Mondes*, to which he was introduced by Renan; cf. Marty *op.cit.* p93.
17 Cf. his statements in the Avant-Propos of the first edition: 'Le point de vue historique se substitue au point de vue dogmatique . . . la grande loi du devenir ou du développement naturel ne leur (sc. les doctrines religieuses) est pas moins applicable qu'aux autres phénomènes terrestres . . . nous usons d'une indépendance entière vis-à-vis des formules successivement consacrées par les dogmatismes du passé'. But: 'pour expliquer clairement

In 1880 Réville was elected to a chair in the history of religions at the Collège de France and in 1886 to the first Presidency of the newly founded Section des Sciences Religieuses, within the EPHE. A number of other liberal Protestants were given posts in the Section including Jean Réville (son of Albert), Auguste Sabatier and Maurice Vernes (editor of the *Revue de l'Histoire des Religions*, founded in 1880 by Ernest Guimet). In congratulating Réville upon his election, Auguste Sabatier wrote, in 1880:

> . . . le positivisme ne pourrait traiter l'histoire des religions que comme l'histoire de la sorcellerie ou de la magie; le catholicisme, hors de son dogme, n'y voit qu'une erreur pernicieuse et invention diabolique . . . ; cette discipline est "fille légitime de la théologie protestante."[18]

Réville himself was always somewhat distrustful of the more theological claims of Sabatier[19] but even when, as President of the Section des Sciences Religieuses, he made official pronouncements about the objectivity of the work of the Section, he could easily lapse into quasi-confessional claims about Christianity. Writing in 1889 about the teaching method employed, he stated:

> Elle est exclusivement historique et critique et, sans oublier la nécessité d'accorder à la plus remarquable et à la plus européenne, à la plus intéressante aussi des religions qui se partagent le monde une part majeure dans la distribution des conférences, les organisateurs de cette section se sont attachés à dresser un plan pour ainsi dire cosmopolite, où toutes les grandes formes de la religion puissent être étudiées dans leurs sources originales.[20]

Here, Réville's 'European cultural tribalism' leads him to assume the self-evident superiority of Christianity, as the most culturally advanced specimen of an underlying substance or object of study called 'religion'. Réville himself lectured on a wide range of non-Christian religions, as well as many aspects of Christianity but it would be true to say that the Section's work on Christian origins was in the hands of a confessional group. Volumes of essays produced by members of the Section[21], and separate monographs sponsored

---

des doctrines qui se relient par une genèse intime à des sentiments d'un ordre tout particulier, il est nécessaire de retrouver en soi-même l'écho sympathique, au moins, des sentiments qui constituent le sous-sol d'une telle histoire' (*Op.cit.* 2nd edition ppXIII, XVII).

18 Quoted in Marty *op.cit.* p93.

19 Cf. his statement: 'J'aimais plus que lui les contours distincts et se détachant en pleine lumière. Je parle ici du théologien', quoted in Marty *op.cit.* p116.

20 *Etudes de critique et d'histoire* (A collection of essays by members of the Section) pXIII.

21 *Etudes de critique et d'histoire* 1889 and 1896; 7 out of 33 essays deal with aspects of early Christianity.

by the Section[22] reveal that this area was handled by Jean Réville, Auguste Sabatier and Eugène de Faye: the last two named also taught at the Protestant Faculty in Paris. These critics genuinely sought to be as unconfessional as possible but their religious positions usually obtrude[23] and it has to be remembered that, together with the *Revue de l'Histoire des Religions*, they were the main French speaking link with German Protestant scholarship[24].

When in 1900 Alfred Loisy sought and secured a temporary position in the Section des Sciences Religieuses through the intermediaries of Paul Desjardins and Gaston Paris, he did not find that A. Réville and A. Sabatier were kindred spirits. Even allowing for Loisy's own prickly character, one can understand his feelings: the Protestants, he thought, were over-full of generosity towards a persecuted Catholic priest and gave the impression that only Protestants could fully understand the Bible[25]. This view was confirmed in Loisy's mind by his inability to secure a permanent post in the Section on the grounds that a Catholic priest could not be expected to deal with the period of origins with sufficient objectivity. In 1904 Loisy found that if he made an ecclesiastical retractation of his 'errors', he would lose even his temporary post at EPHE and he confided bitterly to Paul Desjardins that there was a great similarity of spirit between inquisitors on the right and inquisitors on the left[26].

In order to characterise the ideology of this Protestant 'establishment' one must turn to the writings of Auguste Sabatier. Sabatier

---

22 Jean Réville, *Les Origines de l'épiscopat* (1894); *Le Quatrième Evangile* (1901); Eugène: de Faye, *Etude sur les origines des églises de l'âge apostolique* (1909).

23 Eg. Jean Réville's study of the episcopate stresses the moral and charismatic nature of authority in the early communities; only later did 'sacerdotal ritualism' and 'traditionalism' enter in. E. de Faye *op.cit.* draws heavily upon Weizsäcker, *Die apostolische Zeitalter*, but, untypically among Protestant critics, says of early Christianity that it was 'un phénomène plus social qu'individualiste'. (*op.cit.* p100).

24 These remarks do not take into account the French-speaking Protestant churches and academic institutions of Switzerland; it also has to be remembered that the University of Strasbourg was in German hands between 1870 and 1918.

25 *Mém* II p7.

26 *Ibid* p329. Duchesne had already taught several times at EPHE but in the historical Section; Mayeur, in *Mgr. Duchesne et son Temps* p328 contrasts Loisy, 'qui voulait faire oeuvre d'apologète' (doubtful but it must have appeared so to others) and Duchesne 'le plus laïque des savants de l'Eglise', in their experiences at EPHE. Réville's letters to Loisy show that he personally sympathised with the latter's dilemma, while remaining firm on the attitude of EPHE (BN n.a.f. 15661).

was the outstanding theoretician of Liberal Protestantism in France, without being a party man[27]. G. Weill has pointed out that he managed to reconcile certain competing strains in French Protestantism, for instance, the individualist conception of justification by faith and the 'socialist' conception of the Kingdom of God on earth[28]. He also combined the pietism of the Réveil movement of his youth with an enormous erudition and a complete acceptance of modern methods of Biblical research[29]. His expulsion from Strasbourg in 1873 and his arrival in Paris provided an excellent opportunity to establish a Protestant Faculty under his leadership in 1877, which kept alive the Strasbourg tradition of the scientific study of religion and of high culture. G. Marchal has referred to the 'left-wing' spirit of the Paris Faculty on the dogmatic front (over against the Faculty of Montauban), but a 'deeply spiritual, even mystical' left wing, 'vigorously constructive'[30]. His background and interests made Sabatier a philosopher of religion rather than a systematic theologian, although 'philosopher' must here be taken in a non-professional sense for he saw himself mainly as a critic and historian. His large output included work on the New Testament, notably his study *L'Apôtre Paul* (1870).

Sabatier is however mainly known for his 'symbolist' interpretation of religious phenomena, which can be briefly indicated as follows[31]. True religion, which is the equivalent of God's revelation, is known through symbols, including all belief systems. These can

---

27 On Sabatier (1839–1901) v. *Auguste Sabatier. Sa vie, sa pensée et ses travaux* (1904—four appreciations by friends and colleagues); J. Viénot, *Auguste Sabatier I La jeunesse (1839–1879)* (1927 — Volume 2 was never written); T. Silkstone, *Religion, Symbolism and Meaning — a critical study of the views of Auguste Sabatier* (1968).

28 *Art. cit.* pp223–4.

29 Cf. his replies, recorded by F. Puaux in the commemoration volume of 1904 p49, to critics of his article on 'Jésus-Christ' in the *Encyclopédie des Sciences Religieuses,* where he seemed to be following in the steps of Schérer and Colani. He did not share their scepticism about the Gospel records: 'Je peux affirmer ... après de longues années d'études, qu'il n'est personnage dans toute l'histoire que je connaisse aussi bien que le Christ'.

30 In his introduction to a new edition of Sabatier's *Les Religions d'autorité et la religion de l'esprit* (1956).

31 For summaries of Sabatier's doctrine, v. E. Ménégoz 'La Théologie d'Auguste Sabatier' *Revue Chrétienne* XIV 1901 pp422–430; *ibid*, 'Symbolo-Fideism', *ERE* Vol.12 (1921) pp151–2; G.B. Stevens, 'Auguste Sabatier and the Paris School of Theology', *HJ* Vol.I 1902–3 pp553ff.

never be absolute, since dogma is forever in a state of evolution[32].
'Religion' lies beyond the shifting sands of history and cannot ever
be finally encapsulated, either by orthodoxy or by rational philosophy. Criticism therefore provides a means of exploring and evaluating
the symbols in their constant state of flux. For the Christian, just as
a Canon of Scripture was once providentially bestowed upon the
Church, so now Biblical criticism is a God-given tool to seek out the
essence of religion[33].

A review of relevant sections in Sabatier's major publications will
bring out the bearing of this general philosophy upon the area of
Christian origins and their critical evaluation. In *Esquisse d'une
philosophie de la religion* (1897), Sabatier[34] states that the history
of religions cannot fail to demonstrate the superiority of Christianity:
the religion of the Father and the Son, the concept of the Man-God,
must be the climax of all religious development[35].This is something
he has proved in his own experience; but an objective manifestation
was recently provided in the Chicago Parliament of Religions in
1893[36].Just as the genius of the Judaeo-Christian tradition is found
in the experience of the Old Testament prophets [37], so too the essence
of Christianity is found in religious experience — in the first place
that of Christ himself in his consciousness of filial union with God
the Father[38]. The Virgin Birth and the Logos doctrine are different
ways of expressing this central fact[39]. From the start Christianity
has been an inward power impelling man to surpass himself in the
direction of an unattainable ideal[40]   but it has always been tempted

---

32 Cf. *De la vie intime des dogmes* (1890): the evolution of dogma is made necessary by
   the laws of history, and the rightness of the evolutionary view had been demonstrated by
   Protestant theologians using the historical method; the transposition of early Christianity
   from a Jewish to a Hellenistic setting is an example of this evolution.
33 In his Stockholm lecture of 1897 on *Religion and Modern Culture* (ET 1904) he mentions Renan and Loisy as critics whose use of the new methods has produced conflict
   between the church and 'science' (ET p184–7); nevertheless, 'modern culture acts upon
   the forms of religion by its criticism and religion elevates and purifies criticism by its
   spirit'. (ET p226).
34 ET *Outlines of a Philosophy of Religion* (1897).
35 *Op.cit.* huitième édition p125.
36 *Ibid* pp132–3.
37 *Ibid* pp154, 160.
38 *Ibid* pp183ff.
39 *Ibid* pp189–190.
40 *Ibid* p207.

to deviate from the ideal in one of two ways, either into 'paganism' (the idolatry of creeds and institutions, amoral gnosticism) or into legalism[41]. In spite of these tendencies, early Christianity was nevertheless a classical and creative period and provided it is considered dynamically, it stands as an example and a norm[42]. There were two crucial 'moments' of development in the new religion: the shift of the centre of gravity away from 'hypnotising' messianic expectation towards a 'sanctifying' meditation upon Christ's passion, his teaching and redemptive work[43]; and the subsequent loss of the original Gospel in the dualism produced by forms of organisation, ascetic morality and especially Church dogma[44]. Dogma was unavoidable, but, unlike the Catholic, the Protestant is happy to see dogmas change, die and find new expression through evolution and force of circumstance[45].

In his other principal work, *Les Religions d'Autorité et la Religion de l'Esprit* (1903)[46], Sabatier looks at Christian origins in more detail. The central question is how the Jewish Messianic idea became the Catholic concept of the Church in the third century[47]. Paul's notion of the Church was moral, idealist and transcendent[48]. In the first century the Christian ministry was a spontaneous response to the needs of the moment[49]. But, later, the Gentile Christian church followed a middle path between the theology of Paul (which it found incomprehensible) and the religious institutions of Judaism (with the removal of their more extreme requirements) and so the substructure of Catholic orthodoxy was produced[50]. The wealth and diversity of theologies in the first century were replaced by the mental habits of the synagogue and church life experienced an evolution from pure democracy through republican oligarchy to the

---

41 *Ibid* pp210–212.
42 *Ibid* p222.
43 *Ibid* p231.
44 *Ibid* pp232ff, under the title, 'Le christianisme catholique'.
45 *Ibid* pp251ff.
46 Published posthumously; ET *The Religions of Authority and the Religion of the Spirit* (1904).
47 *Op.cit.* Quatrième édition p55.
48 *Ibid* pp62–63.
49 *Ibid* pp134–136.
50 *Ibid* pp67–8.

monarchical state[51].Sabatier reluctantly admits that, for the Gospel
to be realised at a popular, social level, it could not remain purely
spiritual and had to flow in the religious moulds of the past[52].
But he remains optimistic: the ponderous inheritance of the past has
never quite overpowered the true Christian spirit and the nineteenth
century has witnessed the decline of the religion of priesthood and
the religion of the letter[53].This is in no small measure due to the
critical study of Christian origins, made possible by historical exegesis[54].

These views of Sabatier would not necessarily have been subscribed to by all his fellow Protestants, even in the liberal sector, but they
give an adequate idea of the ideology which pervaded not only the
Protestant Faculty but also the Protestant group at EPHE and a
wider readership in France. Many Catholics, of course, responded
adversely. Marchal claims that Batiffol's *L'Eglise Naissante et le
Catholicisme* was intended as a counterblast to *Les Religions d'Autorité et la Religion de l'Esprit*[55]. Loisy attacked Sabatier in an article
of 1899, taking him to task especially for his individualism[56]. But
there are certain affinities between Sabatier's Liberal Protestantism
and the views of Catholic modernists, for example concerning the
nature and development of dogma[57].Some Catholics indeed recognised similarities between the ideas of Sabatier and those of Newman
and, to that extent, were prepared to give them serious attention,
although obviously not entirely to concur with them[58]. Undoubtedly
Sabatier's work was influential upon the debate which took place in

---

51 *Ibid* pp98—99; 138.

52 *Ibid* p152.

53 *Ibid* p439.

54 *Ibid* p425.

55 In the 1956 edition of the latter work pXXII.

56 A. Firmin (pseudonym of Loisy) 'La théorie individualiste de la religion' *RCF* 1899,
ler janvier pp202—214.

57 On such affinities, as seen by contemporaries, v. 'Ignotus' (a Catholic priest and former
teacher at the Collège Stanislas), 'Protestantisme et Modernisme', *RChr* 1909 I pp425—
433; A.L. Lilley, *Modernism, A Record and a Review* (1908) p184. The affinities were,
of course, not so apparent at the time, because the Modernist position put forward by
Loisy in *L'Evangile et L'Eglise* was conceived as a reply to the Liberal Protestantism of
Harnack. The Church authorities, however, believed the Modernists to have been tainted
by Liberal Protestantism.

58 For details, v. the contribution of B.D. Dupuy in *The Rediscovery of Newman* (1967)
esp. pp153—169.

France during the Modernist period about dogma and to which several non-orthodox contributions were made[59].

It has now become apparent that by the end of the nineteenth century in France, it was customary in some Protestant circles to consider Christianity as one religion amongst others: the highest, unsurpassable example, perhaps, but nonetheless a specimen of the general religiousness of mankind and whose formulae could never be fixed and final. Confirmation of this viewpoint may be found in Jean Réville's Hibbert Lectures on Liberal Protestantism of 1903[60]. He says that modern Liberal Protestantism, under the influence of the history of religious and historical criticism, no longer claims for the Biblical writers any exclusive and supernatural inspiration, either general or partial[61]. The Bible preserves the record of the noblest and holiest religious experiences of mankind, those of the Israelite prophets and of Jesus Christ[62]. But the Gospel of Jesus does not consist of dogma or of ritual; it is a religion of love, whereby religion and ethics are indissolubly associated with conscience; its value is independent of its local and temporary forms[63]. J.E. Roberty, a Protestant pastor, writing in 1910, concludes that the history of Liberal Protestantism over the past 50 years has led to four widely held positions: religious symbolism (A. Sabatier); the faith which saves independently of creedal formulae (E. Ménégoz); social action towards the realisation of the Kingdom of God (T. Fallot, W. Monod); and radical criticism of the Bible and history (T. Colani, A. and J. Réville)[64]. None of these positions excludes, of course, the uniqueness of Christianity but cumulatively they lent themselves to a much more relative view than that held by orthodox Catholics or Protestants.

Sabatier's work had raised hopes for a renewed Protestantism in France, where a truly religious spirit might rise above party conflict. But in a volume of 1911, *L'Orientation Religieuse de la France actuelle*, Paul Sabatier, the historian of St. Francis and general facto-

---

59 V. e.g. E. Le Roy (Catholic lay philosopher), *Dogme et critique* (1905 — placed on the Index); C. Guignebert (rationalist), *L'Evolution des dogmes* (1909).
60 *Le Protestantisme Libéral — ses origines, sa nature, sa mission* (1903); ET: *Liberal Christianity* (1903).
61 ET p31.
62 *Ibid* p33.
63 *Ibid* pp54—58.
64 'Notes sur le protestantisme libéral' *RChr* 1910 I pp391—407.

tum of the Modernist movement (not, it appears, a relation of Auguste), has to conclude that these hopes remain unrealised[65]. The Protestant cause has not prospered in France because of Protestantism 'theologism', 'critical turn of mind' and 'iconoclastic zeal'[66]. So organised Protestantism remained a minority group, sharing something of the opprobrium borne by the Jewish community in the eyes of many Catholics. Nevertheless, Liberal Protestant ideas exercised a widespread diffused influence upon an educated reading public, which was happy to accept a more relative view of Christianity without having to repudiate religion altogether[67]. And in the study of early Christianity, such ideas provided for both Protestant and independent scholars an alternative evaluation of the evidence, over against the predominant orthodoxy of the Catholic Church and one which they could share with many other researchers beyond the confines of French life and thought.

1.4 *THE INDEPENDENT SECTOR*

The difficulties in designating an 'independent sector' over against prevailing Catholicism and the small but influential Protestant group will by now have become apparent. Within Catholicism there were critics claiming independence of ecclesiastical control; Liberal Protestants felt that they embodied a truly independent tradition, avoiding the dogmatism of Catholics and rationalists alike. But Loisy and the EPHE group were more influenced than they may have realised by Catholic and Protestant presuppositions respectively, as they looked into the origins of Christianity. It is therefore necessary to consider certain groups and individual critics who belong to

---

65 *Op.cit.* p214.

66 *Ibid.* p219.

67 Cf. G. Crespy, *Contemporary Currents of French Theological Thought* (1965) p1: 'If French-speaking Protestants publish a great deal of material, it is because many Frenchmen who are not Protestants read it and the cultural setting thus supports and multiplies the efforts of the minority'.

1 The autodidact and socialist writer P.–J. Proudhon (1809–1865) had, for example, written voluminously on early Christianity, both as a literary hack for a Catholic dictionary, and more seriously on his own account. He believed that Jesus survived the crucifixion and secretly organised the early Church for another forty years. V. *Proudhon: Ecrits sur la religion* (1959) ed. Th. Ruyssen.

neither of the two major Christian categories, but who contributed to this area of scholarship. We are not here concerned with the products of gross anticlericalism, or with the unorthodox opinion about early Christianity in the work of political theorists[1], or even with anti-Christian writing with some claims to scientific or literary merit[2]. It is of course necessary to realise that such a polemical tradition existed, reflecting the deep polarisation of French life and thought on religious matters. But we are instead seeking to identify a sector which had some serious academic concern for the study of religion. Inevitably this sector overlaps with the liberal Protestants on the one side and with the rationalists on the other, and we have already seen how Renan himself falls into such a category. But, since we are speaking of very small numbers, it is hardly to be expected that France should have produced anyone else in this sector of Renan's intellectual eminence.

In order to assist our enquiry, we may consult two almost contemporaneous surveys of liberal trends in French religious thought. The first, already mentioned, is *L'Orientation religieuse de la France actuelle* (1911) by Paul Sabatier. In this impressionistic work, the author, having discussed the effects of the war of 1870 upon the conscience of the nation, and described the defects of both the Church and anticlericalism, turns to recent philosophy, notably that of Bergson, Boutroux and William James. The attitudes of these thinkers to religion are positive and hold promise for the future, according to Sabatier, and he even invokes the patronage of J.—M. Guyau, whose *L'irréligion de l'avenir* (1887) is now seen to be more sympathetic than once supposed[3]. The recovery of a new religious sense depends upon an interpretation of history which is no longer dogmatic or materialistic, but which uncovers the inner life of the past and relates it to the present. This interpretation can provide the

---

2   A. Mellor in *Histoire de l'Anticléricalisme français* (1966) considers that the years of the Combes ministry (1902–5) saw 'l'apogée de l'anticléricalisme français' (Ch.XI) and he cites as samples: Durkheim and his colleagues of *L'Année sociologique;* S. Reinach's *Orpheus* (v. below); *La Folie de Jésus* by Binet-Sanglé (Jesus as a madman according to the psychiatry of c.1900); the novel *L'Enfer* by H. Barbusse (about an evil priest); and the literary activity of Anatole France. However the work of Durkheim and even of S. Reinach, has rather more permanent validity than Mellor is prepared to grant.

3   Sabatier, *op.cit.* Ch.VI and VII. Guyau's work ran into many editions and helped to influence Durkheim and Salomon Reinach and doubtless many others of their generation, in their conception of human history as progressive secularisation.

basis for a lay morality and a lay religion[4]. The new orientation is specifically French, owing nothing to the industrial nations, or to German politics and theology[5]. Renan is its true precursor. Its manifestations are to be found here and there in Catholicism and Protestantism, although not officially accepted by either body; but they are also apparent in Free Thought circles. Free thinkers are not irreligious, claims Sabatier and he cites in particular the Ecole des Hautes Etudes Sociales, with its section for the study of religion in relation to society[6] and the Union de libres penseurs et de libres croyants pour la culture morale[7] as independent organisations where religion is taken seriously. There are many references in Sabatier's work to the problem of moral and religious education in the secular State school system and these help to locate the book and its tendencies. Sabatier should be seen as the spokesman of a high-minded element in French society, which welcomed secularisation and the Separation of Church and State because they provided a break with Catholicism and any kind of religious orthodoxy and paved the way for a new religion and a new morality, as yet undefined.

Diametrically opposed to Sabatier's vague optimism was the work published in 1913 by a Bendictine monk, Dom J.–M. Besse: *Les religions laïques: un romantisme religieux*, in which he sought to uncover the anti-Catholic conspiracy threatening France through a series of organisations dominated by Jews and Protestants. Dom Besse was a recognised theologian of *L'Action Française* and, amongst others, his book impressed the young Georges Bernanos, who became a 'camelot du roi' in this right-wing, nationalistic,

---

4 *Ibid* Ch.IX.

5 *Ibid* Ch.X. Sabatier considers that 'l'admirable effort exégétique de l'Allemagne' is largely confined in its value and effects to its home ground, since the Bible has never had so important a place in French life (p170). Harnack is greatly admired in France but his perspectives do not accommodate the French point of view (p173). Cf. similar remarks in Sabatier's Jowett Lectures on *Modernism* (ET 1908) pp78–80.

6 The Ecole was an independent body founded c.1900; v. the account given by its secretary Mlle. Dick May (pseudonym of Mme. J. Weill) in *Le premier Congrès de l'enseignement des science sociales* (1901) p307. The Section for the study of religion was added in 1903 with Théodore Reinach as religious adviser.

7 Founded in 1907 by Jean Leclerc de Pulligny (1859–1939) and incorporating freethinkers (some of them with high official positions in education and State administration) and liberal Protestants in its membership.

monarchist and religiously 'intégriste' movement[8]. Because the work presents a conspiracy theory, it needs to be used with some caution, but the enemies of France unmasked by Dom Besse include the independent sector we are investigating and his polemical intent brings them into sharper focus than is possible in Sabatier's euphoric haze.

Besse refers to four 'lay pontiffs': Paul Desjardins, the former 'neo-Christian'[9], now leading light of L'Union pour la Vérité, who had just acquired the Abbey of Pontigny and inaugurated a series of informal meetings on philosophical, literary and religious topics under the name of 'Décades'[10]; Paul Sabatier; and the brothers Salomon and Théodore Reinach, 'men of government', Jewish, the former of whom had recently published his notorious manual of the history of religions *Orpheus* (1909) and the latter acting as religious adviser to the Dreyfusard Ecole des Hautes Etudes Sociales[11]. The names of Liberal Protestants frequently recur, especially those of Auguste Sabatier and the pastors Wilfred Monod and Charles Wagner[12]. The 'theology' of the 'movement' is traced back to Protestantism generally and in particular to Rousseau, Schleiermacher, Renan, Guyau and Boutroux[13]. Organisations included in the diatribe are

---

8 For the history of the movement, v. Eugen Weber, *Action Française* (1962). For the novelist Bernanos, v. R. Speaight, *Georges Bernanos* (1973). Both these works contain references to the work and influence of Dom Besse.

9 On the 'neo-Christians' of the 1890s, v. A. Houtin, *Histoire du Modernisme Catholique* (1913) Ch.1; A. Baudrillart, *Vie de Mgr. d'Hulst* Vol.II (1914) pp187–198; R. Bessède, *La crise de la conscience catholique dans la littérature et la pensée française à la fin du XIXᵉ siècle* (1975), Pt.III.

10 In 1892 Desjardins had founded L'Union pour l'Action Morale to incorporate freethinkers, Protestants, Jews and Catholics on an antipositivist platform. The 'neo-Christianity' of the Action Morale group, which broke up over the Dreyfus Affair, was replaced by a more secular atmosphere in L'Union pour la Vérité. For the Décades, in several of which Alfred Loisy took part, v. details in 2.2 below.

11 For more details of Salomon Reinach v. below. Salomon and his brothers Joseph and Théodore were good examples of 'emancipated' Jews who achieved high intellectual distinction through the French academic system. Emile Durkheim, born in the same year as Salomon Reinach, was another such. For the position of Jews in late nineteenth century France, v. M.R. Marrus, *The Politics of Assimilation* (1971).

12 Monod (1867–1943) was well known for his preaching and his pastoral and social work; Wagner (1852–1918) had a similar fame, with a special interest in moral education in the State system, over which he collaborated with the freethinker Ferdinand Buisson.

13 Besse resumes this theology in six fundamental points: 1) Humanity has eternal, independent existence, incorporating the attributes of deity; 2) this existence develops in accordance with an undefined progress; 3) each individual leads a double existence:

the Congresses for the History of Religions, the International Congress for Religious Progress[14] and L'Union de libres penseurs et de libres croyants pour la culture morale. Besse has already taken up the phrase of the historian Aulard 'La Sorbonne huguenote' to indicate that the Third Republic is dominated by Protestant and Jewish University men[15]. He has a chapter on 'M. Durkheim en Sorbonne', which describes Durkheim's ideological influence upon the whole French educational system[16]. In a chapter on L'Union ... pour la culture morale, he describes its members as weak but dangerous men, dangerous in virtue of the position they occupy in the State[17]. French Catholicism is encircled by the overlapping membership of L'Union pour la Vérité, L'Ecole des Hautes Etudes Sociales, Durkheim's *Année sociologique* and L'Union pour la culture morale[18].

It is obvious that both Sabatier and Besse are bringing together, for different reasons, certain tendencies which did not have as much in common as they supposed. But their agreement in detecting a recognisable ambiance in the early years of the twentieth century makes it possible to speak of an independent sector, where religious and moral questions received an 'open' treatment, although not without the influence of Protestant and rationalist notions. All of this was naturally anathema to the Catholic mainstream even if not all Catholics shared Besse's paranoia: some indeed felt that rationalism was on the wane[19]. The First World War was to act as partial

---

his own, and the collective existence of humanity; 4) the mutual collaboration between the individual and humanity constitutes the mystery of religion; 5) humanity fulfils its destiny in following the law of progress, in which the individual is swept along; 6) intelligence has no place in this system; religion is based upon feelings and instincts, and its truth need not be discussed (*op.cit.* p64).

14 This had strong support from American Unitarians; the Congress was held in Paris in 1913.

15 *Op.cit.* p121.

16 *Ibid* Ch.XIV. According to Besse, Durkheim too is a lay pontiff: 'A l'exemple de son correligionnaire, M. Th. Reinach, M. Durkheim rêve d'un doctorat en théologie' (p233). On Durkheim v. S. Lukes, *Emile Durkheim* (1973) and W.S.F. Pickering, *Durkheim on Religion* (1975).

17 *Ibid* p268.

18 *Ibid* p306. In spite of their small numbers, the antipathy aroused by such organisations can be gauged from satirical accounts in novels by the Catholic Paul Bourget: *L'Etape* (1902) describes 'L'Union Tolstoï' (Ch.V); and *Le Démon de Midi* (1914) describes 'L'Ecole Libre des Sciences Religieuses' (Ch.X).

19 It is apposite to recall here once again the change in the cultural climate which occurred round about the same time as the Separation of Church and State in 1905. Prior to that

solvent of some of the ideological antinomies in French society but the opposition between Catholics and anti-Catholics was to persist. L'Action Française continued, even after its condemnation by Rome in 1926, to provide a political and spiritual centre for ultra-Catholics; at the other end of the scale, various rationalist groups recruited some of the membership of the pre-1914 independent sector. In particular these rationalist organisations helped to promulgate the quasi-dogma of the non-historicity of Jesus of Nazareth and thus to foster the 'Christ-myth' school of thought, to be encountered later in this study[20].

Among 'independent' critics who did not belong to either the Catholic or the Protestant sector, the first to be mentioned is Ernest Havet, of the EPHE, who produced a four-volume work on *Le Christianisme et ses origines* (1878–84). Havet was a positivist of the old school who declined the first presidency of the Section des Sciences Religieuses on the grounds of age. His denial of any supernatural revelation is to be seen in his choice of epigraph: 'Non fit statim ex diverso in diversum transitus' (Seneca). His Preface states his belief that Christianity is much more Hellenic than Jewish; its beginnings in Judaism were accidental. The first two volumes are therefore devoted to Greek and Roman thought, from Homer to Seneca, showing what was already contained of Christianity in Hellenism. A third volume deals with Judaism: most of the prophetic literature is dated in the second century B.C. because of its close resemblance to Christianity. Only in the last volume does Havet deal with the New Testament, where the 'Galilean element' in Christianity becomes apparent, but even so he sees much Greek influence in Epistles and Gospels. Havet closes the work with a statement of belief in the progress of humanity, but adds that nothing on earth is ever perfect and it is of the essence of religion to impede progress. Havet's devotion to the rationalism of Ancient Greece, revived after the dark night of the Middle Ages with the dawn of the Renaissance, is eloquently described in the funeral oration pronoun-

---

date, the secular rationalism associated with Durkheim and 'l'Université' had been predominant; but in the decade before the outbreak of the First World War, there was a reaction in favour of spontaneous nationalism, with more emphasis upon irrationality and individualism: Bergson replaced Durkheim as a national oracle. Cf. T.N. Clark, *Prophets and Patrons* (1973) pp214–5.

20 V. below 2.5.2 and 4.3.

ced by Renan[21].His contemporaries and subsequent critics were quick to point out the eccentricity of his approach and blamed him for not knowing Hebrew and German[22].Such a work did not inspire much hope for a French independent school to arise in the wake of Renan.

A more promising event was the appointment in 1906 of Charles Guignebert to teach the history of Christianity at the Sorbonne. Guignebert was a historian, without any confessional allegiance, who had come to the study of early Christianity through his doctoral thesis on Tertallian. In the year of his appointment he published his *Manuel d'histoire ancienne du christianisme — les origines,* much more objective in spirit than Havet's work and solidly based upon the most recent literature. This work will be considered in detail below[23]; for the moment we may simply note that, although Guignebert subscribed to the secular republican ideals of his day, his rationalism was not of the extreme variety encountered in Havet[24]. But a single lectureship at the Sorbonne and one or two others scattered through the provinces[25], could not suffice to establish a new independent tradition. Further investment by the State was in any case not to be expected, for the Section des Sciences Religieuses at EPHE carried sufficient guarantees of objectivity, even though, as we have seen, the work on Christian origins carried a strong Protestant bias.

Three years later, in 1909, Alfred Loisy, recently excommunicated, was elected to the Chair of the History of Religions at the Collège de France. Once again, for reasons to be investigated, this appointment did not lead to any significant new academic grouping[26]. But

---

21 'Discours prononcé aux funérailles de M. Ernest Havet le 24 décembre 1889' *OC* II pp1127—1130. 'Jamais croyant ne fut plus fidèle à son dogme que Havet à sa philosophie . . . Son livre des *Origines du christianisme,* qui ne traite qu'un côté du sujet, le traite d'une façon définitive. C'est un livre inflexible. Havet croit au vrai; il ne transige pas'.

22 In his article on 'Historiens du christianisme' in *DACL* VI, II (1925) Leclercq, as a Catholic, is of course very hard on Havet: 'A défaut d'une science approfondie, l'auteur est armé d'un fanatisme agressif, l'accent est âpre et farouche. Pour lui le christianisme n'est pas un fait à étudier, mais un ennemi à combattre.'

23 3.2.1.

24 V. e.g. 3.3 below.

25 E.g. E.—Ch. Babut at Montpellier, with whom Loisy was on excellent terms (cf. below 2.2).

26 V. below 2.1 and 2.2.

the same year saw the publication of a work which brought before the general public questions about the history of religions, including Christian origins, in a sensational way. This was Salomon Reinach's *Orpheus*[27]. Its impact was sharply felt, first, because it was attractively written at a popular level, by contrast with the more learned writings of EPHE, the *Revue de l'Histoire des Religions* and *l'Année sociologique*; secondly, because it was the first manual of the history of religions available in France to include Christianity[28]; and thirdly, because of Reinach's definition of religion, to become notorious, as 'a sum of scruples which impede the free exercise of our faculties'[29]. Reinach saw religions as 'the infinitely curious products of man's imagination and of man's reason in its infancy'[30] and he explained the origins and development of religion largely in terms of taboo. His treatment of Christianity, from its beginnings to the Modernist crisis of the day, was highly unsympathetic and critics of all shades of opinion complained that it was cold, external and unappreciative of religious sentiment[31]. But the work acted as a catalyst upon public and academic opinion, and was widely debated. Within a few years, there were two major Catholic replies, manuals of the history of religions including the history of Christianity[32]. The treatments of Christian origins in these two works remained standard accounts in Catholic circles for many years to come[33].

Reinach's own account appears to have as its principal objective

---

27 Salomon Reinach (1858–1932) had studied at the French School in Athens, became a member of the Académie des Inscriptions in 1896, and in 1902 was appointed Director of the Musée St. Germain. His archaeological and related studies were published in *Cultes, Mythes et Religions* (5 volumes 1905–1923). His own account of the publication and reception of *Orpheus* is contained in Vol.IV of this series, pp438–483, under the title 'De Bello Orphico'. For an assessment of the debate, v. A.H. Jones, 'The Publication of Salomon Reinach's *Orpheus* and the Question of Christian Origins', *Religion* Vol.7 Spring 1977 pp46–65.

28 Reinach *op.cit.* pIX refers to the works of Conrad von Orelli and Chantepie de la Saussaye, which deliberately omit Christianity.

29 'Un ensemble de scrupules qui font obstacle au libre exercise de nos facultés (*Ibid* p4).

30 *Ibid* pIX.

31 V. eg. the reviews of the work by Gabriel Monod (a mediaeval historian and a Liberal Protestant) and Alfred Loisy (writing as an independent) in *RH* Vol.CII pp300–314.

32 J. Bricout et al., *Où en est l'histoire des religions?* 2 Vols (1912); J. Huby et al., *Christus* (1913). Catholics claimed that cheap copies of *Orpheus* were widely distributed in State teacher training colleges: cf. J. Lebreton, *Le Père Léonce de Grandmaison* (1935) p236.

33 Cf. a judgement to this effect in E. Magnin, *Un demi-siècle de pensée catholique* (1937) p37.

the undermining of orthodox Catholic opinion about the institution of the Christian Church[34].The Gospels contain little history, but reflect beliefs about Jesus held between the years 70 and 100 A.D., themselves the result of 'a legendary and expository labour carried on for at least forty years in the bosom of the community'[35]. The appeal of Christianity must have resided in the idyllic tragic beauty of the legend of Christ and in the 'Gospel morality' of Jesus, which was an advance on Pharisaic scholasticism, even if not highly original. But Paul superimposed upon this gentle teaching the harsh doctrines of original sin, redemption and grace, leading to eighteen hundred years of sterile disputes which still hang over humanity like a nightmare. Paul's system of belief would have been repudiated by educated Athenians of the fourth century B.C. Gentile Christianity was a kind of Gnostic sect, which proved superior to other such sects by its greater simplicity and reasonableness and by its moral purity. Early church organisation was uncomplicated and charismatic activity caused problems. The only 'sacraments' were baptism, the Eucharist and the use of holy oil. Ascetic tendencies were to be found but celibacy was not enjoined. Persecutions were sporadic and those persecuted were mainly of the lower classes: pre-Constantinian Christianity was a religion of hard-working humble people, who formed a mutual aid society.

This tendentious account is not of course wholly inaccurate; it should be seen as typical of a period in which academic serenity was still difficult to attain in the independent sector, even on the part of someone as intellectually eminent as Reinach. The entrenched position of Catholicism and the restricted influence of Protestant views inevitably led to polemical writing on the part of independents who wished to abandon any religious a priorism in their work. Renan's polemical intentions were somewhat obscured by his literary and historical gifts, by his own 'philosophy' and by the sheer scale of his

---

34 What follows is taken from Ch.VIII and IX of *Orpheus*, on 'Les origines chrétiennes' and 'Le christianisme de Saint Paul à Justinien'.

35 Reinach came very near to joining the *mythologues*; he believed for example that the Passion Narrative in the Gospels was nearly all constructed upon the basis of Old Testament texts. Later he changed his mind and gave his support to the theories of Robert Eisler: cf. his paper at the Congrès d'histoire du christianisme (Jubilé Loisy) 1927 (reproduced in the published proceedings (1928) Vol.I) on 'Les clous de la croix' and the remarks of Loisy in *Mém* III p528.

enterprise. The more detached view of Guignebert, though not lacking in anti-Catholic animus, had not yet commended itself to those who had spent their lives fighting political and educational battles on behalf of the secular State. In spite of more moderate opinion within Catholicism itself and the presence of a Protestant minority, the history of Christianity was for long to be regarded in France as the province of the 'curés' and the 'anticurés'. Even if this is a crude view, it is possible to locate among the anti-Catholics scholars of distinction, such as Reinach and even so eminent a figure as Durkheim who, although he did not write on early Christianity, embodied the secular ideology of the Third Republic and of the University and who was soon to publish *Les Formes élémentaires de la vie religieuse* (1912), with its reductionist explanation of religious phenomena[36]. Even if his secularism was to be challenged by a changing intellectual climate in the years c. 1905–1910, the hostilities of the past persisted. In these circumstances the 'independent' sector cannot be excepted from the scrutiny of its presuppositions already postulated for Catholic and Protestant critics, when its representatives addressed themselves to the sensitive area of Christian origins.

1.5 *THE RELIGIOUS AND ACADEMIC SETTING*

1.5.1 Ideological Factors

From what has been described above, it is now apparent that there were deep conflicts in French religion and society during the period under consideration. The conflict, for example, between faith and reason corresponded more than in other countries to a political conflict between right and left[1]. In spite of Catholic Thomism and Protestant intellectualism, reason was usually equated with unbelief, and we have noted several examples of the opposition between tradi-

---

36 Durkheim was not of course opposed to all religion as such; cf. his short address on 'Le sentiment religieux à l'heure actuelle' delivered to L'Union de libres penseurs et de libres croyants during their winter lectures of 1913–14 and reproduced in *ASR* 27, 1969, pp 73–77, in which he envisaged new forms of religious belief which might arise in the future.

1 For this argument cf. the remarks of Jean Guitton in *Ecrire comme on se souvient* (1974) p33: ' . . . dans les crises, malgré ceux qui tentent d'établir des ponts, on voit reparaître ces deux religions qui se font guerre comme deux mystiques, c'est à dire sans compromis'.

tional Catholicism and the secular ideology of the State. Such conflicts were of course replicated within the Church itself: Biblical and
philosophical Modernism and Christian socialism and democracy
can be seen as attempts to mediate between opposing poles in French
society; their failure was a sign of the strength of ongoing Catholic
tradition, itself reinforced by the aggressiveness of anti-clericalism.
Catholic apologists attempted at various times to pronounce the
defeat of unbelief, in the intellectual sphere, at least: there was still
no sociological awareness of the extent of 'dechristianisation'. One
of the best general surveys of the evolution of ideas in late nineteenth and early twentieth century France is significantly entitled
'De Taine à Péguy'[2]. Taine stands for the old positivism, devoted
to the cult of Reason, whereas Péguy is the former socialist and intellectual who returned to Catholicism as a fervent defender of the
faith through his essays and poetry. The philosophy of Bergson is
hailed as a major factor in the break with rationalism[3]. But the influence of Bergson's intuitionism and vitalism did not really stem the
tide of secularisation and a Catholic survey of 1937 is not as optimistic as that of 1920 and includes a final chapter on 'The persistence
of areligious, irreligious or anti-Christian tendencies'[4].

It was inevitable that the study of early Christianity should have
been affected by this intellectual and religious climate. Orthodox
Catholics and Protestants tried to preserve the sacred documents
from impious critical hands, and at the same time to find in them
legitimation of their most cherished beliefs; anticlericals, if they took
them seriously, wished above all to show that the documents were far
from infallible and gave no support to orthodox systems. Any serious
'scientific' work could only be found in the thinly-inhabited and
difficult terrain in between the contending forces. In practice, this
meant the work of Catholic 'progressives', of Liberal Protestants and
of those 'independents' who avoided the extremes of dogmatic
rationalism. Each of these categories was able to draw upon established traditions: not only was there the dominant presence of Renan

---

2   G. Fonsegrive, *L'Evolution des idées dans la France contemporaine — De Taine à Péguy*
    (posth. 1920). Fonsegrive was a liberal Catholic lay philosopher who taught for most of
    his life (1852—1917) at the Lycée Buffon in Paris.

3   *Op.cit.* p320: 'C'est alors que Bergson vint, qui par sa critique aigüe de l'intellectualisme
    purement abstrait fournit à Péguy le pont par où il peut s'évader de Taine'.

4   E. Magnin, *Un demi-siècle de pensée catholique.*

behind them, but Catholics had a master in Duchesne, Protestants had a close affiliation with the world of German scholarship and in the independent sector, the school of Durkheim was building a tradition of the scientific study of religion as a social force, as well as the less radical but solid work undertaken in the history of religions at EPHE. These were not exclusive sources of inspiration, because on the one hand, the exegetical achievements of German scholarship could not be disregarded by any critic working in this field and, on the other, sociological approaches did not always find favour with the critics whom we are to consider in detail below. But although there were ample resources for their work, the pressure of social and religious forces in France meant that such critics worked in comparative isolation.

1.5.2 Institutional Factors

This isolation is confirmed by an examination of the academic setting. Our period bears the mark of the fundamental change in the study of religion, away from confessional institutions towards secular institutions. The change can be studied with greater clarity in France than elsewhere, precisely because of the deeply-felt conflicts outlined above[1]. The suppression of the State faculties of theology and their replacement on the one hand by the confessional Instituts Catholiques and on the other by the secular Section des Sciences Religieuses at the EPHE and a few other University appointments, are one indication of this. Another would be the fact that the only discernible French-speaking 'school' of Biblical criticism was created in the ultra-confessional setting of the Dominican Ecole Biblique de Jérusalem, under Lagrange. Within the University, even though ideologically 'l'Université' in the Third Republic operated as a kind of counter-Church, such a school could not take shape. The sociologist T.N. Clark has pointed out that, whereas in the German university system, the 'feudal' professor could create an 'apprenticeship grouping' within a single faculty (leading in the case of our subject to groups of scholars associated with, eg. Harnack, Holl or Bultmann), the

---

1   For much detailed information on these institutional changes, v. E. and O. Poulat, 'Le développement institutionnel des sciences religieuses en France', *ASR* XXI 1966 pp23–36, reprinted (under the name of E. Poulat only) in *Introduction aux sciences humaines des religions* (1970) ed. Desroche and Séguy, pp79–98.

nationally diffused system in France favoured the formation of
'clusters' (eg. the Durkheimians) which were violently reshuffled
every few decades[2]. Added to which, one must point out the extremely small number of independent scholars engaged upon the
study of early Christianity in France, by contrast with the well-
endowed State faculties of theology in Germany. In Paris we may
count the small group at EPHE, the Chair at the Collège de France
(which happened to be occupied by Christian specialists in Albert
and Jean Réville and Alfred Loisy, although this need not have been
so), the lectureship at the Sorbonne and a few Protestants at the
Faculté Protestante. Outside Paris there was a mere handful of
isolated scholars.

Whereas in Germany and England the distinction between the
confessional and the University sectors was blurred almost to non-
existence, its sharp observance in France meant that few scholars
could straddle Church and State institutions. Duchesne, as we have
seen, was an exception to the rule among Catholics and the difficulties were raised in acute form in the case of Loisy's temporary lectureship at EPHE. It was of course more common for Protestants to
hold confessional and secular posts in plurality, as we have noted in
the case of Albert Réville, Auguste Sabatier and others: Maurice
Goguel was to continue in this tradition. There were some Catholic
laymen in the State system, but of those who had professional
interests in religion, most were philosophers; Christian origins were
avoided, either because of the danger of conflict with Church authorities, or because they were considered a clerical preserve, or simply
because the University posts did not exist.

In addition, therefore, to ideological factors, one must include
these institutional and statistical constraints upon French scholarship in a field which in other countries was well-filled with labourers.
The constraints did not have the effect, for reasons sufficiently
indicated, of bringing together those who considered themselves to
be 'independent' into a close formal grouping: we shall find our three
chosen critics working along parallel lines, discussing each other's
work in their publications and occasionally meeting at Congresses
or gatherings organised by some of the minority groups described

---

2 T.N. Clark, *Prophets and Patrons. The French University and the Emergence of the
   Social Sciences* (1973) Ch.2.

under the independent sector. They did however belong to that international community of researchers and writers who read each other's books and articles and who reacted to issues of the moment. Since many such issues were raised by academic developments in Germany, some allusion needs to be made to cultural relationships across the Rhine, before surveying the issues themselves.

1.5.3 Franco-German cultural relationships

In the mid-nineteenth century Renan had been among those who sought to absorb something of the efficiency of the German university system into French intellectual life[1], as well as acknowledging his debt to German Biblical scholarship, mediated through the Strasbourg group[2]. Even after the defeat of 1870, Germany continued to be admired in French University circles for her intellectual achievements, insofar as these could be separated from politics[3]. Promising young scholars were sent to German universities at the State's expense[4]. Duchesne travelled in Germany and absorbed the findings of German historians. It was still however a cause for suspicion in orthodox Catholic circles 'to know German'[5] and this charge was often brought against Loisy in order to cast doubts upon his originality. He always vehemently rejected it, perhaps over-vehemently[6]. His ambivalent attitude towards German Protestant Bible scholarship will be considered below[7].

At the turn of the century, French sentiment towards Germany began to change, with a resurgence of French nationalism and a rejection of such German idols as Wagner and Nietzsche (who had

---

1 Cf. his *La Réforme Intellectuelle et Morale de la France* (1871) esp. Part II section IV (*OC* I pp391—400).

2 As we have already seen, he did not of course agree with all of the Germans' conclusions.

3 According to J.—M. Carré, *Les Ecrivains français et le mirage allemand* (1947) it was a fatal mistake to distinguish between 'L'Allemagne qui enseigne, qui cherche, qui pense' and 'celle qui vient de nous battre' because 'nous ne voulons pas voir que l'Allemagne des Hohenzollern est en train de domestiquer l'autre'. (p109).

4 Cf. C. Digeon, *La Crise Allemande de la Pensée Française 1870—1914* (1959) Ch.7.

5 J. Ratté, in *Three Modernists* (1968) p125 remarks that 'Germanophobia (compounded by *revanchisme* and bitterness over Bismarck's *Kulturkampf*) . . . paralysed Catholic scholarship in France'.

6 Cf. his reply to L. de Grandmaison in *Mém* I pp153—5; and his remarks in 'Le Cours de Renan au Collège de France', *JPs* 1923 pp325—330.

7 V. esp. 2.1—3.

their circles of admirers in France also)[8]. We have already noted the change of climate in the decade before the outbreak of the First World War, with a certain swing in favour of right-wing intransigence in religion and politics[9]. This of itself did not have any immediate effect upon the interchange of ideas in the academic sphere and although Loisy was to be outspoken in his criticism of Harnack's ideology during the First World War[10], the three chosen critics for this study continued to read, discuss and either assimilate or reject German language work in their field.

1.5.4 Contemporary issues in exegesis

In so doing they inevitably responded to some of the burning issues raised in Protestant debate. Some of these were confessional in origin (eg. the nature of dogma, or of ecclesiastical authority) and *mutatis mutandis* were of interest to Catholics. Others were created by 'outside' pressures (eg. the comparison of Christianity with other religions). Ultimately of course most of such issues, of both types, go back to the rise of the historico-critical method and the awareness which it produced of Christianity as a historical phenomenon; early Christianity had to be considered in a dialectical relationship with the culture surrounding its birth, especially Judaism, but also with the developed forms of Protestantism and Catholicism in modern times. In France, these issues were usually delayed in their emergence. We have seen how the whole 'Biblical question' was still being cautiously approached in the Catholic sector in the early years of the twentieth century: it was being mainly considered in relation to the Old Testament[1] and it was the temerity of Loisy in forcing the discussion onto New Testament territory which helped to provoke the Modernist crisis[2]. Only among Protestants and independents could the canonical literature receive critical handling. We have

---

8 Cf. Digeon, *op.cit.* Ch.8—10.

9 In the literary sphere, this is excellently documented in R. Griffiths, *The Reactionary Revolution — The Catholic Revival in French Literature 1870—1914* (1966) esp. Ch.11.

10 V. 2.3 below.

1 Cf. the title of Lagrange's book of 1902: *La méthode historique surtout à propos de l'Ancien Testament.*

2 It was not for instance possible for Catholics to approve of Loisy's attempted refutation of Harnack when, in *L'Evangile et L'Eglise*, he simply denied the authenticity of the saying about the Father and the Son in Matthew 11, 27.

noted how questions about early Christian dogma and ecclesiastical institutions were almost entirely the preserve of confessional writers. Similar reactions greeted the application of comparative methods to the early Christian documents. The insights and methods of the *religionsgeschichtliche Schule* in Germany were repulsed by most Catholic critics, to be championed, conversely, by the independent critics Loisy and Guignebert[3]. The fact that the comparative method was popularised by Salomon Reinach in his *Orpheus* is yet another sign that most of the critical issues in the study of early Christianity were taken up in France in polemical guise, further delaying their resolution in reasonable, objective terms. Even the Christ-myth debate, rampant in Germany in the early years of the twentieth century, was not to be fully aired in France until the campaign of P.—L. Couchoud twenty years later[4].

1.5.5 French historiography

The critics whose views we are to examine all claimed to be historians first and foremost: theologians they were emphatically not, and they all had certain reservations about comparative and sociological approaches. Something should therefore be said, in concluding this description of the setting of their work, about French developments in historiography[1]. The mid-nineteenth century had seen a notable flowering of 'histoire synthétique', with monumental works by Michelet, de Tocqueville, Fustel de Coulanges and, most important from our point of view, Renan[2]. Renan's methods, however, seemed too impressionistic for the positivists of the last two or three decades of the nineteenth century (he was criticised along these lines by eg. Taine and Durkheim) and with the establishment of the historical section of EPHE, there was ushered in a 'règne de la critique', with an emphasis upon the critical use of documents[3]. This trend was reflected in the pages of the *Revue Critique* (for which

---

3   For their rejection, v. the lectures of Lagrange published in 1918: *Le sens du christianisme d'après l'exégèse allemande* Ch.IX; the whole work is a reasoned rebuttal of the successive phases of German criticism, whose fundamental errors are traced back to the 'false mysticism of Luther'. For Loisy and Guignebert, v. below 2.2 and 3.2.2.

4   V. below 2.5.2 and 4.3.

1   For what follows cf. L. Halphen, *L'Histoire en France depuis cent ans* (1914).

2   Halphen, *op.cit.* Ch.V.

Loisy was a regular reviewer). The emphasis upon documentary research meant that many of the leading historians at the end of the nineteenth century began their careers as mediaevalists, eg. G. Monod, who founded the *Revue Historique* (always hospitable to contributions about early Christianity), E. Lavisse (teacher of Guignebert) and Ch. Seignobos (often quoted as a typical upholder of the rationalist ideology of the Third Republic). When Halphen wrote his survey in 1914, he pointed to the high degree of specialisation which had been attained not only by periods, but also by areas (eg. social, religious, artistic and intellectual history, as well as political). But he also noted a countervailing trend, represented by a few high-quality *vulgarisateurs* (among whom he names Duchesne) and by the publication of a new journal, the *Revue de Synthèse Historique*, edited by Henri Berr[4]. Halphen suspected that sociology might provide new guide lines, and this was confirmed by the subsequent career of Berr, to whose hundred volume series *L'Evolution de l'humanité* (which he began to edit in 1920) Guignebert was to contribute his three volumes on late Judaism and early Christianity[5].

By the standards of the secular historian, early Christianity, of the first century or so, might appear a highly circumscribed area and therefore a specialist preserve. According to the swing of the pendulum just outlined in French historical studies, it would perhaps seem to belong to the world of the monograph rather than the overview. But the investment of scholarship in the area, largely due to confessional or, in some cases, anti-confessional interests, has always been out of all proportion to the apparent limitations. It has usually seemed appropriate, in the world of European scholarship, to lavish the closest possible attention upon the origins of a religious movement so rich in consequence and we shall see how each of the independent critics to be investigated below chose to round off a lifetime's researches with a general work on Christian origins occupying several volumes. It is true that Alfred Loisy was a historian of religions, that Charles Guignebert was a general historian who always maintained historical interests outside his specialism and that Maurice Goguel brought to his work, however unacknowledged, a

---

3   *Ibid* Ch.VII.
4   *Ibid* Ch.VIII.
5   For Berr and the contributions of Guignebert, v. 5.1 below.

theological seriousness as well as the interests of a historian. Each could therefore claim wider horizons for their specialist activity. But it was sufficient justification on the part of each critic to be following in the footsteps of Renan, all the more so because Renan's scholarship required updating and also because the religious climate in France, to which Renan had made so ambiguous a contribution, remained charged with suspicion and fanaticism. The independent critic, however much he might be ignored or misunderstood, had a vital role to play, not only in removing some of the prejudice, but also in creating an atmosphere where burning issues could engender more light than heat.

2. LOISY'S WORK ON EARLY CHRISTIANITY 1909—1927 **

2.1 THE CHAIR OF HISTORY OF RELIGIONS AT THE COLLEGE DE FRANCE

According to his own lights, Loisy did not become an independent critic of early Christianity and the New Testament until after his excommunication in 1908. It is true that in the eyes of the Catholic authorities, what he wrote on the subject in the years 1902—1908 went far beyond the bounds of orthodoxy. His two works of apologetics, *L'Evangile et l'Eglise* (1902) and *Autour d'un petit livre* (1903), based upon the large work which he had drafted during his years as a convent chaplain at Neuilly[1], contained much that was unacceptable on e.g. the nature of Biblical authority and inspiration, the divinity of Christ, the development of dogma and the institution of Church and sacraments. His massive commentaries on the Gospels[2] were equally unacceptable in their doubts cast upon the historicity of the Gospel material and the large part ascribed in the creation

---

** The documentation is particularly rich. The third volume of Loisy's *Mémoires* (1931—562pp) covers the period exactly. The writing of the *Mémoires* was prompted by the knowledge that Albert Houtin had left among his papers an incomplete 'Life of Loisy' which Houtin's literary executor, Félix Sartiaux, would not show to Loisy. Sartiaux completed the work but it was only finally published, as *Alfred Loisy — Sa Vie — Son Oeuvre*, by Emile Poulat, in 1960. The last few chapters in Houtin's section (on 'The Life') and much of Sartiaux's section (on 'The Work') give an account of the years under consideration. Since the Houtin-Sartiaux volume is in many ways hostile towards Loisy and the *Mémoires* comprise an elaborate apologia, subsequent criticism has tended to favour one or the other account. Dr. A.R. Vidler has made out a good case in favour of Loisy and against Houtin-Sartiaux in *A Variety of Catholic Modernists* (1970) Ch.2. But Sartiaux's account of Loisy's work as an exegete after 1909 remains almost alone in the field (though cf. F. Heiler, *Alfred Loisy* (1947) Ch.11—16). Loisy's correspondence of the period is also highly instructive; some of this is reproduced in the *Mémoires* but much remains unpublished in the Loisy papers at the Bibliothèque Nationale.

1 The 'Neuilly apologia', fully described in *Mém* I Ch.XV—XVI, is preserved in the Loisy papers in two versions (BN n.a.f. 15634—8).

2 *Le Quatrième Evangile* (1903); *Les Evangiles Synoptiques* (1907—8).

and arrangement of the material to the Early Church. But during these years, Loisy remained a Catholic by conscious choice, in the ever-diminishing hope that his type of criticism might win a hearing within the Catholic Church. When the excommunication decree was finally pronounced, Loisy, who for many years had not subscribed to standard Christian beliefs in his private thinking, simply felt free of any further need to write either as a Christian believer or as a Catholic apologist and free to pursue his study of early Christianity from a neutral standpoint.

Even in the case of a recluse like Loisy, such a study could not of course be undertaken in isolation. For many years, Loisy had been reviewing a regular and voluminous flow of publications on Biblical subjects for the secular *Revue Critique*[3] and for the *Revue d'Histoire et de Littérature Religieuses*[4], which he had helped to found in 1896. He was already much indebted to German Protestant scholarship in the New Testament field, although he consistently criticised the theological presuppositions which Liberal Protestants introduced into their exegetical work[5]. So while he was thoroughly familiar with the trends of scholarly debate, Loisy was at the same time casting around for other schemata than those provided by either Catholic apologetics (however advanced) or Liberal Protestantism for the study of the Christian religion. His work on the Gospels frequently makes the point that one cannot separate the study of the early Christian documents from that of the history of the religion itself: the two were mutually illuminating. From this, it was a logical step to view Christianity, including its origins, among the religions of the world[6].

---

3 Loisy reviewed for the *Revue Critique* from 1889–1927.

4 For example, cf. his use of Jülicher in his lectures on the parables at EPHE in 1901–2, published in *Etudes évangéliques* (1902); and his frequent references to Holtzmann in his work on the Synoptic Gospels.

5 One example from many: Loisy greeted *Die Auferstehung Christi* by A. Meyer (1905) as the most clear and complete book on the subject, but thought it laid too much stress on the religious experience of Paul, which should be considered more in terms of a 'nervous illness' (*RC* Vol.60, 1905, pp186–9).

6 L. Salvatorelli in 'From Locke to Reitzenstein: The Historical Interpretation of the Origins of Christianity' *HTR* XXI (1929) pp263–367 suggests that Loisy's writings of 1902 to 1908 were tending, unconsciously perhaps, in this direction, in his description of Christianity 'as having come about with and through reaction to the successive environments in which it had existed' (p339). Such a description is found, for example, in *Autour d'un petit livre* (1903) pp119–129.

Evidence that Loisy's thoughts were moving in this direction may be cited as follows. In 1904, in reviewing a Manual of the History of Religions by Chantepie de la Saussaye, Loisy regretted that Christianity was not included. The history of religions and its philosophy could only gain by the removal of this 'negative privilege', which was indeed more dangerous than useful to Christianity itself[7]. In 1906 Loisy greeted with approval the volume by Charles Guignebert, *Manuel d'histoire ancienne du christianisme — les origines.* As already noted[8] Guignebert, a secular historian with no confessional allegiance, had recently been appointed to teach Christianity at the Sorbonne, after the Separation of Church and State. He saw the history of Christianity as an aspect of the religious history of mankind[9]. Loisy considered this work to be 'truly scientific' in its absence of confessional prejudice[10]. In January 1907 Loisy stated his position in a letter to Albert Houtin: as a product of humanity, he says, Christianity could never be perfect but it has made its own contributions to the history of mankind.

> Explosion d'illuminisme et de fanatisme comme l'humanité n'en a pas beaucoup vu, il s'est peu à peu assagé, se transformant en un système de croyance qui était de valeur sensiblement équivalent à la philosophie du temps, et en un système de morale, exagéré dans certaines parties, mais qui, après tout, pour la direction de l'individu et l'organisation de la famille, valait mieux que ce qui existait antérieurement . . . C'est pourquoi j'ai toujours considére l'idée fondamentale du protestantisme, le retour au christianisme primitif, au pur Evangile, comme une pure insanité . . . L'établissement chrétien est en liquidation. Mais ce n'est pas un motif pour jeter tout le mobilier à la fenêtre. Mieux vaut transporter doucement, sans rien casser, ce qui est hors d'usage, à ce riche musée d'antiquités qu'est l'histoire des religions'.[11]

When, in the weeks after his excommunication, Loisy was investigating the possibility of being appointed editor of the *Revue d'Histoire des Religions,* he expressed the view that his nomination would signify 'l'inscription définitive de la religion chrétienne dans le cadre de l'histoire générale des religions'[12]; this had not been self-evidently the case as long as the *Revue* was in the hands of the Liberal Protestants of the EPHE. The editorship was vacant, follow-

---

7 *RC* Vol.58 (1904) p2.
8 V. above 1.4.
9 V. below 3.1.
10 *RC* Vol.63 (1907) p268. This review gave rise to a controversy described in *Mém* II pp533–5; cf. also *Quelques Lettres* . . . (1908) pp90ff.
11 Loisy to Houtin 16.1.07 (BN n.a.f. 15718).
12 Loisy to Houtin 10.5.08 (BN n.a.f. 15718).

ing the untimely death of Jean Réville; although Loisy did not secure the position, within a year he had been appointed successor to Réville in the Chair of the History of Religions at the Collège de France. It is not necessary to describe the details of the election[13], but it is relevant to consider the Inaugural Lecture which Loisy delivered at the Collège de France on 24th April 1909[14]. This is a key document for Loisy's thoughts and intentions at the time. It begins with tributes to his predecessors, Albert and Jean Réville, each of whom ranged widely in the history of religions while maintaining a specialist interest in early Christianity. Their Protestant faith did not prevent them from striving towards a real objectivity in their subject; according to Loisy, the struggle against theological control has helped to constitute the history of religions:

> Et tant que l'étude du christianisme n'était pas dégagée parmi nous de tout intérêt théologique ou polémique, l'étude des religions en général était comme paralysée. C'est pourquoi l'émancipation de l'exégèse biblique et de la science des origines chrétiennes a eu pour conséquence directe celle de l'histoire des religions.[15]

Loisy then proceeds to outline his own standpoint and plans. He is at pains to dissociate himself from two positions in particular: those of the rationalists and of the sociologists. The former see in all religions 'une succession de songes incohérents et absurdes', but:

> . . . pour compredre et pour enseigner l'histoire des religions, il n'est pas requis d'y voir la grande folie de l'humanité; . . . 16

sympathy and even indulgence are called for. Such remarks were probably directed at Salomon Reinach's recently published manual of the history of religions, *Orpheus*[17]. The sociological school to whom he refers is of course that of Durkheim and his colleagues of the *Année sociologique*. They are right, says Loisy, to recall the social nature of religion, but their method sets itself up as an exclusive doctrine.

> L'écueil est tout proche, — et je crains qu'on n'y ait déjà touché, — de traiter les religions

---

13 The details are provided in *Mém* III Ch.XLII—XLIII and in *Alfred Loisy Sa Vie — Son Oeuvre* Pt.I Ch.XXI.

14 *Leçon d'ouverture du cours d'histoire des religions au Collège de France* (1909).

15 *Op.cit.* p6.

16 *Ibid* pp25—6.

17 For Loisy's controversy with Reinach v. Loisy, *A propos d'histoire des religions* (1911) Préface and Ch.I—III; Reinach, 'De Bello Orphico', *Cultes, Mythes et Religions* Vol.IV (1912) pp438—483; Loisy, *Mém* III pp142—7; 260—3.

comme des organismes physiologiques de type fixe; de procéder par inductions générales sur des observations partielles; de donner des définitions absolues de certains éléments de la religion, par exemple du sacrifice, comme des réalités partout identiques et immuables; de s'exposer ainsi à constituer une scolastique plutôt qu'une science des religions.[18]

Sociology therefore deserves to be heard as one of several voices — others are comparative mythology, anthropology and philology — which contribute to the comparative study of religion, but none of which can replace the historical method, to which Loisy declares himself committed. The historico-critical method must be applied to the history of religions and thereby uncover the origins and development of their constitutive elements. Significant elements which Loisy hopes to study in this way — not overlooking their mutual links — are sacrifice, divination and prophecy, morality, beliefs, priesthoods and reformations[19]. Sacrifice is to be the starting point, because rituals and customs are the most consistent and revealing elements of a religion.

Loisy at first thought that his work on sacrifice might last for several years and that, having surveyed world religions in this way, he might then return to the origins of Christianity. He laboured immensely on sacrifice, summoning help from specialists[20]; and when his *Essai historique sur le sacrifice* was finally published in 1920, he commented that of all his works, it had caused him the most trouble[21]. But his interests in early Christianity were never crowded out and, as we shall see, he returned to the New Testament and Christian origins sooner than expected, mainly through his enthusiastic welcome given to the methods and conclusions of the *religionsgeschichtliche Schule*. But before turning to that phase of his development, some mention must be made of two small volumes, *Jésus et la tradition évangélique* (1910) and *A propos d'histoire des religions* (1911) which are revealing of his ideas at the time.

The former is a presentation in more popular form of sections of the introductory material in his *Evangiles Synoptiques* of 1907.

---

18 *Ibid* p35. Loisy's remarks echo those of his predecessor Jean Réville in *Les phases successives de l'histoire des religions* (1909) who refers to the 'Einseitigkeit' of the Durkheim group (p223).

19 *Ibid* pp39—40.

20 Cf. his correspondence of the period with Franz Cumont (BN n.a.f. 15644 and 15651); and with Nathan Söderblom (A.H. Jones, 'The Correspondence of Alfred Loisy and Nathan Söderblom' *DR* Vol.94, October 1976 pp261—275).

21 *Mém* III p393.

No longer under any ecclesiastical restraint, Loisy offers unambiguously a view of early Christian religion and literature which anticipates much that was later to be urged by Form critics and Redaction critics. It is not enough, he says, to identify certain sources in the Gospels: the special tendency of each element must be recognised, in relation to the life and faith of a religious 'social organism'[22].

> Les étapes de la rédaction n'ont d'intérêt que parce qu'elles correspondent à des étapes d'opinion et c'est le rôle de ces idées dans le christianisme vivant qui donne véritablement un sens aux opinions et une valeur aux textes.[23]

Literary relationships are far less important than the relation of the texts with the living reality of Judaism and Christianity. Thus, in Loisy's view, the texts lose their status as sacred scripture and become documentary evidence for the history of religions. For example, the Passion Narratives reflect Pauline soteriology, pro-Roman apologetic, Christian exegesis of the Old Testament and the development of legendary motifs. The sayings of Jesus have been shaped in accordance with the needs of catechesis and the miracle stories by developments in Christology. Speculation about the person of Christ and in particular the activity of Christian prophets, has led to the standardisation of certain titles for Jesus and ultimately to the 'high' Christology of the Fourth Gospel. The infancy narratives are a comparatively late form of 'concrete symbol' and 'popular hagiography'. The literary history of the New Testament takes us well into the second century, since it was only then that the authority of the Fourth Gospel became accepted as a definitive statement of the divinity of Christ[24]. Thus, after fifteen years of close work on the Gospels, Loisy was leaving behind source-criticism in favour of tendency-criticism and saw the documents as anonymous, community products, whose literary history must be subordinate to religious developments within the early church.

The composite volume *A propos d'histoire des religions* gives a good idea of Loisy's interests in the years 1909–1910. The first three articles were instigated in various ways by the publication of Reinach's *Orpheus*[25] but two others had special reference to early

---

22 *Op.cit.* p30.
23 *Ibid* p33.
24 These points are taken from *op.cit.* Ch.III 'La tradition évangélique.'
25 'Remarques sur une définition de la religion'; 'De la vulgarisation et de l'enseigement de l'histoire des religions'; 'Magie, science et religion'.

Christianity. 'Jésus ou Christ' had been contributed to the *Hibbert Journal* as a final comment upon a symposium of English contributions on the subject[26]. Loisy attacks the writers for conducting the debate within the framework of a traditional metaphysic which accepts the idea of a God both infinite and personal. One's presuppositions in undertaking historical work upon the Gospels do not have to be taken from Christian theology, for the idea of salvation can now be conceived in wider terms than those of the first century A.D. Liberal Protestant reconstructions fail to do justice to the eschatological Christ. A valid philosophy of religion must cast its net wider than Christianity. The viewpoint of the writers is itself to be seen as a limited and historically conditioned response within a much more varied Christian spectrum[27].

Loisy also included in the composite volume his extended review of *Die Christusmythe* (1910) by Arthur Drews[28]. Although he can agree with Drews about such matters as the legendary nature of some of the Gospel material and the inadequacy of certain Protestant reconstructions of the historical Jesus, he provides a vigorous and detailed defence of the historicity of Jesus of Nazareth. The issue was to re-emerge in his later exchanges with Couchoud[29]; but although Loisy subsequently retracted some of the positions upheld in his review of Drews, e.g. the authenticity of some of the Synoptic and Pauline material and the comparative lack of influence exercised upon early Christianity by the mystery religions, he was never to doubt that there had been a historical person, Jesus, who provided the starting point for the whole Christian movement.

2.2 *THE 'RELIGIONSGESCHICHTLICHE SCHULE'*

The years 1909–1911 were therefore a time of transition for Loisy, of adaptation to a secular existence and, in particular, to the non-confessional treatment of religious subjects. Not only did

---

26 *HJ* Vol.8 (1910) pp473–497.
27 Houtin says, overdramatically, but with some justification, of this article, 'Ce fut le premier grand manifeste de rupture de M. Loisy avec le christianisme' (Houtin-Sartiaux p175) and Loisy was concerned about the painful effect it might have upon von Hügel (*Mém* III pp147–8).
28 'Le mythe du Christ' pp264–323.
29 V. below 2.5.2.

his position at the Collège de France offer him financial security, it provided a base of operations and a setting for his academic work, which otherwise would have been conducted within the complete isolation of his village retreat at Ceffonds. The title of his chair encouraged him in his private conviction that the study of Christianity must be inserted into the general religious history of mankind. But his controversy with Reinach and his difference of opinion with Durkheim showed that he did not intend to join the rationalists[1]; and his review of Drews ruled out any possible collaboration with French-speaking 'mythologues'. Although he remained in correspondence with some of his former Catholic associates (especially von Hügel), he was reluctant to be drawn into any grouping which might constitute a 'school' or 'party'. This was largely a matter of personal temperament but, in addition, the Collège de France post did not entail teaching duties apart from the delivery of lectures, and unless the holder of a chair in that institution possessed the personal charisma of a Bergson, for example, his lectures alone could not serve as the basis for a new corporate venture.

It is true that his association with Paul Desjardins led Loisy to write for the *Correspondence de l'Union pour la Vérité* and to visit the Abbey of Pontigny for colloquia ('Décades') on religious topics during the years 1910–1913, but he remained marginal to the company assembled by Desjardins for the *Union* and the *Décades*[2]. It is also true that during the years 1909–1914 Loisy gathered a group of admirers, some of whom attended his lectures and some of whom wrote for his journal *RHLR*. But of the most promising, two, Ernest Babut and René Duchamp de Lageneste, were killed in the First World War and two others, Louis Canet and René Massigli, eventually left the academic world for diplomacy[3]. In any case, they did not owe exclusive allegiance to Loisy. However, retrospectively

---

1 For a strong refutation of the 'myth' of 'Loisy rationaliste' v. Loisy to A. Gambaro 8.6.13 in M. Guasco, *Alfred Loisy in Italia* (1975) pp276–7.

2 For Loisy's connections with Desjardins and with Pontigny v. *Mém* III Ch.XLVII; A. Heurgon-Desjardins (ed), *Paul Desjardins et les Décades de Pontigny* (1964) (especially the contribution of E. Poulat); H.F. Stewart, 'Pontigny' in *Studies in French Language, Literature and History presented to R.L. Graeme Ritchie* (1947) pp218–224.

3 The correspondence with Babut and Lageneste (BN n.a.f. 15649 and 15658) reveals Loisy in his most affectionate vein. There are tributes to both of them (anonymously) in *Mors et Vita* ([2]1917) pp50–53. Canet later became Loisy's literary executor.

Loisy saw himself continuing the tradition of Renan[4] : he felt that he entered the Collège de France under the patronage of Renan[5] ; he rejected Harnack's charge that the Modernists were crypto-Protestants and claimed that he had been far more influenced by Renan than by Auguste Sabatier[6] ; he quoted Renan's dictum 'on ne fait pas de critique religieux à genoux' against von Hügel's theory of 'successive Christologies'[7]. The question was, how should the tradition of Renan be continued?

Certainly Loisy was in search of a more specific framework for his study of early Christianity: no theological guide-lines remained, there was no immediate academic or quasi-confessional grouping to which he could belong, and the 'historical method' and 'comparative method' to which he subscribed could be widely interpreted. It was perhaps inevitable in the circumstances that during 1911 he should have become a firm adherent of the methods and findings of the *religionsgeschichtliche Schule*. The steps must, however, be examined in some detail because Félix Sartiaux, in his study of Loisy's exegesis, has represented it as a blinding vision leading to sudden conversion, with subsequent attempts to obscure the record[8].

According to Sartiaux, Loisy was at first reluctant to read *Die hellenistischen Mysterienreligionen* of Richard Reitzenstein, which was recommended to him by various friends in the early part of 1911. When he did finally read it, in preparation for his Collège de France lectures in 1911–12 on Greco-Roman cults, it was an 'illumination' and he took over wholesale the idea of early Christianity as a mystery religion, created in the Gentile world, based on the myth of a dying and rising god and incorporating rites of initiation and participation (baptism and eucharist) modelled on the pagan cults. Loisy publicised his new understanding in an article in the *Hibbert Journal* of October 1911, 'The Christian Mystery'[9]. His lectures on the Greco-Roman cults concluded with an account of the rise of Christianity seen from this new angle and were finally published as *Les Mystères païens et le mystère chrétien*. Loisy's

---

4   V. above 1.1.2.
5   *Mém* III p99.
6   Loisy to Houtin 22.8.09 (BN n.a.f. 15718).
7   *Mém* III p179.
8   *Alfred Loisy, Sa Vie – Son Oeuvre* pp203–7.
9   *HJ* Vol.10 pp45–64.

brief comments in the Mémoires, where he refers to his *Hibbert Journal* article as 'assez nouveau' but 'peu discuté', are cited by Sartiaux as a way of glossing over a significant turning point in his thinking.

This account is not entirely convincing. In the first place, Sartiaux, when writing of Loisy's exegesis, had two overriding intentions: to highlight Loisy's lack of originality and to show how he very nearly joined the ranks of the 'mythologues', to which Sartiaux himself belonged. Next, Loisy was perfectly familiar, from his reviewing activity, with the phases of development in the *religionsgeschichtliche Schule*[10]. In *Les Evangiles Synoptiques* Vol.II (1908) Loisy referred to *Les religions orientales dans le paganisme romain* (1906) of Franz Cumont when discussing the institution of the eucharist: Paul and John both drew upon 'des idées communes de sacrifice et de communion qui régnaient dans le monde antique' (*op.cit.* p541). His own *RHLR* of 1900 (first volume in the new series) included articles on the Aesculapius Cult by C. Michel, on Manicheism in the Roman Empire by F. Cumont (with whom Loisy was now in regular correspondence) and a review of Clemen's *Religionsgeschichtliche Erklärung des Neuen Testaments* (1908). If he showed any resistance to the new ideas, it was partly because of their exploitation in some quarters in the interests of the Christ-myth theory, as indicated by his reactions to Drews and Reinach. Then, too, the German critics retained a theological outlook which rendered them suspect to Loisy; he considered the theologian of the *religionsgeschichtliche Schule*, Ernst Troeltsch, to be 'un théoricien extrême de l'individualisme'[11]. A clear distinction must indeed be drawn between the 'history of religions' as it appears in the name given to the German critical movement, which was 'eine durchaus innertheologische Bewegung'[12] and as it was understood by Loisy in his secular French setting. But he was drawn in the Germans' direction not only by the insertion of early Christianity into the context of Oriental and Hellenistic piety

---

10 For example, in 1902 he had reviewed two essays of Reitzenstein (*RC* Vol.53 pp105–6); in 1904, Gunkel's *Zum religionsgeschichtlichen Verständnis des Neuen Testaments* (*RHLR* Vol.9 pp573–4); in 1908 Wendland's *Die hellenistisch-römische Kultur* (*RC* Vol.65 p102). His remarks on Gunkel and Wendland were highly appreciative, if somewhat reserved.

11 *Mém* II p418.

12 Gunkel, writing in 1921, quoted in W. Klatt, *Hermann Gunkel* (1969) p26.

but also because they were moving on, as he himself wished to do, from a purely literary criticism of the texts, exemplified for instance by Holtzmann.

It seems very likely therefore that Loisy was seeking an understanding of early Christianity which would avoid the deformation of history produced by 'théologues'[13] on the right and 'mythologues' on the left. Two years later Franz Cumont complimented Loisy on his Collège de France lectures (which had been appearing in *RHLR*) and advised him to say in an introduction to his book how he differed from such predecessors to left and right[14]. He agrees with Loisy that *mythologues* and *théologues* were both wrong about the debt of Christianity to paganism: it was not that Christianity borrowed its basic beliefs from the mysteries, but that it presented itself to the Mediterranean world as 'un mystère, une économie de salut': 'il n'y a pas eu reproduction, mais transposition'. If Loisy states this clearly enough, says Cumont, even German theologians such as Harnack will be made to understand[15]. It therefore appears that in 1911 Reitzenstein's book acted as a catalyst upon Loisy, suggesting to him the reorientation of some well established ideas: he was now able to associate himself with the new German school of criticism without having to embrace their 'theologism', or having to admit on his own soil that Salomon Reinach was right after all.

The *Hibbert Journal* article presented its main thesis in these words:

> The scheme of Messianic salvation, of which the Galilean prophet thought himself the destined head, became the myth of universal salvation, which the historic existence of Christ served to fix upon earth![16]

Paul was the most important, if not the only worker in this metamorphosis[17]. Gentile converts had been appealing for modes of doctrine and worship which answered their aspirations and they thus helped to create in part the faith they were accepting. Jewish ideas of a suffering servant and of a Christ pre-existent in God had con-

---

13 The word does not of course mean 'theologian', but is a coinage, with strong pejorative overtones, on the lines of 'sociologue' and 'mythologue'.
14 Cumont to Loisy, June 1913 (BN n.a.f. 15651).
15 Cumont to Loisy, also June 1913 (BN n.a.f. 15651) in reply to Loisy's letter of 14.6.13 (BN n.a.f. 15644).
16 *Art.cit.* p51.
17 Loisy told von Hügel that his article presented more solid views than those of Reitzens-

tributed to Paul's religion of cross and exaltation but these were now completed by pagan concepts of a dying god, a divine saviour and an immortal spirit capable of conveying rebirth and immortality. Loisy claimed that in turn, such ideas had influenced the gospel tradition: his short commentary on Mark of 1912 stressed the Pauline influence in this Gospel[18]. The Galilean gospel had almost been lost in Paul's impetuous mysticism and anti-Jewish polemic and even when the first written gospel did something to redress the balance it was still heavily imprinted by the Pauline 'mystery'. It is this mystery which is meant in Mark 4, 11[19]; the Christ of the Transfiguration is a divine saviour-figure[20]; the account of the Last Supper is to be traced back to Paul's 'vision' on the subject[21]. But for a full statement of Loisy's reconstruction of Christian origins at this period one must turn to *Les Mystères païens et le mystère chrétien* and, as it is the first full scale 'scientific' account which Loisy produced, it is necessary to summarise his views rather closely.

In an Introduction, Loisy sets out the general resemblances between the Mysteries and Christianity. In each case a local or national cult grows into a universalist religion offering the assurance of immortality[22]; entry into the scheme of salvation is voluntary and by means of initiation[23]; the rites are dramatic and participatory rather than doctrinal[24]. Loisy warns the reader, however, that the precise relationship between the Mysteries and Christianity is not easy to fathom, if only because of the problems of interpreting the New Testament documents[25]. After five lengthy treatments of the principal Mysteries, Loisy turns to the story of Christian origins.

Jesus may have been the 'chief author' of Christianity but he was

---

tein on the contribution of Paul. In particular, Reitzenstein was wrong to suggest that Paul actually *studied* the Mysteries (*Mém* III p231–2).

18 *L'Evangile selon Marc*. For Loisy's description of the volume, v. *Mém* III p232; it was 'en libraire, un complet fiasco'. He may have been stung into publication by hostile remarks of Lagrange in a commentary on Mark published in 1911; cf. Loisy to Cumont 27.7.11 (BN n.a.f. 15644).

19 *Op.cit.* pp34–5.

20 *Ibid* p120.

21 *Ibid* p405. 'Le Christ de Marc est comme les dieux des mystères: ce qui lui arrive et ce qu'il fait est le type de ce qui doit arriver à ses fidèles et de ce qu'ils doivent faire'.

22 *Op.cit.* p12.

23 *Ibid* p15.

24 *Ibid* p19.

25 *Ibid* p21.

not its 'founder'[26]. He did not concern himself with Gentiles and died a martyr of his Messianic cause, an 'enthusiastic' movement within Judaism[27]. Such 'enthusiasm' among his followers gave rise to resurrection faith, which was essentially the belief that God had not abandoned Jesus, who would swiftly return as Messiah and King and Judge in glory[28]. The community which embraced this faith practised baptism which was both a rite of purification and a rite of incorporation into their brotherhood[29]. They also met for a common meal, where they relived the Last Supper (including the note of hope for Messianic victory); where they acquired a distinctive group-consciousness; and where faith was formed, affirmed and expanded[30].

With the writings of Paul, however, we are in a different world. The nationalist religion of the first Christians has now been transformed 'en véritable mystère'[31]. On the basis of his personal vocation, mediated by a vision of Jesus, 'Paul prétend avoir été mis d'un seul coup en dehors de toute tradition'[32]. Such a vocation is for *all* Christians (cf. Romans 8, 28—30)[33] and is universally available (cf. Gal. 3, 26—27; Romans 3, 29—30; 10, 12)[34]. The Kingdom of God is now realised in the company of the faithful, and the Jesus of history has been replaced by the heavenly Lord (cf. II Cor. 5, 14—19)[35]. He 'is also the Heavenly Man, whose mythology may be glimpsed behind Philippians 2, 6—8[36]; the soteriology based upon this figure is heavily influenced by Greek dualism[37] and can be described as 'l'interprétation morale de vieilles idées mythologiques'[38]. The idea of a mystical virtue inherent in the death of a figure both human and divine, which is capable of redeeming humanity from sin and death, cannot be of Jewish origin and must be derived from pagan sources[39].

---

26 *Ibid* p210.
27 *Ibid* p211.
28 *Ibid* p216.
29 *Ibid* pp220—1.
30 *Ibid* pp221—2.
31 *Ibid* pp231—3.
32 *Ibid* p235.
33 *Ibid* p236.
34 *Ibid* p238.
35 *Ibid* pp241—2.
36 *Ibid* p245.
37 Paul's dualism is not, according to Loisy, to be traced to the rabbis or to Philo.
38 *Ibid* p247.
39 *Ibid* pp248—9.

Paul upholds the myth by tortuous and bizarre arguments, for his rabbinic training did not prepare him to deal adequately with such concepts[40]. The essence of Pauline Christianity is found in the phrase: 'It is no longer I who live, but Christ who lives in me'. (Gal. 2, 20). This Christ is a personal Spirit, communicable to man. The Christian is a 'spiritual man', no longer reliant on wordly wisdom[41]. But for the *teleioi*, there is a *mystērion* (NB I Cor. 2, 6—8), which is to be contrasted with the doctrines of demons, i.e. the other Mysteries[42]. *Charismata* are available for the interior illumination of individuals; Christ is a collective person in the Church but is also the 'soul' of each Christian[43]. It is indeed the idea of the Church which marks Christianity off from the other Mysteries, since it comes from the Biblical tradition, but Paul has incorporated into this idea his own notions of the 'Lord' and of Christ as Spirit[44].

The Pauline sacraments are 'la forme naturelle et l'expression indispensable' of the Apostle's doctrine of justification[45]. In his exegesis of the sacramental passages in Paul, Loisy is at special pains to combat Protestant views. Against Lietzmann and Heitmüller he maintains that Paul did not simply use the Mysteries as illustrations of the moral and spiritual experience of Christians: Romans 6, 3—11 displays a curious but inseparable amalgam of mystical, moral and eschatological ideas[46]. Paul does not speak so much of moral renovation as of the mystical drama of christian initiation[47]. The rites of salvation are in closest association with the 'myth' of salvation, i.e. justification by faith. Baptism and eucharist are brought together by the concept of 'body'; a study of the relveant sections in I Corinthians shows that Paul accepts the idea of a 'sacrement efficace', although he stops short of a 'sacrement magique'[48]. He received his eucharistic tradition by means of a vision and what he offers his Corinthian readers is not so much an explanation of their ritual, but a new

---

40 *Ibid* pp252—3.
41 *Ibid* pp254—5.
42 *Ibid* pp256—7.
43 *Ibid* pp264—5.
44 *Ibid* p266.
45 *Ibid* p269.
46 *Ibid* p272.
47 *Ibid* p273—4. Cf. Loisy to Houtin 11.6.11: The Protestant theologians go into ecstasies over the Pauline phrase 'Christ in me' but do not realise it is more akin to initiation in a tribal religion than to the 'spiritual' concept they imagine (BN n.a.f. 15718).
48 *Ibid* pp280—1.

definition of what they are already accustomed to. It is no longer to be a mere anticipation of the messianic banquet but a commemorative rite of Christ's sacrificial death, with a 'realistic' interpretation of the elements (which incidentally, Protestant critics cannot explain away)[49]. Even the *agapē*-hymn of I Cor. 13 is subordinate to Paul's sacramental outlook:

> ... c'est dans l'eucharistie qu'il voit se perpétuer le gage de l'amour divin dans l'amour du Christ et se réaliser incessamment l'union des fidèles dans le Christ et avec lui.[50]

In a final chapter on 'The Conversion of Paul and the Birth of Christianity' Loisy first analyses Gal. 1–2: much of this analysis reappears in the Commentary on Galatians of 1916[51]. The historical conclusion of Loisy is: 'l'influence de la primitive tradition évangélique aura été assez limité, non seulement sur sa conversion, mais encore sur sa formation chrétienne et sa prédication évangélique'[52]. The main influence in his conversion had come from Christians who were already somewhat Hellenized[53]:

> ... des gens pour qui le Christ commençait de n'être plus le Messie juif mais 'le Seigneur', et à pénétrer plus ou moins dans la sphère de la divinité ... Ce n'est donc pas seulement la conversion de Paul qu'on a besoin d'expliquer psychologiquement, c'est sa conversion au mystère chrétien que l'on doit expliquer historiquement.[54]

Paul was a rabbi (but *not* a pupil of Gamaliel, which is a fictional trait in Acts); from Tarsus he was familiar with the spirit if not the texts of paganism[55]; he was *not* a tortured soul, converted from intrasigent orthodoxy to a 'liberal' faith in God's goodness: rather, in his search for a universal scheme of salvation, he was converted

---

49 *Ibid* pp285–90.
50 *Ibid* p296.
51 V. below 2.3.
52 *Ibid* p317.
53 Bousset had very recently published his *Kyrios Christos* (1913) which is obviously influential at this stage of the argument. Loisy refers to the book on p207 of *Les Mystères* ..., together with other works of the second wave of the *religionsgeschichtliche Schule*. He devoted a review article to Bousset in *RHLR* 1914 pp385–401. Although he questioned some of Bousset's absolute distinctions (Messiah/Kyrios, Messiah/Son of Man) he rallied to the central thesis that just as the first disciples had been able to express their faith in Jesus as 'Son of Man' because that concept lay conveniently to hand, so Gentile converts were able to use the title 'Lord', taken from their own religious culture. Loisy also refers to W. Heitmüller's highly influential essay 'Zum Problem Paulus und Jesus' *ZNW* (1912) pp320–337, which drew attention to the importance of pre-Pauline Hellenistic Christianity.
54 *Ibid* p321.
55 *Ibid* pp321–3.

from belief in a Jewish national Messiah to belief in a divine Saviour who rescues the believer from this world into heavenly glory[56]. The religion he embraced cannot be called syncretism, because he retained Jewish monotheism; his theory of justification by faith was worked out later in his controversy with the Judaizers[57]. His type of Christianity coexisted with others (eg. those of Apollos, or the Jewish Christians) because early Christianity was flexible and these early developments all spontaneous[58]. Jewish Christians were eventually to be left behind, maninly because of their isolation, although not before their reminiscences of the early Jesus had been incorporated into Christian theology[59]. The Fourth Gospel, 'qui s'inspire d'une philosophie mystique plus large que celle de Paul', represents the culmination of this process of incorporation; but it was the 'mystère chrétien' and not the 'gospel of Jesus' which conquered the Ancient World[60].

In his concluding remarks, three points emerge for Loisy's more precise relationship with the *religionsgeschichtliche Schule* and other current scholarship. First, he does not accept the unqualified use of the term 'syncretism' for early Christianity — or even for second century Gnosticism — because in each case religious materials are absorbed by a higher, dominant, principle:

> Dans le christianisme, la philosophie et la mystique païens sont en une certaine mesure absorbées par l'Evangile et utilisées par lui; dans le gnosticisme c'est plutôt l'Evangile qui est absorbée par la philosophie et la mystique païennes.[61]

This passage is directed against H. Gunkel: *Zum religionsgeschichtliche Verständnis des Neuen Testaments* (1903, 1910) where the author had stated 'Das Christentum ist eine synkretistische Religion'[62], but Gunkel's subsequent comments on this remark show that there was no substantial difference between himself and Loisy in their historical judgements (although Gunkel placed more emphasis upon oriental rather than Hellenistic elements):

> Die christliche Religion hat solche fremden Stoff in sich aufgenommen, in eigentüm-

---

56 *Ibid* p324–5.
57 *Ibid* pp334–5.
58 *Ibid* p336–8.
59 *Ibid* p339.
60 *Ibid* p340.
61 *Ibid* p355.
62 1st edition p95 quoted in Klatt: *Op. cit.* p96. Not all of Gunkel's fellow *Religionsgeschichte* were happy with this formulation.

licher und glänzender Weise verarbeitet, denn es ist und bleibt die höchste aller Religionen.[63]

Loisy would have demurred from the theological value judgement in the last clause, but on the question of 'syncretism', their difference was merely semantic, as may be seen more clearly from Loisy's discussion of the term[64].

Next, Loisy takes to task the proponents of 'Christ-myth' theories, among whom he is prepared to place Reitzenstein, because he too, in writing of Paul as an intellectual syncretiser, seems to suggest that religions are mere aggregates of myths; on the contrary, religions are born of the intensity with which certain ideas are held by particular individuals and groups – religions come alive in a human context[65]. This consideration can be made to count not only against those who deny the historical existence of Jesus but also against Gunkel and some of his associates who turn the Jesus of history into a fantom-figure representing 'the moral imperative of religious individualism'. In an important summary statement, Loisy concludes:

> ... ce n'est pas pour l'assimiler aux dieux de mystère qu'on a présenté le Christ comme un Sauveur divin; c'est pour le distinguer d'eux et le mettre au-dessus d'eux qu'on l'a proclamé l'unique et véritable Sauveur. Et le mythe du Christ ne préexistait point au christianisme, il s'est formé et il a grandi avec le christianisme.[66]

However, without acknowledging the fact, Loisy comes closer to Gunkel again in his discussion of 'religious experience', where he denies the possibility, often sought by Protestant exegetes, of distinguishing between 'unimportant' traditional elements and personal intuitions of absolute value. Even in the case of great innovators these intuitions are predetermined by the subject's former knowledge. For example, in considering the originality of Jesus over against Jewish tradition, or of Paul over against the Mysteries, there is a sense in which everything comes from the tradition but it is modified by a perception, a perspective, a synthesis and an intensity of feeling which are distinctive[67]. Thus Loisy posits an interplay of personality and history, which was also an abiding concern of Gunkel[68]; at this stage of his writing, Loisy was content to draw attention to the

---

63 Klatt *Op.cit.* p97.
64 *Ibid* pp356–7.
65 *Ibid* pp358–9.
66 *Ibid* p359.
67 *Ibid* p361.
68 Cf. Klatt: *Op.cit.* p93.

creative role exercised upon traditional elements by Jesus, Paul and others, even if he was later to place more emphasis upon the anonymous collectivity.

Les Mystères païens et le mystère chrétien is sometimes cited as an extreme example of the comparative method, seeking to undermine the originality of Christianity by assimilating it to contemporary cults and religious movements, but the above analysis has shown Loisy continuing to drive a middle way between Protestant theologians and out-and-out mythologisers. In doing so, he upheld the distinctiveness of Christianity, considered historically, but tried, not always successfully, to keep away from arguments based upon its alleged moral or psychological superiority. This depreciation of the ethical and experiential dimensions led him to stress the ritual and social dimensions, true to his Catholic formation and his sustained anti-Protestantism[69]. Here we have another indication of Loisy's academic isolation: he took a great deal from the German comparativists and in that sense can be correctly described as the leading French representative of the *religionsgeschichtliche Schule*. But although they had a common ideological foe in Harnack, Loisy's only personal contacts were with Clemen and, as we have just seen, there was much in the Protestant school's presuppositions which he could not share. Thus, having separated himself from Catholics, rationalists, *sociologues* and *mythologues* in France, Loisy was now keeping his distance from scholars whose views came closest to his own and any hope of a closer association with the German group was soon excluded by the outbreak of the First World War.

2.3 *THE WARTIME PERIOD*

Loisy's occasional writings on the question of the War show that

---

69 In 1911 Loisy had discussed the Harnack-Sohm controversy on the constitution of the early church in correspondence with von Hügel. The latter tended to favour Sohm but, equally surprisingly, Loisy sided with his old adversary Harnack: the charismatic ministry had never existed in a 'pure' form, without a 'legal' structure. 'D'ailleurs, je n'entends pas grand chose aux subtilités de ces messieurs protestants pour échapper au droit divin de l'Eglise . . . le sentiment mystique, dont résulte le prestige du sacré, ne se sépare pas des institutions et des rites traditionnels.' (Loisy to von Hügel 3.1.11 (*Mém* III p213)). Cf. also Loisy to von Hügel of 28.12.13 where he says, concerning *Les Mystères* . . . 'Je n'attends pas beaucoup de succès. Les savants allemands me lisent peu. D'ailleurs, je crois que les savants protestants, — et même les protestants qui ne sont pas savants,

it affected him profoundly. Not only did he suffer personal losses but, like Karl Barth, he was shocked by the support given to the German war effort by leading academic theologians. It was also during the War that he developed his ideas concerning a 'religion of humanity', as expounded in *La Religion* (1917) and subsequent volumes[1]. These reactions, both positive and negative, did not directly affect his exegesis and historical reconstruction of early Christianity, except perhaps his treatment of Paul. In contrast with the German tradition of an interplay between exegesis and theology, he kept his work on the New Testament separate from his more 'philosophical' speculations and it is possible over the next two decades to detect an inverse ratio between his increasing historical scepticism on the one hand and his more positive evaluation of religion on the other.

He certainly felt that there were connections between German nationalism and the prevailing German theologies. In his Journal of 8th March 1915 he wrote that the Germans had adapted a blend of Old Testament nationalism and 'Gospel mysticism' for their own purposes[2]; in writing to Cumont, he denounced Harnack's defence of the historicity of Luke-Acts as part of the great political programme of which the present War is the climax[3]. A letter of August 1915 to Lageneste tells him that his commentary on Galatians is now finished and that the Preface of *Guerre et Religion* (second edition) will have prepared the reader for his views on Paul[4]. Certainly, the

---

— me goûtent de moins en moins, à mesure qu'ils comprennent mieux que je n'ai jamais été orienté dans leur sens.' (*Mém* III p277).

1 Loisy was later to explain that during the War, he received an 'intuition', which he described as 'un sentiment direct, très vif et très sûr, de la vie religieuse dans l'humanité' (*La crise morale du temps présent* (1937) pxii). This was the basis of the 'pan-mysticism' of his later years.

2 *Mém* III p305.

3 Loisy to Cumont 4.6.16 (BN n.a.f. 15644). He had in mind the three monographs *Lukas der Arzt . . .* (1906); *Die Apostelgeschichte* (1908); *Neue Untersuchungen zur Apostelgeschichte* (1911). In a reply of 25.8.16 Cumont agreed: Harnack's theologico-historical scaffolding will not resist a push from Loisy; Harnack is a Prussian lackey (BN n.a.f. 15651).

4 Loisy to Lageneste 6.8.15 (BN n.a.f. 15645). The new Preface states that after generations of exegetical labour, the German scholars now have the aim: 'retrouver l'Allemagne et les Allemands dans tous les coins de l'Ecriture'. In particular Harnack has for several years been active in applying a damper to the freedom of exegesis (*op.cit.* p15). Deissman is also among those accused of 'absorption du christianisme dans le germanisme'

commentary maintains the anti-Protestant strain in Loisy's thinking: in a letter to von Hügel he describes it as:

> . . . une première ébauche du livre que je prépare sur saint Paul et où je pense réussir à le *déprotestantiser,* pour le remettre dans son attitude originale.[5]

The wartime background and these ideological considerations should not however weigh too heavily in our evaluation of *L'Epître aux Galates* (1916), where the main interest lies in the further evolution of Loisy's view of the apostle Paul. The commentary[6], published in popular format, is based upon a lecture course delivered at the Collège de France in 1914–1915. Correspondence of the period is revealing. Cumont, for example, told Loisy that *Les Mystères* . . . had helped him to understand Paul for the first time[7]. In his reply Loisy mentioned his conclusion that no real development is discernible in Paul's thought: he was the least logical of men, using words and ideas at random; the real problem is his conversion and what prepared for it[8]. When, in the following summer, he was preparing his work for publication, Loisy reread Renan (*Les Apôtres* and *Saint Paul*) whom he was amazed to find so timid and conservative in his criticism. To Cumont he said that the Church should erect statues to Renan for his conservative views[9] and to Lageneste: Renan wanted to keep everything in the documents (he showed a surprising confidence in the Acts narrative for instance) and so he compromised by means of his use of 'peut-être'; it is sad that the leading nineteenth century French historian of Christian origins should have dated so quickly, but this is a salutary reminder of how one's own work may appear later[10].

To Cumont: there can be no doubt about the authenticity of

(*ibid* p18). Loisy was however careful to dissociate himself from the rampant patriotism of certain French Catholics: cf. *Mors et Vita* (1916).

5 Loisy to von Hügel (*Mém* III p316).

6 In the Introduction Loisy states that it is not a commentary, properly speaking, but 'une esquisse préliminaire de l'evangélisation chrétienne en ses débuts d'après la source la plus authentique en attendant que l'on se risque à en entreprendre le tableau tant de fois déjà fait et toujours à refaire'. (p4). However the larger part of the book is made up of a kind of running commentary, incorporating some paraphrase (as is usual in Loisy's full-scale commentaries), even if there is no strict exegesis of each separate verse.

7 Cumont to Loisy 14.5.14 (BN n.a.f. 15651).

8 Loisy to Cumont 24.5.14 (BN n.a.f. 15644).

9 Loisy to Cumont 13.6.15 (BN n.a.f. 15644).

10 Loisy to Lageneste 14.6.15 (BN n.a.f. 15645).

Galatians, since no one else could have faked such a mental state[11]. To Lageneste again on 6th August: the commentary is complete; Paul was a visionary who 'saw' events in his own perverse way; Renan had perceived something of Paul's madness and vanity but was over influenced by Protestant ideas of 'religious experience';

> ... je ne connais pas de livre où on ait essayé d'attraper comme je le fais l'esprit de saint Paul en flagrant délit de création *visionnaire* quant aux faits et quant aux croyances ... Vous verrez comme je repêche Barnabé. C'est la meilleure action de ma vie.

(Barnabas has been robbed of his true place in early Christian history because, unlike Paul, he did not leave behind a theological theory of his vocation)[12]. To Cumont again on 26th September: whatever Protestants may say, Paul's conversion was not just a moral crisis, but rather 'une crise mentale et même une crise cérébrale'[13].

In the book itself, the language is equally strong. Having discussed the background of the epistle (the 'North Galatian' hypothesis is accepted, as is the view that Paul's opponents were a deliberately organised Judaizing counter-apostolate, originating from Jerusalem), Loisy puts forward his theory that the sharp antithesis between salvation by faith and salvation by the Law existed only in Paul's mind and did not fairly represent the shades of opinion to be found among Jewish Christians. All of his opponents would have accepted the idea of 'salvation by faith without the law' and even for James, baptism without circumcision was possible. But whereas their position was 'judéo-centrique', 'pour Paul, le salut est purement *christo-centrique*, avec un Christ qui n'est plus vraiment le Messie d'Israël, mais le Sauveur des hommes'[14]. In this situation, neither side was capable of logical thought and the controversy arose from mutual incomprehension. On Paul's side, this was exacerbated by his own temperament: his personal apologia in Ch.1–2 is selective and therefore misleading:

> ... c'est le plaidoyer d'un enthousiaste, d'un visionnaire qui sait fort bien ce qu'il dit, mais qui est parfaitement incapable de critiquer les évolutions de son esprit.[15]

How can he claim, for instance, the complete independence of his revelation when he must have had historical contacts with the Chris-

---

11 Loisy to Cumont 31.6.15 (BN n.a.f. 15644).
12 Loisy to Lageneste 6.8.15 (BN n.a.f. 15645).
13 Loisy to Cumont 26.9.15 (BN n.a.f. 15644).
14 *Op.cit.* pp28–9.
15 *Ibid* p37.

tian movement before his conversion? Can one really accept at face value the declared motives for his visits to Jerusalem, or the alleged division of labour between himself and Peter? If Barnabas had at one time been on an equal footing with Paul, how can the latter now assert his personal uniqueness? The doctrinal section is equally unmethodical, especially in its use of arguments from Scripture:

> . . . si toutefois on peut appeler arguments les interprétations les plus arbitraires et des fantaisies telles qu'on se demande comment elles se sont imposées à un esprit lucide pour être présentées comme des preuves péremptoires d'une doctrine qui, d'ailleurs, ne comportait pas de démonstration?[16]

The only explanation can be that Paul's experience was 'fortement teintée d'illuminisme et non seulement d'une grande exaltation, mais d'une certaine aberration mentale'[17]. Whatever the experience was, it produced 'visions', which the apostle transcribed as 'theories'. Thus one can speak, in Gal 2—5, of a 'vision' of salvation inaugurated by Abraham, to which Jewish speculation and the Gentile mysteries have contributed but a spontaneous product of Paul's mind and therefore, for him, 'reality'; a 'vision' of Christ on the cross; a 'vision' of two women and two sons of Abraham; a 'vision' of a covenant[18].

It is not necessary to consider in any detail the historical reconstructions suggested by *l'Epître aux Galates,* since subsequent publications offer a more synoptic view and in any case Loisy was to revise some of his opinions. But some amplification is required of the judgements pronounced on Pauline theology. Loisy presents Paul's doctrinal system as completely idiosyncratic, illogical and arbitrary. His own language in the body of the commentary is as scathing as that of Paul himself: we meet expressions like 'mirage de mots et confusion d'idées'[19]; 'l'arbitraire de l'interprétation atteint ici au comble'[20]; 'cette fantasmagorie'[21]; 'pensée enfantine'[22]. The basis for some of these judgements is that Paul did not show a 'correct' historical understanding of the Old Testament passages he employs; he is also said to be lacking in mature human judgement. But, at a deeper level, Loisy's moralism makes him very suspicious of Paul's

---

16 *Ibid* p41.
17 *Ibid* p44.
18 *Ibid* p46—8.
19 On 3, 7: p145.
20 On 3, 13f: pp149—50.
21 On 3, 18: p154.
22 On 3, 29: p161.

central doctrine of justification by faith, which he rejects utterly because it is subversive of common morality[23]. His comments on 3,25f are instructive in this regard:

> La loi extérieure ne fait pas la moralité intérieure de l'individu; mais il est d'une enfan-tine absurdité de soutenir qu'elle n'aide en rien l'homme à réaliser cette moralité intime et qu'elle sert seulement à lui révéler le mal qu'il fait, ainsi que son impuissance radicale à faire le bien. Paul invente la philosophie et la psychologie qui conviennent aux besoins de sa thèse.[24]

Loisy's distaste for theological systematising went back to his own seminary days and, in spite of his work as an apologist, it was to remain a constant feature of his career. One must surely allow for this personal element, as well as his single-handed battle against the Protestants, in accounting for the scorn which he pours upon ideas which were to be so influential upon the Christian tradition of centuries to come[25]. Even if his language is somewhat more moderate in his treatment of Galatians 4, where terms like *stoicheia* and *gnōsis* permit allusions to the Mysteries, the overall impression is conveyed of a fanatic who wilfully misunderstood and misrepresented his fellow Christians and who, in so doing, had recourse to wild and desperate arguments conjured up from a disordered imagination. *L'Epître aux Galates* therefore represents a significant shift of opinion away from *Les Mystères* . . . : there Paul had been credited with a highly creative role in the transmutation of Christianity from a Messianic cult into a universal 'gnosis'; now, however, the emphasis is upon his eccentricity over against the main body of Christians. Loisy does acknowledge a genuine historical feature in Paul's concern for the preservation of unity between Jewish and Gentile Christians and this leads to inconsistency in the epistle:

> Sa gnose ne s'accorde pas du tout avec son mysticisme ecclésiastique, qui est d'origine juive, ni tout à fait avec son mysticisme de confrérie, d'union dans le Christ pour l'im-

---

23 Cf. Loisy to Cumont 26.12.15: unless one is a violent Protestant, faith and works are not mutually exclusive, 'attendu que c'est la foi qui fait le mérite des oeuvres et la vertu des rites'. (BN n.a.f. 15644) In a letter to Loisy of 18.10.15, Cumont had speculated that issues similar to those of Galatians must have been raised in the Mystery cults: was faith enough for salvation or was strict observance of the ritual also required? (BN n.a.f. 15651).

24 *Ibid* p159.

25 Cf. his comment in the *Les Actes des Apôtres* (1921): Le rôle de Paul a été possible parce que Barnabé lui avait préparé la voie. Plus tard l'influence de Paul à été considérable, — *sinon toujours heureuse*, — par ses écrits, sur la pensée chrétienne . . . (p576) (My italics).

mortalité, qui paraît bien être d'origine païenne, mais ce n'est pas son illuminisme gnostique qui aura le dernier mot, même chez lui.[26]

But some of the inconsistency must lie with Loisy, who has obviously not yet reached a definitive picture of Paul. He can rightly point to some of the unresolved tensions in the apostle's thought (which are perhaps too conveniently explained away by more orthodox writers as paradoxical expressions of the truth or in terms of Paul being 'all things to all men') and he can rightly question standard Protestant accounts of Paul's theology which refer everything to a moral-psychological understanding of his conversion (though Loisy has his own psychological account to give). But even the historian has some duty to suspend disbelief and take theological ideas alien to himself rather more seriously than this. It is possible moreover that in *Les Mystères* . . . Loisy had not fully absorbed the positions of Bousset's *Kyrios Christos* and not quite accepted the idea of extensive developments of Christian thinking in pre-Pauline Hellenistic Christianity. But, as we shall see, this kind of theory was to make a strong contribution to his further attempts upon the story of Christian origins.

2.4 'LES ACTES DES APÔTRES'

The next phase of Loisy's criticism centres upon his work on The Acts of the Apostles and the massive commentary on Acts which he published in 1920[1]. He was originally stimulated to work on Acts by E. Norden's *Agnostos Theos* (1913) and in a review article devoted to this work[2] he expressed his agreement with Norden that a redactor had interpolated the account of the Ascension and Paul's speech in Athens and gave the opinion that the same redactor might well have worked on the Gospel of Luke also. A letter of Cumont to Loisy shows that they both considered Norden as an ally against

---

26 *Ibid* p107, with reference to Gal 2, 1–2.

1 He in fact completed work on the commentary in the summer of 1916 (cf. Loisy to Houtin 20.9.16 (BN n.a.f. 15718) and Loisy to von Hügel 24.12.16 (*Mém* III p331)) but publication was delayed by the War. He immediately started work on a translation and commentary of the Epistles, hoping, as the letter to von Hügel states, to extract a new synthesis of apostolic history from his labours. Such a volume however did not appear, because of changing directions in his work, but some of the work on the Epistles appeared in print in the *RHLR* articles of 1921 which are described below.

2 'Les écrits de saint Luc' *RHLR* 1913, 4 pp352–68.

the views of Harnack[3] and writing to von Hügel Loisy said he would lecture on Acts during 1914–15: 'Après l'*Agnostos Theos* de Norden, il y a quelque chose à faire de ce côté-là'[4]. In fact, the lectures on Galatians intervened, so that it was during 1915–16 that he lectured on Paul's trials in Acts, in 1916–17 on 'Les premières années du christianisme d'après les Actes des Apôtres', in 1917–18 on Paul's missions (the mid-section of Acts) and Paul's major epistles and in 1918–19 on 'L'Apôtre Paul et le christianisme ¹udaïsant'. These lectures drew upon the work he had completed on Acts and his ongoing study of the epistles and were utilised in a series of articles published in 1920–1 on: the early years of Christianity[5]; early Christian literature[6]; the life and epistles of Saint Paul[7] (as well as further articles on the other New Testament epistles and the Apostolic Fathers). Here we note the alternation: history of the religion – criticism of the documents, always one of Loisy's stated principles in his work on early Christianity. Since these articles comprise a new synthesis in response to the task 'toujours à refaire', an account is required of their main conclusions.

In the period 29–44 A.D. ('période de gestation au terme de laquelle on peut dire que le christianisme est vraiment né') there were three 'moments essentiels': the formation of a first group of believers in Jerusalem, composed of former disciples of Jesus; the formation of a second group, drawn from Hellenistic Jews in Jerusalem, which was almost immediately dispersed; the diffusion of the new faith beyond Palestine and the founding of a mainly Gentile-Christian community in Antioch. 'A ces trois moments se rattachent trois noms: Pierre, Etienne, Barnabé'[8]. The first period is the most obscure but it seems likely that, back in Galilee, Peter was the first to 'see' the Risen Jesus and that when the other disicples had 'seen', the group returned to Jerusalem to await the Parousia[9]. The second group, around Stephen, was attracted by the idea of a heavenly Messiah (rather than a military leader) and with their wider horizons, the Hellenistic Jews

---

3   Loisy to Cumont 21.7.13 (BN n.a.f. 15644).
4   Loisy to von Hügel 28.12.13 (*Mém* III p277–8).
5   *RHLR* 1920, 2, pp161–180.
6   *RHLR* 1920, 3, pp305–325.
7   *RHLR* 1920, 4, pp449–471; 1921, 1 pp76–125; 2, 213–250.
8   'Les premières années du christianisme' p161.
9   *Ibid* pp164–5.

were able to develop hints contained in the teaching of Jesus about the Temple and the Law being superseded; they did not, like Paul later, envisage a complete abrogation of the Law, but their views were quite unacceptable in the religious atmosphere of Jerusalem and therefore they had to leave[10]. In Antioch (and possibly in other centres, although the evidence is obscure) the Hellenistic preachers, under the spontaneous impulse of their faith and the circumstances, admitted Gentiles to the community without any Jewish ritual prescriptions[11]. In such a setting it was possible for the original nationalistic faith to be replaced by the kyrios-cult centred upon a quasi-divine mediator: 'c'est dans ce second foyer de l'Evangile, dans ce premier foyer de l'helléno-christianisme, que s'ébaucha réellement la religion chrétienne'[12]. An atmosphere of enthusiasm prevailed: 'Ainsi fut consommée la pénétration de l'eschatologie juive par le mysticisme oriental'[13]. Barnabas was the leader of this work; Paul, to begin with, only his auxiliary.

Paul, who cannot in such circumstances be regarded as the 'real founder of Christianity' was converted to Helleno-Jewish Christianity in Damascus, not as a result of a crisis of conscience, but more probably after prolonged debates with Christian opponents[14]. But his visionary temperament produced at an early stage his personal notion of the death of Christ as a salutary act for the removal of sin, and this he grafted on to the faith in the cultic Christ which he had received[15]. After a profitless mission in Nabataea, he paid a brief visit to Jerusalem, where he was advised to go to Antioch; there he became one of the 'prophets and teachers' and began his ten-year collaboration with Barnabas. When their preaching to the Gentiles had caused some alarm in Jerusalem, a meeting was held there, which they attended, and it was agreed that their work should continue and regular collections be sent to the mother-community. The crisis was not as serious as some of Paul's letters and Acts suggest[16]. It was Paul's disagreement with Peter in Antioch, described in Galatians 2, which led to his exclusion from the community and

---

10 *Ibid* pp168–173.
11 *Ibid* p175.
12 *Ibid* p177.
13 *Ibid* p178.
14 'La carrière de l'apôtre Paul' p452.
15 *Ibid* p454.
16 *Ibid* p459.

from then on, no longer having Barnabas as his companion, he worked as an independent missionary. Thereafter he regarded anyone who disagreed with him as a 'Judaizer' and insisted upon his own authority. Unfortunately he confused two distinct factors: his personal vocation and the evangelisation of the Gentiles by means of a Law-free Gospel. 'La critique moderne subit encore l'influence de cette vision'[17]. He undertook successful missions in Philippi and Corinth, although trouble soon arose among the Corinthian Christians, due to the influence of Apollos and Peter. Paul managed to effect a reconciliation, but before the end of the first century A.D., the church of Corinth had been brought back into the mainstream of the Christian movement. Paul's final days under house-arrest in Rome reinforce the impression of a marginal figure in the life of the Church: it may in fact only have been through his martyrdom that contending elements in the Church were reconciled[18]. Thus Paul's role in early Christianity was never as great as he himself thought, although he made a considerable contribution, through his apostolic activity and 'son inconsciente adaptation de l'Evangile au courant de la mystique contemporaine'[19].

Christian literature was generated by the ongoing life of the Church and it was specifically born in that situation where Christianity was recognisably a new religion, that is to say in the Hellenistic communities[20]. Apologetic motives were prominent in its production:

> Au fond, sa littérature exprime la conscience de plus en plus claire et décidée qu'il (sc. le christianisme) prend de son autonomie vis-à-vis du judaisme; dans la variété de ses formes, elle atteste le travail spirituel par lequel cette autonomie s'est réalisée, et les efforts de la raison croyante pour étayer la nouvelle foi.[21]

It also corresponded to the activities of Christian preachers and teachers. The 'catéchèse' of the first community merely added to the teaching of Jesus the ideas of his resurrection and parousia, although in the Gentile mission, prominence had to be given to monotheism and moral teaching. This type of basic teaching was used by all Christian missionaries, including Paul, and is to be distinguished from 'la démonstration plus ou moins savante de la nouvelle foi', which can be described as 'une gnose où régna bientôt le mystère' and which was to be found in the teaching of 'les théoriciens du mystère

---

17 *Ibid* p461.
18 *Ibid* p470.
19 *Ibid* p471.
20 'La littérature du christianisme primitif' p307.
21 *Ibid* p308.

chrétien' such as Paul (in Romans), the writer to the Hebrews and (probably) Apollos[22]. The basic *catéchèse* remained very Jewish in tone and is well represented by the Didache. However, 'le mystère ne tarda pas à entrer dans la catéchèse, comme il était entré dans la foi et dans le culte', and thus was created 'une vaste dispute d'exégèse' whereby the substitution of Jesus the Saviour for Jesus the Messiah took place under cover of an arbitrary manipulation of Old Testament texts[23].

Such elements of 'mythe' had already taken hold of the person of Jesus in the Palestinian community, in order to explain how the death of the Messiah had been prophesied, but it was in pagan territory that the idea of the death of Christ as an expiatory sacrifice was elaborately justified by extremes of exegesis. Both in Paul and Hebrews, therefore, we find a 'mythe du Christ', very different from 'la légende de Jésus' preserved in the Gospels; it is in fact a 'Gnostic' gospel which the writers claim to read off from the Old Testament[24]. It was further developed with the delay of the parousia in order to consolidate the place of Jesus as founder of the new religion and to justify developments in Christian belief and practice. The arbitrary illogical character of the early Christian exegesis of the Old Testament is to be explained by charismatic excitement combined with the demands of apologetic. Faith and 'vision' established the relationship between texts. Also in this way a saying could be ascribed to Jesus, or a letter to an apostle, without any consciousness of deliberate fraud[25]. The earliest written documents were probably collections of prooftexts and manuals of ethical instruction, the latter derived from Hellenistic Judaism. The main types represented among extant documents are: gospels ('des christologies et des catéchèses en forme d'histoire'; even the narratives are 'une vision mystique de la carrière du Christ', with a strong influence exercised by Christian ritual); Acts, which is an apologia directed at the Gentile authorities but also 'une instruction morale sur l'histoire apostolique, et une vision mystique de cette histoire'; and the

---

22 *Ibid* p310. Loisy draws attention to the distinction found in I Corinthians 1, 14—3, 2 and Hebrews 5, 11—6, 3 between elementary teaching and a 'higher' understanding of the Christian mystery.

23 *Ibid* p311.

24 *Ibid* p313.

25 *Ibid* p318.

epistles, which apart from moral exhortation, contain varying elements of christology, soteriology and ecclesiology[26]. From the Old Testament and even more distant religious forebears, the writings of the New Testament inherit a liturgical, oracular style, which develops its own rhythmic subtleties, and its distinctive usages imprinted by the new religion itself[27].

These summaries will have given some idea of Loisy's ideas at this time concerning the main developments in early Christian history and literature. The articles in *RHLR* go on to provide analyses of and comments on the epistolary literature of the New Testament[28] but since Loisy's views on the composition of the epistles were to develop somewhat startlingly during the 1920s and 1930s, his ideas can be considered in another context[29]. On the historical side, more stress is laid upon the spontaneous and anonymous nature of the developments: not only is Paul still further devalued in his overall influence, but even the names of Peter, Stephen and Barnabas are little more than labels for the main stages in the process. So too in the literature: the documents are 'occasional', the products of a ferment of religious activity, where only general trends rather than specific names, dates and places can be charted. In order to describe these trends, Loisy now deploys to their full extent, but not always with the requisite precision, a range of terms, notably: 'catéchèse', 'gnose', 'mystère', 'mythe', 'légende', which are well suited to his interpretation. It is interesting to compare this terminology with that employed by Bultmann in *Die Geschichte der synoptischen Tradition* of 1921. Bultmann's categories are predominantly literary (apophthegmata, logia etc.) and he has a more precise understanding of 'legend'. But

---

26 *Ibid* p322.

27 For Loisy's elaboration of this last point, v.2.5.1 below.

28 In *Mém* III 349 Loisy describes work done on the epistles in 1917—18. 'Mon commentaire des Epîtres n'est qu'une longue paraphrase des textes; je n'ai pas eu et je n'aurai jamais le temps de le retravailler à fond pour la publication.' The description fits the *RHLR* articles very well. By publication Loisy presumably meant in full commentary format.

29 V. 2.5.3 below. It should however be noted that in the two articles on the Pauline literature of 1921 Loisy maintained the substantial authenticity of Romans, I & II Corinthians, Galatians, Philippians, Colossians, I Thessalonians and Philemon. Such a position was already somewhat in conflict with the drastic reduction in Paul's influence and the largely anonymous character of early Christian literature which the earlier articles in the series had underlined and it was this problem which Loisy had to resolve in the next phase of his criticism.

as Loisy's review of Bultmann shows, in spite of his general sympathy, he could not himself accept in all its detail the literary
analysis of the 'forms' undertaken by the German critic[30]. Of more
interest to him at the time was the question of the rhythmic style
running through most if not all of the early Christian literature,
itself a reflection of the liturgical and catechetical origins of that
literature. Loisy felt that this approach brought him into closer contact with the religious impulses of early Christianity[31]; but before we
see how he took up and developed the approach, we must first give
some account of the commentary on Acts.

The outstanding feature of this commentary is the author's relentless pursuit through over one hundred pages of introduction and
eight hundred pages of commentary proper, of his central thesis: an
original document of great historical value, written by Luke about 80
A.D., was deliberately falsified by a redactor of the early second
century, writing on behalf of the leaders of the Roman church. Loisy
claims to see so many inconsistencies in the text of Acts as it has
reached us, that they can only be explained by the insertion of crude
'fictions' (a word which is probably the most widely encountered in
this work).

Luke himself ('la figure la plus sympathique, après Barnabé, du
christianisme primitif')[32] had genuine historical motives in producing
his two-volume work (cf. Luke 1, 1–4), and although his original
story of the early Church was inevitably in the nature of 'une légende
religieuse', it contained information which would have resolved the
most persistent problems encountered by modern criticism concerning Christian origins. It contained, for example, details on the following matters: the return of the apostolic group from Galilee to Jerusalem, after the first appearances of Jesus; the rise of the Hellenistic

---

30 *RHLR* 1922 pp452–8. Loisy begins his review by remarking that Bultmann's work is
similar in scope and conclusions to his own lectures at the Collège de France over recent
years. But he finds that in the case of the sayings material, Bultmann's categories are too
overlapping and the analysis too dense: 'il s'agit toujours de dissection plutôt que résurrection organiquement vivante'. In the case of the narratives, there is too much hunting up
of hypothetical literary sources, instead of simply admitting the free creation of material
for the purposes of teaching or apologetics. Loisy reserves highest though qualified
praise for Bultmann's final section in the redaction of the material: 'Comme analyse
littéraire, il ne semble pas qu'on ait jamais fait mieux ni même aussi bien. Mais la méthode
reste trop littéraire et scolastique'.
31 V. 2.5.1 below.
32 *Op.cit.* p89.

group in Jerusalem and Stephen's (legal) trial; the dispersion of the Hellenistic group to Alexandria and other centres; the founding of the Church of Antioch and developments there (including the first charismatic activity); the missionary work of Barnabas and Paul in Syria and Cilicia; the disowning of the extreme Judaizers by the Church in Jerusalem, after private discussions between representatives of Jerusalem and Antioch; Peter's escape from Herod Agrippa to Antioch; Luke's precise involvement with Paul on his missionary journeys; Paul's relations with the Roman Christians and his condemnation and execution in Rome. In some of these cases Loisy starts from genuine obscurities and inconsistencies in the Acts narrative, which call for historical reconstruction by the modern critic. But he is obviously overconfident in claiming to know so precisely what the original document contained and has to draw upon his own previously reached conclusions (themselves, of course, partly based on his interpretation of other early Christian documents).

This valuable information has been denied us because the redactor, acting reprehensibly even for his own day, wished to make the point to the Roman civil authorities that Christianity was not a new sect, but the perfected and authentic form of Judaism[33] and should therefore enjoy the same toleration in, the Empire as that accorded to Jews[34].

> ... il travaillait pour un groupe, dont l'intérêt actuel des communautés chrétiennes, sans mesurer tout le dommage qu'il causerait à la science du XXe siècle, et sans autre préoccupation que de transformer en plaidoyer l'histoire que Luc avait laissée. . .[35]

His method is that of 'travestissement perpétuel'[36], using 'les

---

33 This is the most consistently argued point throughout the commentary and references are legion. Loisy wavers somewhat as to whether the redactor genuinely thought that the differences between Christianity and Judaism were minimal, or whether this is simply part of his apologia: cf. remarks on p830.

34 It is this apologetic motive which leads him, for instance, to provide an outline history of Israel in Stephen's speech (the inadequacy of the Temple is emphasised to make the point that Christians do not need to pay the Temple tax (p321)); to indicate by means of Paul's speech in Athens, that there are affinities between pagan wisdom and the Christian revelation (p662); to distinguish his own standard Gentile Christianity of c. 100 A.D. from Jewish Christianity (wether Palestinian or Alexandrian) (p719); and to suggest, in 26, 26 that the facts about Jesus and the early church were public knowledge (p902).

35 Op.cit. p106.

36 Loisy finds this misrepresentation throughout the book, but it achieves a special intensity towards the end of Acts in the much distorted records of Paul's trials — cf. e.g. remarks on pp889, 906–7.

libres procédés du dédoublement et de la transposition'[37]. He freely invents miracles[38], speeches[39], characters[40] and edifying tales[41] drawing upon models in the Old Testament, the Gospel tradition and the pagan world. His fictions are partly the expression of a systematic conception of the Church, as a spirit-filled community centred upon a spiritual and immortal Christ. The Holy Spirit is active in the appointment of leaders; there is much 'spiritual' activity, such as prophecies and visions, and the redactor attempts to trace this type of activity back to the earliest days, by the interpolation of the fictional account of the forty day period between the Resurrection and the Ascension and the descent of the Spirit at Pentecost [42]. In his efforts to demonstrate the continuity between Judaism and Christianity, the redactor has had to introduce another series of fictions. In reality, the Christian 'mystery' of a universal Saviour had replaced early Messianism, but according to Acts, Peter is credited with having first preached to the Gentiles, sometimes using Pauline language[43], while Paul and Hellenistic Christianity are repeatedly judaized[44]. This judaizing tendency also accounts for features in the book's Christology which are sometimes described as 'primitive': in fact, some of the more mystical elements in Hellenistic Christian-

---

37 Other procedures of which he is accused by Loisy are 'synchronismes' (eg. p686) and 'remplissage' (eg. pp744, 929). Examples of 'dédoublement' are mentioned on pp708—9.

38 E.g. among many others, Peter's miracles in 9, 32—43 are constructed upon models provided by Elijah and Elisha (p431); Paul's miracle on Malta (28, 3—6) is 'embroidered on a given theme' (p924).

39 Virtually all the speeches in Acts are of the redactor's invention, according to Loisy. The 'apostolic preaching' is in fact the standard preaching of his own day; Paul's speech at Miletus has strong resemblances to the Pastoral Epistles; sometimes the redactor makes a special rhetorical effort as in Paul's speeches at Athens and before King Agrippa.

40 Eg. Agabus in 11, 28 and 21, 10: the reintroduction of the same fictional character is said by Loisy to reveal the redactor's 'gaucherie' (p787).

41 Eg. 20, 7—12 (Eutychus); 24, 24—5 (Paul visited by Felix and Drusilla: an example of the redactor's 'faible pour les grands personnages' (p864)). These are only two examples among many alleged by Loisy.

42 For details of the redactor's antedating of the Holy Spirit and its manifestations, cf. Loisy's comments on 1, 5—8 esp. pp152, 154—5, 158.

43 Loisy sees such 'Pauline' language in Peter's speech to Cornelius eg. 10, 34f, 43.

44 The redactor could not deny Paul's reputation, largely fostered by his own writings, as 'the apostle to the Gentiles' but he depicts him as subordinate to the apostles in Jerusalem and emphasises his faithfulness to Jewish tradition: cf. 21, 26; 23, 6; 24, 14. Cf. also the 'fiction' of 22, 21: Paul receives his vocation as apostle to the Gentiles in the *Temple of Jerusalem*. Loisy does however admit that Paul, a highly complex character, remained more Jewish than some of his own theories and some modern commentators

ity have been replaced by the extensive use of the Septuagint and by the standard terminology of the late first century[45]. Paul's idiosyncratic teaching is almost totally absent (although it had not indeed been much quoted in Luke's historical work, where the emphasis was upon 'the facts'). The break between Judaism and Christianity is explained by emphasising at every juncture the opposition and guilt of the Jews and the transition is made to appear more smooth than in reality by the invention of the Apostolic Decree – 'la première des fausses décrétales'[46]. The redactor's Roman outlook is revealed in the prominence given to Peter:

> L'apologie de l'auteur des Actes est donc équilibrée de telle sorte qu'elle représente la fondation du christianisme dans l'histoire des deux apôtres fondateurs de la communauté romaine, réservant à Pierre, comme il convenait pour l'équilibre de la démonstration et de la tradition, la première place et le premier rôle.[47]

The redactor is thus shown up as 'un rhéteur de second ordre, jonglant en avocat avec les idées et les faits'[48].

This commentary is of great interest in the history of interpretation, since it constitutes a break with much contemporary work on Acts and a prelude to later exegesis[49]. It breaks with the tradition of source-criticism, of the type which sought parallel or complementary sources used by Luke[50]. It also breaks with the acceptance of the

---

suggest (cf. 768, 801). For the alleged adherence of Gentile Christians to the Jewish requirements of the Apostolic Decree cf. 21, 25 and Loisy's comments *ad loc.* (p799).

45 Cf. eg. Loisy's comments on *pais* (p230) and *kyrios* (pp212, 464–5); and on Christology generally: pp202ff.

46 According to Loisy the 'Council' of Acts 15 was originally a private meeting which agreed upon the 'collection' among Gentile Christian communities. Neither has the redactor's 'system' (apostolic decisions binding upon the whole Church) anything to do with Paul's theological 'system' in Galatians and Romans: Paul did not embody 'the Gentile question'. The 'Apostolic Decree' breathes the spirit of late first-century writings such as the Pastorals and the Didache (v.comm. *ad loc.* esp. remarks on pp567, 571, 582, 583, 600–1, 608).

47 *Op.cit.* p117. Unhistorical features of Peter's story in Acts, according to Loisy, include not only his miracles (cf. above), but his quasi-episcopal visit to Samaria (8, 14ff), his success in the conversion of the first Gentile (Cornelius Ch.10–11) and his intervention at the 'Council of Jerusalem' (15, 7ff).

48 *Op.cit.* p124.

49 Some indication of Loisy's independence is gained from W.W. Gasque: *A History of the Criticism of the Acts of the Apostles* (1975) p245 n.123 where we are told that the commentary cannot be properly considered, for reasons of space 'and because of the difficulty of fitting it into a systematic outline', although 'it is the only one-man commentary of this century which equals Haenchen's in both volume and ingenuity'.

50 For a description of this phase of Acts criticism, v. Loisy's introduction Section II and the more recent account in J. Dupont, *The Sources of Acts* (1964).

Acts narrative as a reliable historical account of early Christianity[51]. The name of Harnack was associated with both of these positions and we have seen that Loisy had his personal reasons for opposing Harnack's 'campaign', as he called it, on behalf of the historicity of Acts[52]. On the other hand, in its identification of apologetic and theological 'tendencies' in Luke, it anticipates some of the redaction-criticism of Dibelius and Haenchen. Loisy's aversion to 'literary' criticism meant that he did not pick up those aspects of the work of Norden, whose *Agnostos Theos* had set him off on the trail of interpolations, which were to lead into the form-critical concerns of Dibelius. Neither did he wish to write 'a theology of Luke', along the lines of later redaction critics, since his standpoint is that of the historian of religions, rather than the Christian theologian, and he is scathing about the redactor's intellectual achievement[53]. But in its refusal to take the Acts narrative at face value, in its frank recognition of legendary elements and tendentious writing, in its claim to place the book of Acts in the history of early Christianity (rather than to reconstruct early Christianity around the book of Acts) and in its vigorous, trenchant style, Loisy on Acts remains readable and thought-provoking[54].

One must of course refer to the personal appropriateness of Loisy's findings to his own life history. As someone who had tried to be an impartial historian of the early Church, only to be thwarted

---

51 This remark applies to Catholic and orthodox Protestant scholarship. But Loisy, although perfectly familiar with his predecessors, does not stand in the direct line of the Tübingen school of F.C. Baur nor of any subsequent radical scholars, such as B. Bauer, the Dutch school, or F. Overbeck: cf. his comments on these *op.cit.* pp23, 28, 32.

52 Cf. 2.3 above.

53 *Op.cit.* p536. Loisy specifically states that the redactor was not a theologian. There may appear to be some resemblance between Loisy's depreciation of the redactor and the low regard in which the Lucan literature is held by some Protestant exegetes, who find in it the deadly influence of 'early catholicism'. But this latter judgement is based upon a comparison with Paul, who enshrines the true Gospel, whereas Loisy, as we have seen, was equally scathing about Paul. So the only real coincidence of viewpoint is in the condemnation of religious institutionalism, motivated by apologetic concerns.

54 It does have the disadvantage of being over-long; one rather wishes that Loisy had followed the idea he mentioned to von Hügel in a letter of 7.8.20 of rewriting before publication (*Mém* III p395); some repetition and unnecessary paraphrasing might then have been omitted. On the other hand the commentary includes important discussions of such topics as Christian worship and glossolalia, exorcisms and visions, the role of leaders such as Stephen, Barnabas and James, as well as many cross references to other early Christian literature.

by the Roman authorities, he obviously found in this document some striking parallels with his own career[55]. His zeal in unmasking pious fraud comes dangerously close to the tendencies he had decried in Reinach and this personal factor, which is revealed in a host of caustic remarks and some obvious examples of special pleading[56], inevitably detracts from the work's objectivity. But to note this element of personal engagement with the text is to raise the wider question of how far Loisy, as a non-confessional historian of religions, succeeded in producing an objective portrait of early Christianity, when the only evidence comes from the New Testament documents themselves[57].

His work in the period covered by the commentaries on Galatians and Acts and the articles in *RHLR* throws into sharp relief the problems which the secular historian confronts in the circumstances. The confessional writer, however radical, almost inevitably approaches the documents with the idea that they are capable of yielding up 'truth' and even if this turns out to be religious rather than historical truth, his attitude contains positive factors which may influence his historical conclusions. For example, most commentators and historians of the early church, when faced with discrepancies between Acts and the epistles, express a general preference for one or the other source of information. Loisy however is highly

---

55 Cf. A. Omodeo, *Alfred Loisy Storico delle religioni* (1936) 'L'attività dell'ultimo rielaboratore, il Loisy, espertissimo del mondo ecclesiastico, la concepisce un po' troppo simile a quella di certi preti scaltriti e furbi . . . Forse converrebbe esser più moderati'. (pp86–7).

56 Eg. his interpretation of 16,19ff and 19,29ff (disturbances sparked off in Philippi and Ephesus by the Christian preaching); in each case, the main point is said to be: 'le différend qui sépare les chrétiens des Juifs est de nulle importance, et . . . les paiens n'ont pas à intervenir dans cette affaire' (p756), rather than the more obvious emphasis, supported by most commentators, on the political inoffensiveness of Christianity.

57 Loisy's growing aversion during this period to the literary criticism of the New Testament is made clear in his review (*RC* 1922 pp263–5) of Goguel: *Introduction* t.III, much of which is devoted to Loisy's *Actes*. Loisy says that differences between himself and Goguel are not simply due to wrong opinions, but to the confrontation of different methods producing different results. The 'critique littéraire exacte et minutieuse' of a Reuss, Holtzmann or a Wellhausen has rendered remarkable services, but has reached a dead end. Instead, 'il faudra éclaircir le contenu de ceux-ci (sc. les textes) par la comparaison, le pénétrer par une intelligence indéfiniment progressive de son objet, intelligence qui ne consiste pas à résoudre cet objet en abstractions, mais à le réaliser, pour ainsi dire, dans sa vie initiale, dans la vie sociale et individuelle de ceux qui ont conçu et rédigé les textes.'

critical of both and is indeed antagonistic towards both Paul and the redactor of Acts. He cannot trust them as historians and, interestingly enough, he has a fairly low view of both as religious thinkers (in spite of his originally more positive estimate of Paul in *Les Mystères* . . .). He therefore has to take as his starting-point a schema derived from a general understanding of how Christianity developed in its early years, namely the three-stage theory which he labelled 'Peter-Stephen-Barnabas'[58]. In fact this turns out to be a valuable heuristic device and something like it is still being employed by those engaged in traditio-historical investigations in early Christian doctrine. The history of religions, although too narrowly conceived in terms of the Mysteries, also provides Loisy with insights, especially in the collective and ritual aspects of his study. But even if one shares something of his opposition to an over-literary approach, his handling of the documents produces a certain dissatisfaction. Whatever their historical deficiencies, the documents deserve a more positive religious evaluation than that which Loisy accords them. In particular, his scorn for theologians precludes a more sympathetic study of the theological positions held by Paul and the redactor of Acts. We have seen how the setting of Loisy's academic work and his own personal history made it difficult for him to achieve a serenity of gaze. But even judged as a historian, Loisy is disappointing in not achieving greater accuracy of focus upon the writers concerned. In the following years, he came increasingly to see the New Testament documents as disparate and anonymous, but in the Acts commentary, Paul is still a sufficiently recognisable and influential historical figure for a more consistent view to have been held of his doctrines; and even if the redactor was only an ecclesiastical lackey, his religious milieu called for closer definition. There is, for example, uncertainty about the mixture of Jewish and Gentile elements and of charismatic and institutional elements, in the 'standard' Christianity of c.100 A.D. which the redactor is said to represent. Where, however, Loisy must be applauded, is in seeking to submit the documents to historical

---

58 This schema is, of course, in part derived from the Book of Acts (one would not know anything of Stephen and the Hellenists from the epistles) and Loisy is therefore open to the charge of circularity, which can be brought against many radical critics of Acts. His own escape from the circle is in positing the original source worked over by the redactor and this would be perfectly legitimate were it not for his overconfidence in claiming to identify the source in such detail.

rather than theological control: the latter was the more easy course and still affected the work of even the more advanced Protestant scholars and the documents themselves propose theological critieria; so without any external checks upon dates, places, authors or tendencies to guide him, Loisy chose the more arduous path, which was to lead him ever further away from commonly accepted results.

2.5 FROM 1921 TO THE 'JUBILE LOISY' (1927)

The years 1921 to 1927 saw important developments in Loisy's work on early Christianity, even if the results of this thinking were not to become fully apparent until his *La Naissance du christianisme* of 1933 and its satellite volumes. During the early 1920s, he published a translation of the New Testament, with brief introductory remarks on each of the books: *Les Livres du Nouveau Testament* (1922);[1] and a series of large-scale commentaries: *Le Quatrième Evangile. Les Epîtres dites de Jean* (1921)[2] (a complete revision of his earlier commentary of 1903), *L'Apocalypse de Jean* (1923)[3] and *L'Evangile selon Luc* (1924)[4]. A commentary of similar scope on Matthew was completed but remained unpublished[5]. He was lecturing on the

---

1 Loisy's journal of 4.7.21 records his decision to publish this translation, which he had made over the years, when he realised that a full-scale commentary on the Epistles would take longer than expected (*Mém* III pp406–7). He consulted friends on the project and accepted the advice of Louis Canet that the Gospels should follow the Epistles (Canet to Loisy 19.10.21 (BN n.a.f. 15650)); and the advice of Cumont to include 'apocryphal' books (Cumont to Loisy, undated letter of late 1921 (BN n.a.f. 15651)): the Gospel and Apocalypse of Peter are put in an Appendix (cf. *Mém* III p414). For Loisy's problems with the proofs of this work and his preparation of a second edition, v. below 2.5.1. n. 10 and 22.

2 Loisy worked on this during the summer of 1918 (cf. Loisy to von Hügel 7.5.18 (*Mém* III p362)). In Loisy to Cumont 14.8.18 (BN n.a.f. 15644) he says that it contains less on redactional matters than the 1903 edition but more on the question of the origins of the Fourth Gospel, especially in relation to the Mysteries. The work was completed on 27th March 1921 (*Mém* III p406).

3 This was begun in 1918 (cf. *Mém* III p362); it was revised for publication in 1921 (cf. Loisy to von Hügel 17.10.21, in which Loisy acknowledges a debt to R.H. Charles, although not sharing his conclusions (*Mém* III p413)).

4 *Mém* III p454 mentions that this commentary was his main task during 1924.

5 The manuscript survives among Loisy's papers (BN n.a.f. 15641). Autograph notes of 1938–9 explain that he could not bring himself to destroy it, even if it was not quite worthy of publication. It was begun in 1919 (cf. Loisy to Cumont 8.6.19 (BN n.a.f. 15644)) and resumed in 1925 (cf. *Mém* III p473). At the time, Loisy gave pressure of work and finance as reasons for not publishing (Loisy to Cumont 2.8.25 and 28.10.26 (BN n.a.f. 15644)).

Gospels at the Collège de France and the final volume of *RHLR* in 1922 contained lengthy articles on *L'apocalypse chrétienne* and *La légende de Jésus*[6]. It is not possible here to give a full account of these labours. We can merely note that Loisy continued to review and to publish across the whole spectrum of Biblical studies. He was to return again to the religion of Israel[7] and maintained a steady interest in apocalyptic as a significant link between Judaism and nascent Christianity[8]. All aspects of the New Testament came under his scrutiny. But it is possible to separate out certain major concerns which preoccupied Loisy during these years and which contributed towards his final synthesis. They are also chosen to illustrate his interaction with contemporary criticism and, simultaneously, his attempt to pursue independent lines of enquiry. These concerns are: the question of 'le style rythmé'; the 'Christ-myth' question; and problems concerned with the dating and composition of the documents, especially the Pauline corpus.

2.5.1 Le Style Rythmé

The importance of this topic for Loisy may be gauged from his devoting a chapter to it in his *Mémoires*[1]. The main statement of his case was made in an article of 1923[2] but his interest in the subject was aroused in the early months of 1922, when he was correcting the proofs of *Les Livres du Nouveau Testament*. As related by Loisy his 'discovery' that most of the books of the New Testament were composed in rhythmic strophes was more or less spontaneous[3], but a number of writers at the time were working along similar lines. One can mention H. Cladder, *Unsere Evangelien* (1919)[4]; R.H. Charles, *Revelation* (1920)[5]; the work of the anthropologist Wilhelm

---

6 *RHLR* 1922 1,78−113; 2,215−253; 3,394−422; 4,433−476.
7 *La Religion d'Israël* (3rd edn. 1933).
8 His lectures at the Collège de France in 1924−5 were devoted to 'L'apocalyptique juive' and in 1925−6 to 'L'idée messianique et les origines du mouvement chrétien'. In the same years he taught courses at EPHE on Daniel and Ezekiel.

1 *Mém* III Ch. LVI.
2 'Le Style rythmé du Nouveau Testament' *JPs* mai 1923 pp405−439.
3 *Mém* III pp431−2.
4 Mentioned by Loisy in *L'Evangile selon Luc* (1924) p64. Cladder (1868−1920) was a Jesuit with a special interest in the Semitic form and content of the Gospels.
5 Loisy reviewed Charles very favourably in *RC* 1921 pp121ff.

Schmidt[6]; P.–L. Couchoud, *L'Apocalypse. Traduction du poème avec une introduction* (early 1922)[7]; an article by R. Schütz on the Epistle of James[8].

It is quite impossible in these circumstances to assess the precise influences upon Loisy: his own account seems rather naïve, although the outline is probably correct; but there was no single unacknowledged influence, as suggested by Sartiaux. In *Le Quatrième Evangile* (1921) Loisy had in fact printed in verse form, although not in regular strophes, much of the discourse material. These sections he calls 'morceaux de prose rythmée', derived from the earliest source of the Gospel; they were:

> ... rédigés dans le style mystique dont le plus ancien modèle est pour nous celui des incantations babyloniennes, – mais le type s'en rencontre un peu partout dans les cultes primitifs; – ce style était devenu celui des mystères, sans cesser d'être celui des incantations magiques.[9]

Thus basic notions in the theory were already present in Loisy's mind when he corrected the proofs of, first, the Epistles and 'saw' that passages he had left in prose were equally susceptible to a rhythmic treatment. And working later in 1922 on the Gospels, he came to accept the view of Schmidt that the narrative sections, as well as the discourses, had the same potentiality. It was too late to make more than a few alterations to the Epistles in *Les Livres du Nouveau Testament*[10] but Loisy immediately devoted himself to

---

6   This was reported in *RHR* janvier-avril 1922. In *Mém* III p431–2 Loisy says that Houtin drew his attention to the article in a letter of 23. 7.22 and that it caused him 'un grand émoi' because Schmidt included the Gospel narratives, as well as the discourses, in his enquiry. But he had already referred to Schmidt's work in a letter to Cumont of 1.4.22 (BN n.a.f. 15644). There he states that Schmidt is probably right, but: ' . . . je le soupçonne d'arrière-pensée apologétique . . . sa découverte . . . est loin de garantir l'historicité des récits'.

7   In *Alfred Loisy, Sa Vie – Son Oeuvre* pp209–10 Sartiaux accuses Loisy of suppressing all mention of Couchoud's work, which was his main source of influence. But Couchoud's work was itself an adaptation of the Charles commentary, with which Loisy was familiar. NB Goguel's review of Couchoud in *RHR* 85, 1922, p209 which takes up the question of the *style rythmé*, mentioning earlier work by J. Weiss, Blass and D.H. Müller.

8   *ThB* February 1922; mentioned by Loisy in *Mém* III p432 as contemporaneous with his own work on the Epistles.

9   *Op. cit.* p63.

10 In the final printed version the following sections are printed in strophic form: most of the sayings-material in the Gospels; the discourses and a few of the disciples' sayings in the Fourth Gospel; the speeches in Acts; most of Romans and I Corinthians; much of II Corinthians; selected passages in the remaining books except that all of the following are rendered strophically: James, I–III John, Revelation; and none of the following: II

testing the hypothesis to its fullest extent and finding it proven to his own satisfaction. He devoted his 'leçon d'ouverture' at the Collège de France to the subject on 2nd December 1922 and sent von Hügel the Christmas present of a strophic transcription of I Corinthians 11 and 13. In answer to doubts raised by von Hügel, Loisy explained this 'epistle' is made up of 'textes oraculaires, faits pour être déclamés publiquement, presque chantés, dans l'assemblée de la communauté' and suggested that one should read the story of calming of the storm in Mark 4,35—41 as a 'petite chanson' in six strophes of four lines each[11].

These examples recur in Loisy's article of 1923, to which we now turn for a full statement of his position. Having mentioned that a number of recent studies have appeared on the subject[12] he first considers the literary forms, mainly by use of examples[13]. Not only is the whole of I Corinthians constructed rhythmically, but also the more classically 'correct' writings, Hebrews and James; and even the derivative Ephesians ('véritable galimatias') breaks down easily into strophes. Discourse material is obviously constructed in this way and Loisy suggests examples not only from the Gospels (including the Sermon on the Mount and the Johannine discourses which are 'odes mystiques sur certains thèmes doctrinaux') but also from Acts (Paul's speech in Athens). He then passes to narratives and gives the parallel accounts of the calming of the storm; each has its own rhythm, showing it to be 'une leçon de foi qui se déroule et se chante'. The Johannine narratives are more elevated in tone and can thus be classified as 'dramatisation liturgique'. The narratives in Acts are also designed for edification and therefore, although there is a certain loss of 'souffle mystique', the declamatory form has been retained. In all these examples there is a wide variety of metric and strophic

---

Thessalonians, Philemon, II Peter. One small piece of Gospel narrative receives strophic treatment (by an oversight?): Luke 7,29—30. All extensive O.T. quotations are presented strophically.

11 For details of this exchange v. *Mém* III pp438—9.

12 Loisy gives no names. Typically, the article does not discuss the work of other scholars. Loisy only considered critical opinion in detail in his book reviews and in the introduction of his major commentaries.

13 These are: I Cor. 11, 2—16; 13, 1—12; Mark 2, 17 and 19—22; Matt. 6, 1—6 and 16—18; Acts 17, 22—31; John 15, 1—10; 17, 24—26; Mark 4, 35—41; Matt. 8, 23—27; Luke 8, 22—25; John 18, 28—38; Acts 8, 3; 9, 1—9; 22, 4—9; 27, 9—15.

forms[14] and although the French translation which Loisy provides is highly literal, in order to keep close to the Greek original, no attempt is made to suggest any normative verse patterns. The point is made at several junctures that the establishment of the original rhythmic shape enables the critic to detect interpolations and redactional activity.

Thus the New Testament documents are not 'popular' literature, nor are they greatly infuenced by Classical Greek 'Kunstprosa'[15]. They are certainly influenced, via the Septuagint, by the oracular and liturgical forms of the Old Testament, whose own prototypes are to be found in Babylonian religious literature[16]. Both Babylonian and Hebrew texts are however to be considered as 'fonction directe de la vie religieuse et sociale des peuples qui les ont produits'. It is therefore possible to establish, for example, a direct parallel between the solemn introduction to the Hammurabi code and the opening verses of the Epistle to the Romans: 'On peut réellement comparer l'apôtre prédestiné du Christ au vicaire prédestiné de Marduk . . . les deux parlent ou plutôt chantent la même langue'. Such forms themselves derive ultimately from 'la parole magiquement efficace' of primitive incantations[17] but have been moulded by aesthetic feeling and liturgical practice. These 'mystical' forms, adapted to the needs of public lection, explain the nature of the New Testament writings. Critics have been misguided in looking principally for doctrines or history: 'ces écrits sont en rapport avec l'économie naissante du culte chrétien'.

Epistles and Gospel sayings comprise oracles of the living Christ to be declaimed for the religious and moral instruction of the community. Gospel narratives form 'le poème liturgique du salut' from baptism via the salvific acts of Christ to crucifixion and resurrection[18].

---

14 Lines have anything between 3 and 21 syllables in the French translation and strophes range between 3 and 10 lines in length.

15 Even Luke 1, 1–4 is made up of two four lined strophes.

16 It must be remembered that Loisy first established his critical reputation as an Assyriologist and Hebraist.

17 This conception is directly apparent to Loisy in such passages as Rev. 1, 1–3; 22, 18–19; I Cor. 14, 37.

18 Cf. for a contemporary parallel, G. Bertram *Die Leidensgeschichte Jesus und der Christuskult* (1922) whose author concludes: 'Die Leidensgeschichte Jesus ist die Kulterzählung des Christentums' (p96). Bertram was to attend the Congrès Loisy in 1927 but his paper on the Form-criticism of the story of Jesus walking on the water, was to prove incomprehensible to most of his hearers. Loisy however offers a summary and positive evaluation of Bertram's position (*Mém* III p531).

The dramatic nature of the stories explains many of the variants between Gospels and, in particular, the Synoptics correspond to the Paschal observance of Rome and John to that of the Quartodecimans in Asia. The Acts of the Apostles are also a sacred history, designed for public reading. It may be admitted that the broad sweep of this kind of argument is impressive, but the one or two examples provided by Loisy do not unfortunately permit its verification in any detail.

Loisy believes that such a theory will contribute to textual, literary and historical criticism of the New Testament. It will help to pick out doctrinal and redactional glosses (although of the examples he gives[19], most could be recognised on grounds of content, as well as style). It will throw into relief the composition of certain passages eg. the insertion of the healing of the woman with the issue of blood into the story of Jairus' daughter and that of the Barabbas episode into the Johannine passion narrative. It is not intended to replace critical analysis and it cannot claim to pass final judgement on questions of authenticity; it is however specially informative on the origins of the Gospels. The carefully balanced utterances attributed to Jesus belong more naturally to the activity of Christian prophets in the early church:

> ... nos évangiles se chantent. Ils représentent dans l'ensemble une légende prophétique et une liturgie. Ce qu'ils expriment est le culte de Jésus dans les premières communautés.[20]

It would be very unwise however to use the theory in support of the non-existence of Jesus[21].

Loisy never had the opportunity to publish extensively on this question. Although he completed a manuscript for a second edition of *Les Livres du Nouveau Testament*, there was no call for its publication[22]. The only places where his revised findings appear are in the Commentary on Luke of 1925, in which the whole of the

---

19 Matt. 1, 25a; John 17, 3, 12b; Luke 2, 18, 35a, 51b.
20 *Art.cit.* p439.
21 *Mém* III 442 informs us that this final point was directed against P.–L. Couchoud and the publicity surrounding the latter's forthcoming *Mystère de Jesus*; v. below 2.5.2.
22 Cf. *Mém* III p407. The manuscript is preserved among Loisy's papers, BN n.a.f. 15639–40. It was compiled and readjusted over a period of at least eleven years (the Preface dates from after the publication of *La Naissance du christianisme* (1933)). Nearly everything in the Gospels is in verse-form; in the case of the Epistles, Loisy reverted to prose in a number of substantial sections; generally speaking, he dropped some of his elaborate strophic arrangements in favour of more loosely constructed couplets and triplets.

translation into French is printed in strophes and in *Remarques sur la littérature épistolaire du Nouveau Testament* of 1935 where all the quotations are similarly printed. Loisy hardly attempted to refine or reinforce his theory by detailed published work on the texts, or by bringing forward parallels[23]. The theory was well received by some of his associates at the time[24], but did not create any impression in the world of New Testament scholarship. At the Congrès international d'Histoire des religions (Congrès Renan) in October 1923 Loisy presented a paper on I Corinthians 11 where he analysed two 'instructions': the first, on the veiling of women, occupies four 9-line strophes; the second, on the Eucharist, six 9-line strophes, each of which has four distichs and one tristich[25]. Together 'les deux instructions forment une sorte de poème didactique, on plus exactement d'oracle conçu en termes choisis et cadencés'. The style is however *sui generis* and no rhythmic rules can be derived from verse or prose forms in Classical Greek, nor, on the other hand, from popular speech. When Maurice Goguel asked, at the end of the paper, how Loisy established his divisions into lines and strophes, since neither length nor syntax came into it, Loisy made the astonishing reply:

> La séparation des lignes et des strophes se fait d'une manière expérimentale: la déclaration à haute voix, voilà ma méthode. En principe il y a partout une cadence rythmique, mais non strophique déterminée.[26]

There was obviously little future for a theory so subjectively based.

Another reason for the eclipse of this theory, apart from Loisy's own lack of documentation and its championing by the *mythologues,* was the appearance on the scene of Marcel Jousse S.J.[27] Loisy

---

23 His lecture course at EPHE on 'Le style rythmé' (1924–5) did not appear in print.

24 Cf. Houtin to Loisy 24.4.23 (BN n.a.f. 15655); Turmel to Loisy 7.8.23 (BN n.a.f. 15662); Cumont to Loisy 9.8.23 (BN n.a.f. 15651). Cumont hopes that at Dura-Europos, where he is soon to excavate, texts of Oriental hymns will be found to back up Loisy's theory. Couchoud fulfilled Loisy's fears by becoming an advocate of the theory: he sent a communication to the Société Ernest-Renan on possible rules governing the rhythmic style of the Pauline epistles (résumé in *RHR* 90, 1924, pp171–3; cf. *L'Evangile selon Luc* (1924) p64).

25 *Actes du Congrès* . . . Vol.II (1925) pp321–9.

26 *Ibid* p329. *Mém* III p448 omits this crucial exchange, so damaging to his position and simply reports his very general point about affinities between the New Testament and poetic sections of the Old Testament.

27 For the life and work of Jousse (1886–1961) see Gabrielle Baron, *Marcel Jousse* (1965). Unfortunately, this volume reads more like hagiography than sober biography.

had mentioned to von Hügel, as early as March 1923: 'un jésuite français s'apprête à vulgariser la découverte (de W. Schmidt), "qui ruine la critique de Loisy", à ce qu'il prétend'[28]. Jousse had come to Paris in 1922 to study experimental phonetics under Rousselot, psychology under Janet and Dumas and ethnology under Mauss, having previously acquired proficiency in Hebrew and Aramaic and carried out ethnographical research in America. His researches and publications in Paris were devoted to the recovery of the *ipsissima verba* of Jesus, whom he customarily referred to as 'Rabbi Iéshoua'. He vowed to demonstrate scientifically the literal authenticity of the words of Jesus in all four gospels, by removing the 'envelope' of 'Greco-latinism'[29] and thus revealing the oral, rhythmic, pedagogic and ethnic qualities of true 'Iéshouisme'. The advance publicity for his volume of 1925: *Etudes de Psychologie linguistique: le Style oral rythmique et mnémo-technique chez les Verbo-moteurs* claimed that it would reduce to nothing 'l'hypercritique superficielle de M. Loisy sur les textes du Nouveau Testament'[30]. Against Loisy's assumption: 'Rythmique, donc poétique, donc mythique', he proposed the argument 'Rythmique, donc pédagogique, donc historique'[31].

The terminology and style adopted by Jousse were involved and obscure (eg. he referred to the parables as 'récitatifs mnémoniquement rythmo-mélodiques')[32] and Loisy commented to Houtin 'Le livre est très curieux, savant à sa manière . . . Ce P. Jousse est une brute savante dans le genre de Mauss, et il est de plus théologien'[33]. But Loisy did consider that his own theories had been provided with a broader base and more detailed illustration through the work of Jousse on the Targums and other sources, however outrageous his style and however lacking he might be in any notion of Biblical criticism[34]. Jousse, through his publications, his phonetics laboratory

---

28 *Mém* III p439.

29 Cf. also his statement 'Enlevez le gréco-latinisme, et il n'y a plus de modernisme'. (Baron, *op.cit.* p52).

30 Turmel sent this notice to Loisy in a letter of 5.4.25, suggesting that Loisy should ask the editor of the *Journal de Psychologie*, Meyerson, if he could review Jousse's work there. (*Mém* III p473).

31 Baron *op.cit.* p118.

32 *Ibid* p124.

33 Loisy to Houtin 11.5.25 (BN n.a.f. 15718).

34 For Loisy's evaluation in full v. *Mém* III 474–5 and his review in *RC* 1925 pp264–266,

and his theatrical presentations, managed to create a stir in ecclesiastical and intellectual circles[35] and among New Testament scholars
who gave serious attention to his views were Maurice Goguel and
Léonce de Grandmaison S.J.[36] Thus Loisy's own campaign on behalf
of 'le style rythmé' suffered from neglect by New Testament scholarship and outflanking by Jousse[37].

There are undoubtedly obsessive aspects in his presentation of
this theory. Although he had many other concerns at the time, this
particular idea is described and conveyed rather in the nature of a
vision[38]. It seems as if Loisy was in search of a 'key', or cohesivé
principle which would bring together the findings produced by historical and literary analysis. It was consistent with his previous work
that he should find such a key in the ritual and social dimensions of
early Christianity but it was also typical that he should refuse to
align himself with contemporary critics who might have seemed to
be allies. Wilhelm Schmidt and Marcel Jousse were suspect because,
whatever their scientific credentials, they were theologians with a
vested interest in the historicity of the Gospels; Rudolf Bultmann
was hopelessly wedded to literary criticism[39]; the *mythologues*

---

with its final comment: 'Trop de zèle'. There are further comments for and against
Jousse in the unpublished commentary on Matthew (BN n.a.f. 15641 fol. 32–34).

35 See the list of publications in Baron *op.cit.* pp89–93.

36 Jousse continued to expound his views to the end of his life, although largely forgotten;
eg. in 1955 he protested against Bultmann with the words 'Mimisme Paysannisé *et non
pas* Mythisme Algébrosé' (Baron *op.cit.* p274). He is however cited as an authority in
B. Gerhardssohn, *Memory and Manuscript* (1961).

37 Loisy was not attracted to theories, which like that of Jousse, sought confirmation of
the words of Jesus in the Aramaic background: cf. at this period G.H. Dalman, *Jesus-
Jeschua* (1922) and C.F. Burney, *The Poetry of our Lord* (1925). In his review of Dalman, Loisy wrote: 'la question n'est pas tant de savoir comment elles (sc. the words of
Jesus at the Last Supper) ont pu être dites en araméen, que de voir si elles peuvent
s'entendre autrement que par rapport à la cène pratiquée dans les communautés chrétiennes'. (*RC* 1924 p190).

38 Cf. remarks in *Mém* III pp432, 436, 437; and the interview with Loisy in F. Lefèvre, *Une
Heure Avec . . .* (1924) pp193–201, where Loisy nominates *Les Livres du Nouveau
Testament* as his favourite book among his publications.

39 *L'Evangile selon Luc* (1924) p22 refers to Bultmann's 'souci . . . de rigoureuse (et irréalis-
able) classification'.   For Loisy at this time the Form critics were scarcely to be distinguished from source-critics because of their reliance upon literary analysis. Cf. his
review of Streeter, *The Four Gospels* (1924) for a characteristic statement: 'Et tout
cela encore est très ingénieux, subtilement déduit, habilement défendu. Une seule chose
y manque, l'intégration de ce travail d'écriture, si singulier, dans la vie des premières
communautés. Ce sont remarques de critique purement textuelle et littéraire, sur lesquelles on pourrait discuter indéfiniment sans avancer beaucoup la question fonda-

were rationalists and amateurs[40]. Loisy's theory, if accepted, might therefore demonstrate his true independence, just as he had previously sought the middle way between *mythologues* and *théologues*[41]. This in a way it did but it was not the right theory. It is not necessary to demonstrate here the inadequacy of the proposed all-purpose 'key', since its pretensions have been shown up in merely describing it; we may simply note that it was plausibly founded in Loisy's own academic background (Assyriology, Hebrew, the history of religions, as well as the New Testament) and that it did serve as an antidote to over-literary and over-theological views. It was to remain a permanent feature of his subsequent work, even if it lost some of its prominence as other ideas came along[42].

2.5.2 The Christ-Myth Question[1]

The Christ-myth question during these years centred upon the publication by P.–L. Couchoud in 1924 of *Le Mystère de Jésus*, a small volume, engagingly written, but hardly a work to carry weight in the academic world. In order to understand its impact, it is necessary to say something about Couchoud himself and his relationship with Loisy at this time, which will also involve introducing other associates of both men. Loisy did not publish specifically on the Christ-myth question during the years 1921–27[2]; but his *Mémoires*

---

mentale: le caractère et les conditions historiques de ces écritures qu'on appelle évangiles'. (*RC* 1925 p380).

40 V. below 2.5.2.

41 V. above 2.2.

42 Sartiaux in *Alfred Loisy; Sa Vie – Son Oeuvre* p211 gives a wrong impression when he says that in *La Naissance du Christainisme* (1933) the theory has lost much of its importance.

---

1 There appears to be no definitive survey of Christ-myth theories. There are some useful references in W.G. Kümmel, *The New Testament – a History of the Investigation of its Problems* p447 note 367; some of the proponents and antagonists give an outline of the debate, eg. A. Drews, *The Christ Myth* (ET 1912) Prefaces; M. Goguel, *Jésus de Nazareth, Mythe ou Histoire?* (1925) Ch.1; in popular vein, H.G. Wood, *Did Christ Really Live?* (1938). Of special value for this section is M. Goguel, 'Recent French discussions of the historical existence of Jesus' *HTR* XIX 1926 pp115–142. For the place of these theories in the history of ideas cf. C.Maignial, 'Brèves notations sur le mythisme dans l'histoire des religions et devant la foi' in *Cahiers du Cercle Ernest-Renan* No. 82 Oct. 1973 pp2–15.

2 Loisy had made his opposition to Christ-myth theories clear in his review-article devoted to Drews: 'Le mythe du Christ' *RHLR* (1911) Ch.V. However radical his Gospel criticism

and correspondence show that he was much preoccupied with the activities of Couchoud and that, even if this episode deals more in personalities than in the history of interpretation proper, it nevertheless occupies an essential place in Loisy's development.

Couchoud was a doctor by profession, and the personal physician of the novelist Anatole France, whose fierce anticlericalism is a well known feature of his writing[3]. Couchoud became interested in Christ-myth theories after reading Reinach's *Orpheus* and started to attend Loisy's lectures at the Collège de France. He was encouraged in his literary and historical ambitions by Anatole France, and their correspondence reveals Couchoud's devotion and gratitude for France's support[4]. Loisy claims that as late as 1st March 1923 he was unaware of the inspiration which France had provided for Couchoud's ideas, and that on the occasion of his only meeting with France he denounced the Christ-myth thesis roundly when asked for his opinion[5]. In December 1920, Couchoud had written to Loisy, ostensibly to ask for his interpretation of three verses in Paul's writings (Galatians 1,19; II Corinthians 5,16; Galatians 4,4) which seemed to suggest that Paul knew nothing of an earthly Jesus, but setting out his own views at some length[6]. The Christ-myth theory also received a boost during 1920 by the publication of Drews's book *Das Markus-Evangelium*, which Loisy reviewed in *RHLR*[7].

It was hints such as these which led Loisy to comment in writing

---

became, he consistently maintained this opposition; Sartiaux, in *Alfred Loisy, Sa Vie — Son Oeuvre* Pt. II Ch.II, is unable to claim Loisy for the *mythologues,* even though he demonstrates Loisy's increasing scepticism about the historicity of the Gospels.

3   V. eg. *L'Eglise et la Republique* (1904).

4   Published as nos. 99—104 (1968) of *Le Lys Rouge* (Société A. France). In 1914 France told Couchoud that *Le Problème de Jésus* by Guignebert (1913) had not succeeded in refuting those who deny the 'humanity' of Jesus; in 1917 they discussed Loisy ('Saint Alfred de Ceffonds') whose *La Religion* had just appeared: he turns out to be a theologian in disguise, 'un solitaire qui ne sait rien de la vie', a bookworm too embroiled in his texts; later in 1917 Couchoud expounds his theory that the books of the New Testament comprise two groups, those prior to 70 A.D. where Jesus is known in visions as a manifestation of Yahweh and those after 70 A.D. where his (mythical) earthly story is evolved; finally in 1923 Couchoud sent France the proofs of an article which would form the preface to *Le Mystère de Jesus*, with profuse thanks: 'Vous savez que je vous ai donné mon coeur'.

5   *Mém* III pp437—8.

6   V. *Mém* III p443.

7   *Mém* III p408 records that Houtin, in a letter of 28.7.21, considered Drews to be more important than Guignebert, whose *Christianisme antique* (1921) also had just appeared. Loisy dissented sharply from this view.

to Cumont, that the *mythologues* were mounting a campaign. He states his own principles as follows:

> ... ce n'est pas le mythe qui crée la religion, c'est la religion qui crée le mythe. Bien que le christianisme soit fondé en un sens sur le mythe du Christ, ce n'est pas le mythe qui a créé la religion chrétienne, c'est la foi qui l'a exploité au profit de Jésus et de son culte.[8]

Even, he says, if there are not four consecutive lines in the gospels which are 'rigoureusement historiques et authentiques' this does not mean that Jesus did not exist[9]. This position was fully argued in the *RHLR* articles of 1922 on 'La légende de Jésus,' and other articles in the same volume contain remarks directed at the *mythologues*. An opening lecture at the Collège de France of December 1921[10] quoted Nietzsche on Jesus: 'Un fondateur de religion peut être insignifiant: une allumette, rien de plus', although according to Loisy, it can be said of the earthly Jesus that he had a profound sense of humanity, in its wretchedness and its need of solace, and this was enough to start the blaze[11]. An article on parallels between the Passion of Marduk and the Passion of Christ[12] disallows any direct influence, although allowing cultic influences via the Jewish Passover; it concludes with a warning against those who think that historical criticism is 'un jeu d'imagination ou un amusement d'esprits subtils'[13]. We have already seen how Loisy inserted a similar warning, specifically directed at Couchoud, at the end of his article on *'Le style rythmé'*[14].

During 1923 Couchoud began the campaign which Loisy had foreseen. His article 'L'Enigme de Jésus' was published in *Le Mercure de France* of 1st March and replies by the Protestant Maurice Goguel and the Jesuit Léonce de Grandmaison appeared in the same journal on 1st June and 15th August respectively. In the same year he published an article in the *Revue de l'Histoire des Religions* on 'La reconstitution et le classement des lettres de saint Paul'[15] where he

---

8 Loisy to Cumont 6.8.21 (BN n.a.f. 15644).

9 Loisy to Cumont 1.11.21 (BN n.a.f. 15644).

10 'De la méthode en histoire des religions', published in *RHLR* 1922, 1 pp13–37.

11 Sartiaux, *Alfred Loisy, Sa Vie – Son Oeuvre* p209 thinks that Loisy only just stepped back at this point from joining the *mythologues*.

12 'La Passion de Marduk' *RHLR* 1922, 2 pp289–302.

13 *Art. cit.* p302.

14 V. above 2.5.1.

15 *RHR* 87, 1923, pp1–31.

claimed that the authentic epistles may be broken down into twelve separate letters of Paul. He was acquiring collaborators, notably Prosper Alfaric, a former priest now lecturing in the history of religions at Strasbourg[16]; Albert Houtin, who had also left the church and who was well known through his historical and biographical writings as the publicist of Modernism[17]; and Joseph Turmel, a priest without faith living in Rennes, who had collaborated in Loisy's *RHLR* over many years under a variety of pseudonyms[18]. Of these three, Alfaric was the only declared *mythologue* but they all now entered Couchoud's ambit. Houtin and Turmel, for example, were recruited to write volumes for a new series edited by Couchoud: 'Christianisme'; plans for this were laid during 1923 and Couchoud's own *Mystère de Jésus* was to be No. 3 in the series[19]. He was able to recruit other more eminent collaborators, e.g. the philosopher Alain and the historian Aulard, and Loisy agreed to provide a popular version of his commentary on Acts[20]. Houtin, who was Loisy's regular informant on religious publications and events when the latter was away from Paris, seems to have been acting at this stage as an agent for Couchoud: he transmitted to Loisy Couchoud's opinion that Mark's gospel is a *haggada* based on Paul[21] and later stressed that Paul Desjardins and Sartiaux were both enthusiastic about Couchoud, in spite of Loisy's attempts to dissuade Sartiaux[22].

---

16 For Alfaric (1876–1955) v. his autobiography *De la foi à la raison* (1958) and the collection of his writings in *A L'école de la raison,* a memorial volume (n.d.). His pamphlet 'Le Problème de Jésus' reprinted in the latter volume (originally Cahier No.1 of Le Cercle Ernest Renan (1954)), describes how he had moved on to the 'mythologue' position after studying Renan, Loisy and Guignebert. Loisy, who had helped Alfaric when he left the priesthood, was amused to hear that he had been congratulated by Duchesne for his study of the Simonians, since Alfaric claimed that Simon Magnus was a cult-deity, *like Jesus!* (Loisy to Cumont 17.1.22 BN n.a.f. 15644).

17 For Houtin (1867–1926) v. his two volumes of autobiography. *Une Vie de prêtre* (1926) and *Ma Vie Laïque* (1928). For his close if not cordial relationship with Loisy over the years and Loisy's severe judgement of Houtin after the latter's death v. *Mémoires* III Ch.LVIII and Vidler, *A Variety of Catholic Modernists* Ch.2.

18 For Turmel (1859–1943) v. below 2.5.3.

19 For a general account of the series, after about 20 volumes had appeared v. M. Goguel, 'Recent French Discussions of Christianity: the Series 'Christianisme' ' *HTR* XX 1927 pp63–104.

20 He did not accede to Couchoud's later requests to produce a popular edition of *Les Mystères* . . . and to edit his correspondence with von Hügel for publication in the series.

21 Houtin to Loisy 24.4.23 (*Mém* III p443). In *Le Mystère de Jésus,* Couchoud actually says: 'l'évangile de Marc est un *midrach* sur le mystère chrétien' (p56).

22 Houtin to Loisy 20.8.23 (*Mém* III p446).

Meanwhile, Loisy was confiding his views about Couchoud to Cumont; he admits that Couchoud can write well but:

> . . . il déraisonne en matière d'histoire religieuse. Du reste, le meilleur garçon du monde. Le vieux diable d'Anatole France l'encourage . . . On ne s'improvise pas critique et historien, quand même on aurait du génie. Car les mythologues sont tous comme les sociologues de l'école Durkheim, ils ont tous du génie. Nous autres, infortunés éplucheurs de textes, nous ne sommes que de vieilles ganaches.[23]

It is not necessary to provide an analysis of Couchoud's work, *Le Mystère de Jesus*, but merely to note some of its features. It has a pronounced literary tone: the first chapter relates a conversation about the Buddha and Christ, set in a Japanese garden. Then the author traverses Russia by train, noting the churches in village after village and is made to realise that Jesus is the 'Master of the West'; he is 'la structure intime des scoiétés d'Occident'[24]. Couchoud writes lyrically, even religiously, about this 'Christ of faith'; simple believers are right: 'Jésus, c'est le bon Dieu. C'est le *Mahadêva* d'Occident, qui a chassé tous les *dêva*'.[25] But the Master of the West has no historical basis and the book concludes with a lay-sermon:

> Historiens, n'hésitez pas à rayer de vos cadres l'homme Jésus. Faites entrer le dieu Jésus. Aussitôt l'histoire du christianisme naissant sera mise à son vrai niveau. Elle se montrera neuve et haute . . . Et vous, croyants . . . aurez-vous peur d'une réalité spirituelle, vous dont la noble fonction est de maintenir les réalités spirituelles?[26]

Couchoud compares the Jesus of Renan with the Jesus of Loisy[27]. The latter is undoubtedly a more probable figure, historically speaking but since all that is known of his life may be summarised in six lines, has Loisy gone far enough? Loisy has challenged the *mythologues*: 'où est l'allumette?'[28] and Couchoud takes up the challenge[29]. He finds the heart of the problem in the interpretation of seven or eight texts in the writings of Paul[30], and his conclusion after analysing these is:

---

23 Loisy to Cumont 5.5.23 (BN n.a.f. 15644).
24 *Op.cit.* p17.
25 *Ibid* p101.
26 *Ibid* pp185—6.
27 *Ibid* Ch.V.
28 In his article in *RHLR* 1922 pp13—37.
29 *Op.cit.* p76.
30 Phil. 2, 6—11; Col. 1, 15—20; Gal. 4, 4—5; I Cor. 2, 6—8; I Cor. 15, 3—8, 25—28, 44—49; I Cor. 11, 23—25; I Thess. 4, 15—17. Couchoud, under the influence of 'Delafosse' (v. 2.5.3 below) later modified his treatment of the Pauline epistles (cf. *Mém* III p443).

Il n'y a dans Paul aucune allusion à un personnage historique du nom de Jésus. Le Messie Jésus Fils de Dieu est le héros d'un apocalypse. Et il est l'objet d'une expérience mystique. C'est le dieu d'un mystère. Le dieu ni le mystère ne sont encore historisés.[31]

In the course of his analysis, Couchoud claims that Loisy's approach has already been superseded:

Jésus a été conçu dans l'esprit raisonnable et mystique du XVIIe siècle, puis à la mode philosophique de l'Encyclopédie, puis dans le goût romantique d'un Renan, puis par Loisy sous le jour cru du matérialisme historique. Aujourd'hui le progrès de la méthode sociologique ouvre des vues nouvelles. Je crois que vers 1940 Jésus tout entier aura passé du plan des faits matérials dans celui des représentations mentales collectives.[32]

Such an evolution, in Couchoud's view, would take us back to the original faith in Jesus. A historical Jesus undermines the truly religious nature of Christianity[33]. It was not until the beginning of the second century that certain Christians, under the pressure of such factors as the delay of the parousia, political developments and liturgical needs, began to suggest that 'l'histoire mystérieuse de Jésus' had taken place on earth[34]. It was in this way that the Gospel tradition was inaugurated.

The reactions of Loisy to this book are interesting to compare with those of Goguel and Guignebert. Goguel replied with his own volume of 300 pages[35], Guignebert, after some delay, with a long, highly detailed and crushing review[36]. Loisy on the other hand confined himself to a five-page review[37] (hostile, certainly), but he also chose to review Goguel's reply with some asperity[38]. Couchoud is an easy prey to Loisy's pen: the style of a novelist does not suit a historian; sociology is incapable of deciding historical questions; the author's Pauline exegesis is inexact, fantastic and 'abracadabrant'; he is a neophyte in both exegesis and sociology; 'sa thèse atteste surtout un effort extraordinaire d'imagination'[39]. But Goguel on his

---

31 Op.cit. p145.
32 Ibid p107. The language of the last sentence is of course that of Durkheim. Couchoud lived long enough to have to retract his prediction about 1940: cf. Le Dieu Jésus (1951) p50.
33 Cf. eg. Ibid p108.
34 Ibid pp158ff.
35 Jésus de Nazareth, Mythe ou Histoire? (1925).
36 RHR 94, 1926, pp215—244.
37 RC 1924, pp447—451.
38 RC 1925, pp343—347.
39 Cf. Couchoud to Houtin 3.11.24 (BN n.a.f. 15696). Couchoud expresses admiration for Loisy's Evangile selon Luc, although he knows that he himself will be sharply reviewed

side has wrongly posed the question in asking 'mythe ou histoire'? He tries to present a human person, also considered to be divine, as the unique and total cause of Christianity. But the 'personality' he ascribes to Jesus is of his own making and cannot be proved to belong to history — it is in fact easier to determine the place of myth in the formation of Christianity than it is to assess the personal action of Jesus and thus, paradoxically, Goguel plays straight into the hands of the *mythologues,* by presenting his own historicisation of the myth. Although Goguel provides some useful arguments, he is open to criticism in his exegesis of both Paul and the Gospels[40] and needs to recognise that everything said by New Testament critics about sources, authorship, stages of redaction and dates is more or less conjectural.

Here we see Loisy once again treading the path of independence. He was suspicious of Couchoud and his associates. In spite of the strain of religiosity running through *Le Mystère de Jésus*, it is apparent from the volumes of the series 'Christianisme' that rationalism and anticlericalism were contributing factors to the enterprise. Houtin and Turmel, as renegade priests, certainly came into the category of rationalist and even if Loisy shared their antipathy towards the Roman ecclesiastical system, his general lectures at the Collège de France during these years formed part of his own anti-rationalist campaign[41]. Also, in his estimation, Couchoud's organising genius and brilliant writing and even his publications in the weighty pages of the *Revue de l'Histoire des Religions*, could not possibly compensate for his lack of grounding in the basic philological disciplines of Biblical studies. But Goguel's counterstatement smacked too much of 'critical orthodoxy'. Not only had Goguel rejected the validity of Loisy's conclusions on Acts and on the question of the 'style rythmé' but he continued to propound Liberal Protestant views on the personality of Jesus and to practise the type of literary criticism

---

by Loisy. However, he thinks that Loisy is now closer to his own position than to that of Guignebert. This opinion may appear to receive some confirmation from Loisy's and Guignebert's respective reviews but Couchoud was mistaken if he thought that Loisy had any intention of joining him.

40 Eg. he uses Pauline passages which are probably not authentic and labours too hard to remove crassly mythical elements from Pauline soteriology; he does not allow sufficiently for Old Testament influence upon the Passion Narrative.

41 V. esp. the collection *Religion et humanité* (1926).

upon the New Testament documents which Loisy regarded as effete. It might be tempting to suppose that Loisy was restrained from joining the *mythologues* by the distant influence of his Catholic upbringing and his former work as an apologist, but there is no evidence of this from his general writings of the period. He appeared to be quite detached from any confessional leanings and the example of a Guignebert or a Bultmann is to hand in order to show that Loisy's position, of maintaining the historical existence of Jesus while having to admit almost complete ignorance about his life, is a reputable one for the historian to uphold.

To conclude this section, we may briefly note the subsequent dealings between Loisy and Couchoud. The latter undertook to organise a Congrès d'Histoire du Christianisme in honour of Loisy in 1927[42]. Loisy was suspicious that the event might turn out to be a manifestation in favour of the *mythologues*[43] and his fears were shared by Franz Cumont[44], who resigned from the *comité de patronage* for this reason. But Loisy was able to secure a radical revision of Couchoud's original plans and the Congrès was held, in April 1927, to Loisy's almost complete satisfaction[45]. When in 1937, Couchoud published *Jésus le dieu fait homme*, Loisy replied with one of the last volumes of his vast output: *Histoire et mythe à propos de Jésus-Christ* (1938). Couchoud's suppressed wrath erupted in a virulent note[46]. However, he was able to write with some objectivity about Loisy in *Le Dieu Jésus* of 1951 and the book contains some interesting reminiscences[47] as well as a more general

42 V. Loisy's account of events in *Mém* III Ch.LIX.

43 Cf. Couchoud to Loisy 7, 9 & 12.6.26 (BN n.a.f. 15651); these letters reveal that Loisy had expressed himself forcibly on Couchoud's 'dogmatism' and the possible domination of the Congrès by anticlericals, *mythologues* and 'scientistes'.

44 Cf. Cumont to Loisy 3 & 10.7.26 (BN n.a.f. 15651); Cumont suggests that without Catholics and orthodox Protestants, the Congrès will not be representative and that even if Loisy has lacked recognition in the past, he is greater in his isolation than he would be in the company of the 'infimes mythologues'.

45 Its proceedings were published in three volumes in 1928 under the title *Congrès d'Histoire du Christianisme*.

46 Couchoud to Loisy 4.6.38 (BN n.a.f. 15651); 'Un ami m'apprend que vous avez consacré un opuscule entier à mon dernier livre. Je ne le lirai pas, car j'apprends en même temps qu'insignifiant pour la critique, il est curieux seulement par la haine qu'il exprime. Je suis assez fier de la haine que je vous ai inspiré par les services que je vous ai rendus. Il faut avoir des ennemis: ça tient chaud. Mais je regrette, pauvre homme, après vous avoir cru quelque chose, d'etre obligé de tant vous mépriser.'

47 On Loisy v. esp. pp43–48.

account of the history of interpretation seen through the eyes of an intelligent Frenchman. That this man had been able during the 1920s to occupy such a prominent place in French academic debate on Christian origins is, however, a good indication of the sheer underinvestment in this area in the non-Catholic sector[48].

2.5.3 The Influence of 'Delafosse'

'Henri Delafosse' was one of fourteen pseudonyms used during his lifetime by Joseph Turmel, until he was finally unmasked and excommunicated in 1930, at the age of 71[1]. The writings of 'Delafosse' during the years 1921–1927 are alleged to have exercised an important influence upon Loisy, which Loisy was reluctant to admit[2]. These writings are devoted to a 'Marcionite' view of the New Testament and other earlier Christian documents, assigning dates of c.150 and later to the final redaction of this literature. Certainly Loisy in *La Naissance du Christianisme* and its associated volumes rallied to a second century dating for most of the New Testament, including the Pauline epistles. His work on the Gospels and Acts had already taken him into the second century for the final stages of redaction[3] but in *Les Livres du Nouveau Testament* of 1921 he still regarded the bulk of Romans, I and II Corinthians, Galatians, Colossians, Philemon and Philippians as authentic. Here his

---

48 Another man of letters who joined the *mythologues'* crusade was Edouard Dujardin (1861–1949) who staged a play in 1923: *Le mystère du dieu mort et ressuscité*, and wrote four volumes (1927–1945) under the title *L'histoire ancienne du dieu Jésus*. He was refuted by Loisy in *Autres mythes à propos de la religion* (1938).

1 On Turmel, v. F. Sartiaux, *Joseph Turmel — prêtre, historien des dogmes* (1931); K.–P. Gertz, *Joseph Turmel (1859–1943) Ein theologiegeschichtlicher Beitrag zum Problem der Geschichtlichkeit der Dogmen* (1975) (with bibliography of Turmel's published and unpublished works). For the pseudonyms, v. L. Saltet, *La Question Herzog-Dupin* (1908); J. Rivière, *Le Modernisme dans l'Eglise* (1929) Sixième Partie Ch.II; Sartiaux, *op.cit.* (pp112ff on 'Delafosse'); Gertz, *op.cit.* (3.5.1.10 on 'Delafosse').

2 The charge is made not only by Turmel himself (v. below) but notably by Sartiaux in *Alfred Loisy, Sa Vie — Son Oeuvre* pp211–223; cf. also T.F. Glasson, 'Loisy on Christian Origins' *Mod. Ch.* XLI, 1951 pp317–23.

3 Eg. the unpublished commentary on Matthew suggests somewhere between 100 and 125 (but nearer 125) for its final redaction (BN n.a.f. 15641 fol.30); *L'Evangile selon Luc* (1924) suggests 125–150 (p62); *Le Quatrième Evangile* (1921) suggests 130–150 (p69). But second century dates for the Gospels were already a feature of *Jésus et la Tradition Evangélique* (1910): v. above 2.1.

views changed drastically and the influence of Turmel[4] has therefore to be investigated with care[5].

Turmel, under a variety of names, had been a regular contributor to the *Revue d'Histoire et de Littérature Religieuses* since 1898. He was a specialist in the history of Christian doctrine[6] but his use of pseudonyms enabled him to write on many aspects of Christian history and belief from a non-orthodox point of view: he was a priest without faith who had decided to remain in the Church and attack it from within. His production of articles was voluminous and it was overreliance upon his contributions to *RHLR*[7], as well as financial problems, which induced Loisy to close the journal in 1922[8]. There was however no real collaboration between the two men: Turmel was even more of a hermit than Loisy, with no teaching commitments and few ecclesiastical duties. Loisy did not consult him about closing *RHLR* and Turmel was deeply disappointed at the decision, since he was now deprived of the only outlet for his writings[9].

In April 1922 he had sent Loisy an article on the Ignatian Epistles, which denied their authenticity and attributed them to an anti-Marcionite author. Loisy at first had doubts about printing the article but a second reading led him to accept the force of the argument[10]. The article appeared in the final numbers of *RHLR* and

---

4 In what follows we shall refer mainly to 'Turmel', using 'Delafosse' with reference to publications under this name.

5 The documents for this investigation comprise: (a) an abundant correspondence of some 60–70 letters written by Couchoud, Houtin, Loisy and Turmel; (b) Loisy's account in *Mémoires* III; (c) Turmel's account in *Après Cinquante ans d'Etudes* Ch.XIII (typescript, BN n.a.f. 15756, no date, but this chapter was abbreviated for *Comment j'ai donné congé aux dogmes* (1935)) and in *Histoire des dogmes* t. IV (1935) p475 and t.V (1935) p572; (d) Sartiaux's account in *Joseph Turmel* and in *Alfred Loisy, Sa Vie – Son Oeuvre*; (e) the publications of 'Henri Delafosse'.

6 He published *Historire de la théologie positive* (1904–6) under his own name; much of his published work deals with the patristic period. After his excommunication he published *Histoire des dogmes* in 6 volumes (1931 6).

7 In 1921 ten out of fourteen of the main articles were by Loisy or Turmel; in 1922 fifteen out of nineteen.

8 *Mém* III p422.

9 Turmel to Houtin 7 and 20.5.22 (BN n.a.f. 15735); Turmel to Loisy 29.8.22 (BN n.a.f. 15662).

10 *Mém* III p434. Loisy wrote to Turmel: 'l'ensemble de l'argument m'a paru très concluant, même sur l'article de Marcion' (quoted in Sartiaux, *Joseph Turmel* p114). In the *Mémoires*, however, Loisy only mentions his acceptance of the inauthenticity and relative lateness of the Ignatian Epistles, but not the anti-Marcionite thesis.

Turmel expressed his gratitude for Loisy's support of his theory[11].
In writing to Turmel, Loisy mentioned a possible inference:

> La question des *Pastorales* se trouve ainsi placée dans un jour nouveau. La première à Timothée n'a pris sa forme traditionelle qu'après la publication des *Antithèses*.[12]

Turmel foresaw even greater consequences:

> La littérature ignatienne faisait un peu l'office d'une maîtresse poutre pour certaines pièces dites apostoliques. Son effondrement aura inévitablement des conséquences que vous signalez et sur lesquelles l'avenir seul nous donnera des précisions.[13]

In 1923 Turmel had the good fortune of being approached by Couchoud, via Houtin, with the idea of writing a volume·on Ignatius for the series 'Christianisme'[14]. So recently condemned to silence, in his own view, by the closure of *RHLR*, he now saw a new future opening up before him and he went on to produce a number of volumes for the series, including six signed 'Delafosse'[15]. The volume on Ignatius was held back by Couchoud, partly on account of its length and also to bring forward Turmel's work on the Fourth Gospel[16]. Then, towards the end of 1923, Houtin told Turmel that he had spoken about 'Delafosse' to the editor of the *Revue de l'Histoire des Religions,* Paul Alphandéry, who had agreed to accept whatever 'Delafosse' might care to submit[17]. Turmel lost no time and in 1924 there appeared articles on the Synoptic Gospels and Paul[18], to be followed in 1925 by a long review of Harnack's *Marcion*[19]. Thus Turmel was drawn into the circle of Couchoud, Houtin and

---

11 Turmel to Loisy 16.4.22 (BN n.a.f. 15662).

12 Sartiaux, *Joseph Turmel* p114. Loisy accepted Turmel's argument that I Timothy 6, 20 referred to Marcion's work and mentioned this possibility in *Les Livres du Nouveau Testament* p207. Turmel claimed, with good reason, that his own manuscript article had led to the inclusion of this reference (*Après cinquante ans d'etudes* p217).

13 Turmel to Loisy 29.8.22 (BN n.a.f. 15662).

14 Couchoud to Houtin 28.2.23 (BN n.a.f. 15696). Gertz *op.cit.* 7.3.6 does not allow sufficiently for this new opportunity supplied by Couchoud.

15 *Le Quatrième Evangile* (1925); *Les Ecrits de saint Paul* 4 vols. (1926—8); *Les Lettres d'Ignace d'Antioche* (1927).

16 Couchoud requested the latter work early in 1924; cf. Turmel to Loisy 14.4.24 (BN n.a.f. 15662) where Turmel says that Loisy's commentary of 1921 was of great assistance. The work was completed by mid-1924 (cf. Turmel to Houtin 30.6.24 (BN n.a.f. 15735) but Couchoud considerably abridged Turmel's manuscript (cf. Houtin to Turmel 23.8.24 (Draft preserved in BN n.a.f. 15735)).

17 Houtin to Turmel 9.10.23 (draft preserved in BN n.a.f. 15735).

18 'Les rapports de Matthieu et de Luc' *RHR* 89 pp1—38; 'Nouvel examen des epîtres pauliniennes' *RHR* 89 pp193—224.

19 *RHR* 92 pp169—179.

(later) Sartiaux[20] and although he remained a recluse and did not actually sever relations with Loisy, his new associates were closer to him ideologically[21]. He was therefore to find himself included in Loisy's anger directed at the *mythologues* and the treachery of Houtin. These personal dealings have to be borne in mind in this enquiry[22].

It is not necessary to discuss Turmel's ideas on the Marcionite origin of the Fourth Gospel and the anti-Marcionite nature of the Ignatian Epistles, except to note that Loisy consistently opposed the first hypothesis[23], while remaining sympathetic to the latter. In both cases Turmel was to revise his earlier published opinions[24]. Neither does the name of Harnack enter the debate as much as one might expect. The latter's momumental work on Marcion of 1921[25] may have encouraged Turmel's pan-Marcionism, although the evidence is disputed[26]. Turmel's 1925 review of Harnack concentrates upon the reconstruction of the 'Apostolikon' and 'Evangelium' (Marcion's version of the Epistles and Gospels respectively); Harnack is said to accept too uncritically the statement of Tertullian that Marcion suppressed whole passages of the New Testament: they simply did not exist. The review concludes:

M. Harnack a droit à nos remerciements pour nous avoir restitué *l'Evangile* de Marcion et son *Apostolicon,* mais ces deux livres ne peuvent en aucun degré être considérés comme les témoins de l'Evangile de Luc et de dix des épîtres pauliniennes avant 140.[27].

---

20 Loisy saw close affinities between Houtin and Turmel in particular: each had come to see in the Church 'une maîtresse perpétuelle de "pieux mensonges" ' (*Mém* III p434; cf. pp479, 505, 558). Loisy claims never to have shared their hatred for Christianity and Catholicism.

21 In acknowledging *La Religion,* Turmel had told Loisy that the view that morality rests on religion is like the Hindu belief that the earth rests on an elephant (Turmel to Loisy 20.6.17) (BN n.a.f. 15662)). He told Houtin, concerning his new volume on the Mass: 'elle contredit l'orthodoxie du Vatican, mais elle contredit aussi l'orthodoxie de Ceffonds' (Turmel to Houtin 29.10.25 BN n.a.f. 15735).

22 For Loisy's repudiation of Houtin, v. *Mém* III Ch.LVIII; and for its repercussions upon Turmel, v. the concluding remarks of *Après cinquante ans d'études* Ch.XIII. Gertz *op.cit.* 7.4.1 accepts too easily Turmel's version of the relations between himself and Loisy.

23 Cf. his review of *Le Quatrième Evangile* in *RC* 1925 pp237–243.

24 Cf. *Alfred Loisy, Sa Vie – Son Oeuvre* p211 n.9; *Mém* III p435.

25 *Marcion: das Evangelium vom fremden Gott.*

26 Gertz *op.cit.* 5.2.2 and 7.1.2 accepts Turmel's claim that he reached his views independently of Harnack.

27 *RHR* 92 p178. Loisy considered that this review, with its gratuitous mention of *L'Evan-*

Thus the ground is cleared for the fuller views of 'Delafosse', and in particular his theories about the epistles, where he is said to have influenced Loisy.

Turmel began his analysis of the epistles in his *RHR* article of 1924. He examined seven passages in turn, and considered that in each case an original Marcionite text had been subsequently glossed by a Catholic editor[28]. Thus the general conclusion is reached:

> . . . l'école marcionite, aux environs de 140, a interpolé les lettres de Paul pour y loger sa doctrine. Mais l'école catholique à partir du milieu du second siècle, s'est livré à un travail analogue . . . Il appartient à l'étude patiente de nos textes d'aller plus loin et de nous dire ce qui revient à chacune de ces deux éditions.[29]

Loisy was not impressed by this article: 'Il n'est pas permis de présenter sur quatre ou cinq points d'aiguille une conclusion aussi générale', he told Houtin. 'Delafosse' should have started from the Marcionite text as known from Tertullian[30]. But meanwhile Turmel had been extremely active: two volumes on Paul were ready by January 1925, on Romans and I Corinthians[31], but they had to take their turn in the 'Christianisme' series and so did not appear until the following year[32].

These works and the two succeceeding volumes on the other New Testament Epistles, are not commentaries; for each epistle there is an introduction, followed by a translation with variations in the typography to indicate the stages of redaction. The introductions do not inspire confidence: there is hardly any discussion of contemporary exegesis[33]; as in the *RHR* article, Turmel seizes upon individual

---

gile et l'Eglise was a counterblast to his own adverse criticism of *Le Quatrième Evangile* by 'Delafosse' (*Mém* III p497).

28 The passages are Romans 16, 25—26; Ephesians 3, 3—5; I Timothy 6, 20—21; Ephesians 2, 15; Romans 6, 3—13; I Timothy 2, 11—14.

29 *RHR* 89 p224. Turmel viewed this article as a curtain-raiser for his volumes on Paul; cf. Turmel to Houtin 25.8.24 (BN n.a.f. 15735).

30 Loisy to Houtin 21.8.25 (BN n.a.f. 15718); for this exchange of opinion with Houtin cf. *Mém* III pp479—81.

31 Turmel to Houtin 19.1.25 (BN n.a.f. 15735).

32 Cf. Couchoud to Houtin 8.7.25 (BN n.a.f. 15696): Houtin is to retain the manuscript of the volume of I Corinthians until Romans has appeared. Couchoud abridged the Romans volume, as Turmel discovered from the proofs, although the author was satisfied that the essential remained. (Turmel to Houtin 19.9.25 (BN n.a.f. 15735): he says he is hopeful his work will show up the scribblings ('grimoire') of the exegetes.)

33 For standard commentary points, Turmel often refers to patristic and mediaeval authorities.

verses and even words, in order to press his hypothesis[34]; arbitrary links are established between concepts in the epistles and elements of Marcionite and anti-Marcionite theology. With these arguments we need not be closely concerned, as Loisy was to reject most of them. What requires attention is the final picture of the epistles as composite documents, having undergone several stages of redaction[35]. Diagram 'A' at the end of this section summarizes the results of the thorough analysis carried out by 'Delafosse', in the case of those major Pauline epistles recognised as largely authentic by Loisy in *Les Livres du Nouveau Testament* (1921). It rapidly reveals the confidence with which 'Delafosse' recognised glosses and interpolations, even when they consist of single phrases or words.

Loisy's review of 'Delafosse' on Romans is a vital document for his changing views and requires quotation at some length[36];

> Il est à présumer que la critique retiendra quelque chose et même beaucoup du classement de sources que M.D. a pensé établir d'un seul coup et d'une manière définitive par la seule force de son raisonnement; mais ce ne sera probablement pas sans changer ses étiquettes et ses dates, ni sans appeler d'autres preuves.[37]

Then, having agreed that sections of Romans are interpolated (eg. 1, 18–32; all of chapter 2) and having suggested that Turmel's Marcionite passages could well be in the nature of mystical 'gnoses', he concludes:

> Il se peut que la rédaction de l'épître aux Romains soit aussi compliquée que le dit M.D., peut-être même l'est-elle encore plus, mais elle se sera effectuée en d'autres conditions et avant Marcion.[38]

Thus Loisy, although not accepting the dating and provenance for the epistle suggested by Turmel, is here prepared in principle to

---

34 Eg. *meteschēmatisa* in I Cor. 4, 6 is alleged to reveal the fundamental principle of the Marcionite editor.

35 For the brief indication of writers and commentators who have suggested such compilation theories v. J.C. O'Neill, *Paul's Letter to the Romans* (1975) pp285–315 under the names: Barnikol, B. Bauer, Loisy, Manen (van), Michelson, Pierson, Weisse; cf. also entries under Bultmann, Marcion and Schweitzer. For more details on B. Bauer and the Dutch school, v. A. Schweitzer, *Paul and his Interpreters* (ET 1912) Ch.V. The Dutch radical tradition was continued by G.A. van den Bergh van Eysinga, who wrote about it in *Die holländische radikale Kritik des Neuen Testaments* (1913) and who contributed *La Littérature chrétienne primitive* (1926) to the series 'Christianisme'.

36 *RC* 1926 pp241–5. It is quoted by Sartiaux in *Joseph Turmel* p115 and by Turmel himself in *Après cinquante ans d'études* p213. Loisy, significantly enough, only refers to it in passing (*Mém* III p500).

37 *Art.cit.* p243.

38 *Ibid* p245.

jettison the authenticity of large sections of Paul's major epistle, in favour of the idea of a compilation, at a fairly late date, of anonymous writings. He was to be much harder on 'Delafosse' in his review of the volume on I Corinthians, but in rejecting the author's 'conjectures' he again gives an indication of his own view of the provenance of the material, if it is not to be assigned to Paul:

> On peut croire que M.D. abhorre le mysticisme et qu'il n'admettrait pas d'argument expliquant par la mentalité mystique et les croyances mystiques les textes auxquels il ne trouve aucun sens en dehors de son hypothèse.[39]

Further evidence of Loisy's position is gained from the brief summaries which remain of his lectures at EPHE. During 1925–6 he lectured on 'La rédaction des épîtres de Paul' with reference to I Corinthians and concluded that in that epistle not only Ch.13 (the *agapē*-hymn) but also important sections in Ch.7 (on marriage and virginity), Ch.11 (on women's veils and the Eucharist), Ch.12 and 14 (on spiritual gifts) and Ch.15 (on the resurrection) were originally independent of their context[40]. In the following year, the course was specifically devoted to the theories of 'Delafosse'[41]. Loisy accepted that I and II Corinthians were compilations, not only of authentic letters of Paul but also of 'd'autres instructions, soit doctrinales, soit disciplinaires'. Romans is 'un recueil d'enseignements, progressivement élaborés autour d'une lettre authentique de Paul'. There are however no signs of Marcionite teaching[42].

At this point in his career, Loisy moved into retirement[43] but a public utterance of 1927 made his position more generally known. At his own *Jubilé*, he read.a paper on I Corinthians 11, written under the stimulus of Lietzmann's *Messe und Herrenmahl* (1926)[44]. He accepts a distinction between the 'cène eschatologique' of the first Christians and the 'cène mystique' of I Corinthians, but concludes that the second must be a later development, to be dated at the end

---

39 *RC* 1927 p133.
40 *Annuaire de l'EPHE – Section des Sciences Religieuses* – 1926–7 pp35–6.
41 Cf. *Mém* III p517.
42 *Annuaire de l'EPHE – Section des Sciences Religieuses* – 1927–8 pp39–40.
43 He resigned from EPHE, was replaced by his suppléant, Jean Baruzi, at the Collège de France, and ceased to write for the *Revue Critique*.
44 The paper was published as 'Les origines de la cène eucharistique' in *Congrès d'histoire du christianisme* I (1928) pp77–95. When he reviewed Lietzmann's book, he raised the question of whether I Corinthians 11 on the Eucharist and the 'gnose du salut' in the central chapters of Romans could possibly go back to Paul (*RC* 1927 p335).

of the first century or the beginning of the second. The implications of the paper aroused comment when it was delivered[45] and it is alleged by Turmel and Sartiaux as a clear example of Loisy's unacknowledged borrowing from 'Delafosse'[46]. But the EPHE lectures, though unpublished, had prepared Loisy's ground, and later in 1927 he was to acknowledge the contribution of 'Delafosse', when he rebuked Goguel for not taking the compilation theories more seriously[47]. However, his desire to distinguish between the acceptable and unacceptable aspects of the theories of 'Delafosse' undoubtedly create the impression of ambiguity, described by Sartiaux as 'une mélange d'adhésion et d'hostilité'[48] and this ambiguity was further compounded by the personal and ideological factors mentioned above.

The final evidence for Loisy's estimate of the Epistles has to be taken from *Remarques sur la littérature épistolaire du Nouveau Testament* (1935), which lies outside the scope of this section. But the name of Turmel is frequently mentioned[49] and its conclusions must be summarized, all the more as they show continuity with what we have gleaned of those held in 1927. An attempt is made to present Loisy's findings in Diagram 'B', at the end of this section. Direct comparison with Diagram 'A' is largely precluded, mainly by Loisy's desire not to be 'systematic', but it can be seen that he allows even less of the Pauline epistles to be authentic than 'Delafosse' had allowed and that they are reduced to many disparate sections. Loisy's terminology is revealing: 'théories', 'instructions', 'enseignements', 'moralités', 'gnoses', with much use of the adjectives 'mystique' and 'gnostique', all applied to the 'morceaux détachés'. Thus the picture is created of isolated elements of tradition brought together through liturgical use and ascribed to the apostle of the

---

45 Guignebert said that such a theory might lead to a complete readjustment of received opinion about the evolution of Christianity in the first century, to which Loisy replied that such 'accidents' are not unknown (*Mém* III p529).

46 *Après cinquante ans d'études* p215; *Alfred Loisy, Sa Vie — Son Oeuvre* p213.

47 *RC* 1927 pp413–5, in a review of Goguel's *Introduction au Nouveau Testament* IV ii (1926). Loisy does not of course suggest that all the theories of 'Delafosse' should be accepted. Against the 'outrageously systematic' conclusions of 'Delafosse', he offers a provisional analysis of Romans, mentioning 'une apologie de l'apostolat de Paul' and 'une gnose mystique du salut' by different hands, as well as various 'suppléments'.

48 *Alfred Loisy, Sa Vie — Son Oeuvre* p213.

49 Turmel is granted the merit of having posed the problem in correct terms, but is again

Gentiles. The material is therefore anonymous and may not be precisely dated, although some relative datings are suggested when two or more passages are compared. A general impression is conveyed of a late first-century or early second-century provenance for most of the material.

In conclusion, it seems that Loisy was ungenerous in not acknowledging more freely Turmel's decisive role in triggering off a new phase of criticism. But he was clear and consistent in stating which aspects of 'Delafosse' were acceptable and which were not[50]. Turmel and Sartiaux complain that Loisy took two basic concepts from 'Delafosse': the idea that only a kernel of the so-called authentic epistles really goes back to Paul; and the idea that they are largely second-century compilations, incorporating sizeable 'gnostic' elements. On Loisy's side it might be claimed that he was already uneasy about conflicting elements in 'Pauline' thought when he published *L'Epître aux Galates* in 1916[51]; that he had mentioned a number of probable interpolations in the Epistles in *Les Livres du Nouveau Testament* (1922)[52]; that he had mentioned the compiled nature of certain epistles in his article on 'Le style rythmé'[53] and that he always rejected Turmel's rigid classification of the material and his pan-Marcionism. Certainly Loisy had already decided, on historical grounds, that Paul was a marginal figure in early Christianity; and, in the case of the Gospels, he had come to see them as comparatively late compilations of anonymous materials. The new theory offered him the possibility of dissolving a body of material which, if ascribed to a single author, remained an impressive individual achievement, even if the ideas it contained were eccentric in the early Church and repugnant to the modern mind. This could well explain the alacrity with which Loisy embraced the new approach.

---

accused of 'scholasticism' (*Op. cit.* pp6–7). Loisy's new view of the epistles had become apparent in *La naissance du Christianisme* (1933) and Turmel claimed that he should have been given credit for a good twenty or so of Loisy's observations in that volume, although he was grateful for Loisy's adhesion to his standpoint in the face of both orthodox and independent critics. (*Histoire des dogmes* IV (1935) p475). He also claimed that in *Remarques* ... Loisy was using the same critical sieve as himself (*Histoire des dogmes* V (1936) p572).

50 Gertz *op. cit.* 7.4.2 again accepts too readily the Turmel-Sartiaux version of Loisy's borrowings.

51 V. above 2.3.

52 I Cor. 13; Romans 13.1–7, 8–10; I Thessalonians 2.13–16, 3.3–4, 4.13–5.11.

53 Cf. above 2.5.1; *art. cit.* p428, with reference to I and II Corinthians and Philippians.

Loisy's use of the theory was, however, much more supple than Turmel's, reflecting his awareness of ritual, social and 'mystical' elements in early Christianity and he was deliberately reluctant to ascribe dates and places[54]. So there was not such a sharp turn in his critical evolution as might appear; as in the case of the *religionsgeschichtliche Schule*[55], Loisy took a newly published work as a catalyst for his own further development. The new departure, if not unprepared for, was however sufficiently startling for a closer account to be required of how he had reached his conclusions and this might have involved more generous references to Turmel. We have seen how the interplay of personalities and events during these years made such an acknowledgement too much to expect.

H. Delafosse, *Les Ecrits de Saint Paul*   DIAGRAM 'A'

	Paul	Marcionite Redactor	Catholic Redactor	
			I	II
ROM	$1^{1-17*}\ 3^{27}-4^{25*}$ $9^1-10^{21*}\ 15^{8-33}$ $16^{1-2.19-23}$	$1^{4\dagger}\ 3^{21-26}4^{15.25}$ $5^1-8^{39*}\ 9^{5b}$ $12^1-13^{14*}\ 16^{17-27*}$	$1^{3b.18-32}$ $2^{1-29*}3^{1-20}$ $5^{9.15\dagger}\ 7^{7-25}$ $8^{3a.9b.11.14-17}$ $8^{23.26\dagger.36}$ $9^{1\dagger.5\dagger.14-29}$ $11^{1-36}\ 13^{1-7}$ 14^{1-12}	2^{14-15} $14^{13}-15^7$
I COR	$1^{1-9*.10-16}\ 4^8$ $5^{1-2.6-7a}$ $11^{2.17-22*.33}$ $16^{1-12.15-21}$	$1^{2b.5b.17-18.20b-30}$ $2^{1-8}\ 2^{10}-3^{15}$ $3^{18-19a}3^{21}-4^{6a}$ $4^{6c-7.9-21}$ $5^{3-5a.7b-13}$ $6^{9b-13.15-16a}$ $6^{17-18.20}\ 7^{1b.7-9}$ $7^{28b-35}\ 11^{20b.22a}$ $11^{23-32*.34}\ 15^{22}$ $15^{45-52a.52c-58}$ $16^{13-14.22-24}$	$1^{12\dagger.19-20a.31}$ $2^9\ 3^{16-17.19b-20}$ $4^{6b}\ 5^{5b}\ 6^{1-9a}$ $6^{14.16b.19}$ $7^{1a.2-6.10-28a}$ $7^{36}-9^{12a}$ $9^{13-14.19-27}$ $10^{23}-11^1\ 11^{3-10}$ $11^{13-16.17\dagger.18-19}$ $11^{24-29}\ 12^{1-4}$ $12^{7-11.13.31}$ $14^{1b-33a.36-40}$ $15^{1-21.23-44.52b}$	$1^{12\dagger}\ 9^{12b}$ 9^{15-18} 10^{1-22} 11^{11-12} $12^{5-6.12}$ 12^{14-30} $12^{31b}-13^{13}$ 14^{1a} 14^{33b-35}

(Continued on page 123)

(Continued from page 122)

	Paul	Marcionite Redactor	Catholic Redactor
II COR	${}_1^{1-2.\,8-11}$ ${}_1^{15-20.\,23}$ ${}_2^{1-13}$ ${}_6^{11-13}$ ${}_7^{2}-{}_8^{8}$ ${}_8^{10}-{}_9^{14}$ ${}_{10}^{1-2a*.\,9-11}$ ${}_{11}^{6b-12a}$ ${}_{12}^{13}-{}_{13}^{2}$ ${}_{13}^{10a.\,12-13}$	${}_1^{3-7.\,12-14.\,21.\,24}$ ${}_2^{14}-{}_4^{5}$ ${}_4^{6b-12}$ ${}_4^{15}-{}_5^{1}$ ${}_5^{3b.\,4b}$ ${}_5^{6}-{}_6^{10}$ ${}_6^{14-16a}$ ${}_7^{1}$ ${}_8^{9}$ ${}_9^{15}$ ${}_{10}^{2b-8}$ ${}_{10}^{12}-{}_{11}^{6a}$ ${}_{11}^{12b}-{}_{12}^{12}$ ${}_{13}^{3-9.\,10b.\,11.14}$	${}_1^{22}$ ${}_4^{6a.\,13-14}$ ${}_5^{2-3a.\,4a.\,5}$ ${}_6^{16b-18}$.
GAL	${}_1^{6-7}$ ${}_3^{6-9.\,11-12.\,14a}$ ${}_3^{15-18.\,19b.}$ ${}_3^{28b.\,29}$ ${}_4^{11-23}$ ${}_4^{28-31}$ ${}_5^{7-12}$ ${}_6^{11.\,17}$	${}_1^{1\ 5*.\,8-17}$ ${}_1^{21}-{}_2^{2a}$ ${}_2^{3-14}$ ${}_2^{18}-{}_3^{1}$ ${}_3^{3-4.\,10.\,13.}$ ${}_3^{19a.\,26-28a}$ ${}_4^{1-4a.\,5.\,7}$ ${}_5^{1-6.\,13-26}$ ${}_6^{7-10.\,12-16.\,18}$	${}_1^{18-20}$ ${}_2^{2b.\,15-17}$ ${}_3^{2.\,5}$ ${}_3^{14b.\,19c-25}$ ${}_4^{4b.\,6.\,8-10}$ ${}_4^{24-27}$ ${}_6^{1-6}$
COL	${}_4^{7-8.\,10-11}$ ${}_4^{15*.\,18a}$	${}_1^{2-14.\,18a.\,19-21}$ ${}_1^{22-23a.\,26-28}$ ${}_2^{2-3.\,6-12a.\,13-15}$ ${}_3^{1}-{}_4^{3a}$ ${}_4^{5-6.\,12}$ ${}_4^{16-17.\,18c}$	${}_1^{1.\,15-17.\,18b.\,22\dagger.\,23b-25}$ ${}_1^{29}-{}_2^{1}$ ${}_2^{4-5.\,12b.\,16-23}$ ${}_4^{3b-4.\,9.\,13-14.\,18b}$
PHIL	${}_1^{1-2*.\,12-18}$ ${}_1^{25-26}$ ${}_2^{19}$ ${}_2^{22}-{}_3^{1a}$ ${}_4^{2-3}$ ${}_4^{10-22}$	${}_1^{3-11.\,19-24}$ ${}_1^{27}-{}_2^{8}$ ${}_2^{12-18.\,20-21}$ ${}_3^{1b-20a}$ ${}_4^{1.\,4-9.\,23}$	${}_2^{9-11}$ ${}_3^{20b-21}$
I THESS	${}_1^{1-10}$ ${}_2^{17}-{}_3^{13}$ ${}_4^{9-12}$ ${}_5^{1-9.\,11}$	${}_4^{1-8.\,13-14.\,17-18}$ ${}_5^{10}$	${}_2^{1-16}$ ${}_4^{15-16}$ ${}_5^{12-25}$ ${}_5^{27-28}$(further addition ${}_5^{26}$)
PHMN		all †	vv. 23 and 24†

* excepting minor glosses;   † single words or phrases

---

54 Here one must differ from a remark of Marcel Simon who considers that in this phase of his criticism, Loisy was judging Paul by the over-exact standards of Descartes or St. Thomas Aquinas. ('The Birth of Christianity', *FF* 1948 p138).

55 Cf. the suggestion concerning his use of Reitzenstein above 2.2.

A. Loisy, *Remarques sur la littérature*   DIAGRAM 'B'
    épistolaire du Nouveau Testament

ROMANS

Fragments of an original letter: 1^{1-7} 15

Eschatological theory of salvation: 1^{8-17} $3^{27}-4^{24}$ 9–11 15^{8-12}

Mystical theory of salvation: 3^{25-26} 5–8 (3^{21-24} is a 'suture')

  (but NB additions: $5^{5.9}$; attempted reconciliation of the two theories: 7^{7-25}; Ch.8

  heavily glossed: vv. 3a. 9. 11. 14–17. 23. 26–27. 36)

Polemical hors d'oeuvre: $1^{18}-3^{20}$

Sundry moral 'instructions': 12 $13^{1-7.\ 8-10}$ $14^{1}-15^{7}$

GALATIANS

Possible fragments of an original letter: 1^{6-7}

Eschatological theory of salvation: $3^{6-9.\ 11-12.\ 14a.\ 15-18.\ 19b.\ 28b-29}$

  $4^{11-20.\ 21-23.\ 28-31}$ (4^{24-27}'Catholic' addition)

Mystical theory of salvation: $1^{1-3.\ 11-12}$ $2^{14.\ 18-21}$ $3^{1.\ 3-4.\ 10.\ 13.\ 19a.\ 26-28a}$

  $4^{4-5.\ 7}$ $5^{1-6.\ 13-26}$ $6^{7-8.\ 12-16}$

Later addition: 1^{18-20}

I & II CORINTHIANS

The real Paul: I Cor $1^{1-3.\ 4-16}$ II Cor $1^{1}-2^{13}$ 7^{5-16} 8–9

  (Ch.10–13 include fragments of a 'severe letter')

The 'mystical' Paul: I Cor $1^{17}-4^{6}$ II Cor $2^{14}-6^{13}$ (1st panegyric) 10–13

  (2nd panegyric, dating from second century)

Erratic block: II Cor $6^{14}-7^{1}$

Detached items:

  I Cor 5–6 (genuine Paul with interpolations)

  I Cor 7 (not from apostolic age but before Montanism)

  I Cor 11^{3-16}, 12, 14 (3 pieces of similar provenance but 14^{33b-34} is a later

          interpolation)

  I Cor 11^{17-34}, 5^{7-8} and 10^{1-22} (of similar provenance)

  I Cor 15 (of mixed origin; basic document in such vv. as 20–22, 45–51, 53–58)

I THESSALONIANS

Paul's letter: 1, $2^{17}-3^{2a}$ 3^{5b-13} 5^{26-28}

Later insertions: 2^{1-16} (by supporters of Paul)

          3^{2b-5a} (persecution)

Moral 'instructions': $4^{1-7.\ 17-18}$ (mystical), 4^{9-12} 5^{1-11} (practical; 5^{10} mystical gloss)

Detached items: 5^{12-24} ('moralité' of c.120–130)

          4^{13-18} (resurrection; 4^{15-16} eschatological gloss)

(Continued on page 125)

(Continued from page 124)

PHILIPPIANS

Two letters of Paul: (a) 4^{10-22}

(b) 1^{1-2}. 12–18. 25–26 2^{19}. 22 2^{30}–3^{1a}

Christological poem: 2^{6-11}

Gnostic, mystical teachings: 1^{3-11}. 19–24 1^{27}–2^4 2^{12-18}. 20–21 3^{1b-20a}. 20b–21

COLOSSIANS

Possible note by Paul: 4^{7-11}

Christological poem: 1^{15-20}

Gnostic passages: 1^{1-14}. 21–23a. 26–28 2^{2-3}. 6–15 3^1–4^{3a} 3^{5-6} 4^{12}. 16–17

Redactional additions: 1^{23b-25} 1^{29}–2^1 2^{4-5}

PHILEMON

Authentic, but no connection with 'Colossians'

2.6 *CONCLUSIONS*

By 1927 therefore all the ingredients were present in Loisy's mind for his final synthesis in *La Naissance du christianisme* of 1933. Much that he had stated in the *RHLR* articles of 1920–22 was to reappear there[1] but he did not find it an easy book to write[2]. The main features were of course established: very little can be known about the Jesus of history[3]; early Christianity went through a series of transformations, whereby the Messianic resurrection faith of the first disciples was transformed into the cult of a heavenly Lord, offering universal salvation; Paul did not have the principal role in this transformation, since the lead in the direction of the Gentiles had been taken by Stephen's followers and figures such as Barnabas. But the more recently acquired views of Loisy concerning the nature and dating of the documents, especially the Epistles, meant that developments in the first century A.D. were rendered

---

1 V. above 2.4.

2 Cf. Loisy to Cumont 7.8.27 (BN n.a.f. 15644): 'Plus j'avance et plus je sens le besoin de nuancer et d'affermir mes conclusions'. It is like being caught up in Penelope's web. Loisy to Bremond 24.8.27 (text by courtesy of E. Goichot) speaks of 'un terrain mouvant'; 'plus j'avance et plus je vois la nécessité de refondre tout ce travail pour la publication'. Cf. also *Mém* III p518.

3 Sartiaux, *Alfred Loisy, Sa Vie- Son Oeuvre* p218, provides a useful summary of Loisy's modifications in his account of the historical Jesus (although he is over-insistent on the discontinuities in the critic's thought).

increasingly obscure. In reducing still further the significance of Paul, Loisy also deprived himself of evidence for the fundamental developments he had once been prepared to ascribe to pre-Pauline Hellenistic Christianity. As a historian, he had to abandon the attempt to provide a strict chronological account of Christian origins[4].

As many critics have complained, *La Naissance du christianisme* gives a highly negative impression and has therefore often been considered to be 'rationalist' or 'positivist' in inspiration[5]. But we have seen how Loisy was attempting to reconstruct early Christianity as a historian of religions, sensitive to ritual and collective elements[6] but with a hypercritical view of the documents. There can be no doubt that he wished to make early Christianity 'come alive' (his work on 'le style rythmé' is evidence enough of that) but the more usual ways of doing so were not open to him. He could not adopt a doctrinal approach, since early Christian doctrines were alien, confused and often absurd; nor a retelling of the history through outstanding personalities, since the personality of a Jesus or a Paul was no longer accessible to the modern critic and in any case the significant developments were anonymous; nor, in spite of his bulky commentaries, could he attempt a documentary, literary reconstruction because he regarded source-criticism, and even form-criticism, as a dead end. Moreover, one looks almost in vain for additional insight into early Christianity in Loisy's non-specialist works of the period; references to the first Christians are sketchy and slight among hundreds of pages of writing on religion, faith, morality and mysticism'.

There is much honesty in this evolution of ideas but the characteristic which emerges most strongly is that of ferocious independence[8]. Loisy was under a permanent constraint to differentiate

---

4   V. details in 5.2 below. For his own view of the problems involved, cf. 'Le problème des origines chrétiennes' (originally a lecture of 1931) in *Le Mandéisme et les origines chrétiennes* (1934) pp159–174, where Loisy insists strongly on the non-historical nature of the documents.

5   V. eg. the comments of H.G. Wood, *Jesus in the Twentieth Century* (1960) pp96–110; Sir M. Knox, *A Layman's Quest* (1969) pp119–21. Cumont anticipated such critics: 'A la vérité certains se plaindront que vous ayez si peu de certitudes à leur offrir. Il est toujours difficile de pratiquer *l'ars nesciendi'* (Cumont to Loisy 26.11.33 (BN n.a.f. 15651)).

6   Significantly he chose to speak at both the Congrès Renan in 1923 and his own Jubilé in 1927 on the Eucharist in I Corinthians 11.

7   Cf. eg. *La Religion* (2nd edn. 1924) pp174ff; *Religion et humanité* (1926) pp200ff.

8   Cf. Sartiaux in *Alfred Loisy, Sa Vie – Son Oeuvre* p291: 'Loisy appartient à cette caté-

himself from all others in the field: Catholic theologians and exegetes; their Protestant counterparts (however liberal); the sociologists, especially those of the influential Durkheim school; rationalists, anticlericals and *scientistes*; the whole tribe of *mythologues*; Marcionites and all who practised a thoroughgoing literary exegesis of the New Testament[9]. It would be possible to show how, in reality, he owed something to each of these groups, but his temperament and the circumstances of his life made alliances impossible for him. Even the writers of the *religionsgeschichtliche Schule*, with whom he shared strong historical interests and an aversion for purely literary criticism, were too theological for his tastes.

The case of Loisy raises in acute form therefore the problems of the independent critic of early Christianity. The confessional critic looks back to the first century A.D. in the belief that he will find something there of permanent value. But for those outside any established hermeneutical tradition, all the questions are seemingly open. Nevertheless, these critics too belong in a sense to the history of Christianity: just as Loisy saw the first Christians as an example of Mediterranean religiosity, so he himself may now be seen as a product of his times — his ecclesiastical training, his initiation into historical methods by Renan and various German critics, the conflicting ideological forces of his country and his period and the academic setting of his critical work. The freedom of a secular critic also has its constraints, all the more so in a culture where he is working against the ecclesiastical and academic streams[10]. To be a non-Catholic and furthermore a non-Protestant scholar in this field, during the period we have been considering in France, was to be an outsider indeed. In that situation, to have maintained a distance from the ideological world of the rationalists and their associates must be seen as a remarkable personal achievement, but also as a stance which could not, of itself, guarantee the sureness of the results.

---

gorie d'esprits qui pensent toujours contre quelqu'un'.

9 A further sign of his independence is the comparative lack of reference in his published work to the views of other scholars in the field; cf. Houtin in *Alfred Loisy, Sa Vie — Son Oeuvre* p179.

10 Interestingly, Loisy rejected theories of far-reaching secularisation; e.g. in reviewing Aulard on *Le Christianisme et la révolution française*, which argued for widespread dechristianisation in France at the time of the Revolution, Loisy commented: 'A considérer les profondeurs de l'âme, on pourrait aussi bien soutenir que la déchristianisation n'a été et n'est encore que partielle et superficielle.' (*RC* 1925 p239).

3. GUIGNEBERT'S WORK
ON EARLY CHRISTIANITY 1906—1933

3.1 APPOINTMENT AT THE SORBONNE

Charles Guignebert was a historian who happened to specialise in early Christianity. As a student at the Sorbonne, he had become the favourite pupil of the historians Lavisse and Guiraud[1] but he also sat at the feet of Renan[2]. During the customary period spent teaching in lycées in the provinces[3], Guignebert presented his doctoral thesis on Tertullian: 'Etude sur ses sentiments à l'égard de l'Empire et de la société civile', in 1902 in Paris[4]. It was through this work that he found his way into early Christianity, although, as the title indicates, the early Christians were never to be studied in isolation from the general political and religious life of their times. In 1905—6, Guignebert, who now had a post at the lycée Voltaire, gave a 'cours libre' on Christian origins at the Sorbonne, which reached publication as *Manuel d'histoire ancienne du christianisme — Les origines* (1906). This will be considered more fully below.

In 1906, Guignebert was appointed full-time to the History section of the Faculty of Letters at the Sorbonne. The appointment had a political significance, as it came in the wake of the Separation of Church and State. Under the new Law, the Protestant Faculty lost its official status at the Sorbonne and became a 'free' independent faculty (Catholic institutions were already quite separate from

---

1 According to Marguerite Brunot, 'Charles Guignebert (1867—1939): Sa Vie et son oeuvre', *Annales de l'Université de Paris* 1939 no.3., p365. (Mlle Marguerite Brunot, daughter of the philologist Ferdinand Brunot, was for many years Guignebert's academic assistant; she prepared the posthumous volume *Le Christ* (1943)).

2 Mentioned by E. Poulat, *Alfred Loisy, Sa Vie — Son Oeuvre* (1961) p359.

3 He taught, briefly at Evreux and Pau, and for a longer period at Toulouse. E. Poulat in *Histoire, dogme et critique* (1962) p377 mentions that during 1903, Guignebert gave a public lecture in favour of Loisy in Toulouse, to counteract the lectures of Batiffol, then Rector of the Institut Catholique there.

4 Its date of publication was 1901.

the State). It was felt desirable to make an appointment for 'l'histoire ancienne du christianisme': the state of governmental feeling at
the time would never have countenanced a Catholic appointment and
even a Protestant might have been *persona non grata*. Guignebert,
who always claimed to be quite detached from any confessional
interests, was the ideal choice[5]. He was to hold the position for the
rest of his academic career, until his retirement in 1937[6].

His introductory remarks to the lecture course of 1906—7 are of
interest here. They do not constitute a full statement of policy but
indicate his thinking at the time of his assumption of duties. He pays
tribute to the scholars of the Protestant Faculty, who, by contrast
with their Catholic counterparts, were able to combine a deep faith
with a remarkable freedom of outlook; but the confessional nature
of the institution with its obligation of ministerial training, inevitably
kept the general public away. The Section des Sciences Religieuses
at the EPHE attracts future specialists and is by its very nature ill
fitted to fulfil an important task of higher education: 'à mettre au
point pour le grand public instruit, les résultats obtenus par les
recherches des érudits'[7]. It is precisely this more modest and more
general type of teaching which arouses alarm; nobody objects to
future *pasteurs* learning the basic facts of their religion, or to highly
specialised researchers publishing obscure tomes, but something
serious aimed at a wider audience is suspect. The alarm is felt not
only by the clergy of various churches who have their vested interests
but more especially among educated Frenchmen who do not wish
their prejudices to be disturbed. Although the Frenchman prides
himself upon his intellectual curiosity and his lack of reverence for
established authority, it has become traditional in France not to treat
religious matters with serious objectivity. Frenchmen adopt various
attitudes, such as the following:

> . . . une position de combat pour ou contre, ou une attitude d'indifférence bienveillante
> ou malveillante, mais il ne les fondent que sur un *a priori*, et on étonne beaucoup la
> plupart des gens en leur disant que l'histoire chrétienne n'est pas nécessairement un

---

5 His detachment from presuppositions is, of course, part of the object of the present
   study; but we may note, for the present, the comment by M. Brunot *art.cit.* p366 that
   he never experienced any religious crisis and that his interest in early Christianity was
   purely intellectual.
6 In 1919 he was promoted from 'chargé de cours' to 'professeur titulaire'.
7 GP ESE 3.

arsenal de polémique d'où les armes ne sont pas toutes éprouvées, mais qu'elle est tout comme une autre digne de retenir l'attention, capable d'intéresser passionément un homme qui réfléchit, susceptible d'être étudiée et expliquée comme toute autre forme de développement de l'humanité.[8]

Much of the reaction to the work of Renan or of Loisy is to be explained by this challenge to complacency.

French religious education remains largely at the level of the catechism. The omission of religion from secondary education (probably to be explained by the same official circumspection which excludes the study of recent history) is the principal reason for the extremely low level of public interest and understanding. Guignebert is therefore grateful for the opportunity which is now his:

. . . de démontrer que l'histoire chrétienne est une histoire comme les autres; que les faits qui la constituent sont des faits comme les autres, qui nous sont connus par des textes accessibles comme d'autres à la recherche critique, poussée en dehors de toutes les confessions, dans l'absolue sérénité de l'indifférence scientifique.[9]

There seems to have been a perfect correspondence between the requirements of the State and the University on the one hand and the intentions of Guignebert on the other. Essentially a University man himself, having no direct acquaintance with confessional institutions, Protestant or Catholic, the new lecturer approached his task with an objectivity which Renan would have approved: Christianity was an aspect of the general religious evolution of humanity. The remarks quoted above show that he was intent upon steering a middle path between the confessional critics — who could not have been easy with the phrase 'indifférence scientifique' — and the polemics of rationalist opponents of Christianity, who might have been hoping for a more open declaration of support from Guignebert. In choosing to attack the ignorance and the indifference of the general public, Guignebert was hoping to provide a way through the embroiled situation which, as we have seen, existed at the time of the Modernist crisis.

It will be convenient at this point to survey the University teaching which Guignebert provided during his tenure at the Sorbonne. Some of it is related to his published output, but much of it did not appear in print. It is generally agreed that Guignebert was an excellent teacher[10]; it should be remembered that he did not confine him-

---

8   GP ESE 6.
9   GP ESE 8.
10 According to Loisy in *RHR* 1940 p179, Guignebert was essentially '*le* professeur',

self entirely to the teaching of Christianity, but regularly taught courses on French history and civilisation[11]; nevertheless most of his lectures were devoted to 'l'histoire de l'antiquité chrétienne'. His lecture notes for many of his courses, mostly written out *in extenso*, have fortunately survived. They are an eloquent testimony to his profound knowledge of the ancient sources, his close attention to the contributions of modern scholars, whether Protestant, Catholic or independent, and his considerable skill in organising his materials in an orderly and attractive way for his hearers[12].

In the opening lecture referred to above, Guignebert stated his intention of proceeding to the general history of the Church in the second and third centuries, having already covered the first century in his 'cours libre' of the previous year. He envisaged this history in two aspects: the self realisation of the new religion vis-à-vis the Roman State and pagan society; and the internal constitution of Christianity, as it separated from Judaism and developed its own distinctive doctrines, organisation and practices. The latter question involved the Hellenisation of Christianity in both spirit and dogma, as well as the details of its own internal life. The two sides of this history are brought together in the Constantinian compromise.

This scheme took five years for its realisation[13]. Another five years were then devoted to a detailed study of the results of the Constantinian settlement, i.e. the Church in the fourth century[14]. Guignebert obviously attached special value to the period of Christian

---

devoted to his subject and its diffusion; cf. also M. Brunot, *art.cit.* p368.

11 M. Simon in *RHR* 1940 p181 remarks, 's'il possédait admirablement sa spécialité, il mettait cependant une certaine coquetterie à ne pas s'y cantonner de façon exclusive'.

12 A complete list of the lecture courses is given by M. Brunot, *art.cit.* pp372–3. These are divided into 'Cours Publics', and 'Conférences Ouvertes', the latter being mainly N.T. exegesis. The lecture notes which survive, now in the possession of Prof. Marcel Simon of Strasbourg, cover the years 1906–1921, 1928–1937 for the *cours publics* and 1915–1925, 1928–1933 for the *conférences ouvertes*. Of those which have not survived, it would be of great interest for this study to have the *cours publics* of 1921–1928 on the earliest years of Christianity and the Commentary on Acts of 1933–4; but it seems highly probable that these were retained by Mlle Brunot for the preparation of the posthumous volume *Le Christ* (1943). Much in the *cours publics* is devoted to the 2nd–5th centuries: these will be used selectively for our purposes. The courses of exegesis comprise some 2000 pages. For purposes of reference, the general designation GP ('Guignebert Papers') will be used to indicate this source, followed by an abbreviated title. For a complete list of these manuscripts, v. Bibliography.

13 1906–1911.

14 1911–1916.

consolidation in the second century and processes which led to its adoption as a State religion during the fourth century[15]. But he did not lose sight of the earliest period, because in 1911 he initiated his series of 'Conférences Ouvertes' under the rubric 'Lecture pratique du Nouveau Testament'[16]. Then, in the 'Cours Publics', having considered Church history down to the East-West schism[17], and having taken a close look at the methodology of his subject[18], he returned to the first century A.D. in a series of lectures which served as a basis for his volumes in the series, 'L'Evolution de l'humanité'[19]. In the last decade at the Sorbonne, while still pursuing his New Testament exegesis, Guignebert investigated different aspects of early Church history. He lectured on the Church of Rome from the first to the fourth centuries; on the origins of the Greek schism; and on religious politics and religious life in the Roman Empire in the first and second centuries A.D.[20].

This record of a lifetime's teaching reveals a remarkable devotion to the original intentions behind the teacher's appointment. Single-handed, Guignebert undertook to expound the origins and early history of Christianity[21], a task which in England or Germany might have been shared by two or three scholars. He was however quite content that the task should be undertaken within a department of history, because this offered some guarantees of objectivity, not easily obtained in a confessional institution. As a historian, he took a wide view of the period of 'origins': he diagnosed some kind of *terminus ad quem* to have occurred with the Constantinian settlement, before which the interaction of Church and State is just as important an object of study as the purely internal growth of Christianity — although so called 'internal' developments often need to be explained by interaction with the environment. But the very concept of *terminus ad quem* is relative in the historian's eyes and the

---

15 Matters of Church and State were of course most apposite so soon after the Separation in France; but Guignebert refrains from drawing parallels and his writings on contemporary religion were of a more popular nature.

16 For details, v. below 3.4.

17 1916–1921.

18 For details, v. below 3.5.

19 1921–1928. For details, v. below 5.1.

20 1929–1937.

21 For the chronological limits he assigned to 'l'histoire ancienne du christianisme' v. below 3.5.

'settlement' under Constantine did not inhibit Guignebert from taking the history of Christianity beyond that date. On the other hand, the historian of the early church cannot afford to neglect the foundation documents and Guignebert lavished upon these the same microscopic attention which the New Testament specialist would require. Here then is a most impressive range of activity across the canonical and patristic literature, as well as the relevant documents from Judaism and late Antiquity. This expertise, centred upon his teaching duties, is the heart of Guignebert's achievement, although the mere relating of his work at the Sorbonne does not do justice to the breadth of his interests. We have not satisfactorily indicated, for example, his preoccupation with the problem of the Jesus of history, his ability over the whole span of Christian history, including a close interest in contemporary religious problems, his concern for the pedagogy of history and others. Neither will these necessarily be adequately reflected in the pages which follow, although it should emerge that his publishing activity was firmly anchored in the teaching he gave, even if not solely dictated by it.

It is convenient to mention at this point that soon after his appointment to the Sorbonne, Guignebert began to contribute, to the *Revue Historique*, a series of 'Bulletins historiques' at first under the title 'Histoire du christainisme', then 'Antiquités chrétiennes' and at a later date, 'Histoire des religions'. Twelve of these *Bulletins* appeared between 1907 and 1937, each of them reviewing a large number of recent publications, including not only New Testament and patristic titles, but volumes on the Old Testament, Church history of various periods and the general history of religions. Guignebert also became a frequent reviewer in the *RHR* and in *Scientia* but these regular and massive contributions to the *Revue Historique* are to be seen as an important expression of his concern to place the study of Christianity within the sphere of historical research. Quite frequently in his reviews he distinguishes sharply between historical and confessional writings: for the historian, the latter only have interest insofar as they illuminate the contemporary religious scene.[22] In this, he tried to remain faithful to the principle enunciated at the opening of his first *Bulletin*:

---

22 Eg. in reviewing Batiffol, *L'Eglise naissante et le catholicisme* (1909) while admiring the writer's virtuosity, Guignebert stated that no non-dogmatic historian could accept the

Les temps semblent décidément venus où le gros des hommes instruits admettent que la critique historique peut légitimement appliquer ses méthodes aux idées et aux choses de la religion chrétienne, où les préoccupations de polémique ne trouvent plus guère place que dans les écrits des hommes incapables d'apprendre et de penser.[23]

3.2 PUBLISHED WORK ON EARLY CHRISTIANITY 1906–1910

This section will consider the *Manuel* of 1906, already mentioned, and a summary version of Christain origins which Guignebert contributed to the international journal *Scientia* in 1910[1]. It will also examine a work executed in great detail: *La Primauté de Pierre et la venue de Pierre à Rome* (1909).

3.2.1 Manuel d'histoire ancienne du christianisme — Les origines

The *Manuel* is a compact volume of some 550 pages, in the format of a *manuel scolaire*. An *avertissement* states that it is intended as a 'manuel purement laîque' for the general public, not for experts. It is in no way beholden to theology and the author will have been rewarded for his pains if he succeeds:

... à replacer sur le terrain historique des questions primordiales que les préoccupations confessionnelles et politiques en ont si longtemps écartées.[1]

The Introduction draws attention to the complexity of the emergence of a new religion, to the inadequate state of the documentation, to the convergence of Jewish and Greek elements in early Christianity and to the process of conflict and compromise whereby Christianity became the State religion of the Roman Empire. The modern reader notes from the bibliography how little was available in this field in French at the time: Duchesne's *Histoire ancienne de l'Eglise* is nominated as 'le meilleur manuel français'[2]. In a chapter on 'The Sources', Guignebert ranges at first over the first three cen-

---

book's conclusions. (*RH* t.100 p168). He similarly rejected the Protestant assumptions in Eugène de Faye, *Etude sur les origines des Eglises de l'âge apostolique* (1909) (*RH* t.107 p110).

23 *RH* t.95 (1907) p381.

1 *Scientia* Vol.VIII (1910): 'Les origines chrétiennes' pp123–145; 'L'évolution du christianisme ancien' pp375–402.

1 *Op.cit.* ppIII–IV.
2 *Ibid* pVIII; cf. 1.2 above.

turies, designating as categories 'Livres d'instruction' (of the narrative type, to which the Gospels and Acts belong and of the didactic type, to which the Epistles belong); 'Oeuvres de polémique' (apocalypses, apologias and polemical works proper); 'Documents hagiographiques'; and 'Quelques ouvrages purement narratifs' (Eg. Eusebius, but all such works are selective and tendentious). A more particular survey of the New Testament documents accepts a two-source theory for the Synoptics, although their final redaction by anonymous compilers must be placed between 98 and 117 A.D.; dates the Acts of the Apostles at the end of the first century or the beginning of the second; allows Galatians, I and II Corinthians and Romans to be by Paul, I and II Thessalonians and Philippians to be very probably by Paul; casts doubt on the authenticity of Colossians, Ephesians and Philemon; dates Hebrews during the reign of Domitian and Revelation c.95 A.D.

In his chapters devoted to 'background', Guignebert emphasises the differences between the Judaism of Palestine and that of the Diaspora. Christianity was to inherit the 'exclusivisme intolérant' of Palestinian intransigence, but in reacting against Pharisaic formalism, it used the Hellenistic Judaism of the Diaspora as a bridge to the Gentile world[3]. In the pagan world, philosophy was deviating into mysticism because of 'la nullité de la science'[4] and Christianity was able to provide a synthesis which satisfied some men's aspirations 'par sa souplesse, son ampleur, sa clarté et sa puissance d'expression'[5].

The life of Jesus is shrouded in mystery. His baptism probably marked 'une crise intérieure'[6]. Like a prophet, he spoke and healed, aided by 'des qualités personnelles de charme, d'esprit, de séduction et de simplicité'[7]. He was probably put to death by the Romans on a Messianic charge. Guignebert discusses the Resurrection at some length[8]. All that can be deduced from I Corinthians 15 is that, apart from his own vision, Paul simply reproduced what he had been told by apostles and disciples. From the Synoptics one must conclude

---

3 *Ibid* pp116—8.
4 *Ibid* pp142—4.
5 *Ibid* p154.
6 *Ibid* p179.
7 *Ibid* p180.
8 *Ibid* pp187—98.

that the disciples became convinced of the reality of the Resurrection on the strength of later visions but it is impossible to say when these visions occurred, because of the natural tendency to refer them back to Easter morning. An empty tomb was indeed discovered by the women but, leaving aside the orthodox account of the Resurrection (which is beyond the bounds of normal discussion) one is left with an arbitrary choice between the possibility that Jesus was not really dead and departed after being in a coma, and the possibility that the body was stolen. On the question of the visions, there are, apart from the orthodox standpoint, three possible theories, from which the individual may choose according to his 'disposition d'esprit':

(a) they were contagious hallucinations, as brilliantly defended by Renan;

(b) they were the transposition into material facts of the act of faith which accepted that Jesus was now alive with God, an interpretation supported by Loisy;

(c) they were pure invention, in order to demonstrate that Jesus was the awaited Messiah (but Guignebert thinks that this explanation is simplistic and attributes too much guile to the first disciples).

In a chapter on the teaching of Jesus[9], Guignebert is at pains to show that it gives no support to later ideas about the Incarnation, the Trinity, the Atonement and the Church. Jesus did not see himself as the miraculously conceived Son of God, the Second Person of the Trinity, the Saviour of the World and the Founder of the Church, with its dogmas and sacraments. It is not even possible to say with some modern theologians, that such doctrines were implicit in the teaching of Jesus: the debate between Harnack and Loisy shows how impossible it is to decide what the earthly Jesus thought of his own person, apart from the probability that he believed himself to be the Messiah. He certainly did not have it in mind to found a new religion. His own personality as a reformer determined to breathe a new spirit into Judaism was more important than his (not very original) teaching; his simple doctrine became the complicated orthodoxy of later years because the Kingdom which he preached did not appear.

The Acts of the Apostles has to be used with the greatest caution, since it combines some genuine historical information with much in

---

9 Ch. VI: 'L'enseignement de Jésus'.

the way of legendary traditions. Since the first Christians expected that Jesus, now Messiah at God's right hand, would shortly return to inaugurate the Kingdom, the organisation of their community was quite spontaneous and lacking in any theoretical basis[10]; the emphasis in the teaching was practical rather than intellectual[11]. Elements of church organisation in Jerusalem began with the appointment of officials to receive gifts, such as those brought by Paul, and the setting up of a presbyterate to decide on the official attitude to Gentile Christians. Here may be seen the beginnings of the break with the synagogue. Later, some Christians left Jerusalem to reinforce the small communities in Galilee, where memories of Jesus circulated, soon to be preserved in the Synoptic Gospels. After 70 A.D., the former Jerusalem community tried to reorganise as a 'mother church' with legitimate supremacy, but it was too late: the Christianity of Jerusalem had failed by remaining too faithful to the teaching of Jesus. The sterile dream of the Parousia and legal practices adequate for a closed, exclusive group had immobilised this religion and the future had passed to other places.

Guignebert devotes two chapters to Paul. Following Auguste Sabatier, whose study of Paul he considers to be the best in French, he begins with an account of Paul's temperament (ardent, effusive, speculative, rabbinic, uniting 'sensibilité de femme' and 'virilité d'action')[12]. Upon this foundation, it is only the *forms* of Paul's thinking which changed. In spite of his misgivings about Acts as a historical source, Guignebert follows the accounts contained therein of the missionary journeys. Paul's speeches were composed by the author of Acts, but the sermon at Pisidian Antioch does give a fair idea of what Paul taught[13], whereas the speech in Athens is a prototype for all oblique exegesis which, in its desire to conciliate, merely leads to misunderstanding and deception[14]. The meeting in Jerusalem reflected in Acts 15 and Galatians 2 led to a separation of responsibilities, rather than an understanding, 'et cette solution bâtarde ne tarda pas à engendrer de graves conflits'[15]. The quarrel between

---

10 *Ibid* p259.
11 *Ibid* p263.
12 *Ibid* p287.
13 *Ibid* p302.
14 *Ibid* p313.
15 *Ibid* p309.

Peter and Paul at Antioch took place soon afterwards. Paul may have been released after his arrest and journey to Rome but it is impossible to say if he went to Spain; his death, like that of Peter is surrounded by legend.

The essence of Paul's religion is to be found in such verses as Galatians 1,16; 2,20 and Philippians 1,21[16]. We are far from the teaching of Jesus with its themes of peace and love:

> Le Jésus de Paul est une construction subjective, une combinaison de logique et de la métaphysique d'un pharisien appliquées à quelques faits réels; c'est une *gnose*.[17]

Paul is only united to the historical Jesus by a single theme:

> . . . l'élan de confiance et d'amour vers Dieu, le Père de qui seul dépend la grâce du salut.[18].

I and II Corinthians and Galatians reveal that forms of organisation in the Pauline churches were rudimentary, still not much beyond the 'démocratisme anarchique' of Jerusalem but Philippians shows that some advance had been made, drawing upon Jewish and pagan models[19]. The end of charismatic dominance is only found in the Pastorals at the end of the first century A.D., although even there the insistence on church order and sound doctrine represents an ideal not yet achieved.

The importance of Paul has often been exaggerated, merely because of his strong personality and the state of our documentation. In the early church he was easily misunderstood and quickly forgotten, although he left his mark with his doctrine of Christ as the New Adam and the impulse he gave towards docetism, 'issu du dédain de Paul pour la vie terrestre du Maître, et de son désir de l'exalter jusqu'à Dieu'.[20]

Guignebert has an ingenious and not implausible arrangement for the rest of the New Testament and related material. Under 'L'influ-

---

16 *Ibid* p339. Here Guignebert agrees with A. Sabatier that Paul's conversion provided the essence of his Gospel.

17 *Ibid* p344.

18 *Ibid* p352. In a note on Goguel's *L'Apôtre Paul et Jésus-Christ* (1904) Guignebert remarks that he cannot understand the author's conclusion that the radical transformation of the teaching of Jesus by Paul represented the Apostle's faithfulness to his Master (*Ibid* p370).

19 In his treatment of these organisational questions, Guignebert acknowledges his debt to J. Réville, *Les Origines de l'épiscopat* (1894).

20 *Ibid* p369.

ence de la spéculation juive' he includes Revelation as an example of 'spéculation purement juive'; and the Fourth Gospel, the Epistles and Hebrews, as examples of Alexandrian-type exegesis producing specimens of Christian 'gnosis'. He summarises the doctrinal contribution of this literature as follows:

L'Apocalypse restera le grand magasin à images, la grande inspiratrice de l'art eschatologique; le IVe Evangile et les *Epîtres* le grand arsenal des arguments propres à fonder la divinité de Jésus-Christ et la Trinité, et la ressource suprême des orthodoxes, quand il deviendra nécessaire d'interpréter l'espérance première de la *parousie*.[21]

All such ideas are as equally removed from the Jesus of history as those of Paul. Traces of such 'gnosis' may also be found in Colossians, the Pastorals, II Peter and Jude. Jewish speculation therefore prepared for the onward march of Christianity towards philosophical Hellenism; at the same time, its very excesses called forth the need of stable forms of doctrine, discipline and church organisation.

Under 'Les Eglises judéo-chrétiennes' Guignebert groups together the Synoptic Gospels, James and the Didache[22]. All of these represent a non-speculative type of Christianity, revealing various degrees of legalism. Without the Synoptics, the heavenly Christ of Paul and the Incarnate Logos of Johannine speculation would have soon eliminated any trace of the human life of Jesus[23]. The Didache shows originality in attributing spiritual functions to administrative functionaries; it also exhibits the rudiments of a *regula fidei* and of an established ritual: 'les trois éléments réunis feront l'Eglise'.[24] But generally it was the lack of speculation in the communities responsible for the literature which led to their progressive isolation.

Under 'the Church of Rome', Guignebert concludes as follows. Paul's epistle to the Romans gives good indications that the Roman congregation was predominantly Jewish: if, however I Peter and Hebrews are Roman in origin[25], they prove that it was Judeo-Alexandrian liberalism rather than Paulinism which led the Roman Christians to a universalist outlook. No doubt the cosmopolitan environment also helped; but, in general, the spirit of Rome was juridical

---

21 *Ibid* pp414—5.
22 The Christian communities of this tendency were to be found, according to Guignebert, in Galilee, Syria and even Arabia (*ibid* pp425—8).
23 *Ibid* p430.
24 *Ibid* p450.
25 Guignebert cannot finally decide between Rome and Alexandria for the place of origin of Hebrews.

and organisational rather than speculative. This is exemplified in I Clement where growing ecclesiastical authority clamps down on anarchic democratism and the pretentions of laymen and, possibly, charismatics. In order to satisfy the mass of the faithful the highly varied theological notions of the first generation had to be reduced to a mediocre rule of faith: here is the germ of the Catholic Church.

The *Manuel* concludes with an assessment of the state of the Church at the end of the first century. The historical Jesus has been left far behind, but Christianity is still dominated by the Jewish spirit in its various guises.[26] It has however separated from Judaism as a religion (helped by Paul's estimate of the Law, by its success on Gentile soil and by the destruction of the Temple) and has become the object of sporadic opposition by the Roman State. On the doctrinal level, there was probably an early version of the Apostles' Creed in Rome at the end of the first century: even if it did not refer to any doctrine of Redemption, this idea was universally accepted[27]. Trinitarian developments were largely in the future. Ritual forms were just beginning to acquire fixity and were mostly derived from Judaism, although pagan ceremonialism was soon to precipitate the formation of a Christian liturgy, just as Hellenistic thought was to hasten the establishment of Christian dogma[28]. The Catholic *idea* was still unborn, although the community of the faithful 'in Christ' created bonds corresponding to the name of 'Church'. Catholic unity had to await a uniformly constituted clergy, and moves in this direction can be discerned, such as the control of charismatics and itinerants, the ascription of religious functions to administrative officials and the concentration of both religious and administrative powers in the hands of a single official. The Ignatian epistles confirm these developments towards catholicism:

> Tout y pousse les fidèles: le sacerdotalisme juif, l'esprit d'organisation et d'uniformité de Rome, l'exemple même de l'Etat romain; et, d'autre part, l'audace croissante des *loups*[29].

Social expansion of Christianity was mainly among the lower classes: the aristocrats sometimes cited during the reign of Domitian were more likely to have been Jewish proselytes with Christian ten-

---

26 Ibid p482.
27 *Ibid* pp488–9.
28 *Ibid* p508.
29 *Ibid* p515.

dencies; the upper classes would not be attracted to Christianity until Greek philosophy had involved itself with the new religion.

This extensive summary of the *Manuel* has been provided, partly because it is the first full statement by Guignebert on Christian origins and upon this basis it will be possible to chart subsequent changes of opinion; and partly because it is a significant publication in the independent sector, with real claims to impartiality by comparison with the views of other 'independents' such as Havet or Reinach. It was greeted as such by Loisy[30]. It remains a very satisfactory achievement by virtue of its balance: doctrinal, social, ritual, ethical and organisational aspects are all considered and the interior life of the Church is set over against the wider religious and political currents in the Roman Empire. In this, it reminds us of Renan, although Guignebert's view of the documents marks a distinct advance upon Renan, who, it will be remembered, held out against critical developments in Germany and the *Revue de Strasbourg* group in France.[31] Guignebert also follows Renan in taking a wider view of early Christianity than that of many Protestant exegetes, who were content to investigate the New Testament period as an enclosed, normative entity. There is of course a heavy debt to Protestant critics and some of their presuppositions have been incorporated: not only are A. Sabatier, J. Réville and others acknowledged by name, but Guignebert makes free use of such antitheses as 'foi-confiance'/'foi-croyance', faith/dogma, plasticity/fixity, practical/intellectual. He also allots a pivotal place to Paul, although pointing out that his place may not have been quite as important as the state of the documentation makes him appear. Guignebert's highly negative view of the Gospels as historical evidence for the life and teaching of Jesus must have appeared polemical to confessional critics of the day but he always maintained this viewpoint, although, like Loisy, he equally resolutely refused to join the ranks of the *mythologues*. It was perhaps because Guignebert did succeed in offering a a synthesis of early Christianity which did not completely suit the needs of any of the contending parties of his day: traditionalist or modernist Catholics, conservative or liberal Protestants, or bellicose rationalists, that his very worthy *Manuel* did not excite the response

---

30 Cf. above 2.1.

31 Guignebert warns his reader of Renan's limitations: 'Il faut se méfier du charme profond qui se dégage de ces livres; sa séduction cache quelques pièges'. (*op.cit.* pIX).

which greeted Loisy's 'little red books' of 1902–3 or Reinach's *Orpheus* of 1909.

3.2.2 'Scientia' articles

The articles in *Scientia* of 1910 present two main points of interest as compared with the *Manuel.* They attempt to explain to the multidisciplinary academic readership of this journal some of the problems connected with the field of Christian origins; and they offer some modification of the assessment of Paul. According to Guignebert, the disinterested researcher, especially in Latin countries[1], is not only up against public ignorance and indifference but also such factors as these:

> Préjugés héréditaires, qui *tabouent* encore plusieurs grosses questions, intérêts divers, religieux, moraux ou même sociaux . . .; crainte légitime de verser sans le vouloir dans la polémique . . . d'autre part, lacunes, doutes, ignorances décourageantes que confessent tous les vrais savants, hardiesses téméraires, hypothèses prématurées ou un peu scandaleuses, comme celles qui tendraient à rejeter jusqu'à l'existence du Christ, heurts de systèmes et querelles d'érudits; enfin nécessité d'un effort assez pénible pour suivre des enquêtes compliquées et des raisonnements tortueux.[2]

In spite of all such discouragement, many basic questions have to be answered; they are concerned with 'le principe et "l'essence" (*das Wesen*) du christianisme, le sens et l'économie de l'évolution chrétienne'[3]. It must be a fundamental assumption of such research that Christianity has evolved by constant readaptation to changing circumstances:

> Toute oeuvre humaine ne vit qu'en se transformant et elle ne se transforme qu'en empruntant aux milieux successifs où elle se transporte, les éléments qui lui permettent de s'adapter à leurs exigences ou à leurs besoins. Le christianisme a toujours subi cette loi et il a vécu; s'il veut s'y soustraire, il périra: c'est le suprême enseignement de l'histoire.[4]

It is somewhat in line with this general principle of transformation by assimilation that we find a highly significant shift of emphasis in what Guignebert has to say about Paul. In the *Manuel,* Paul's type of speculation, especially about Christ as second Adam, is

---

1 Guignebert mentions that only two French universities have teaching posts for early Christianity and that his own students in Paris are mainly Americans and Germans: 'pour le commun de nos étudiants, l'étude des origines chrétiennes est encore et justement considérée comme une spécialité du luxe'. (*art.cit.* p125).

2 *Art.cit.* p126.

3 *Ibid* p130.

4 *Ibid* pp401–2.

ascribed to a background of both rabbinic and Diaspora Judaism. Hellenistic influences were of course to be found in the latter, but a general impression was conveyed in the *Manuel* that Christianity was not profoundly affected by Hellenism until the second century, and that it remained essentially Jewish in spirit until at least 100 A.D. Now Guignebert states that because for Paul Christ had replaced the Law and its requirements, and because Messianic ideas did not interest the Greeks, a religion of salvation was necessary, *like the Mystery religions*. Paul's doctrines of a heavenly Man and of an expiatory sacrifice whose benefits were available by faith opened the way for later Gnostic systems and was itself *'une gnose syncrétiste'*[5]. The common meals of the first Christians were transformed into a sacrament and Christians happily accepted this *'morceau de paganisme'* as legitimate 'majoration'[6]. Already therefore in the first century Christianity appeared as an *oriental religion*, offering a *mystical salvation* through a divine mediator[7]. In these statements the influence of the *religionsgeschichtliche Schule* is becoming apparent. We have already seen how c.1910 Loisy declared his support for the new insights of the 'school'[8]. Guignebert too was to accept its findings with enthusiasm, although exactly when and under whose influence is not entirely clear. In a review of Clemen, *Religionsgeschichtliche Erklärung des Neuen Testaments* (1908) Guignebert merely commented that it admirably filled out the work of Anrich, Wobbermin and Soltau[9]; but he greeted Reitzenstein, *Die hellenistischen Mysterienreligionen* (1910) as a major advance of scholarship:

> Pour la première fois, ces présomptions si importantes trouvent . . . au moins une consolidation précise, au moins une complète démonstration, grâce à une étude minutieuse de divers textes de Paul . . . par rapport à la langue des mystères . . . Tout n'est pas assuré de ce qu'avance M. Reitzenstein, mais son petit livre inaugure véritablement tout un ordre de recherches dont je crois que l'avenir montrera la fécondité.[10]

So there is sufficient evidence, if not of a very precise nature, to

---

5 *Ibid* p381. My italics. The *Manuel* refers to Paulinism as 'une gnose' but without the epithet 'syncrétiste'.
6 This term, with the sense of 'addition' or 'inflation', ie. the natural process whereby religious ideas are magnified and elaborated under the influence of faith, is one of the most frequently encountered in the vocabulary of Guignebert.
7 *Ibid* p388. Again, my italics.
8 Cf. above 2.2.
9 *RH* t.103 (1910) p351.
10 *RH* t.110 (1912) p345.

show that at the time of writing his *Scientia* articles, Guignebert was responding to the later phase of the German *religionsgeschichtliche Schule,* with its emphasis upon the affinities between early Christianity and the Mystery religions. This idea was to become a permanent acquisition in his interpretation of Christian origins, although it never led him to deny the Jewish roots of Christianity, nor indeed the Jewish elements in Paul's thinking. But his own fundamental position of tracing the origins and development of early Christianity within the framework of the social, religious and political life of the Roman Empire, and his evolutionary view of history mentioned above must have predisposed him strongly to take the new German work into his own reconstruction.

3.2.3 La Primauté de Pierre

It was possibly to maintain his scholarly reputation established by his doctoral thesis on Tertullian that Guignebert published *La Primauté de Pierre et la venue de Pierre à Rome* in 1909. This is no popular manual but a searching examination of the question of Peter in the early Church; it studies all the relevant texts from the New Testament and the patristic period and shows a complete familiarity with the current literature in French, English and German. Nevertheless, the choice of subject cannot have been made on grounds of scholarship alone, even if it offered the opportunity to range over several centuries and take into account those matters of religion and Empire which had already engaged the critic's attention in his work on Tertullian. The *Avant-Propos* makes this quite clear, for here Guignebert launches a much more vehement attack than we have encountered so far upon the confessional critics. Even if they do not wilfully misrepresent the evidence, he says, they are so blinkered by prejudice and by the requirements of theology and polemic that their clamour prevents the more reasonable approach and conclusions of some recent work on Peter from being heard. The future perhaps belongs to the methods recently tried out by such critics as S. Reinach, J.M. Robertson and W.B. Smith[1]. These are surprising names, because Robertson and Smith were advocates of the Christ-

---

1 *Op.cit.* pV.

2 Theological concerns are prominent, for instance, in O. Cullmann, *Petrus. Jünger, Apostel, Märtyrer* (1952 and 1960; ET 1953 and 1962).

myth theory, to which Reinach also came close. We can only assume that at a time when the Catholic Church was at its most vigorous in repressing progressive trends in Catholic intellectual life, the exasperation of Guignebert induced him momentarily to consider joining the *mythologues*, although he never in fact did so. However in that climate, even if his intentions were reasonably serene, his own work could not but be regarded as an *oeuvre de combat,* all the more because his own conclusions were opposed at every step to those of Catholic orthodoxy. But as a historical and resolutely non-theological approach to a topic which has always remained a largely confessional preserve[2], *La Primauté de Pierre* can still be consulted; the author's conclusions remained unchanged throughout his life[3].

Here a mere outline of those conclusions can be given. Historical information about Peter as disciple and apostle is extremely uncertain[4]. Matthew 16,18–19, Luke 22,31 f and John 21,15 ff may all be described as 'Petrine apologetic'. None of these texts supports the idea of a special mission conferred upon Peter during the lifetime of Jesus[5]. The authority of Peter in the early Church was of an entirely personal nature[6]. As far as one can tell, his missionary activity was entirely confined to Palestine[7]. None of the three traditions about Peter's coming to Rome — in the company of Paul; by himself to commence an episcopate of twenty-five years; in connection with Simon Magus — can find any solid historical support[8]. It is easy to demonstrate the legendary character of Peter's dealings with Simon Magus and of other stories of his activity in Rome[9]. It is perfectly feasible for the early Christians to have known that Peter died by crucifixion (cf. John 21,18–22) without knowing where the execution took place and it was natural, in such a state of ignorance, for Rome to be chosen as his appointed place to die[10]. Guignebert's own hypothesis (which, he emphasises, is necessarily

---

3 He took up the question again in his lecture course of 1928–9 (GP OER); he also maintained his thesis *versus* Lietzmann in 'La sépulture de Pierre' *RH* 1931, pp224–53.
4 *Op. cit.* Ch.I.
5 *Ibid* Ch.II.
6 *Ibid* Ch.III.
7 *Ibid* Ch.IV.
8 *Ibid* Ch.VI. Guignebert rejects the authenticity of I Peter, which he ascribes to a 'deutero-Pauline' school of c.100 A.D.
9 *Ibid* Ch.VII.
10 *Ibid* Ch.VIII.

conjectural) to account for the growth of the Peter legend is as follows[11].

At the beginning of the second century, it was known that Paul had died in Rome under Nero (this was substantially correct) and it was believed that he had been buried on the Ostia road (also highly probable). In the first half of the second century Peter and Paul became symbols of Jewish and Hellenistic Christianity respectively and therefore legendary enemies. In particular, Peter had to be seen as Paul's equal and a 'rigorous parallelism' demanded that he should have exercised a ministry and met with a glorious martyrdom in the capital of the Empire. However, with the eclipse of Paulinism on the one hand and isolation of the Jewish-Christian sects on the other, a new phase of legend-making reconciled the two apostles, who were now thought to have been fellow workers in founding and administering the Church of Rome, before their joint execution. The traditional site of the execution of the Christians martyred by Nero, on the Vatican hill, was the obvious place for Peter's death, and when his remains were 'discovered' on the Appian Way in 258 A.D., their presence in that place was explained in terms of a temporary resting place to avoid profanation. A third phase of development in the story involved the subordination of Paul to Peter and the latter's status as the first bishop of Rome during an episcopate of 25 years[12].

This study of a single topic inevitably bears some of the marks of the controversy it seeks to avoid, but is perfectly consistent with the general picture of early Christianity presented in the *Manuel.* Guignebert agreed with Renan that the first 150 years of Christianity are historically obscure, but he did not allow the historian as much liberty of conjecture as Renan thought desirable. Negative conclusions are the only honest conclusions in many cases. The confessional historian, even when trained in historical critical method, seeks from the meagre documentation the maximum of 'fact'; his secular equivalent regretfully recognises that the documents — whether Gospels, epistles or Acts — were not written to provide such information. Guignebert therefore has to take them as evidence for the standpoint of the writer and his times, rather than for the events they claim to describe. It might be possible to charge Guignebert

---

11 *Ibid* pp372–9.
12 This hypothesis is repeated in almost identical terms in GP OER 113–4.

with undervaluing the evidence in places but his wider view of Christianity over two or three centuries in the Roman Empire made him more likely to adopt this critical position. In the case of Peter, his reconstruction carries much weight, if not final conviction. In the case of the crucial transfer of Christianity during the first century from its Jewish matrix to a Gentile environment, he readjusted his views when presented with the evidence from the Mystery religions, but this was not so momentous a shift for him as it seems to have been for those with an exclusive or overwhelming interest in the Biblical documents.

3.3 *GENERAL WRITINGS ON RELIGION RELEVANT TO THE INTERPRETATION OF EARLY CHRISTIANITY*

3.3.1 'La Grande Revue' articles

We have already noted Guignebert's more general interests as a historian and his view of Christianity as a component in the total religious history of mankind. From 1908 onwards he published a number of articles in *La Grande Revue* and in 1910 a book, *L'Evolution des dogmes,* in which theoretical and methodological questions relating to his work were discussed. *La Grande Revue* was a not very demanding literary and philosophical journal and the contributions of Guignebert are in the category of 'higher journalism'[1]. A series of them was devoted to the contemporary Modernist crisis and these were republished in a volume *Modernisme et tradition catholique en France* (1909)[2]. But here too, questions of Biblical interpretation as well as contemporary religious history were aired for the wider public. So this is a phase of Guignebert's work which needs to be examined for the light which it may throw on his presuppositions and working principles.

As Loisy pointed out, the book on Modernism was mainly concerned to show that the orthodox Catholic position was no longer tenable, largely because of the progress of Biblical criticism: therefore, those attempting to reform the Church from within were

---

1 Some of them were review-articles of recent books; others appeared under the heading 'Questions religieuses contemporaines'.
2 The five articles originally appeared between 25th October 1908 and 10th January 1909; in book form they are prefaced by an extra chapter on 'Le Problème'.

doomed to failure from the start[3]. Guignebert is at pains to stress the disparate and composite nature of the New Testament material which, having issued from different writers, milieux and phases of speculation, presents 'discordant variations on the common theme of the Messiahship of Jesus'[4]. A non-confessional examination of the Synoptic Gospels shows that Jesus did not teach the three fundamental dogmas of the Incarnation, the divinity of Christ and the Atonement. Neither did he legislate for ritual or for Church organisation[5]. Catholicism is a syncretism, 'un mélange d'éléments hétérogènes', whose dogmas, rituals and forms of organisation were collected from various sources to compensate for the non-arrival of the Parousia[6]. Its dogmatics can no longer have any objective historical value and it must therefore lose that supernatural authority which its adherents claim, but if it recognises this, it is capable of further evolution and can thus retain the allegiance of honest religious men, for whom faith is more important than papal authority[7].

Similar attitudes emerge from other articles of the period. Guignebert expresses general approval of the book by 'Pierre Saintyves', *Le Discernement du miracle* (1909)[8]. Neither the historian, nor the scientist, nor the philosopher nor the theologian can offer any certain means of discernment.

> Ainsi que l'expérience religieuse, dont il (sc. le miracle) est, en définitive, une des formes les plus grossières, il ne se produit et n'acquiert une valeur que dans la conscience religieuse des hommes; il ne saurait être ni object de démonstration, ni élément d'argumentation apologétique pour réduire les incrédules, encore moins matière à discussion scientifique[9].

On the other hand, it is unfortunate that the concept of 'libre pensée' has become monopolised by fanatics:

> ... incapables de comprendre un état d'esprit qui n'est pas la leur, un amour, une joie, un espoir, qu'ils ne partagent pas, mais prompts à mépriser, ils ressemblent aux fanatiques confessionels et non point à ces chercheurs de vérité, libérés de toute entrave dogmatique, qui veulent encore plus comprendre qu'apprendre, et vont élargissant leur

---

3 Cf. *Mém* III p235.
4 *Op.cit.* p46.
5 *Ibid* p91.
6 *Ibid* p92.
7 *Ibid* p114, 151.
8 In a review article in *La Grande Revue* t.61 (1910) pp150–6. 'Saintyves' was the pseudonym of Emile Nourry (1870–1935), who had trained for the priesthood but who took up the double career of publisher under his own name (he published many of Loisy's books) and of folklorist under the pseudonym.
9 *Art.cit.* p156.

capacité d'aimer à mesure qu'ils savent plus et mieux.[10].

But this desire to understand and therefore to love could not be extended to institutions which by their repressive nature made the pursuit of scientific truth impossible. In a piece on the condemnation of Duchesne's *Histoire ancienne de l'Eglise*[11] Guignebert writes that the Catholic church has shown once again that orthodoxy is irreformable and therefore itself stands condemned:

> . . . nous tenons une preuve nouvelle de l'impossibilité d'un accord entre la théologie et la science. L'un des deux doit périr par l'autre; à moins, et c'est ma conviction profonde, que l'une déjà ne soit morte et que des manifestations comme celle qui a chassé M. Loisy de l'Eglise et celle qui vient d'y humilier Mgr. Duchesne ne soient tout simplement destinées à nous donner l'illusion qu'elle vit encore.[12]

3.3.2 'L'Evolution des dogmes'

Guignebert had a special fondness for this work[1], which it is difficult for the modern reader to share, since it contains much repetition and clearly owes much to Auguste Sabatier and other Liberal Protestants (a debt which is several times acknowledged). The controversy aroused by *Dogme et critique* (1906) of Edouard Le Roy (placed on the Index for its philosophical pragmatism) gave Guignebert the impulse to write more discursively on religion. He chose in particular to show how a dogma is a 'living organism which is born, develops, changes, grows old and dies'[2] and the work is therefore somewhat of a personal statement, which probably accounts for its place in the author's affections. Dogmas, he believes, obey a 'law of evolution', which continually undermines the claim of dogma itself to be immutable and eternal[3]: this is the dilemma faced by intelligent believers of the present day[4].

Guignebert's debt to Liberal Protestants may be seen, for example,

---

10 From an article 'Questions religieuses contemporaines' in *La Grande Revue* t.68 (1911) pp168–78, in which Guignebert reviewed five recent books, including two by George Tyrrell.
11 'La condamnation de Mgr. Duchesne', *La Grande Revue* t.71 (1912) pp833–8.
12 *Art.cit.* p838.

1 According to M. Brunot, *art.cit.* p367.
2 *Op.cit.* p1.
3 The phrase 'law of evolution' is used throughout, eg. on p1 and, at the end, pp341–2: in the second case Guignebert explains the phrase to mean *the fact that* dogmas evolve, rather than any predictable sequence of evolution.
4 *Ibid*, p301.

in his distinction between 'foi-confiance' and 'foi dogmatique' and in the antithesis between the religious experience of the individual, which is at the heart of any new 'revelation' and its subsequent congealment in a dogmatic formula or Holy Book[5]. In more rationalist vein, he distinguishes between the simple believer, or the mass of the faithful on the one hand and the intellectual or theologian on the other: the former has traditionally provided the raw material upon which the latter performs his subtleties of interpretation[6]. In a more deistic frame of mind, Guignebert contrasts two categories of dogma: 'fundamental propositions' (such as the existence of God and life after death) characterised by simplicity and ubiquity; and affirmations which are said to be complicated and irrational (such as original sin and the Trinity). It is these in the latter category, only justifiable by an appeal to revelation, which 'are born, evolve, change, live and die'[7].

Guignebert is more convincing when, for example, he describes the birth of religious experience in relation to the cultural environment; 'revelation', he says is:

> ... un réflexe de la conscience d'un homme, particulièrement sensible aux impressions religieuses, un mouvement de son coeur, qui se communique à son esprit, dans une ambiance où ont agi sur lui ces désirs mêmes, ces aspirations et ces espoirs, qui se retrouvent sous des formes plus ou moins heureuses dans sa révélation.[8]

He is also interesting on 'le milieu dogmatique': ancient Alexandria, mediaeval Paris, certain centres of Arabic culture, were all specially conducive to the development and elaboration of dogma[9].

Guignebert wishes his remarks to apply to religion generally and therefore illustrates his arguments with examples from Judaism, Islam and Buddhism. But these references tend to be incidental and it appears that the general principles about 'tradition', 'interpretation', 'Holy Book', 'rule of faith', 'progress in dogma' etc. are drawn in the first instance from the author's specialist studies. He returns continually to Christianity and to the early Church in particular;

---

5 V. eg. the conclusion of the chapter on 'La révélation et l'inspiration', pp65–7.
6 V. eg. pp106–11 for a description of the procedures of 'theology' which, by its very methods, loses touch with the original sources of inspiration. Cf. also p163–4: 'La foi populaire produit la matière des dogmes ... la forme regarde les théologiens'.
7 Ibid pp34–8.
8 Ibid p66. This could of course be read as sheer determinism, but, as a historian's description of the interplay of personality and culture in the origins of a new religious movement, it is a valuable statement.
9 Ibid Ch.VI.

we may therefore survey this volume for further evidence of the critic's views about the period of Christian origins.

The apostles' 'dogmata' were 'simple rules of practical life', and even Paul's 'metaphysics' kept the appearance of 'un fait révélé'. It was only later that Greek culture superimposed itself on the 'Christian hope' and transformed the 'foi-confiance' of the first disciples into 'foi de doctrine'. Gospel dogma was replaced by scholastic dogma, conceived in the spirit and by the procedures of pagan philosophy[10]. In this process, the increasingly professionalised clergy were the main agents[11]. Most of the earliest Gentile converts were not sufficiently educated to realise the discrepancies between Paul's preaching and Hellenistic culture. But the influx of more educated converts changed the situation: flexible apostolic doctrine was eventually filled out with Hellenistic intellectualism[12].

But it is the dogmas of Christology which Guignebert quotes most frequently, in order to supply examples of his main contentions[13]. Christology was born of the natural desire of the followers of Jesus, for whom he stood above all men, to increase his status more and more, and of the theological organisation of this desire by men filled with Greek notions of the nature and activity of God[14]. The earliest Messianic faith — 'majorante et illogique' — had to be transformed for Greek comprehension into that of a 'Son of God' (now taken literally rather than metaphorically), pre-existent, dying for the salvation of the world. Whether he was thought to be adopted or engendered as Son of God, the natural progression was set in motion for Jesus to be called 'God' himself. In popular faith it was possible to assert both the divinity of Jesus and traditional monotheism simultaneously, but eventually this inconsistency had to receive theological attention[15]. The Jewish scriptures provided a powerful

---

10 *Ibid* pp27–8.
11 *Ibid* p31–2. Pejorative references to the clergy in the writings of Guignebert reveal a strain of anti-clericalism typical of his period. Cf. a remark at the end of the articles in *Scientia* that the overwhelming impressions in the triumph of Christianity in the Roman Empire are 'la puissance du sacerdotalisme' and 'le développement monstrueux de la théologie'. (*art.cit.* p399).
12 *Ibid* p186.
13 *Ibid* pp168–70; 188–96; 199–202; 285–303. This last section surveys the development of Christology from the beginnings to the present day.
14 *Ibid* p170.
15 *Ibid* pp188–9.

element in Christological development: once Jesus was acknowledged as Messiah, proof texts from the Old Testament were heaped upon him; Greek Christians, at some time between 80 and 100 A.D., evolved the dogma of the Virgin Birth on the basis of the Septuagint version of Isaiah 7,14. But as yet, there were no Christian scriptures as such and Christological development was variegated and undisciplined. Paul's doctrine of the atonement and the Johannine Logos doctrine are examples of this variety and of potentiality for the future. The original disciples could never have accepted that Jesus was either *a* god or God incarnate. But their resurrection faith tended to obliterate the human Jesus and to elevate him ever nearer to God. Fear of anthropomorphism led to the identification of the resurrected Messiah with the celestial beings of Jewish and Greek speculation. Only then was confirmation of the divine status of Christ sought in the Old Testament, by means of ingenious exegesis. Such 'faith' had probably decided by the first quarter of the second century that Jesus was God; 'metaphysical logomachy' then had to be employed to explain the inexplicable[16].

These excerpts suffice to show how Guignebert reiterated in different contexts a number of basic contentions, themselves derived from certain distinctions, such as those already mentioned as deriving from Protestant, rationalist and deistic sources. What he has to say as a historian about the slow but inevitable codification and institutionalisation of a new religious movement holds true in a general sense, but one is struck in *L'Evolution des dogmes* by a relative lack of documentation. Even in such a semi-popular work, one might expect more references to the early Christian texts and in particular to be informed what precisely are the relative amounts of Judaism and Hellenism, of 'faith' and 'speculation' in the writings of Paul, John and Luke. Anti-Catholic animus is, of course, apparent, especially in the wedge which Guignebert drives between the historical Jesus and later doctrines of the Incarnation and Trinity; his rationalist stance may be seen in his aversion for 'theology' which, historically, has been destructive of 'le sentiment religieux' and of true mysticism. His rationalism also finds strong expression in the chapter on 'La mort du dogme'[17], where he states that, in the last analysis,

---

16 *Ibid* pp285–93.
17 *Ibid* Ch.XIII.

Jesus either was, or was not, the Son of God, very God etc. Dogmas die, not only from negative criticism, but because a new intellectual climate is created in which they are no longer tenable. It is not dogma, but the desire for dogma, which survives in the hearts of religious men. But his is not a thoroughgoing or aggressive rationalism. Guignebert concedes that further religious evolution may be expected, for not even the 'libres croyants' like Auguste Sabatier and Jean Réville have attained to 'pure' religion[18]:

> ... l'homme ne cessera d'être "un animal religieux", comme il est "un animal politique", et ses aspirations religieuses ne trouveront jamais leur forme parfaite plus que ses agitations politiques ne l'immobiliseront dans les cadres d'une constitution définitive. Si pareils phénomènes pouvaient se produire un jour, l'homme ne serait plus l'homme.[19]

3.3.3 'Pour l'exégèse'

In this important article of the same period[1], Guignebert undertook to defend the exegesis of texts in the study of early Christianity against recent criticism (unspecified) asserting that 'religious instinct' is more important than critical sense[2]. Exegesis is accused of being never-ending, never reaching firm conclusions and of being oversubjective. But Guignebert states in reply that the imperfections of exegesis are common to those found in any intellectual enterprise. Exegesis is only one hundred years old and has operated under adverse conditions, coming under attack from confessional quarters and liberal romantics alike. Exegetes tend to belong to one of several warring factions or, even more dangerous, to harbour unconscious presuppositions. Their worst vice is certainly oversubtlety and here Guignebert's reply is clear: exegesis must abdicate its claims to explain everything and learn to say more often 'I do not know'[3].

---

18 Cf. a statement of Guignebert in the article 'Dogme', *Revue de Synthèse Historique* t.XLIX (1930) pp39–46: 'La *religion pure*, amorphe n'existe pas. Toute croyance tend nécessairement à une expression dont le terme est l'affirmation dogmatique. Le mythe lui-même aboutit au dogme, qui l'organise, le prolonge et finalement le remplace'. (p41).
19 *Ibid* p344.

1 'Pour l'exégèse,' *Correspondence de l'Union pour la Vérité* No. 10 1er juin 1910 pp409–28; No. 11 1er juillet 1910 pp465–72.
2 The criticism might well have come from those members of the Union pour la Vérité, characterised by Guignebert as liberal romantics wishing to preserve the 'faith of the simple'.
3 'L'avenir de l'exégèse tient à mon sens à la courageuse limitation de son ambition' (*art.cit.* p422).

Such modesty will reduce risky hypotheses and the tendency to lapse into subjectivism, although it does not exclude attention to detail.

Guignebert concedes that an over-preoccupation with words, at the expense of facts and ideas, may distort interpretation but even this is not so great a danger as that to be apprehended from criticism based on 'commonsense' or on 'religious experience'; such criticism can lead to the errors of, e.g. Tolstoy's version of the Kingdom of God, or various Liberal Protestant and Modernist reconstructions. Where agreement seems impossible, it is necessary to enquire how important certain questions are: for example, we know that Mark and Q were sources of Matthew, but we shall never know the exact stages of the redaction of Matthew and so it is better to call a halt; similarly we shall never know exactly what Jesus said at the Last Supper but we do know that he did not intend to institute a sacrament. In the case of Paul, once the incoherences of his thought are fully acknowledged, the *loca desperata* can be marked off as impossible to interpret and attempts to find a religious system in his epistles can be abandoned. True exegesis does not claim infallibility or any kind of metaphysical status but is content to be an auxiliary of historical enquiry. As such, its role will often be more negative than positive, in having to disengage the facts from the parasitic constructions of legend and tradition and in having to admit that the facts when disclosed cannot be meaningfully pieced together. An example of this would be the question of the Papacy and the essential matter of whether Peter went to Rome: 'A ces diverses questions, la critique des textes, *et elle seule*, peut au moins chercher à répondre'[4].

The final conclusion of Guignebert is worth quoting in full, since it admirably prefaces his own exegetical labours, to be considered in the next section:

Je conclus: les résultats où nous mène la critique des textes chrétiens anciens ne sont ni parfaits, ni complets, ni toujours définitifs, c'est entendu, mais, toutes proportions gardées, d'autres sciences de la nature ou de l'homme n'arrivent pas à une stabilité beaucoup plus grande. On leur fait crédit pourtant; on leur passe leurs tâtonnements, leurs expériences, leurs retours et leurs erreurs, sur ce que, de temps en temps, elles découvrent une vérité profitable; l'exégèse, née tardivement, dans de fâcheuses circonstances, constamment entravée par des préjugés et des haines, obligée de vivre sur un sol ingrat et rude, condamnée aux besognes arides et patientes, par elle-même assez revêche et rébarbative quoi qu'elle en ait, toucherait jusqu'au fond de l'infortune si les honnêtes

---

4   *Ibid* p467.

gens lui refusaient l'encouragement de leur estime et la récompense de leur attention.[5]

The 'honnêtes gens' to whom Guignebert made his appeal were doubtless the high-minded members of the Union pour la Vérité who could well have been impatient with Biblical criticism for its apparent aridity and inconclusiveness. In admitting that these qualities are necessarily part of the exegetical task, Guignebert wished to dispel attempts, Protestant, Catholic — or Tolstoyan — at theological reconstruction based on the early Christian texts. Any such attempts, in his view, undermine the objective work of the historian: indeed, some of his statements give the impression that the only interest of the documents is to provide information about historical events. We have already seen however, from his lecture courses and published work, that Guignebert was equally interested in the *ideas* of the early Christians and in tracing the development of these ideas through the texts. The patient labour he was prepared to expend upon exegesis, however unrewarding the results might be, is also to be gauged from his unpublished *cours d'exégèse,* to which we now turn.

3.4 THE COURS D'EXEGESE (1915–1933)

This section will survey the exegetical work of Guignebert, which he steadily maintained from 1911 to 1934. It will consider the following courses, for which the manuscripts have survived:

1915–1917 I Corinthians
1917–1919 II Corinthians
1918–1919 Philippians
1919–1922 Romans
1921–1922 Colossians
1922–1925 The Fourth Gospel
1928–1933 The Gospel according to Matthew.

The format of these manuscripts is as follows. In nearly all cases, Guignebert kept general introductions and conclusions to a minimum; an exception is the Fourth Gospel which has an Introduction of over 100 pages and a concluding summary of 35 pages. For the commentary proper, he wrote out his own French translation in large script, a few verses at a time, sometimes one verse only, depending

---

5 *Art.cit.* p471.

on the amount of comment required. Alternative translations, in French, German and English (eg. Moffatt) are sometimes quoted in difficult cases. In smaller script, surrounding the translation and extending beyond it if necessary, is the commentary. This deals, first, with textual and linguistic points, and then proceeds to possible interpretations. It may involve cross references to other literature, not only early Christian, but also from the Old Testament and Judaism, and from paganism. In all of this commentary work there is frequent reference, expressing both agreement and disagreement, to the principal modern authorities. The total effect is therefore of extremely dense writing. At times Guignebert added, at the end of important sections, a summary of his views, indicating the relevance of his conclusions for the understanding of the writer, or of early Christianity. There is no indication of how this material was delivered orally to the audience at the 'Conférences Ouvertes', although Mlle. Brunot has left a brief description of these sessions[1]; obviously none of these courses was intended for publication for, although the information assembled was in most cases adequate for a large-scale published commentary, it would have needed a more rigorous lay-out.

3.4.1 The Pauline Epistles[1]

With the possible exception of Romans 16 and a few minor glosses[2], Guignebert regards the five epistles under consideration (I and II Corinthians, Philippians, Romans and Colossians) as authentic. He is extremely cautious in all his remarks on questions of

---

1 M. Brunot *art.cit.* pp368–9: she says that Guignebert preferred these sessions with his 'initiates' to his more general lectures; Greek New Testament in his hand, he explained the text verse by verse; his thorough preparation (having consulted the texts and the authorities, he would pace up and down his study, humming a tune before reaching his own conclusions), enabled him to refer each verse to its original historical milieu, unless it was hopelessly obscure.

1 Guignebert's comments, quoted below, on specific verses are to be found in the mss. *ad loc.*, unless otherwise stated.

2 Eg., it is possible that a difficult passage like I Cor.11, 2–16 (on the veiling of women at worship) contains interpolations, but these can only be hypothetical and Guignebert expresses distaste for such desperate expedients; it is more satisfactory to assume occasional glosses, added in an attempt, however futile, to clear up obscurities in the original (GP I Cor. 230). Similarly, Guignebert is inclined to think that I Cor. 14, 34–35 is inauthentic, but, he says, this can be no more than an impression.

authenticity, interpolations and partition: he concedes, for example that there may perhaps have been another letter to Corinth between I and II Corinthians as they stand and that II Corinthians 6,14–7,1 and 10–13 could have been separate epistles but rejects as hazardous 'le tri aventureux des chapitres' by critics such as J. Weiss and Loisy, which is motivated by their desire to recover the lost, 'severe' letter.[3]

The value of the epistles is, of course, purely historical, in the light which they throw on early Christianity and on Paulinism in particular. I and II Corinthians are very important for 'l'intelligence de la primitive communauté de terre païenne', although II Corinthians is of less value and interest, on account of its frequent obscurities: even this epistle does however provide incidental information, all the more valuable precisely because it is uncontrived and so it can be described as 'bon type d'un genre de document généralement assez sûr'[4]. The interest of Philippians is in its 'ton', its 'allure', its glimpses of mystico-gnostic ideas, and especially the Christ-hymn of Chapter 2[5]. Colossians can be seen as a logical conclusion of Pauline religion[6], providing us with good information about the religious ambiance, especially the 'religion of the elements' at which Paul's Christology and cosmology are directed[7]. Romans is not to be taken as a theological treatise; rather, Paul is commending his religion as 'un principe de la vie morale et garantie de salut'; it is therefore an essential document for the understanding of Paulinism, whose twin bases are ethics and soteriology[8].

Most instructive for Guignebert's understanding of the epistles are his frequent remarks about Paul's style and argumentation. He often complains of incoherences, obscurities and contradictions, nowhere

---

3   GP II Cor. 165. In his commentary, when confronted by changes of style or tone, Guignebert is very cautious in drawing any far-reaching conclusions: eg. I Cor. 4, 14 displays a spontaneous rhetorical device; having noted various caesuras in Philippians, Guignebert concludes, 'En somme, je ne crois pas qu'elle soit faite de pièces et de morceaux' (GP Phil. 55).

4   GP II Cor. 167.

5   GP Phil. 55.

6   It is because of affinities between Colossians and earlier epistles, where Guignebert's hearers have already become accustomed to discover 'gnostic' elements, that he asserts its authenticity.

7   GP Col. 65–67.

8   GP Rom. Prolégomènes IX (a).

9   GP II Cor. 29; other verses in this epistle which are singled out for their obscurity are 2,15–16; 5,21; 7,5; 8,18; 9,14; 10,13–16; 11,4; 11,16; 13,7–8.

more than in the case of II Corinthians, where, having completed his commentary of the first chapter he sums up his impressions with the words 'décourageant', 'obscur', 'tendu', 'diffus', 'maladroit', 'gauche'[9]. Guignebert does not shirk the task of weighing the possibilities of interpretation in each instance but even after this process, he is often compelled in all honesty to admit his incomprehension. On one occasion (Romans 5,7) he seems surprised to find Paul speaking plainly: 'Paul n'est pas incapable de dire à l'occasion même des choses simples'. Indeed, in Romans generally, one finds 'moins de laisser-aller dans l'improvisation qu'ailleurs'[10]. But there is good reason for the prevailing lack of logic: Paul is not writing as a theologian but as a 'sectaire' and a 'myste'[11]. In Romans 4,13, for example (where these two terms appear in the commentary) Paul does not offer us history but, as usual, 'impressions', 'sentiments', 'conceptions "mystiques"', 'révélations' which seek to express themselves as 'history' and 'logic'. I Cor. 5,7 is one of the best examples of Paul's method, which is 'l'engendrement des idées par les mots et les images' and 'leur succession incohérente en logique apparente, très cohérente *en image* et dans la pensée de l'auteur, ou, du moins, dans son imagination'. In commenting on Col. 2,14, where the idea of the Law being nailed to the cross is 'une figure', Guignebert refers approvingly to a statement by Dibelius about the abundance of 'figures' in early Christianity. Not that Paul's imagery is always successful: having paraphrased Romans 6,16, Guignebert concludes: 'comme toujours, le parallélisme de Paul cloche'. One can sometimes find a religious or pastoral motivation for Paul's obscurities: I Cor. 9,14 betrays 'la souplesse pratique de Paul missionnaire'; I Cor. 11,5 is 'dans la ligne de la sophistique'; and the difficulty in I Cor. 14,24 results from its being 'plutôt un procédé de bataille que de démonstration'[12].

In general, one should not press words too far, or expect Paul to have had clear definitions of his own terminology: Romans 7,15, for instance, does not teach a doctrine of human irrespon-

---

10 GP Rom. Prolégomènes IX (b).

11 Even the term *hagios* in 1,7 is to be seen as typical of a closed circle of initiates. Cf. also the idea of separation from the world in Rom. 12,2 which is 'propre aux initiés mystiques'.

12 For the combative nature of Paul's writing cf. also Romans 1,21, where Paul assumes 'mauvaise volonté' on the part of the Gentiles which, Guignebert says, is neither logical nor reasonable, but necessary for Paul's argument.

sibility, however it may sound; it is doubtful if Paul had the same clear notion of different meanings of *nomos* in Romans 7,22—23 as modern commentators claim to possess. In the section Romans 8—11, one should not look for coherent doctrine or rigorous solutions, especially on the problem of predestination and free will, because Paul is not speaking 'en théologie'. The 'désordre' of 8, 37—39 is 'celui de l'inspiration'; the doxology of 9,5, where Christ is called 'God'[13], would have been unacceptable to Paul himself theologically but feasible in terms of the Christian cultus and piety; in 9,23, where Paul is 'tout à son affaire', he seems to teach an uncompromising predestination, which he could not really have believed, in view of his appeals elsewhere for conversion and moral effort. At the end of Chapter 11, sensing some of the theoretical problems inherent in his religious position, Paul 'se tire d'affaire en mystique, par une effusion', i.e. the doxology of 11,33—36. In some final remarks on Colossians, Guignebert sums up these judgements in the words 'on parle de théologie, c'est de mystique qu'il faut parler; le théologien raisonne . . . le mystique imagine'[14].

Paul's Christianity may be traced back to before his conversion. In commenting on Romans 7, which may be taken as, in part, autobiography[15], Guignebert hazards the guess that as a result of his moral struggle in failing, as a Jew, to live up the requirements of the Law, Paul had already come to believe in the need of some kind of direct mystical communication with God. Hellenistic Christians of Antioch filled the need by introducing him to the cult of the Lord Jesus. In Antioch, attitudes towards the Jewish Law were dictated more by practice than theory, but Paul elevated the rejection of Law in favour of Christ to the level of principle[16]. It was probably the

---

13 Guignebert reaches this conclusion on the basis of the context and by comparison with other Pauline doxologies.

14 GP Col. 67.

15 Eg. on 7,8: 'Paul présente ses propres expériences, en l'espèce, comme typiques'. Guignebert rejects the suggestion of Lagrange that Paul's ego might represent Adam as 'tendentious' (on 7,9). Guignebert is fairly reticent about Paul's personality, although he concludes from II Cor. 10,9—10 that Paul may have been hypersensitive and depressive and thinks that the 'thorn in the flesh' of II Cor. 12,7 could perhaps have been a nervous illness. On the basis of II Cor. 11,3 he says that Paul must have considered any opponent of his to be a false apostle; however, he explains Paul's apparent tolerance in Philippians 1,18 by saying that Paul's opponents might have attacked his person rather than his teaching and that Paul was indifferent to personal attacks.

16 CP Rom. 187.

paradosis of Antioch which he himself preached and to which he refers in I Cor. 15,3 But, in the view of Guignebert, the Hellenistic Christianity of Antioch was already well-developed beyond the thinking of the Jerusalem community and influenced by notions from pagan philosophy and religion. The stages in this evolution and in Paul's own further development, are not however made entirely clear in these commentaries. This is no small part due to Guignebert's extensive use of the terms 'mystère', 'mystique', 'gnostique' and their cognates. Unfortunately these are not clearly defined and all one can say is that they do not refer specifically in many cases to the Mystery religions as such, or to the developed Gnosticism of the second century; rather, they are characteristic of Paul's religious world, in his personal thinking and in the communities he founded and they are particularly associated with all kinds of religious speculation and with the Christian cultus. Such widespread usage does not permit close analysis and it is easier to follow the ideas of Guignebert in an examination of the more significant passages.

In I Cor. 1–2, Guignebert concludes that Paul had presented Christianity to the Corinthians as 'une *vie* nouvelle *par* le Seigneur Jésus' but that some of them at least, probably those of the Apollos party, quite understandably took it to be 'une nouvelle mystère'. The practice of baptism would further have encouraged this idea[17]. Paul's own religion was more concerned with 'the Gospel' than with the founding of an institution, with 'foi mystique' than with ritualism[18]; his preaching of the Cross was 'le mystère de la mort et de la résurrection du Christ'. 'Tous ceux qui croient à la *vertu* de cette croix seront sauvés; ceux qui la traiteront de *folie* seront *perdus*'[19]. All believers are 'spiritual', *pneumatikoi*, and Paul's distinction between the *nēpioi* and the *teleioi* should not be overpolarised[20].

The special teaching which Paul made available for the *teleioi* was 'la grande gnose paulinienne', as distinct from the practical missionary catechesis, and doubtless contained esoteric instruction with vocabulary derived from the Mysteries, although generally, Chris-

---

17 GP I Cor. 55.
18 GP I Cor. 56.
19 GP I Cor. 59.
20 With reference to the use of *teleios* in Philippians 3, Guignebert concedes to Dibelius that it may be taken *cum grano salis* in v.12 but in v.15 it must be a technical term from the Pauline mystery, similar to the usage in Colossians 1,28.

tianity was not a highly esoteric religion[21]. Paul's teaching on the
Eucharist in I Cor. 10 and 11 reveals his sacramental realism and the
term *koinōnia* means mystical union through cultic activity[22].
It was this realism which made him displeased with the eating and
drinking at the Corinthian assemblies, to the exclusion of real communion with Christ[23]: 11,29 indicates that the eucharistic elements
are to be distinguished from ordinary food. The fact that Paul had
to intervene shows that there was no single presiding celebrant and
that the assemblies were characterised by 'anarchie fraternelle et
pneumatique'[24]. This is confirmed by the instructions which Paul
gives on the question of the charismata in Ch.12 and 14[25].

After a very lengthy discussion of II Cor. 3, Guignebert reaches
these conclusions. First, for Paul, Christ and the Spirit were two
'grandeurs' which almost, if not quite, coincide: the remarkable
statement of 3,17a is the basic affirmation of Paulinism — 'le paulinisme est un pneumatisme'[26]. Next, the earthly Jesus had become
the heavenly Christ by means of the cultic experience of the
community (cf. the intended contrast with synagogue worship in
3,14) although Paul may well have been the first to state the identification of Kyrios and Spirit. Thirdly, the abstract notion of 'Spirit'
is now concretised in the Kyrios, who is both Saviour and the essence

---

21 Since Paul had praised the 'gnosis' possessed by the Corinthians in 1,5, Guignebert is
surprised by the statement in 8,1, which depreciates gnosis at the expense of agape;
he paraphrases: 'Yes, we all have gnosis, but there is gnosis and gnosis and the true
variety is to be judged by its fruits, especially *agapē*'.

22 GP I Cor. 210. Commenting on Philippians 1,5, Guignebert remarks that *koinonia* is a
difficult word to translate into French; it expresses the idea that Christians 'sont entrés
au plein de l'Evangile, qu'ils se le sont assimilés'.

23 GP I Cor. 236.

24 GP I Cor. 239.

25 GP I Cor. 256 *ter* refers to 'ce temps de pneumatisme anarchique'; Guignebert thinks
that the *agapē*-hymn of I Cor. 13 *may* have been inserted as a warning against pride and
the neglect of fraternal duty, although Paul is not specific about this (GP I Cor. 265).
This 'anarchy' also expressed itself in speculation, eg. the references to 'another Jesus',
'another gospel', 'another spirit' in II Cor. 11,4; Guignebert thinks that in the conditions
of spiritual effervescence which prevailed in Corinth, it is impossible to identify these
tendencies.

26 Cf. the paper presented by Guignebert at the Jubilé Loisy in 1927: 'Contribution à
l'étude de l'expérience chez Paul. Remarques sur 2 Cor. 3,15–17', *Congrès d'histoire du
christianisme* (1928) t. II pp7–22, where he concludes: 'L'instinct de sublimation,
d'exaltation de l'objet du culte, inhérent au culte lui-même, oblige Paul à placer le Seigneur aussi près que possible à Dieu: en l'identifiant à l'Esprit, il le hausse autant qu'il
est permis de le faire sans ébrécher son monothéisme' (p21).

of Christian life. However, Paul, under the influence of Jewish monotheism, does not say that Christ is God, or that the Christian becomes Christ, and this is where his teaching diverges from the Mystery religions proper. Also, his emphasis is more social than the individualism of the Mysteries; in Christianity it is the believer who is absorbed into the deity and not vice-versa[27]. Further comments on this epistle reveal, however, that Guignebert considered Paul to have derived not only vocabulary but essential ideas from the Mysteries. The train of thought in 4,10 reveals the essential idea of the Mysteries, that the believer repeats the pattern of suffering laid down by his Lord; the idea in 5,15 of mystical death and life in Christ is taken straight from the Mysteries[28]. On the basis of 5,7 it would be true to say that Paul was more 'croyant' than 'voyant', but his visions were the real foundation of his faith and this is confirmed by 12,2—4, where his 'mystical realism' is apparent[29].

At the end of Ch.5 of Romans, Guignebert looks back in summary fashion at Paul's teaching on justification by faith. Whether justification is taken to be primarily 'l'octroi présent de la justice' or acquittal on the day of judgement, it is conveyed by the grace of God to those who believe in the Lord; believers are those who have accepted the truth of Paul's gospel and who have been initiated into the Christian mystery. Faith may be defined as 'un état interne et subjectif et une adhésion externe et objective à des croyances et à des rites, l'agrégation à une *koinōnia* religieuse'[30]. The Christian 'mystery' blazes forth in the baptismal passage in Ch.6. In 6,2 'Paul rappelle l'essentiel de son mystère' and the idea of death to sin by death with Christ in 6,3 is 'le principe du mystère salutaire'. In a general remark, Guignebert gives his own assessment of such thinking:

> Tout le *Mystère* n'est en somme qu'un jeu de *similitudes* et d'*assimilations* mystiques qui, considerées humainement, ne sont que des apparences et des à-peu-près; mais c'est là en quelque manière la règle du genre: il suffit que le parallélisme des actes et des gestes qui entraîne parallélisme des destinées, soit établi entre le myste et Dieu.[31]

Guignebert agrees with Loisy against many Protestant critics that

---

27 GP II Cor. 56—66. The idea of absorption into the deity is also to be found, according to Guignebert, in Paul's account of his vision in 12,4.

28 This 'mystical' interpretation of the theme of apostolic suffering reappears in Guignebert's treatment of Col. 1,24—27, where he complains, however, of Paul's obscurity.

29 GP II Cor. 143.

30 GP Rom. 133—4.

31 GP Rom. 143.

for Paul baptism was not simply the symbol of moral renewal, but a divine drama and that there is no dichotomy between justification by faith and Paul's sacramental view of baptism[32]. Essential aspects of the Christian mystery are further to be found in Romans at 7,4; 8,11; 8,26; and 14,7—8. In 8,11 there is the suggestion of a 'refrain cultuel' or 'sentence de catéchèse' and the cultic milieu is never far from Guignebert's mind when he expounds the meaning of Christ-mysticism in Paul.

In the case of Colossians, however, he is rather more aware of the overriding polemical intentions of Paul. The heretics envisaged prac-tised a religion of the 'elements' (*stoicheia*) which on the basis of parallels from Babylon, Palestinian Judaism and Hellenism, could have been a kind of Jewish gnosis, where the Jewish and Hellenistic elements can no longer be disentangled[33]. Against this speculation on the role of intermediary aeons, Paul sets forth his doctrine of Christ, as agent of creation and unique mediator. But although for Paul the heretics are indulging in mere human wisdom as they seek to modify the basic Christian mystery (Guignebert uses the verbs 'com-pléter', 'nourrir', 'intellectualiser', 'approfondir' of their efforts)[34], he is nonetheless indebted to such thinking himself. For example, he summarises his own teaching, in 1,28, in terms of *sophia* and *teleiōsis;* his combination of *eikōn* and *prōtotokos* has parallels with the Greek-Egyptian theology of Plutarch and Philo;[35] he has a mystical theory, in 2,2—3, of the relationship between *sunesis, gnōsis* and *agapē*; the contrast between the old and the new *anthrōpos* in 3,9 is also couched in mystical terminology. Such an overlap of usage between Paul and his opponents can be understood when it is remembered that Christianity at this stage of its development was 'essentiellement une *vie*': 'une vie cultuelle' (worship of the Lord Jesus) and 'une vie morale' (based on the antithesis between 'flesh' and 'spirit')[36].

So far, we have attempted to remain faithful to the anti-theologi-cal thrust of Guignebert's exegesis by not considering his views under doctrinal headings. But as he himself freely makes use of terminology

---

32 GP Rom. 147. He refers to Loisy, *Les Mystères Païens et le mystère chrétien* p192.
33 GP Col. 26, 48, 65.
34 GP Col. 39.
35 GP Col. 29.
36 GP Col. 51.

such as 'christologie' and 'sotériologie', it seems permissible to round off our survey of his commentaries on the Pauline epistles by considering his treatment of such themes, with the strong proviso that, in his view, Paul was not a systematic theologian and that theological exegesis is likely to distort a genuine understanding of Paul.

Nearly half of his commentary on Philippians is occupied by a very detailed treatment of the Christ-hymn in 2,6–11; much of this reappeared in a paper which he gave at the Congrès Renan in 1923[37] and it may be regarded as an assessment of Pauline Christology in general. Having reminded his hearers that the passage is rhetorical and in the nature of a passing allusion, so that Paul did not anticipate that his every phrase would be closely dissected, Guignebert examines the main ideas of the hymn. It affirms the pre-existence of Christ and this concept must be traced to the heavenly Man of the Mysteries, rather than the pre-existent Messiah in the Book of Enoch or the writings of Philo. Against later orthodoxy, Paul was happy to express adoptionist notions of Christ (eg. Romans 1,2–3, Galatians 4,5–6), but the fundamental affirmation of Paul's Christology is possibly II Corinthians 3,17 and here Guignebert repeats remarks we have already noted[38]. It was in particular 'l'instinct de sublimation de l'objet du culte' which elevated Jesus to his God-like status[39] and this in turn was bound to imply his pre-existence, the incarnation now appearing as a kind of parenthesis in his divine life. Christ has therefore realised 'sa raison d'être fondamentale', although Paul avoids Docetism and retains the idea of an eschatological fulfilment in the future[40]. In Paul's thoughts, the Kyrios-Pneuma is always subordinate to God; the phrase *en morphē theou,* like the possible use of *theos* for Christ in Romans 9,5, is not a studied usage but springs from piety and, in any case, Paul's attention was so concentrated on the death of Christ, that he did not take a close interest in these other matters. We can however say that for Paul the divinity of Christ was relative and that the *morphē theou* was the equivalent of that *doxa* which had appeared to him on the Damascus Road.

---

37 'Remarques d'exégèse sur Philippiens 2,6–11' *Actes du Congrès international d'Histoire des religions tenu à Paris en octobre 1923* (1925) Vol.II pp290–316. References below are to this published version.

38 V. above n.26.

39 *Art.cit.* p306.

40 *Ibid* p308.

Behind the idea of the voluntary *kenōsis* of Christ lies 'toute une mythologie', probably that of pre-Christian Jewish gnosis (eg. the Simonians thought that created powers tried to seize equality with the Supreme Being)[41] but the evidence is very thin. The significance of the name *kyrios* which is ascribed to Christ Jesus as a result of his obedience is that it combines the O.T. name for God and the title often given to the saviour gods of the Hellenistic world. Guignebert's conclusions are therefore that Christ in these verses is not the consubstantial Son of Trinitarian theology, nor a divine hypostasis; that the main features are derived from a mixture of gnostic ideas and the mythologies of the mystery religions (Paul 'nous apparaît ici en pleine action gnostique')[42] and that the passage is difficult for us because we do not know the whole mystery, although its rhythmic, even psalmic nature shows its close links with the Pauline community at worship[43].

Guignebert sees no essential difference between this Christology and that of Colossians 1,15–20, although in the latter there is more of a cosmological emphasis, directed against the heretics. In both passages, 'Paul affirme sans discuter et même sans développer'[44]. Neither should too much weight be placed on Romans 1,3–4: the first readers would not have expected any 'deep' meaning in a salutation and Sanday and Headlam are mistaken to suppose that the passage is already fairly 'advanced' along Trinitarian lines[45]. I Corinthians 15,28 is thoroughly monotheistic, although Paul does not, unfortunately, explain the nature of the Kingdom of God and the Kingdom of Christ respectively, or how the transition from one to the other is achieved.

Guignebert considers Paul's anthropology to have originated from Jewish and Greek sources[46], although it is the Hellenistic contrast

---

41 A slip of paper in the manuscript commentary reveals that this suggestion about Philippians 2,6 being a direct riposte to the Simonians was made to Guignebert by P. Alfaric in a conversation on 20.3.21.

42 On p314 Guignebert has explained that when Paulinism is described as 'une gnose', this refers more to his 'esprit' or his 'tendances', than to his 'fonds d'idées et de concepts religieux'.

43 *Art. cit.* p316.

44 GP Col. 25.

45 GP Rom. 15.

46 Eg. when Christians are called *pneumatikoi* in I Cor. 2,13–15, this is a Greek notion, overlaid by the Hebrew idea of the infusion of the spirit.

of 'flesh' and 'spirit' which mainly attracts his comments (cf. II Cor.4,16; Rom.7,14) and which strikes him as a complete antithesis. It is true that Paul speaks of a resurrection *body:* II Cor.5,14 probably means 'We do not wish to die, but to be clothed with our spiritual body, without passing through death'; but Rom.8,23 should possibly be taken to mean deliverance *from* the body by which man belongs to fallen creation. Paul's Jewish notion of a resurrection body caused difficulties for Hellenistic Christians as revealed in I Cor. 15; they preferred the notion of the immortality of the soul but Paul was probably not as far from their idea as he – or they! – supposed[47]; his use of *ōphthē* for the resurrection appearances of Christ, for example, leaves open the nature of the object of the visions and by no means entails a corporeal resurrection[48]. Neither does Paul explain the nature of the resurrection body and how it might be reconstituted from the elements of the mortal body[49]. Similarly, the discussion of 'flesh' and 'sin' in Romans 7, in the absence of definitions, leaves us in the dark about Paul's real meaning, although he seems to imply that as long as man is 'in the flesh', he is open to attack from the deadly powers of sin[50].

Jewish and Hellenistic elements also come together in Paul's soteriology: in Romans 3,21–25 we observe the Jewish idea of redemption by blood being grafted on to the pagan notion of vicarious sacrifice. When these verses speak of 'all' being justified, this means that all are given the possibility, but it is those with faith in the saving mystery who in fact escape sin and the spiritual death it entails[51]. Again, in Ch.5,18–19 Paul teaches that just as each man's sin brings about his own death (there is no 'doctrine' of original sin here: man only inherits from Adam 'l'aptitude à mourir')[52], so it is the individual who is granted salvation[53]. On a wider scale, Paul saw the evolution of humanity in three stages: Adam, Moses and Christ,

---

47 GP I Cor. 294.
48 GP I Cor. 290.
49 GP I Cor. 306.
50 GP Rom. 171. Guignebert brings out the mythological overtones in Paul's anthropology when he says, concerning the moral struggle of 7,22–23, 'il serait facile de transformer cette lutte en un drame dont le Christ et Satan sont les acteurs'.
51 GP Rom. 90.
52 *Katestathēsan* and *katastathēsontai* in 5,19 should be taken in the 'weak' sense of a general disposition; there *is* more evidence in favour of 'original' sin in 5,12, but this only goes to show that Paul did not have any consistent teaching.
53 GP Rom. 128–9.

God directing the process according to the principle of election, with the aim of realising his kingdom. He must eventually choose 'all', but all *nations* rather than all men. Election by free grace is the centre and pivot of Paul's soteriology but although his picture of salvation-history in Romans 9–11 leads him inevitably to touch upon the problem of the predestination of the individual, this is not fully resolved and we are left with the two sides of the same coin: 'appel à la foi' and 'élection au salut'[54]. The essence of soteriology is therefore to be known by God[55]. A most important verse for Paul's soteriology is II Cor 8,9, which shows how the Incarnation is the essential prerequisite of the Cross, although once again, Paul does not explain the *modus operandi* by which the 'Lord' became incarnate.

Paul's ethics have a mystical transcendental basis, as may be seen in Col. 3,1–4[56]; 'le grand précepte chrétien' in the same chapter (3,14) is all the more necessary in the absence of competent church authority — later, clericalisation will remove this 'conception de secte'. I Corinthians 6 shows that Paul drew upon Stoic ethics; the sexual morality in Ch.7 reveals a practical strain (absence of distraction, nearness of the End) and an ascetic strain, more Greek than Jewish[57]. Christianity did offer a new moral ideal in the Ancient World, although Paul's argument in Romans 1 that moral degradation in pagan society is a punishment sent by God is a partisan Christian judgement[58]. So, however banal some of Paul's instructions may sound (eg. Rom. 12,9) it has to be remembered that he was laying the foundations of Christian morality. He was also dealing with questions of immediate concern, which is why, for instance, some of the discussion about the 'weak' and the 'strong' in Rom. 14 remains obscure for us[59].

So, for Guignebert, the epistles are tantalising documents, telling the historian much about early Christian beliefs and community life

---

54 GP Rom. 271–8.
55 GP Rom. 282.
56 GP Col. 52.
57 GP I Cor. 176.
58 GP Rom. 47–8.
59 Eg. in 14,16, which no one can possibly understand. The chapter probably envisages *individuals* (the 'weak') who follow ascetic practices, who *may* have been Jewish in origin; but 'Paul reste dans le vague'. (GP Rom. 337).

but in oblique fashion, without defining terms, or clarifying situations which were well known to Paul and his readers, but which are forever lost to history. Such imprecision does in part correspond to the imprecision of the beliefs and the church-situations themselves, at a time when speculation often went unchecked and there were minimum forms of organisation. For any understanding, the chaos of ideas has to be compared with whatever other information is to hand about the religions of the Roman Empire in the first century, A.D. and this comparison does, according to Guignebert, help us to realise the sectarian, enthusiastic, 'pneumatic' nature of the new religion and its indebtedness to current ideas and forms of Hellenistic religion, as it rapidly left behind its Palestinian origins. More confirmation for this picture comes from the Fourth Gospel.

3.4.2 The Fourth Gospel

In order to present in summary fashion the main ideas of Guignebert on the Fourth Gospel, it will be sufficient to draw upon his own fairly extensively expressed conclusions at the end of four hundred pages of commentary, which he delivered over a three year period to his classes[1]. As he had indicated in his Introduction, the history of criticism stands as a warning of the problems to be encountered in reaching firm conclusions: Loisy, for example, had changed his mind significantly between his two commentaries of 1903 and 1921. But Guignebert had at least decided in his Introduction that the Fourth Gospel was an anonymous writing from the province of Asia, written in the period 100–115 A.D. The general conclusions take up this point in more detail: the Asian Hellenistic milieu, similar to the environment detected in the Pauline epistles, could not be satisfied by the Palestinian type gospel found in the Synoptics and therefore the Fourth Gospel corresponds to the aspirations of such a milieu.

The general features of John which strike Guignebert are, first, its 'pneumatic' character, by which he means that the episodes have been chosen to represent theological truth; the author allegorises on the life and words of Christ rather as Paul allegorises on the Old Testament. Next, the gospel is replete with symbolism, extending to persons, places, things, numbers and miracles. Judas is unbelieving

---

1   The last page carries the date 2nd March 1926.

Judaism; in the story of the raising of Lazarus, Martha is the Jewish Christian community, Mary the Gentile Christian community and Lazarus humanity at large. The episode at Cana means 'la substitution d'une économie spirituelle du salut à l'économie externe et insuffisante de la Loi'[2]. The original aims of the Gospel are not quite so clear: Wrede was too 'einseitig' to call it an apologia, although this element is present, especially in the emphasis upon the Judaean ministry of Jesus and the associated denigration of Galilee. It is not however possible to prove a deliberate polemic directed against the followers of John the Baptist, as Goguel asserts. Polemical elements are present and could have been aimed at the non-Jewish religious tendencies in Asia. Guignebert agrees with Wetter that under influence of liturgy and polemic, the Fourth Gospel sets forth Christ as the perfect Mystery, against the claims of other mystery cults (10, 1–6 and 12,26 can be interpreted in this way, although the latter only with 'beaucoup de bonne volonté')[3]. Probably the main aim of the work is 'Messianic' i.e. to show Jesus as the true Messiah, but it is not a theoretical treatise: its mystical nature reflects a genuine milieu.

On questions of 'background', Guignebert considers in turns the relationship of the Fourth Gospel to the Synoptics, Paul, the Mysteries, gnosis and philosophy. He stresses that the world of the Synoptics is entirely different; John has borrowed sayings from Mark and Luke but sometimes these are transformed almost into their opposite (eg. 11,47–48; 16,32). The disciples appear in another light:

> ... il n'est plus rien dit de l'humble condition des disciples ... c'est en face de la doc‐ trine de la messianité comprise au sens paulinien, tout le tableau de l'enlèvement du péché du monde qu'ils se trouvent placés dès l'abord.[4]

The Fourth Gospel is in fact a systematic presentation of the Pauline gospel. It took shape in Pauline communities, taking up and remoulding Palestinian traditions about Jesus (the 'elementary' Paulinism of Mark was felt to be inadequate). The Fourth Gospel develops Pauline ideas of predestination and reprobation and the abrogation of the Law for the believer who has faith; but its Messianic doctrine is more transcendant, its idea of resurrection more spiritual, and its Christology advances beyond the Christ hymn in

---

2 GP Jn. 417.
3 GP Jn. 421.
4 GP Jn. 423.

Philippians 2, even if the Logos doctrine is already implicit in Paul. 'C'est par le Quatrième Evangile que *vit* le paulinisme'[5].

Traces of the Mystery religions may be found, not only in the idea of rebirth by initiation (Ch.3) but also in such verses as 10,30; 14,7; 16,20; 17,23. But most important are the general affinities with gnosis. 'Knowledge' in the Fourth Gospel is equated with faith, and although more intellectual in conception than in Paul, is basically a *mystical* knowledge[6]. The competing strains of Docetism and anti-Docetism (the former to be found in eg. 2,4; 7,10) shows that an original document of (unconsciously held) Docetic sympathies was later readjusted in a more orthodox sense[7]. Unlike the later Gnostic systems, the Fourth Gospel retains the Old Testament, stresses moral obedience and has no elaborate angelology but 'le Logos-Jésus tend perpétuellement à l'être idéal'[8] and so, 'le Quattrème Evangile est un témoin du gnosticisme asiate, autant par ses adhésions que par son opposition aux thèses gnostiques'[9]. On the other hand the work is not in direct relation with any of the current systems of Greek philosophy; it merely uses occasional words and ideas which were widespread and Guignebert rejects interpretations of the Prologue which allege a debt to Philo. The important trend is towards mysticism, not metaphysics.

The sources of the Gospel can never be finally unravelled, because the author was not a compiler. He composed freely, in poetic fashion, in support of the contention in the Prologue that Jesus is the incarnation of the Logos. Endless debates about the respective contributions of the Synoptics, oral tradition and a *Sonderquelle*, and the touting of partition theories and revisionist theories, tend in any case to detract from the Fourth Gospel as 'vision mystique'[10]. Guignebert pays close attention to Loisy's theory of three strata associated with successive redactors but has to describe it as hypothetical. He agrees that complete unity of composition is unlikely,

---

5 GP Jn. 424.
6 Guignebert does not here refer to the fact that the nouns *gnōsis* and *pistis* do not themselves appear in the Fourth Gospel.
7 Guignebert accepts some of the evidence offered by 'H. Delafosse' in *Le Quatrième Evangile* (1925) in favour of this latent Docetism, but rejects his ideas about the Marcionite origin of John (GP Jn. 428).
8 GP Jn. 429.
9 GP Jn. 430.
10 GP Jn. 434.

but the text supports equally the hypothesis of 'retouches sporadiques et restreintes en étendue sur un fond ayant déjà la *teinte* qui nous paraît caractéristique du Quatrième Evangile', and the hypothesis that it was a final rewriting which supplies the 'teinte'[11].

The historical value of the Gospel, in spite of Goguel's pleading, must be pronounced minimal for the life of Jesus. Nowhere can a definite historical reminiscence be proved, nor even a solid probability. Everything already said about the nature of the work (eg. its symbolism and its mysticism) militates against such information being found; its historical value is therefore in the evidence it provides for the ideas of the author and his environment.

His ideas are to be described as 'religion' rather than 'theology'. One should not overstress his speculative ambitions. But he is not as 'personal' or as 'pragmatic' as Paul because his religion results 'd'une éducation chrétienne et d'un enseignement réglé, pas d'expériences plus ou moins dramatiques'[12]. He speaks of redemption less objectively than Paul, because for him it is an 'enlightenment', the knowledge of living truth. His point of departure is the dualistic cosmology which posits two opposing worlds: he retains the God of the Old Testament but this God is now only known through Jesus as Revealer. His religion centres upon Christ and the Church and rests upon three cardinal ideas: Jesus Christ in his person is the revelation of God; his special work was to give *life*; this life is communicated by union with Christ.

The humanity of Jesus is not denied but what interests the author is the pre-existent Son of God, Logos incarnate. 'L'homme Jésus n'est que *Logophore*'[13]. The manner of the Incarnation is undefined. 'Son of God' indicates a perfect union and inter-dependence and is a term derived from the Hellenistic milieu. The phrase *egō eimi* implies that Jesus is Son of God because he reveals God. The author is untroubled by questions of 'subordinationism' or 'the two natures', although his Christology is well on the way towards the identity of Father and Son and the Trinity.

By contrast with Paul, for whom the mission of Christ was to die, in the Fourth Gospel, the sacrifice of the Logos is to take flesh and

---

11 GP Jn. 439.
12 GP Jn. 442 bis.
13 GP Jn. 444.

his work is not to reconcile man to God by crucifying sin but to bring the saving revelation of God and of 'life'. Jesus does not need to teach about God, since he is himself Word, Truth, Life and Light. His death is only one episode in his earthly life, his return to the invisible. He draws men to himself but he does not redeem humanity.

Therefore, salvation is not so much a modification of human nature as the transference of life and light to the elect, who follow their psychopomp-redeemer. Salvation in theory is for all but in practice restricted to the faithful few ('idée de secte close')[14]. Their mystical faith in Christ (cf. eg. 3,36; 6,40) excludes the necessity of an 'intellectual' doctrine of justification and is produced by a *vision* or Christ (cf. 6,36). This faith requires the sacraments for its completion, Christ himself being 'une sorte de sacrement vivant'[15], but' the sacraments are dominated by the idea of a 'love-covenant' and this marked an advance upon the sacrificial language of Paul. The corollary of the union between Christ and the believer is the union of believers in the community of the Church, which is indwelt by Christ and by the Holy Spirit and so constitutes 'le dépôt authentique et qualifié de la révélation du Seigneur et le séjour de l'Esprit qui le prolonge'[16]. The author of the Fourth Gospel followed the decisive step taken by Paul in transferring eschatology to the present time and such verses as 14,21–22 and 28 show that he did not envisage a Parousia; the very different point of view found in eg. 6,39–40 and 44 must indicate the intervention of a later redactor.

These two opposing outlooks lead Guignebert into a final, personal evaluation of the Fourth Gospel; their coexistence in the same document, he says:

> . . . nous permet de saisir sur le vif la lutte de la religion de l'esprit et celle du mythe matérialiste. Il est remarquable que ce n'est pas l'esprit qui a triomphé dans l'ortho-doxie et que la thèse johannique authentique est demeurée une audace incomprise et même réprouvée. Elle constitue aujourd'hui une hérésie très lourde: c'est celle de tous les esprits libres qui restent déistes et même chrétiens en essayant de se dégager de la mythologie où s'affirme la marque du temps et du milieu où la foi première est née.
>
> Sur un autre point toutefois le Quatrième Evangile marque comme un recul et il n'y a pas à regretter, du point de vue théologique, qu'il n'ait pas été suivi: son Christ n'est pas le Sôter des pécheurs; il ne s'intéresse qu'à son troupeau; qui n'est pas de ses brebis n'est rien pour lui. Cet amour restreint des frères s'explique dans un groupe clos et battu en brèche par l'animosité du dehors.[17]

---

14 GP Jn. 447.
15 GP Jn. 448.
16 GP Jn. 448.
17 GP Jn. 451.

3.4.3 The Gospel according to Matthew

In this commentary Guignebert is not quite as pessimistic as in the case of John about recovering genuine historical memories of the earthly Jesus. He does allow that some sayings might be genuine[1], but, in general, much of his exposition is devoted to showing that both sayings and incidents are historically improbable. Moreover, by contrast with the commentary on John, he is not able to suggest a convincing and consistent *Sitz im Leben* for the Gospel as a whole. In his concluding remarks[2] he states that Matthew must date from after the separation of Judaism and Christianity, when 'the Christian community' was in existence and Christology was under way ('en marche'). There is hardly any Pauline influence and the Gospel is therefore addressed to a quite different world from that of Paul and John. The fact that most of the material which Matthew has added to Mark is the form of 'fictions sorties de la tradition élaborée, ou constructions issues de sa propre apologétique' reduces the historical worth still further, so that it brings us more 'obscurité' than 'lumière' on the subject of Jesus. The Gospel was probably written in Palestine-Syria right at the end of the first century A.D. or at the beginning of the second. Whatever the sources used, its fundamental unity of composition is to be gauged from redactional habits, constant features of style and the 'hypnosis' exercised upon the writer by numbers such as 3, 5 and 7.

But beyond this, Guignebert does not attempt to pinpoint the religious background more clearly. In spite of his frequent use of 'polémique' and 'apologétique' to explain features of the narrative, these terms remain at a very general level. For example, 7,6 (pearls before swine) is a saying more appropriate in the early church than during Jesus' ministry; the false prophets of 7,21—23 belong to 'la période première de la vie de l'Eglise chrétienne'. The story of the centurion in 8,5ff presupposes the existence of the Gentile church, just as that of the Canaanite woman in 15,21ff is intended to justify a *fait accompli*. The 'scribe trained for the Kingdom of heaven' in 13,52 is a Christian teacher of a kind known to the writer; the warning against false teaching in 16,12 is a mark of Jewish-Christian

---

1 Eg. 6,9—10 (the eschatological petitions of the Lord's Prayer); 19,9 (the teaching of Jesus on divorce); 19,12 (the saying about eunuchs).
2 GP Mt. Conclusion III—IV.

tensions; the procedures for dealing with the erring brother of 18,15ff are those of Christian community practice. There are a few Hellenistic traits: Guignebert readily accepts that the vocabulary and liturgical style of 11,25ff demonstrate the affinities of this pericope with the Mysteries and deserve its description as an alien 'thunderbolt';[3] *palingenesia* in 19,28 shows the lateness of the saying, intended to encourage the faithful in 'the apostolic age'; the use of 'Lord' in 21,3 reveals that we are far from Jerusalem. The parable of the Marriage Feast in 22,1—13 must date from post-70 A.D. and that of the Sheep and Goats in 25,31—46 seeks to place Christ's envoys in the shadow of his presence and assimilate them to him, so that it must have been written with 'the apostolic preachers' in mind. Such examples show that Guignebert did not consider the state of the text and the analysis of its putative sources were able to reveal at all clearly the stages of redaction or the possible historical situations to which they might be ascribed[4].

The commentary includes a number of excursuses — although not labelled as such — on important features of the Gospel. In a discussion based on 1,20—22, Guignebert concludes that the virginal conception of Jesus is the final 'stage of faith' reached by the New Testament.

> Il a été fait Messie par la résurrection; il a été proclamé tel par la Transfiguration; il a été adopté à cette qualité au baptême; il y était destiné à sa naissance. Sa naissance a été le plus décisif des signes: voilà les principaux jalons de cette foi majorante.

Here at least we have a chronology of the tradition, relative to events recorded in the Synoptics. But in a long discussion of 'the Twelve', based on 10,1ff, Guignebert simply comes to the negative conclusion that such a group of twelve disciples carries no historical guarantees, and that Paul does not appear to have known them. The 'Tu est Petrus' pericope of 16,17—19, is again subjected to lengthy treatment[5]. It may have been intended to raise the status of Peter relative to that of James, or simply to rehabilitate him after his

---

3   'Il y a là un ton de gnose qui ne se retrouve pas ailleurs dans la Synopse'.

4   The commentary on Matthew was written between 1928 and 1933. In 1933 Guignebert published his *Jésus*, in which he welcomed the efforts of the Form-critics to provide a systematic approach to the prehistory of the tradition, although he did not consider that their method was specially new, or that all their conclusions were obvious. (1969 edn. pp54—55).

5   GP Mt. 342—364; cf. *La primauté de Pierre* 15—66.

denial of Jesus but the important points are that Jesus never thought to found a Church, that the Kingdom was transformed into the Church by the passage of time ('la durée') during the apostolic generation and that authority in the Church was vested not in Peter, but in the Church itself and its leaders, under the inspiration of the Spirit. Matthew 26,14–16 evokes an analysis of the Judas tradition with the result that Guignebert associates himself with Havet, Jülicher, Klostermann and Bultmann in believing that the treason of Judas was a legend. 'Elle répond à une note de symbole et aussi au désir populaire de *personnaliser* les responsabilités'.

Unfortunately the commentary on the later chapters becomes sketchy and even inconsistent. Guignebert was content for some of the material to fall back on his previous course on Mark and consequently overlooks several important points. He does not comment on the 'Matthean exception' in 19,9 and omits separate consideration of the man without a wedding garment in 22,11–14. Nor does he have anything to say about the *theologoumenon* in 27,52. This is therefore a disappointing end to a commentary which itself does not have the interest to be found in Guignebert's work on Paul and John. In any case at the period of writing, Guignebert was engaged in the close analysis of the Synoptic tradition which he published as *Jésus* in 1933 and it is fairer not to probe the commentary on Matthew for any further insights but rather to rely, in this instance, upon his published findings.

3.4.4 General characteristics

Guignebert's exegetical work exhibits four main characteristics. First, he practises assiduously his own stated principle of agnosticism[1]. If a word or a verse is obscure, if there are historical events or literary processes forever lost to view, then, having considered the possibilities, he is content to record a negative judgement. Such ignorance is sometimes imposed by the Westerner's inability to penetrate Oriental thought forms and therefore the 'scholastic' methods of the confessional exegete are quite inappropriate[2]. Not infrequently Guignebert asserts his agnosticism in the face of theological exegesis; this is particularly so in his treatment of the Gospels and is undoubt-

---

1 V. above 3.3.3.
2 Cf. remarks to this effect in GP Rom. 191 and 283.

edly conditioned by the fact that when he was writing, Catholic exegesis did not permit doubts to be cast upon the substantial historicity of any of the Gospel episodes. But it can equally apply to the epistles: for example, Guignebert rejects the attempt of Lagrange to expound a Pauline 'paradox' about the Law in Romans 7,13, where in fact Paul's obscurity of expression simply leaves us in the dark.

Similar motivation can be invoked for the second characteristic: Guignebert devotes more space, proportionally, to passages which were to become important as the Scriptural basis for essential Christian doctrines of later orthodoxy. We have noted his treatment of Romans 8–11 (on questions of predestination), Philippians 2 (on Christology, to which should be added his exposition of the Johannine prologue), Matthew 1 on the Virgin Birth and Matthew 16 on Peter and the Church. In each case there is an underlying desire to show that much in established Christian dogma was secondary in relation to earlier thought forms. Even if the Fourth Gospel offers a bridge in the direction of creedal religion, it too must not be interpreted by use of a theological yardstick. So Guignebert returns repeatedly to the fundamental discontinuities in early Christian thought — between Jesus and the Hellenistic churches, between the period of free, unbridled speculation and the age of codification.

Next (and this point hardly needs to be argued) there is the ceaseless pressing of evidence, in the case of Paul and John, in favour of the positions of the *religionsgeschichtliche Schule*. We have already deprecated the overgeneralised use of terminology in this quarter but the work of Guignebert stands as an important historical representative of a school of thought which, bereft of theological presuppositions, may here be found in a purer and more thoroughgoing condition than elsewhere.

Finally, one must refer to Guignebert's acknowledged use of contemporary exegesis. He readily states his debt to other commentators, sometimes taking one particular commentary as his main source, or sparring partner, eg. Lagrange on Romans, Toussaint on Colossians, Loisy on the Fourth Gospel. Even if he does not agree with the religious standpoint of the writer, he does not automatically disagree with every judgement expressed, although he is naturally quick to detect presuppositions in the confessional exegete. By contrast with Loisy, who in his commentaries surveys the history of criticism in the Introduction, but ignores his fellow critics in the body of his exegesis, Guignebert engages in careful, patient and fair debate with named authorities. These are the mental habits of the University trained man, by contrast with those of the ex-seminarian. He is speaking to a University audience accustomed to such procedures; and thus we are reminded again of Guignebert the educator, hoping to initiate his benighted countrymen into the mysteries of exegesis. It was doubtless on account of the comparatively modest aims of this enterprise that the commentaries did not reach publication in their present form; rather, they were intended to serve as auxiliaries to the work of historical reconstruction undertaken elsewhere.

3.5 *INTRODUCTION A L'ETUDE DE L'ANTIQUITE CHRETIENNE* (1919–1921)

This lecture course is deserving of separate treatment because here Guignebert set out the methodology of his subject. He explained to his regular hearers that he had preferred to spend some years on practice rather than theory; his *cours d'exégèse* had supplied glimpses of his work in the laboratory (or kitchen), but the time had now come for a full treatment of questions of method[1]. Volumes by Wernle and Birney Smith were useful but envisaged the future theologian and omitted (or avoided) many questions[2]. 'Nos entretiens seront austères; j'espère qu'ils ne seront pourtant pas ennuyeux ni morts'[3]. They are designed, not for the researcher, but for the newcomer to the subject, who wishes to *know* and to *understand*[4].

The Prolegomena introduce a basic distinction between 'l'histoire ecclésiastique' and 'l'histoire de l'Eglise'.

> L'histoire ecclésiastique est, au vrai, la forme narrative de l'apologétique; l'autre histoire est une étude entièrement désintéressée et scientifique d'un certain nombre de faits, de sentiments, d'idées du passé.[5]

There are no problems in finding examples of statements by Catholic historians in favour of the former view, including writers con-

---

1 GP IEAC I–III.
2 Wernle, *Einleitung in das theologischen Studium* ([2]1911); G. Birney Smith (ed) *A Guide to the Study of the Christian Religion* (Chicago 1917).
3 GP IEAC XIII.
4 GP IEAC III.
5 GP IEAC I.

sidered to be 'liberal' and even those whose methods have every appearance of being 'scientific'[6]. But, says Guignebert, history is not 'naturally Christian', as such writers assume, and the history of Christianity includes the vices, the virtues and, above all the mediocrity of general history[7]. History does not of itself support a metaphysic or a theology: these have to be imposed from without.

Scientific history, by contrast, is neutral and starts from uncertainty in a desire to gain knowledge. It may not possess the exactitude of the natural sciences but it shares their spirit: '*chercher* pour *savoir, et savoir* pour *comprendre*'[8]. Such history (unlike 'érudition', which goes back to the Renaissance) originated in the nineteenth century, by the application of objective methods to the study of texts. There is a difference between 'objectivity' and 'impartiality'. For example, Renan is impartial, but not entirely objective, because he introduces too much 'sentiment' into his study of the documents. On the other hand, it is characteristic of English writers to be objective in their methods and partial in their findings[9].

The phrase 'antiquité chrétienne' refers to the first five hundred years or so of Christianity, the period during which Christian faith became an autonomous religion and an 'organised doctrine' and when the Church developed and finally took its place in the Ancient World. Later events, such as the barbarian invasions and the split between East and West, take us into the Middle Ages, where both the documentation and the spirit of the times are distinct from the earlier period. Not that 'Christian antiquity' is completely homogeneous but the questions it raises differ in degree rather than in kind[10].

Under the heading 'Connaissances préalables', Guignebert lists the areas of knowledge with which some familiarity is desirable for the historian of this period. In several cases he stresses that it is not so much the amount of knowledge as a feeling for the 'spirit' of the discipline which is called for. The list is as follows: general history (especially 'institutions' and 'society'); languages (ancient and

---

6 The 'déformation confessionnelle' is all the more dangerous when it is masked by 'une apparence scientifique plus ou moins consciemment truquée' (GP IEAC 5).

7 GP IEAC 2.

8 GP IEAC 6.

9 GP IEAC 7.

10 GP IEAC 7–8.

modern: without these one is condemned to the interpretations of others); present-day Christianity (a study of the 'point de départ' is helped by a knowledge of the 'point d'arrivée'); theology (whose 'spirit of immobility' is in direct contrast with that of history); history of religions (the best antidote for the illusions created by ecclesiastical history); philosophy (including the judicious use of psychological insights); and a 'religious sense' meaning, not confessional belonging, but a sympathy with one's subject. The list is instructive for Guignebert's general position. His absolute distinction between theology and history, for example, has an anti-clerical aspect, for he challenges the assumption that theology is a clerical preserve and calls for its demystification. He refers to Batiffol, Turmel and Loisy whose attempts at 'théologie positive' (for Guignebert, a contradiction in terms) have brought them into conflict with the Church authorities[11]. By means of the history of religions 'le christianisme cesse d'être un phénomène historique, isolé, singulier, exceptionnel, miraculeux, pour entrer dans une série connue de faits humains'[12]. The study of Christianity has been marred by German metaphysics (eg. Schleiermacher, B. Bauer and even D.F. Strauss) and by an over-use of psychology, necessary though this is in moderation (cf. the 'invention' of Binet-Sanglé and the 'complétion' of Renan)[13]. However, without the 'religious sense' one can equally fall into rationalistic or sentimental interpretations. 'Il faut se garder, comme d'un péril mortel, des préjugés et même des préoccupations confessionnelles, comme aussi des suggestions sentimentales'[14].

The lecture course proper is devoted to 'Les Moyens d'Investigation' and of its three major divisions, the first, on criticism of the texts, is by far the longest (the others are on archaeology and on liturgical and juridical sources). The types of text considered are scriptural, patristic (the Fathers proper, heterodox writings and conciliar decrees), Jewish and pagan, hagiographic and inscriptions. It is not necessary to amplify these sections in turn, because our interest is in the first Christian century only, but a selection of

---

11 GP IEAC 9–10.
12 GP IEAC 10.
13 GP IEAC 12.
14 GP IEAC 14.

comments may offer further insights into the presuppositions of Guignebert.

He devotes much space to problems of Old Testament interpretation, because 'la religion chrétienne n'a pas fondamentalement une autre base que l'Ancient Testament lui-même'[15]. He insists on the circumstantial and utilitarian nature of the New Testament writings[16]. He introduces his students to the main problems of text and canon for Old and New Testaments. In a section on exegesis generally, he repeats many points from his 1910 article. There is the same vigorous repudiation of all a priorism, theological, philosophical, confessional, apologetical. More space is devoted to the history of exegesis. After the formulation of the principles of scientific exegesis by Spinoza and the initial application of these principles by Richard Simon, it was not entirely fortunate that the task was taken up by German rationalism. Scientific work was often overtaken by a concern for system-building, as in the case of F.C. Baur: 'il a construit avant d'avoir étudié assez et éprouvé les matériaux'. Similar speculative tendencies may be found in the social sciences, and it is not easy to make some people understand:

> . . . que l'exégèse est oeuvre de patience plus que de génie spéculatif, qu'on la possède par enquête de détail plus que par 'l'inspiration de génie'.[17]

In contrast with the German critics, says Guignebert, we are like the physicist who studies the facts and allows them to suggest their own explanatory formulae, rather than the mathematician who seeks the confirmation of preconceived formulae. There is however some value in conflicting interpretations, insofar as these cancel each other out, leaving behind only what is of permanent worth.[18]

The major current issues in New Testament study are: the composition of Mark; the composition and historical value of John; the basic eschatology of the Gospels; the composition of Acts; the intellectual formation of Paul; the composition, sources and tendencies of Revelation. More generally, major interest is concentrated upon the relation between the spirit and the letter of the New Testa-

---

15 IEAC 36.
16 GP IEAC 90.
17 GP IEAC 103. Cf. a very similar comment of Loisy directed at sociologists and *mythologues,* in Loisy to Cumont 5.5.23 (BN n.a.f. 15644; quoted above 2.5.2).
18 GP IEAC 93.

ment and the Hellenistic religious milieu in which it took shape. On this question one should consult the works of Wendland, Clemen, Reitzenstein, Böhlig, Loisy, Perdelwitz and Boll. For an appreciation of the present state of New Testament studies one should read Loisy, *Les Mystères paiens et le Mystère chrétien* (1919); Deissman, *Licht vom Osten* (1908); Case, *The Evolution of Early Christianity* (1914); and especially Bousset, *Kyrios Christos* (1913). This reading list helps to place Guignebert himself in the history of criticism, and comes as added confirmation of his position, with Loisy, as leading French exponent of the *religionsgeschichtliche Schule*.

The final remarks of the lecture course, in abbreviated form, also state Guignebert's position concisely:

> Complexité de la science de l'antiquité chrétienne. Nécessité partout de bien poser les questions, et de bien marquer les limites de l'information; réaction indispensable contre l'*a priori*, le confessionnel et l'esprit de construction.
> Etat actuel: résultats encourageants. Indifférence en France.[19]

3.6 *POPULAR PRESENTATIONS (1914–1922)*

In accordance with his declared policy of combating public indifference and of instructing the uninitiated, Guignebert published four volumes devoted to the origins and history of Christianity in popular format:

1914 *Le Problème de Jésus*
1921 *Le christianisme antique*
1921 *La vie cachée de Jesus*
1922 *Le christianisme médiéval et moderne*

The two volumes on Jesus appeared in the 'Bibliothèque de culture générale', the others in the 'Bibliothèque de philosophie scientifique', where *L'Evolution des dogmes* also belonged[1]. They are therefore in the category of 'haute vulgarisation'. Somewhat more in the nature of personal reflections was the volume of 1922 on *Le Problème religieux dans la France d'aujourd'hui*. In pursuit of the diffusion of knowledge, Guignebert also wrote articles and delivered 'extra-mural' lectures; among the latter we may cite those addressed

---

19 GP IEAC 172.

1 In the *Avant-Propos* of *Le Christianisme antique* (p7) Guignebert says the work is a sequel to *L'Evolution des dogmes,* in the form of a practical application of the principles he had there enunciated.

to l'Union des libres penseurs et des libres croyants pour la culture morale in 1926 and 1928[2].

The volumes on Jesus take up specific questions. *Le problème de Jésus* reviews the theories of non-historicity put forward by Kalthoff, Jensen, Robertson, Smith and Drews. There is a good section on 'les antécédents historiques' which, as Goguel remarked, does more justice than Schweitzer's *Von Reimarus zu Wrede* to the views of the English deists and the French *philosophes*[3] and, in general, the documentation is very thorough. Guignebert ascribes a minimum of historicity to the Gospels but he rejects the views of the *mythologues,* partly for their preconceived systems and partly because their position raises impossibilities for history. Most of all, Guignebert feels, in both the Synoptics and, rather differently, in Paul, the humanity of Jesus is assumed *in spite of* the writers' conviction that he was a divine figure[4]. He accepts the charge of the *mythologues* that liberal theologians have tried to produce a human Jesus acceptable to the modern mind, but they have also been responsible for 'un vaste travail critique' of great value to the historian[5]. Guignebert returned to this problem in 1928, in the lecture referred to above, at a time when the views of Couchoud (a philosopher and therefore a systematiser, notes Guignebert)[6] were under debate and his position is the same. Even though the amount of historical information in the Gospels shrinks like the 'peau de chagrin' at every investigation[7], there is a distinction to be made between the (comparatively) human figure of Jesus in the Synoptic tradition and the divine Christ of Paul, John, Revelation and the opening chapters of Matthew and Luke. Against the *mythologues* it must be asserted that the former representation was historically prior to the latter[8].

La Vie cachée de Jésus reviews the religious background of Jesus

---

2 'Les Mystères d'immortalité and 'Les livres saints' in *Dieux et Religions* (1926); 'Le Jésus de l'Histoire' in *Jésus et la conscience moderne* (1928). Guignebert was not a member of the Union and in a letter to Houtin of 21st October 1922 he says that he will probably never join this group of searchers for 'la Vérité' (with a capital V), although he does ask Houtin to provide a room for their meetings at the Musée Pédagogique.

3 Goguel, *Jésus de Nazareth, Mythe ou Histoire?* p10.

4 *Op.cit.* pp151–7.

5 *Ibid* p159.

6 *Art.cit.* p10.

7 *Ibid* pp26–27.

8 *Ibid* pp12–13.

and the narratives of Matthew 1–2 and Luke 1–2. It concludes that
there can be no direct certain knowledge about the childhood of
Jesus, or his 'intellectual, religious and moral formation'[9]. This is in
conformity with the principle which Guignebert had already enunciated in his *Scientia* articles: 'Le problème de la levée de Jésus se
ramène donc historiquement à une étude du milieu où il a vécu'[10].

Le christianisme antique presents a whole series of variations when
compared with the *Manuel* of 1906 but, as Guignebert mentioned
in the *Avant Propos*, his conclusions are based upon fifteen years of
teaching at the Sorbonne and the new emphases should therefore not
surprise us. The Introduction suggests that rather than seek the
essence of 'religion', it is more profitable to study religion*s* historically. One must expect to find differences between social classes:
the religion of educated men will not be the same as popular religion
and the latter is naturally prone to syncretism and 'endosmosis'.
Two chapters on Jesus are mainly concerned with the Palestinian
background, for the only method of understanding his emergence
is the study of his religious milieu[11]; he himself is best compre-
hended in the category of 'prophet'. The 'foi-confiance' of his disciples raised him from the dead, by a process of 'collective visions'
resulting from 'mental contagion'[12].

In writing about the apostles, however, Guignebert immediately
takes leave of Palestine, describing not only the Diaspora but also
Jewish syncretistic cults (Mandaeans, Hypsistians, Sabazians, Nazor-
eans) which testify to the heterodoxy of non-Palestinian Judaism
and explain the ease with which Christianity passed into the Hellenistic world in centres such as Antioch. Chapters on 'le milieu
paulinien' and 'la formation chrétienne de Paul' describe the Mystery religions whch, however much they themselves were later
affected by Christianity, provided Paul with basic mythological
and ritual models[13]. As a Jew, it is unlikely that Paul studied in

---

9 *Op.cit.* p.164.
10 *Art.cit.* p135; cf. above 3.2.2.
11 *Op.cit.* p40.
12 *Ibid* p63.
13 In his article 'Les Mystères d'immortalité' Guignebert gives seven reasons for the triumph
   of Christianity over the Mysteries: 1. it rejected voluntary syncretism; 2. it was young
   enough and flexible enough to absorb the truly religious substance of the Mysteries,
   retaining its firm basis in monotheism; 3. its Lord was a living person, with personal
   witnesses, not a mythical being; 4. it had a strong moral content; 5. its rituals were

Jerusalem and his Christian training must be attributed to the Hellenistic community of Antioch. In Antioch, the 'Messiah', the 'Son of Man' and 'Servant' of the original apostolic preaching had been replaced by the 'Lord'; future eschatology had given way to his cultic presence; and Paul derived from this milieu the basic contention of his soteriology, that 'Christ died for our sins'.

This greatly reduces Paul's originality, but his involvement in the problem of the admission of the Gentiles and his Christological and soteriological 'gnosis' make him a central figure:

> Il n'a pas fondé le christianisme, s'il faut le définir l'adaptation du messianisme juif au salutisme hellénique, mais, sans lui, le christianisme pouvait ne pas être.[14]

After these chapters on Paul and Hellenistic Christianity, the rest of the book treats thematically the subsequent development of Christianity up to the time of Constantine. The themes are: the autonomy of Christianity, the founding and organisation of the Church, the constitution of doctrine and discipline, the conflict with the State and society, the sense of triumph. Here Guignebert treads familiar ground. Christianity at the beginning of the second century was an independent religion but still in a rudimentary state in its dogmas, rites and institutions[15]. It was this plasticity, combined with an exclusivism derived from Judaism, which enabled it to gain ground by means of an unconscious syncretism. The idea of the Church was generated by the transplantation of the Christian hope from Palestine on to Greek soil and hence its universalisation[16]. Whereas at the beginning of the second century, to become a Christian was easy, involving a few simple beliefs and submission to baptism as a means of repentance and renewal[17], tendencies were at work to produce a much more elaborate system by the end of the same century. Christological speculation (of three main types: Pauline, Johannine and Docetic) and philosophical influences, the development of the catechumenate and the ritualisation of the Eucharist, the evolution of the episcopate and the beginnings of the

---

comparatively simple; 6. it was able to reconcile the notions of 'immortality' and 'resurrection'; 7. it was more open than the other Mysteries and formed a mutual aid society. (*art.cit.* pp86—7).

14 *Ibid* p138.
15 *Ibid* p144.
16 *Ibid* p163.
17 *Ibid* p185.

penitential system, all conspired to produce a highly regulated religious organisation. If, after temporary setbacks occasioned by conflicts with the Roman Empire, Christianity was able to establish itself as superior to its major rivals, Neoplatonism and Manicheism, it was because over three centuries it had learned the virtues of tact and flexibility. It had acquired a 'sense of life' whereby it absorbed its rivals' tendencies, holding them in balance so as to appeal to the religious cravings of the age[18]. But there is a sense in which Christianity always remained an oriental religion in its origins (Judaism) and its fundamental character (a mystery of salvation) and therefore a sense in which Western man has never been Christian[19].

This semi-popular history of early Christianity shared the character of the earlier *Manuel* in not falling squarely into the province of either the 'curés' or their opponents. Catholics could well have felt it was a rationalist tract when, for example, they noted the titles of the last two chapters of its companion volume, covering the nineteenth and twentieth centuries: 'Le libéralisme, la critique et la science contre la théologie' and 'Le triomphe du romanisme'. But rationalists might have hoped for the author to subscribe to the *mythologues'* position and to draw more obvious lessons from features such as clericalisation. Certainly Guignebert wished to present the Church of the early decades as a remote and strange phenomenon, all the more so by its affinities with irrational Hellenistic religion and to stress the discontinuities between Jesus and the early Christians and between the faith of the early generations and the later constructions of theology. But his tone remained that of the historian rather than the controversialist. In the history of criticism the stress upon Hellenism at the expense of Judaism may appear one-sided and therefore antagonistic; but, as in the case of the commentaries, the work is a serious attempt to make available in French the findings of the history-of-religions method, which many confessional critics rejected out of hand.

3.7 *CONCLUSIONS*

It is possible to characterise the achievement of Guignebert in a

---

18 *Ibid* pp252–3.
19 *Ibid* pp255–261.

series of antitheses which demarcate him from his confessional counterparts. The most basic antithesis is undoubtedly that between history and theology. Theology means system, immobility, speculation and partisanship. History means 'life', evolution, hard fact and objectivity. Guignebert was deeply convinced that a theological stance jeopardised a real understanding of history[1]. He also does not seem to have entertained any serious doubts about the ease with which impartiality can be practised. It was simply a matter of refraining from passing judgement. He is reported to have spoken as follows:

> Pour sa part il (Guignebert) se refuse à n'importe quel étage de l'histoire de juger. Comprendre doit être le dernier degré du résultat à atteindre; quand on y est parvenu, on peut expliquer si l'on veut, mais dans aucun cas on ne doit *juger* . . . Il a toujours dit à la Sorbonne tout ce qu'il a voulu dire, en choisissant seulement un peu ses mots, parce qu'il n'a jamais porté l'ombre d'un jugement.[2]

He was proud of the fact that, having lectured on the Reformation, he was approached by some of his hearers who wished to know if he was a Catholic or a Protestant[3]. Early Christianity need be no exception to the general rule. 'Explanation' does not amount to 'judgement'.[4] When however we turn from the modern historian to early Christian history itself, the weak link in this first antithesis is the concept of 'speculation'. This could surely be a sign of 'life' rather than immobility. Guignebert does not wish to detract from the creativity of the earliest phases of Christianity and so he distinguishes between the 'religious' or 'mystical' speculation of Paul, John and other writers of the first two or three generations, and the philosophical thought which characterised the second-century Apologists and which contributed to the general codification of Christianity as an autonomous religion. The distinction is obviously questionable and there seems to be no very cogent reason for the

---

1 He did of course distinguish amongst theologians. Cf. *Dieux et religions* pp159–160, where however he stresses that the more objective the theologian becomes, the lower his standing in the eyes of ecclesiastical authority.

2 From the report of a discussion following a lecture by Guignebert on 'La pédagogie de l'histoire'; v. *Bulletin de la société française de pédagogie*, no.7 (1921) p212.

3 *Art.cit.* p198.

4 For Guignebert's severity towards confessional writings, cf. his review article devoted to L. de Grandmaison, *Jésus-Christ* (1928) a monument of French Catholic scholarship (*RHR* t.99 (1929) pp30–39): 'Je ne prétends pas qu'il n'y ait rien à louer dans ces deux gros volumes, j'entends rien du point du vue de l'histoire, car de celui de l'apologétique tout est peut-être louable; je n'ai pas à en décider'. (p38). But it should at the same time be remembered that Guignebert had been equally severe with P.–L. Couchoud, *Le Mystère de Jésus* (1925) (review in *RHR* t.94 (1926) pp215–244.)

secular historian to refuse to speak of the 'theology' of Paul and John. Here of course Guignebert finds common ground with Protestant theologians and his notion of a decline from early creativity into dull and repressive orthodoxy probably owes more to certain Protestant presuppositions than he might have acknowledged[5]. But he immediately draws away again from the Protestants, by taking as his common purview the whole sweep of early Christianity from its beginnings to Constantine and beyond. There may be a difference of quality between the 'anarchical' religion of the first century and the creeping ecclesiasticism of the second but for the historian, the latter is equally to be investigated. It is true that Catholic writers have also commonly taken the wider view but there could be no real confusion between their aims and those of Guignebert. The Catholic emphasises continuity and growth under divine guidance, as the forms of Catholicism emerge more and more clearly, while for Guignebert the process of adaptation by assimilation leads to startling differences of belief and practice from one century to another. So, in his general scope, which he would claim to be that of the 'scientific' historian, he stands over against attitudes commonly assumed by both Protestant and Catholic writers on his period.

A further antithesis which is not unconnected with the foregoing is found in Guignebert's reminder about the 'mediocrity' of history. The Christian writer naturally fastens upon saints, martyrs, theologians, persecutions and councils as the highlights of history. But Guignebert's sensitivity on matters of apologetics and hagiography lead him to stress anonymity, collectivity and, for example, the sporadic nature of persecution and the attitudes towards nascent Christianity not only on the part of State officials but also of popular opinion. It was typical of him that he should write an article 'Les demi-chrétiens et leur place dans l'Eglise antique'[6]. The 'half-Christians' of pre-Constantinian Christianity were not heretics but individuals and groups who, although they had strong links with the Church, nevertheless maintained contact with paganism. Their numbers were not inconsiderable, as Christian polemic indicates, and they probably rendered service to the Church in difficult times and smoothed the transition from paganism to Christianity

---

5 Certainly Loisy, writing both as a Catholic and as an ex-Catholic did not make this kind of distinction.

6 *RHR* t.88 (1923) pp65–102.

as a State religion. Guignebert accepts that further classification and research is required on this subject, but as a historian he is here shedding light on an area likely to be neglected by the confessional writer.

It has also emerged clearly from our study that Guignebert differed from Catholics and (most) Protestants in regarding Christianity as *a* religion and not *the* religion. Although his own excursions into comparative religion were on a fairly general level, he did not doubt that the history of Christianity should take its place in the history of religions. Certainly early Christianity could never be studied as an absolutely unique phenomenon, isolated from its environment. It was this perspective which led Guignebert to emphasise, over against the confessional writers, the strangeness or the 'otherness' of early Christianity, the impermeability of its Oriental assumptions to Western scrutiny. It is in this sense that Guignebert's comparativism and anti-confessionalism hang together.

To designate Guignebert as an 'anti-confessional' in this way is certainly to capture one aspect of his work. In particular he wished to deflate the claims of Catholic orthodoxy as they were still customarily legitimated from the early Christian documents. Ecclesiastical tradition and scientific exegesis were implacably opposed[7]. Contemporary Catholicism also required to be cut down to size. The much vaunted religiosity of the French people has been greatly exaggerated: 'Le peuple de France n'a pas de grands besoins religieux'[8]. The Catholic 'revival' before the First World War was not very widespread or profound: 'ces garçons si décidés n'étaient que des *pragmatistes fidéistes*'[9]. A member of the Académie Française once described Guignebert, not malevolently, as 'religieusement aveugle'[10] and all accounts suggest that he had no personal inclinations towards religious belief. In the absence of more personal writings, it is impossible to say if this negative aspect of his personality was bound to express itself an anti-religious stance. All one can say

---

7 'La "tradition" qui complète le Livre, et l'interprétation, qui l'élargit et l'assouplit jusqu'aux limites du possible, et qui parfois les dépasse, prolongent son action au delà du temps qui l'a vu se constituer. L'exégèse scientifique, au contraire, tend toujours à l'y ramener et à l'entendre dans sa relation historique avec ses origines véritables'. From an article 'Livre', *Revue de Synthèse Historique* t.XLIX juin 1930 pp46–48.
8 *Le Problème religieux dans la France d'aujourd'hui* (1922) p232.
9 *Op.cit.* p256.

is that this was more likely to be the case in France than elsewhere and that in the circumstances, Guignebert was comparatively restrained. We have already noted some of his strictures upon the extreme forms of rationalism.

Certainly one could describe his own history-writing as 'rationalist', 'positivist' and 'evolutionist', although these terms could equally be applied to most modern historiography. More seriously, he appears to us simplistic in suggesting that neutrality is achieved by an absence of 'judgement': non-judgementalism can be its own ideology. It seems quite possible that, if he had been writing some thirty years later, Guignebert might have modified his extreme concentration of interest upon the Mystery religions, in the direction of heterodox Judaism; but he is unlikely to have changed his views about the Jesus of history and the immense qualitative gulf between the first Palestinian community and the developed forms of Catholic orthodoxy. Arguments about acorns and oaks were the recourse of the theologian. Such a resolute historicism undoubtedly blinded Guignebert to continuities of early Christian life and thought and prevented him from gaining a positive appreciation of 'tradition' as an empirical religious phenomenon. But he insisted that religions require sympathetic treatment and, in this, he saw himself as a disciple of Renan. His own attitudes are well expressed in his contribution to the Renan centenary of 1923[11]. Renan was right to oppose 'theology':

> C'est son mérite d'avoir affirmeé que l'histoire des religions est une histoire comme les autres et que la théologie n'est point recevable à opposer ses raisonnements et ses conclusions aux faits bien établis.[12]

But as the final apostrophe relates, Renan has instilled in his followers a love of the subject:

> Tu as aimé la religion et tu nous a enseignés que toutes les formes sous lesquelles elle a successivement vécu dans le monde ont droit à notre respect et d'aucunes à notre amour ... tu as revendiqué résolument, en face de tous les dogmatismes, et comme personne encore ne l'avait fait, les droits imprescriptibles du libre examen, de la critique et de la raison. Il t'en a coûté cher; mais si tu as lutté, tu as vaincu et nous te rendons, d'un coeur reconnaissant, grâce de ton courage, nous qui, aujourd'hui vivons sur ta victoire.[13]

---

10 André Siegfried, at the reception of Daniel-Rops. V. *Edouard Le Roy et son fauteuil* (1956) Pt II (no pagination). For details of this statement v. 5.3. below.

11 'Renan et nous'. *Revue de l'Université des Bruxelles* no.3 (1923) pp229–259.

12 *Art.cit.* p242.

13 *Ibid* p257.

4. GOGUEL'S WORK ON EARLY CHRISTIANITY 1920—1940

4.1 INTRODUCTION

Unlike that of Loisy, the career of Maurice Goguel was unmarked by dramatic incident and the course of his critical opinions remained unwavering for half a century. There are minor exceptions to this rule: for example, in an article of 1948, 'De Jésus à l'apôtre Paul'[1], he no longer finds himself satisfied with what he had written on the subject in L'Apôtre Paul et Jésus-Christ of 1904; but it is noteworthy that his major volumes on early Christianity of 1946—7 contain many references to earlier published work, going back to 1902, with scarcely any revisions of opinion[2].

This unity of outlook can be partly explained in institutional and confessional terms. As student, teacher and finally as Doyen, he was for over fifty years associated with the Protestant Faculty in Paris. He was at the same time a University man, a regular contributor from 1907 onwards to the Revue de l'Histoire des Religions and successor to both Loisy and Guignebert in their posts at the Sorbonne[3]. We have already noted the strong links between Liberal Protestants and the secular University system[4], typified above all by Auguste Sabatier, who was Goguel's teacher. Goguel was to remain faithful throughout his life to the spirit of Sabatier and E. Ménégoz[5], even when such a position had become unfashionable[6]. His visit to Ger-

---

1 RHPR XXVIII—XXIX pp1—29.
2 La Naissance du Christianisme mentions minor changes of opinion about Paul's journeys (pp36 and 322) and about the composition of Ephesians (p439—40).
3 He succeeded Loisy at EPHE in 1927 and took a temporary position in the Faculté des Lettres when Guignebert retired in 1937.
4 V. above 1.3.
5 Together known for their 'symbolo-fideism'. Cf. Protestantisme français (1945) p318 where Goguel mentions symbolo-fideism, Ritschlianism and the Biblical criticism of J. Réville and A. Lods as abiding influences.
6 For the differences of outlook which became apparent during the 1930s between Goguel and his younger colleagues much influenced by Karl Barth, cf. M. Simon in The Primi-

many in the early years of the twentieth century did nothing to disturb such an influence, since he was impressed above all by the teaching and personality of Wilhelm Herrmann[7], to whom he devoted his doctoral thesis[8] and whose saying 'Die erste Pflicht der Religion ist Wahrhaftigkeit' he took as his motto.[9]

As the choice of thesis indicates, Goguel contemplated for a time taking up systematic theology as his life's work, but finally opted for the New Testament because he considered that the historical basis of Christianity needed to be firmly established before the theological task could be properly undertaken[10]. He therefore came to regard himself as a historian and his published work reflects this stance. Significantly, Goguel did not write commentaries, nor did he crown his career with a Theology of the New Testament[11]. His two major achievements were the (uncompleted) *Introduction au Nouveau Testament* (1922—6) and his trilogy on Christian Origins (1932—1948)[12]. A personal statement towards the end of his life is entitled 'Témoignage d'un historien'[13]. His books and articles frequently, of course, took up questions of exegesis and interpretation and important sections of the trilogy are devoted to the teachings of Jesus, Paul and others but nowhere does Goguel overtly attempt a normative theological synthesis. His concern was with the historical interpretation of the New Testament documents which at the same time provided him with a chronological limit beyond which

---

tive *Church* (ET 1963) pp7—11 and J. Daniélou in *Protestantisme français* (1945) pp437—8; for Goguel's own ultra-symbolism, based on Sabatier, cf. *Protestantisme français* p330, repeated in *La Naissance du christianisme* pp25—6.

7 Brief impressions of his time in Berlin and Marburg are recorded in 'Lettres d'Allemagne' *Revue Chrétienne* 1904 pp82—84, 165—168; he is appreciative of Harnack and Gunkel (whose approach is one of the most promising of recent developments) but reserves highest praise for Herrmann, who reminds him of Sabatier in his combination of intense religious conviction with complete freedom of historical enquiry.

8 *Wilhelm Herrmann et le problème religieux actuel* (1905).

9 Freely translated by Goguel himself: 'il ne peut pas y avoir de religion en dehors du respect inconditionné de la vérité et de la réalité.' (*Protestantisme français* p319).

10 Cf. his opinion recorded by P.—H. Menoud *Verbum Caro* IX (1955) p3: three lifetimes are needed for the researcher, the first to master the languages, the second to do history and the third for 'le problème dogmatique'.

11 O. Cullmann in *Vorträge and Aufsätze 1925—1962* (1966) p673 explains this latter deficiency with reference to his liberal protestant prejudices.

12 *La Vie de Jésus* of 1932 was however to be replaced by a much rewritten second edition: *Jésus* (1950).

13 *Protestantisme français* (1945) pp318—352.

he did not frequently stray.

In order to describe and to evaluate Goguel's work on early Christianity, a narrative technique is hardly appropriate. This was useful in the case of Loisy, in order to chart the fluctuations of his critical opinion but Goguel's consistency means that it is not necessary to trace his development over the years. Nevertheless it will assist comparison with both Loisy and Guignebert if a limited period of his career can be chosen and such a period presents itself in the years 1920–1940. By 1920 his reputation was established, although the War had prevented the publication of large scale works. But during the next two decades Goguel was to produce eleven major volumes and some seventy articles. His *Introduction au Nouveau Testament* gathered up much of his previous work, as did a work on texts and editions[14] and a translation (with others) of the New Testament into French[15]. His involvement in the Christ-myth debate led to articles, some in more popular vein and to his refutation of Couchoud: *Jésus de Nazareth, Mythe ou Histoire?* (1925) His teaching at EPHE resulted in the publication of *La Foi à la résurrection dans le christianisme primitif* (1933). His final historical synthesis was inaugurated with *Au seuil de l'evangile: Jean Baptiste* (1928) and *La Vie de Jésus* (1932) and a mounting series of articles during the late 1930s suggests that the two volumes on the early church would have been published earlier, had not the second world war intervened. By 1940 there are therefore sufficient indications of what those volumes would contain for a provisional estimate to be made of Goguel's achievement. In stopping short of the works themselves we are repeating the procedure adopted in the case of Loisy and Guignebert.

Before turning however to consider Goguel's work in detail, some justification is needed of his inclusion in the category of 'independent' critic. His name is to be found cited with those of Loisy and Guignebert as one of the foremost non-Catholic French investigators of early Christianity in the first half of the twentieth century[16], and to have worked as a Protestant critic in a predominantly Catholic milieu does in itself constitute a measure of independence. But we

---

14 *Le texte et les éditions du Nouveau Testament* (1920).
15 *Le Nouveau Testament. Traduction nouvelle … sous la direction de Maurice Goguel et Henri Monnier.* (1929).
16 Eg. by M. Simon in *The Primitive Church* (ET 1963) p7.

have already seen that there was a well-established Protestant intellectual tradition in France, notably in the history of religions. Writers in this tradition were inclined to stress their objectivity and independence of theological control and Goguel was no exception. We shall in fact find that he shared some of the religious, if not strictly theological, presuppositions of his fellow Protestants and to that extent he may be considered a confessional writer. But a *prima facie* case in favour of his independent status is created not only by his own assertions — uttered in all good faith — of impartiality but also by his personal eminence. Alone in France he embodied a critical position which might be described as 'moderate to radical' and which, however common-place in England or Germany, set him apart in his own country, standing as he did between Catholic critics and conservative Protestants on the one hand and the more thoroughgoing historical scepticism of Loisy and Guignebert on the other.

A brief survey of Goguel's work on early Christianity prior to 1920 needs to be inserted at this point, with special reference to some of his presuppositions and working methods. We must refer first of all to *L'Apôtre Paùl et Jésus-Christ* of 1904, because this work is mentioned in at least two important histories of interpretation[17], although it should be remembered that it was written as a thesis for the author's licenciate, before he had given up thoughts of becoming a systematic theologian. It presents a contrast with Goguel's later work in combining history and theology. The author's historical concern is expressed in his preface: 'N'est-il pas indispensable, en effet, de connaître la révélation divine qu'est le christianisme, avant de philosopher sur elle?'[18] and in the first part of the book: 'The Facts'. But the main body of the work is devoted to 'The Ideas', where Goguel undertakes a series of comparisons between the teaching of Jesus and the teaching of Paul, under such headings as 'The Person and Work of Christ', 'Morality' etc. Goguel does not shirk the contrasts, which he sees as most striking in Christology and soteriology and he sees Paul as the true originator of Christian theology; but there is a lingering regret:

---

17 A. Schweitzer, *Paul and his Interpreters* (ET 1912) pp159–160; W.G. Kümmel, *The New Testament. The History of the Investigation of its Problems* (ET 1972) pp293–5.
18 *Op.cit.* pii.

On peut dire que chez Jésus, la réalité vivante est presentée toute nue et sans aucun apprêt. Chez Paul, la vie n'a certes pas disparue, mais elle est enveloppée dans des formules qu'il faut traverser pour arriver jusqu'à elle ... Comme les mots, les doctrines théologiques n'ont en elles-mêmes aucune valeur, mais elles expriment des expériences religieuses qui sans elles risqueraient de passer sans laisser de traces durables.[19]

Thus the original Gospel of Jesus and the basic Christian experiences had to be preserved and Christianity demarcated from Judaism, by the use of dogmatic formulae. Goguel always exhibited this ambivalent attitude towards dogma, ritual, institution and moral code in early Christianity[20].

His definitive transition from theology to history is apparent in the thesis he wrote for the doctorate of letters: *L'Eucharistie des origines à Justin Martyr* (1910). In a chapter on 'Method' he considers various possibilities: the mythological approach of Reinach, the dogmatic method of the theologians, the 'hierological' approach of G. d'Alviella[21], the 'logical' method of A. Schweitzer, and the 'method of erudition' practised by K.A. Goetz. All of these he finds wanting, and in particular he calls for the 'establishment of the facts' over against the dogmaticians. He himself is committed to a historical method[22]. He is particularly opposed to the comparativists, as represented by G. d'Alviella, and the following statement will help explain why Goguel kept himself aloof from the *religionsgeschichtliche Schule*, active at this period[23]:

L'idée sur laquelle se repose cette méthode (sc. the 'hierology' of G. d'Alviella) est qu'il y a un développement en quelque sorte fatal de la religion et que le repas de communion est un moment de ce développement... Le développement du Christianisme a eu quelque chose de spontané et d'individuel, il a été spécifiquement différent du développement des autres religions et c'est se condamner à ne pas pouvoir saisir ce qu'il y a de plus

---

19 *Ibid* pp372–3; 376.

20 Although his thesis on Herrmann of 1905 is not strictly concerned with early Christianity, one can mention here its conclusions. Herrmann's theology, says Goguel, constitutes 'une digue victorieusement opposée aux excès de la méthode spéculative'; it also attempts to take account of modern historical criticism by a) seeking the revelation of God and the basis of faith in history while b) constituting theology so as to leave critical science at complete liberty, fearing nothing from its results; c) attempting to synthesise 'la conscience moderne et l'esprit de l'Evangile'; d) by recognising that religion is not 'affaire de formules mais affaire de vie'. (*op.cit.* p259).

21 Count E. Goblet d'Alviella (1846–1925) held a chair in the history of religions at the Free University of Brussels and had outlined his comparative approach, under the name of 'hierology' at the Oxford Congress of 1908.

22 Cf. Loisy's commitment to the historical method in his inaugural lecture of 1909, above 2.1.

23 Goguel consigns 'Les repas religieux en dehors du christianisme' to an Appendix.

caractéristique en lui que de vouloir l'expliquer entièrement par des lois générales du développement de la religion.[24]

Goguel's divisions are entirely chronological, but his choice of Justin Martyr as a *terminus ad quem* may reveal confessional concerns: in Justin he sees the culmination of a process whereby a real meal was transformed into an imitation meal, ie. a rite, and thus Justin is not only an end term but a beginning. A Protestant was more likely than a Catholic to see things in this way.

In 1913 Goguel was one of many speakers who addressed the Sixth International Congress for Religious Progress, held that year in Paris and supported by a variety of liberal Christians including a sizeable American Unitarian contingent. His subject was 'L'étude critique des origines chrétiennes et le progrès religieux'. His conclusions are worth quoting. Historical criticism of the New Testament documents is a factor in religious progress, he claims, for the following reasons:

1° D'abord parce qu'elle met en lumière à propos d'un example type les conditions du progrès religieux.
2° En second lieu parce qu'elle dissocie l'expérience religieuse chrétienne de conceptions et de théories qui parce qu'elles ont vieilli sont devenues des obstacles au développement de la vie religieuse.
3° Enfin parce que dégageant des éléments secondaires qui obscurcissaient la personne historique de Jésus de Nazareth, elle met l'âme en présence de la puissance qui, à travers les siècles, reste la source la plus pure de l'expérience religieuse et parce que, d'autre part, elle facilite cette expérience en mettant en lumière celles qu'ont faites les grandes personnalités des premières générations chrétiennes.[25]

Important ideas for Goguel's critical stance are here made clear: Christianity as an example of 'religion' more generally[26]; the overlaying of essential Christianity, conceived as a religious experience, by non-essential ideas which only have a temporary value; Jesus himself as the 'power' of Christianity and the importance of 'personality' as a factor in early Christianity.

4.2 'INTRODUCTION AU NOUVEAU TESTAMENT'

Goguel did not complete this important project; but the five

---

24 *Op.cit.* pp27–8.
25 *Travaux du 6e Congrès International du Progrès Religieux* (1913) p204.
26 Cf. his saying in *Protestantisme français* p319 that, as a Lutheran, he feels himself to be 'plus religieux que chrétien, plus chrétien que protestant, plus protestant que luthérien'.

volumes published between 1922 and 1926[1], amounting to some 2,500 pages, cover most of the New Testament: only Hebrews, the Catholic Epistles and Revelation awaited his attention. Such a work by an independent critic was much needed in the French-speaking world, since the only other serious works available in the *Einleitung* category were those of the conservative Swiss Protestant F.-C. Godet[2] and the Catholic E. Jacquier[3]. Goguel faithfully reports the history and present state of critical opinion on major New Testament issues and on many points of detail, but also draws his own conclusions. The work therefore provides important evidence for his conception of early Christianity at the time of his reaching full critical maturity. He aims to follow 'une méthode exclusivement historique'. He recognises that even the words 'nouveau testament' may strike some as more dogmatic than historical, but since the formation of such a collection of books and its influence upon the Christian church are in themselves historical facts, he does not see the need to change the title to *Histoire de l'ancienne littérature chrétienne*[4].

From the volumes on the Gospels the following points may be noted. Discussion of the Synoptics is much concerned with source-criticism, although Goguel mentions, without evaluation, the more recent work of Wrede, J. Weiss, Wellhausen and Loisy[5]. He accepts the two-source theory[6], but he thinks that the sayings-collection existed in two separate 'branches', as known to Matthew and Luke respectively. Other sources used by the Synoptic writers are heterogeneous and cannot always be identified[7]. The early Church had a triple interest in preserving the Gospel tradition: the life of Jesus was the 'terrestrial episode' in the drama of salvation; the personality of Jesus had created an ineffaceable impact; the teaching of Jesus was relevant to the problems of Christians. Corresponding to these three points of view ('points de vue spéculatif, sentimental, moral') were the Passion Narrative, the stories about Jesus and the sayings of

---

1 I *Les Evangiles Synoptiques* (1923), II *Le Quatrième Evangile* (1924), III *Le Livre des Actes* (1922), IV *Les Epîtres pauliniennes (Première Partie)* (1925), V *Les Epîtres pauliniennes (Deuxième Partie)* (1926).

2 *Introduction au N.T.* (1893 ff).

3 *Histoire des Livres du N.T.* (1903–8 and many subsequent editions).

4 III pp6–7.

5 I pp48,100ff.

6 Cf. Goguel's major treatment of this question (the most important in the French-speaking context) *L'Evangile de Marc dans ses rapports avec ceux de Matthieu et de Luc* (1909).

Jesus, the second and third categories as yet uncoordinated[8]. This stage of development is reflected in Paul's writings. Mark and the sayings-collection then represent two types of 'edification', at the next stage[9]. But neither Mark, nor Matthew and Luke when they combined the two types, can be considered as theologians. Each is dominated by his sources and the beliefs of his time. There is, for example, no real 'Paulinism' in Mark[10]; apologetic and ecclesiastical tendencies in Matthew were found by him in his sources[11]; Luke's universalism is inherited from Paul but is no longer polemical[12].

The Fourth Gospel, by contrast, is 'une oeuvre nettement théologique'[13], without serious historical or narrative interests. Its arguments are presented 'par juxtaposition et non par enchaînement'[14] and its contemplative tone contrasts with the vehemence of Paul. Examination of the possible sources does not confirm the hypothesis of a *Grundschrift,* whether a historical document (Spitta) or a lyrical poem (Wellhausen, Schwartz and Loisy): composition was much more complex, including some ancient and historically reliable sources[15]. The book's religious thought presents a unity, but it is mystical rather than systematic, reflecting the collective experience of the Church. Johannine Christology is 'essentiellement la traduction d'une expérience religieuse'[16] and in Johannine soteriology we find 'la combinaison de deux éléments hétérogènes, de l'expérience mystique et de la tradition dogmatique antérieure'[17]. Goguel quotes with approval the works of the Swedish *Religionsgeschichtlicher* G.P. Wetter, allowing for the admixture of Jewish and Hellenistic elements in the Fourth Gospel and he finally shows how its teaching must be contrasted with and subsequent to those of Jesus and of Paul, although prior to that of Ignatius[18].

The nature of the Gospel material, as described by Goguel, places

---

7 For Matthew v I pp421ff and for Luke I pp494ff.
8 I pp41–2.
9 I pp272–3.
10 I pp358ff.
11 I pp434ff.
12 I pp518ff.
13 II p212.
14 II p226.
15 II p470.
16 II p482.
17 II p495.
18 II pp525ff.

restrictions upon our knowledge of Jesus, although in an 'Introduction' he does not have the opportunity to show the extent and the consequences of these restrictions; but his view does not allow for any corresponding gain of knowledge of the early Church, as Loisy and Bultmann in their different ways were urging at the same period. Even though he favoured in principle the attempt to go beyond source criticism and study the history of the tradition[19], the disparate and amorphous nature of the sources and his unwillingness to recognise 'tendencies', in the Synoptic writers at any rate, made his conclusions vague and unevocative. The Fourth Gospel is a more distinct entity in the life of the early Church, but even here Goguel's use of the category of 'religious experience' somewhat clouds his analysis. But his caution is salutary and, as we shall see, was to serve him well in his evaluation of the *mythologues* and the Form critics. It is also interesting to note that Goguel's mistrust of comparative studies for the understanding of early Christianity is suspended in the case of the Fourth Gospel.

The three volumes on the Acts of the Apostles and the Pauline epistles go beyond the normal limits of an 'Introduction' and provide a highly detailed analysis of Acts and a biography of Paul, into which are inserted chapters on the separate epistles, in the supposed order of composition. Nevertheless, this does not amount to a history of early Christianity, since Goguel is preoccupied with questions of textual and literary criticism. It provides however a solid critical basis for his subsequent historical work and some indication needs to be given of his main critical conclusions and of the historical picture which begins to emerge from this massive and intricate study.

Goguel considers that the source-criticism of Acts has been overdone: the Old Testament has proved an untrustworthy guide in the matter, since the New Testament writers are not simple compilers and the writer of Acts in particular qualifies as an author, using his sources with considerable freedom[20]. He is not a historian, being guided by 'pragmatism', meaning his ideas about universalism and his apologia in favour of Paul[21]. He is not, however, representing a

---

19 In his article on Form criticism (*RHR* 1926 – for details v. below 4.4) Goguel states that his article 'La nouvelle phase du problème synoptique' *RHR* 1907 pp311–344 had called for 'l'élaboration de l'histoire de la tradition'.

20 III pp57–60.

21 III p50.

fixed theological position, or *Tendenz*, and it is important in critical work on Acts to proceed from the particular to the general and not try to trace a single guiding thread[22]. The first part of the book is heterogeneous and even though the second part has more unity of purpose, its narrative is still 'surchargé, mutilé, incohérent'[23]. The writer is without distinct theological aims and presents a 'projection' which is 'toute naive et spontanée'[24]. Contradictions are allowed to remain unchecked: one strain in the book represents Christianity as a continuation of Judaism, even Paul appearing as an observant Jew, while on the other hand Stephen's speech denotes a sharp break; in Christology, advanced Pauline notions coexist with the archaic elements in the early speeches[25]. Goguel's hypothesis to account for this state of affairs is that 'Luke' wrote a history of Christianity from the death of Jesus to the arrival of Paul in Rome but that this narrative was adapted by the 'writer to Theophilus', who did not always realise its historical value and introduced other material from a variety of sources. A later interpolator further modified the text by adding the story of the Ascension and few other items[26]. Thus the historical value of Acts is neither very high nor very low. Unhistorical elements include the day of Pentecost, the conversion of Cornelius, the Council of Jerusalem, Paul's trial before Herod Agrippa and the speeches ascribed to Paul at Pisidian Antioch, Athens and Miletus. On the other hand there are sufficient indications in both narratives and speeches of ecclesiastical and theological conceptions which antedate those of the redactor to guarantee the general course of events as described by Acts. The book thus remains 'l'une des bases les plus essentielles sur lesquelles repose l'histoire du Christianisme ancien'[27].

Goguel makes many references to Loisy's recently published commentary on Acts, especially in his 'analyse critique du récit'[28]. He feels generally that, over against Harnack, Loisy has correctly

---

22 III p109.
23 III p154.
24 III p167.
25 III pp361—2.
26 III p352.
27 III p367.
28 For his further views on Loisy's commentary v. Goguel's report to the Société Ernest Renan (*RHR* LXXXIV 1921 pp300—304) and his article 'La critique actuelle des Actes et le commentaire de M. Loisy' *RHPR* I 1921 pp446—463.

taken his point of departure in the extensive redaction of a single original source by a later editor. But he doubts whether the original work of Luke was such a plain and 'modern' piece of history writing as Loisy imagines; and he cannot see that all the obvious omissions and additions made by the redactor correspond to his alleged ecclesiastical concerns[29]. Goguel therefore most frequently disagrees with Loisy when the latter conjectures too confidently what stood in the original source and at the same time offers reasons for its 'removal' in conformity with the *Tendenz*[30]. Goguel also attributes historical value, even if limited, to sections described by Loisy as entirely fictional and this applies particularly to episodes in the life of Paul[31]. But he agrees with Loisy about the fictional nature of the miraculous elements and of certain characters, eg. Agabus, and he is prepared to follow Loisy quite closely in his reconstruction of events after Paul's arrest in Jerusalem until his arrival in Rome.

Goguel is consequently cautious in using Acts for the biography of Paul. He recognises that the second-century apocryphal Acts add very little to our historical knowledge, and he therefore contents himself with an outline of Paul's movements, drawing upon the evidence provided by the epistles and filling in with well-qualified conjectures. The most striking example of this method is in his very elaborate reconstruction of Paul's dealings with the Church of Corinth. He concludes that Paul changed his mind five times on the question of his second and third visits to Corinth[32]; corresponding to these fluctuations is Goguel's rearrangement of I and II Corinthians into six different letters, as well as some fragments[33]. It is true that elsewhere the story provided by Goguel does not reach such a pitch of elaboration, but this serves as a measure of his speculation.

He accepts as authentic: I and II Thessalonians (but II Thessalonians was originally addressed to Beroea), Philippians (not to be partitioned), I and II Corinthians (partitioned as above), Galatians,

---

29 III p346.
30 E.g. Loisy's treatment of the encounter between Peter and Paul at Antioch and of Paul's dealings with the church of Corinth.
31 E.g. the conversion narrative and the accounts of the first and second missionary journeys.
32 V pp60–61.
33 V p86; Goguel stresses that his conclusions on the Corinthian correspondence represent what he has taught for fifteen years at the Protestant faculty and have not been influenced by recent publications of Loisy and of Couchoud. For Loisy's reply to Goguel, cf. *Mém* III p519 and above 2.5.3.

Romans (the original text extended from 1,1 to 16,23) and Colossians. Ephesians was originally a homily, possibly by Tychicus, which was both a 'transposition' and a 'vulgarisation' of Paulinism[34]. The Pastoral epistles include some genuine Pauline fragments but like Colossians and ·Philemon, these reflect Paul's captivity in Caesarea, rather than in Rome, and as Philippians was written in Ephesus, none of the so called 'captivity epistles' may be used as evidence for the end of Paul's life. The letters, considered from a literary point of view, are neither everyday correspondence, as typified by the papyri, nor formal *Kunstprosa.* They are raised from the 'occasional' category by their spiritual level and the power of Paul's personality and also by their subsequent liturgical use[35].

The man Paul was of excitable temperament, prone to depression and resentment. His upbringing in Tarsus had made him familiar with the Greek religious world but his own ideas always remained basically Jewish[36]. His first contact with Christianity could well have been hearing Stephen speak in a Hellenistic synagogue in Jerusalem. His conversion was a violent reversal of values, for which there must have been psychological preparation, although not to be conceived as frustrated moral striving or an unconscious admiration of the Christians whom he persecuted[37]. He preached in Arabia, made a brief visit to Jerusalem and was then commissioned for his preaching task by the church of Antioch, although he later worked independently. As he travelled from one major centre to another, he relied on irrational 'guidance' through both visions and circumstances. He left others to provide the details of organisation[38]. Upon his own admission, he was not a brilliant preacher but his ideas of salvation and immortality corresponded ,to the deepest needs of the men of his time: he spoke of a cosmic drama of man's Fall, salvation and forgiveness through the Cross, the age of the Holy Spirit and a final victory[39].

---

34 Goguel later changed his mind about Ephesians and concluded that it contained an authentic Pauline core, with interpolations: 'Esquisse d'une solution nouvelle du problème de l'Epître aux Ephésiens' *RHR* CXI 1935 pp254–284;CXII 1935 pp73–99.
35 IV pp44–5.
36 IV Ch.III.
37 IV p204. Here Goguel deliberately parts company with many other Protestant exegetes and comes closer to Loisy's position. V. also his article: 'Remarques sur un aspect de la conversion de Paul' *JBL* LIII 1934 pp257–268.
38 IV p240.
39 IV pp253ff.

His ideas underwent development but this was more to do with circumstances, eg. disputation with Jews, evangelisation of Gentiles, than with psychological change. It is not possible to posit a decisive shift, for instance, in his eschatology as a result of his experiences in Ephesus (the view of Auguste Sabatier) where he overcame his fear of death and so no longer anticipated the Parousia in his own lifetime[40]. Some differences may be explained by the situation in the churches to which he wrote. The eschatologies of I and II Thessalonians may be accounted for by two different recipients[41]. In Corinth he was faced with a resurgence of 'paganism' (cf. the Hellenistic anthropology enivsaged in I Cor. 15 and the libertinist trends in sexual morality and commensality with non-Christians)[42]. Galatians is an outpouring directed at the Judaizing campaign which threatened his converts[43]. Romans, written to a Church which was predominantly Gentile, had the specific aim of warning the Christians of Rome that a similar campaign might soon reach them[44]. Colossians was intended to combat a syncretistic gnosis, which it is impossible to define closely, but which was half way between the position of the 'weak' in Romans and I Corinthians and the false teaching attacked in the Pastorals[45]. In his writing, Paul makes abundant use of imagery, derived from physical laws, human relations, trade and agriculture, warfare and the games; sometimes this imagery has a contrived air[46].

These views of Goguel give some idea, not only of his conclusions on critical questions, but also of his estimate of Paulinism. He makes it clear that he is not providing a complete account of Paul's theology but his delineation of biographical and circumstantial factors introduces us to his own non-systematic view of Paul. It is the religious experience of the apostle, expressing itself in changing situations, mainly through concepts inherited from Judaism, which is primary: this experience become available in his preaching to his hearers, as the answer to their own religious needs. It is precisely

---

40 IV pp414–6.
41 Goguel concludes that II Thess. was originally addressed to Beroea (IV pp335–7).
42 V pp93ff.
43 V pp166ff.
44 V pp290–2.
45 V p524.
46 IV pp173–5.

this experience which is lacking or modified in the non-authentic epistles. The ecclesiasticism and 'allegorised' eschatology of Ephesians would not have been Paul's chosen way of making his 'mystical experience' more widely available'[47]. In the Pastorals:

> Entre la fonction de l'apôtre et sa vocation, c'est-à-dire son expérience, il n'y a plus le rapport direct qui est si frappant dans les épîtres authentiques.[48]

This stress upon religious experience betrays Goguel's Liberal Protestant background and is a constant feature of his writing, especially on Paul. The *Introduction au Nouveau Testament* did not permit him to develop his ideas fully, but we may note that this factor provides at least one test for what is authentic and central in the Pauline corpus.

Here then the documentary foundations for Goguel's historical work are laid. A painstaking analysis of Gospels, Acts and Epistles reveals the limits of their use in historical reconstruction; but the general conclusion is not entirely negative: it is still possible to relate the history and trace the religious thought of Jesus and the early Church, even when much remains obscure. Goguel accepts a high degree of obscurity with regard to the sources behind the documents: these may not be reconstituted so as to provide direct evidence of early Christianity. Nor is much to be gained from comparative studies. Alone among the New Testament writings the Fourth Gospel and the authentic epistles of Paul have a distinctive theological position (Hebrews, the Catholic epistles and Revelation not entering into the picture). Since the life and work of Paul are comparatively well documented, he is bound to emerge from this literary-critical survey as the central figure in early Christianity, a position which was maintained in Goguel's subsequent historical writing. We have seen how Loisy at this period was attempting to undermine both the preeminence of Paul and the sway of a purely literary criticism of the New Testament. Goguel, in spite of his agreement with Loisy on many points of detail, represented a perfect target for Loisy's attacks. If Loisy had known that Goguel was devoting a lifetime to the historical study of early Christianity so that others might then proceed to the dogmatic task upon more secure foundations, he would have been confirmed in his suspicions.

---

47 V p470.
48 V p536.

Although the *Introduction au Nouveau Testament* appeared in the series *Bibliothèque Historique des Religions* and although it has good claims to impartiality, it remains a confessional work in a recognisable academic tradition. It was Goguel's achievement to make that tradition available to the French-speaking world, but without any real modification of assumptions, or any radical reorientation of critical trends.

4.3 *THE CHRIST-MYTH DEBATE*

Goguel became deeply involved in the debate surrounding *Le Mystère de Jésus* by Couchoud[1]. He replied to Couchoud's article 'L'énigme de Jésus' which heralded the book[2], engaged in public debate with Couchoud[3], gave semi-popular lectures on the subject and wrote a number of articles[4]. But his complete reply is found in *Jésus de Nazareth, Mythe ou Histoire?* (1925) which, being a work of circumstance, is rather more lively in tone than most of Goguel's publications, although no less thorough. Goguel's involvement, as may be gauged from his article describing the debate[5], came from his concern that Couchoud's views would have great influence in France upon a public which lacked the most elementary knowledge of Christian origins[6]. The popular republican press had taken up Couchoud's ideas with enthusiasm[7], and although more serious commentators had noted the ideological bias in Couchoud's position[8], a historical reply was called for. Goguel was also concerned

1   For the general bibliography of this debate v. above 2.5.2.
2   In an article in the *Mercure de France* 1st June 1924.
3   Under the auspices of *L'Union pour la Vérité*, published in the *Correspondence de l'Union* (1925) pp9–61.
4   'La réalité historique de la personne de Jésus' *Revue de christianisme social* 1925 pp191–204; 'La vie et la pensée de Jésus, leur rôle dans le christianisme primitif' *RHPR* 1925, pp509–539.
5   'Recent French Discussion of the Historical Existence of Jesus' *HTR* XIX 1926 pp115–142.
6   In an article 'Recent French Discussions of Christianity: the series "Christianisme"' *HTR* XX 1927 pp63–104. Goguel concluded that the series edited by Couchoud, in which the latter's *Mystère de Jésus* had appeared, even if not systematically anti-Christian, would not contribute greatly to the education of the French public in the history of religions.
7   Goguel mentions *Le Quotidien, Le Progrès Civique, L'Oeuvre.*
8   Goguel mentions articles in *La Semaine Littéraire, Le Journal des Débats, Revue de Synthèse Historique.*

that within Protestantism, in the face of dogmatic orthodoxy[9], a 'fruitful partnership of science and faith' should be established:

> The study of theology, whether it starts from experience, from speculation, or from tradition, is legitimate only if it abides in harmony with the results of historical enquiry. It may transcend these but not contradict them.

The future of Protestantism and even the future of religion in France was at stake[10].

Our concern is not to follow the debate in all its details but to extract from *Jésus de Nazareth, Mythe ou Histoire?* (this work resumes his ideas on the subject) further indications of Goguel's view of early Christianity. In a number of sections, e.g. on the history of the Gospel tradition, he merely repeats what he had very recently published in his *Introduction au Nouveau Testament*. But his response to Couchoud is suitably wide-ranging. One of the interesting features of the Christ-myth theories is that they cull evidence from many sources: Old Testament, New Testament, Church Fathers, Gnostic and pagan religions. Goguel shows himself accomplished in these fields and also to have a firm grasp of the history of interpretation so that Couchoud is himself placed in historical context[11]. But the main area of discussion is that of the New Testament documents. In the examination of these Goguel is in pursuit of an answer to a question of fact: Are there valid historical proofs for the historical existence of Jesus? Against Couchoud's idea that the problem of Jesus is unique and therefore enigmatic, Goguel insists that a clear distinction must be maintained between the facts and their interpretation and that the problem of Jesus cannot be exempted from the normal processes of historical enquiry[12].

It is this principle of distinguishing fact from interpretation which serves Goguel as a guiding thread through his consideration of a variety of material. For example, the *mythologues* make much of Docetism in the early Church, but 'le docétisme est une opinion théologique, ce n'est pas une affirmation historique'[13] and the very ingenuity of the Docetists witnesses indirectly to their manipulation

---

9   In his article 'The Religious Situation in France' *Journal of Religion* 1921 pp561—577 Goguel noted that a dangerous ultra-conservative party had arisen within French Protestantism.

10 *Art. cit.* pp141—2.

11 NB Ch.I: 'Les théories de non-historicité'.

12 *Op. cit.* pp32—4.

13 *Ibid* p87.

of a historical tradition. The phrase *ta peri tou Iēsou* means the events of the earthly ministry of Jesus, rather than any doctrine about a mythical Jesus[14]. But more importantly, the principle is applied both to the theology of Paul and to the composition of the Gospels. After an exposition of Paul's soteriology, Goguel draws attention to the disjunction between 'justification' as a present experience and the final 'redemption' which is still awaited[15]. The ideas themselves are drawn from the Jewish scheme of salvation, but the introduction of an interim period into that scheme is the result of the earthly appearance of Jesus:

> La doctrine paulinienne provient ainsi d'un dislocation de l'oeuvre rédemptrice. Elle n'a donc pas une source unique; elle n'est pas née de l'élaboration ou de la transformation d'un mythe, mais résulte de l'interprétation par une doctrine préexistante d'un fait historique, constitué par la vie et par la mort de Jésus et par la foi à sa résurrection.[16]

Similarly with the Gospels. Upon analysis, they reveal that from the earliest stage of their composition, 'un plan dogmatique' had replaced the true historical course of events[17] (for example, the historical reason for Jesus going to Jerusalem was to escape from Herod Antipas but this has been replaced by the theological notion of his necessary suffering and death in the holy city)[18]. If, as the *mythologues* claim, the Gospel tradition were the projection into history of a myth, or ideal drama of redemption, the Gospel story would be homogeneous. But in reality:

> Le cadre a été élaboré par la réflexion dogmatique, les éléments du récit n'ont pas été créés en fonction de ce cadre, mais empruntés à la tradition pour le remplir.[19]

The *mythologues* say that important elements in the Gospel story have been created out of Old Testament prophecy, but analysis shows that the truth is much more complex and that four categories may be distinguished[20]: creation, as alleged by the *mythologues* (especially in the birth and infancy narratives); modifications in the story based upon O.T. prophecies; a direct influence of the O.T. on the events themselves; and the later recognition of parallels between historical events and O.T. 'prophecies'. In three of these four

---

14 *Ibid* p72.
15 *Ibid* pp159ff.
16 *Ibid* p170.
17 *Ibid* p257.
18 *Ibid* pp254–5.
19 *Ibid* p257.
20 *Ibid* pp201ff.

cases, the difference between fact and interpretation has to be observed[21].

Goguel allows for a limited influence upon the Gospel tradition of factors which for the *mythologues* are all-important. Folklore has provided motifs such as the earthquake at the crucifixion and Jesus walking on the water, but these are additions to the tradition at some literary stage of development[22]. Words of Jesus may not be ascribed to inspired persons or visionaries in the early Church, since I Corinthians makes it clear that the first Christians distinguished carefully between a 'word of the Lord' and any human utterance[23]. There is no literary evidence for stories of e.g. miracles occurring in the early Church being transferred back into the life of Jesus: an examination of parallels between the Gospels and Acts show that the stories in Acts are always secondary[24]. Loisy's liturgical theories lack verification because no laws have yet been discovered for 'le style rythmé' and in any case there is no evidence from the first century A.D. for the liturgical reading of the Gospels. Any ritual influences upon the tradition are very·restricted[25].

Two substantial sections of the book are devoted to Paul and to the problem of the resurrection[26]. In the case of Paul, Goguel notes his efforts to maintain fellowship with the apostolic leaders in Jerusalem who based their authority upon contacts with the earthly Jesus, in spite of his own quite different conception of apostleship, derived from a revelation of the heavenly Christ[27]. The texts from Paul's epistles used by Couchoud to buttress his theory are examined in turn and none is found to exclude the idea of an earthly Jesus[28]. For instance, the Christ-hymn in Philippians 2 was addressed to Christians who already knew the Gospel story and the mythical elements which are undoubtedly present therefore serve as comment and speculation rather than substance[29]. Paul's Christology moves

---

21 *Ibid* p214.
22 *Ibid* pp258—60.
23 *Ibid* pp260—3.
24 *Ibid* pp263—7.
25 *Ibid* pp267—71.
26 Ch.V and VI: 'L'Apôtre Paul et la tradition évangélique' and 'La Théologie de l'Apôtre Paul'; Ch.XI 'L'Origine de la foi à la résurrection et son rôle dans le christianisme primitif'.
27 *Ibid* pp103—7.
28 *Ibid* pp107ff.
29 *Ibid* p118.

from the humanity of Jesus to his divinity; similarly his soteriology precedes and develops into cosmology[30]. In the deutero-Pauline literature these processes are taken even further, so that doctrines take pride of place over the history of which they originally constituted the interpretation. But the authentic epistles presuppose a Jesus who lived, acted, taught and died. We do not know the full extent of Paul's teaching, but he had no need to argue for the historicity of Jesus since it was taken for granted by all[31].

It was entirely appropriate for Goguel to complete his book with a consideration of the resurrection, for here questions of history and faith, of fact and interpretation are at their most thorny. At first he appears to play straight into the hands of the *mythologues,* for he asserts:

> Le fait décisif dans la genèse du christianisme n'a été ni la découverte du tombeau vide, ni les apparitions de Jésus à ses disciples, mais la foi à la résurrection. En matière religieuse, ce qui importe, ce ne sont pas les faits mais les idées et les sentiments.[32]

A comparison of I Corinthians 15 with the Gospel narratives shows that there are two conceptions of resurrection in the New Testament, that of a heavenly Christ who appears from time to time and that of a resurrected Jesus who resumes his earthly life. The first of these is the earlier conception, found in Paul, while the second, intermingled with the first in the Gospels, is influenced by apologetical motifs. There was a tendency therefore to 'materialise' or to 'concretise' resurrection faith[33]. But Goguel parts company with Couchoud by insisting that this faith was 'étroitement solidaire' with the death of Christ, a historical fact. The 'Messianic faith' created by the bonds between Jesus and his disciples during his lifetime was not entirely shattered by his apparent failure, but only shaken and then reasserted on a transcendental plane[34]. Goguel does not therefore place great store by the historicity of the resurrection narratives themselves; for him, the historical reality of Jesus is so well established by other means, that he can posit a religious experience as the historical core of nascent Christianity. This position might create theological problems in orthodox circles, but in

---

30 *Ibid* pp119–20.
31 *Ibid* p135.
32 *Ibid* p272.
33 *Ibid* pp283–5.
34 *Ibid* p302.

the present context it can be seen as a sign not only of Goguel's liberal presuppositions but also of his confidence and honesty in replying to the *mythologues*.

In spite of Loisy's reservations about *Jésus de Nazareth, Mythe ou Histoire?*[35] as a reply to Couchoud, it was necessary for such a reply, based upon a traditional literary-historical analysis of the texts, to be attempted. Goguel was the critic in France most competent to do so and he had no difficulty in producing ample evidence to destroy Couchoud's hypothesis. But in independent circles, his position could be seen as over-cautious. His confidence in the continuity between Jesus and Paul and his conclusion that Paul's theology was rooted in the humanity of Jesus, were not shared by those who had been influenced by the *religionsgeschichtliche Schule*. When Goguel gave a paper on the resurrection at the Congrès Renan in 1923, he was accused by Guignebert of not having made plain the differences between the Palestinian and the Hellenistic milieux[36]. In his Gospel criticism he did not welcome the ideas of the Form critics, as will be explained below. So his work could obviously not find favour with Loisy, who was preoccupied at the time with escaping from the impasse of traditional critical methods and for whom even the Form critics were too traditional. Guignebert and Loisy both affirmed the historical existence of Jesus, as the indispensable starting point for a new religious movement but Goguel, allowing more historical value to the Gospels, believed that the personality of Jesus was a decisive factor in early Christianity.

It might have made his reply to Couchoud more effective and his position vis-à-vis the radical critics more clear, if he had outlined the stages of development of Christianity in the first century of its existence, as he was later to do in *La Naissance du Christianisme* and *L'Eglise Primitive*. But the Acts of the Apostles only came into the Christ-myth debate incidentally and therefore the main ingredients in the early Church, according to Goguel appear to be: a diffuse Gospel tradition, which in spite of its systematic rearrangement in the canonical Gospels, retains much valuable information about Jesus and which has not been radically distorted by apologetic or ecclesiastical factors; the personality of Jesus, whose influence was transmuted into resurrection faith; the central figure of Paul who, while conver-

---

35 Cf. 2.5.2. above.

36 'Le Christ ressuscité et la tradition sur la résurrection dans le christianisme primitif' *Actes du Congrès d'histoire des religions* II (1925) pp225–253.

sant with the Gospel tradition in its precanonical stages, evolved his own theology by adapting Jewish ideas in the light of his religious experience; and the subsequent codification of doctrines at the expense of experience. This was not in any way a final picture, but in the mean time it was one of Goguel's virtues to acknowledge the inconsistencies, both in Paul and in the Gospels; a 'ragged' picture was to be preferred over against the smooth reconstructions of the *mythologues*, not only as some guarantee of the historicity of Jesus but also as a more faithful indication of the nature of the documents and thereby of our historical knowledge of early Christianity.

4.4 *SOME GENERAL PRINCIPLES*

A good indication of Goguel's position, supplementing those aspects of his work already surveyed, may be gained from his reactions to the emergent school of 'Form criticism' in Germany. His views are contained in an article of 1926[1] and in his inaugural lecture at EPHE in 1927[2]. The latter also enshrines his own working principles and some further idea of these, as related to the Gospels, may be found in a semi-popular address of 1928[3].

Goguel sees in the new school of criticism 'un système de construction plutôt qu'un procédé d'investigation' and he notes that Butlmann in particular is a disciple of Karl Barth, which may in part account for his conclusions. His historical agnosticism may derive from a desire to secure an absolutely certain minimum of historical knowledge, however small, envisaged mainly in terms of a basis for theological construction (an irrealisable hope, according to Goguel)[4]. So although Goguel was himself anxious to create a secure historical basis to be made use of by systematic theologians, he was adamant in maintaining the autonomy of the historical task against

---

1   'Une nouvelle école de critique évangélique' *RHR* XCIV (1926) pp114–160.

2   'L'orientation de la science du Nouveau Testament' *RHR* XCVI (1927) pp297–339.

3   Delivered in response to a paper of Guignebert on 'Le Jésus de l'Histoire' at a meeting of 'L'Union de libres penseurs et de libres croyants pour la culture morale' held on 15th January 1928; published in *Jésus et la conscience moderne* (1928) pp28–39.

4   *Art.cit.* p116. Goguel refers in particular to Bultmann's article 'Das Problem einer theologischen Exegese des Neuen Testaments' *Zwischen den Zeiten* 3, 1925 (ET in *The Beginnings of Dialectic Theology* ed. J.M. Robinson (1968) pp236ff). He also considers that Bultmann's short book *Jesus* (1926, ET 1934) shows that he is approaching the Gospels as a theologian rather than a historian; this is confirmed by Bultmann's theory of history as a dialogue between past and present.

premature invasion by theological interests and one is reminded of
Loisy's stand against Catholic theological imperialism twenty-five
years before. Goguel is perturbed by the loss of interest in history
on the part of these critics; an air of scepticism and historical agnosticism has overtaken New Testament scholars as a result of Gospel
criticism in particular and this is reflected in the preoccupation with
form over substance and in the oblique approach of recent work
(titles like *Hauptprobleme* and *Grundfragen* have become more
common than 'histories' or 'lives').

Goguel considers that the Form critics have overstressed their own
originality: E. Reuss, Jülicher, Baldensperger, J. Weiss, Loisy, Gunkel
and Bousset had all anticipated them in various ways, as well as their
acknowledged forebears Wrede and Wellhausen. Their results are vit-
iated by several factors. They call attention to social, collective and
cultic features and suggest that the Gospels are impersonal products,
whereas it is necessary to point to the individual influence exercised
by the evangelists in the selection and presentation of their material[5].
They attempt to categorise all the Gospel pericopes, but their terminology is deficient and with good reason: 'L'imprécision de la
terminologie est directement fonction de l'imprécision de la définition des types'; the admission of a category *Mischformen* proves that
abstract schemes are being operated at the expense of the complex
reality of the Gospel tradition. The new critics draw parallels with
the laws of epic poetry and this produces some interesting insights
but the comparatively short period of time involved in the writing of
the Gospels and the constant, direct religious nature of the material
as developed in the apocalyptic, charismatic atmosphere of the early
Church, place severe limits on the use of these parallels.

Dibelius is to be criticised on several counts[6]. The relationship
between early Christian preaching and the Gospel narratives was
more complex than he suggests: the former could have been influenced and engendered by the latter, since the preaching was not a primary and irreducible datum. It is incorrect to describe the final form
of the Gospels as 'mythical', as it is simply 'l'explication historique

---

5 Cf. Goguel's comment on G. Bertram, *Die Leidensgeschichte Jesu und der Christuskult*
   (1922): 'Il n'y a pas seulement dépendance des récits par rapport au culte, mais il y a
   aussi, et c'est même ce qui nous paraît le plus primitif, dépendance du culte par rapport
   aux récits'. (*Art.cit.* p152).
6 In his *Die Formgeschichte des Evangeliums* (1919; ET 1934).

du christianisme qui a revêtu un caractère religieux'. (The only truly 'mythical' section of the Synoptic Gospels is Matt. 28,16ff).

Bultmann obviously exaggerated in supposing that all the Gospel material has been influenced by such factors as the accentuation of the miraculous or the prophetic interpretation of history[7]. Most of his *apophthegmata* do not make sense if removed from their (historical) setting. His standard pattern for miracle stories is simply required by the events described and the Gospel miracles are related with sobriety when compared with the Hellenistic parallels. In the Gospel tradition generally, Bultmann does not allow for 'une tendance à la dislocation' over against the 'tendance à l'unification et à l'organisation' which he underlines. Like Bousset he makes too absolute a distinction between Palestinian and Hellenistic Christianity.

In favour of the Form critics, then, it can be said that they have drawn attention to the following points: the Gospels are witnesses to the faith of the early church; the Gospel tradition is not inert but corresponds to the life of the early church; it is important to study the *form* of the Gospel narratives. None of these points is new, although the study of the forms has been neglected hitherto and both Dibelius and Bultmann have provided many useful comments on points of detail. The defects of the school have been made plain: their insufficient acknowledgement of older critics; their over-rigorous classification; their failure to appreciate that a single form does not necessarily correspond to a single *Sitz im Leben*, so that their work loses touch with living reality (this is described by Goguel in the Pascalian phrase: 'prépondérance de l'esprit géometrique sur l'esprit de finesse')[8].

Goguel's inaugural lecture sets the Form critics in the wider context of New Testament studies generally. He begins by enunciating some principles of his own. Any work of synthesis must be based upon a rigorous and strictly documentary method, which proceeds from the simple to the complex, from the known to the unknown. The comparative method should be used with great caution. Literary criticism comprises a 'travail préparatoire' providing 'matériaux prouvés' for the history of early Christianity. When that history is attempted, it is wise to keep separate 'l'histoire des faits' (the life of

---

7   In his *Die Geschichte der synoptischen Tradition* (1921; ET 1963).
8   A phrase already used by Loisy in his review of Bultmann; v. above 2.4.

Jesus, the spread of Christianity in the first century A.D., the life of Paul, the history of rites and institutions)and 'l'histoire des idées et des sentiments' (formerly known as 'la théologie biblique du Nouveau Testament'). Goguel sees the present crisis in New Testament studies as a crisis of growth: critics like Holtzmann and Weizsäcker had conveyed the impression that moderate, definitive solutions to the main problems were within reach, but that has not happened. The reasons are, first 'la laïcisation de la critique', meaning that the theologians have been joined by non-confessional critics, reflecting general progress in the history of religions; and, secondly, increasing specialisation (cf. the growing number of monographs) which has discouraged works of general synthesis: that of J. Weiss[9] remained incomplete and the volumes of E. Meyer[10], like the series *Beginnings of Christianity*[11], are collections of detailed studies.

If one looks for example at the problem of Jesus and the Gospels, which is the single most important issue in New Testament scholarship, one finds that the merging consensus at the end of the nineteenth century was shattered by the work of Wrede, J. Weiss and Wellhausen, all of whom rejected the historicity of the Marcan outline, and now Bultmann has followed in the steps of Albert Schweitzer in denying the possibility of a life of Jesus. But Goguel does not share this extreme pessimism. Even if one must admit to gaps in our knowledge, it should be possible to write a history of Jesus and the early church:

> ... dans laquelle les grandes lignes apparaîtront avec une clarté suffisante et d'une solidité de tous points comparable à ce qu'il est possible d'atteindre en matière d'histoire ancienne.[12]

Such an effort will be some kind of recompense for the solid achievement of the nineteenth century critics, even if they were wrong about definitive solutions just around the corner. Goguel is concerned about resurgent confessionalism in New Testament studies, as variously exemplified by Lagrange and Bultmann. Twenty years ago, he says, no one would have challenged the need for history without a priorism but now the historical and philosophical categories are again confused. But the quest for objectivity may not be

---

9 *Das Urchristentum* (1914–17).
10 *Ursprung und Anfänge des Christentums* (1921–23).
11 Ed. F.J. Foakes-Jackson and Kirsopp Lake (1920ff).
12 *Art.cit.* p333.

abandoned, since there will always be historical problems to solve. Whatever their shortcomings, the Form critics have at least directed us to an important principle:

> ... l'histoire d'une religion, de sa naissance, de son développement et même de ses déviations ne peut être comprise que par la psychologie de la religion en général et de la religion considérée en particulier.[13]

Goguel does however call for a positive appreciation of the facts of early Christianity and considers that the critic, in pursuing his task, should be ready to assume 'une âme chrétienne'.

Whether or not Goguel was correct in deducing this demand for empathy and the importance of religious psychology from the work of the Form critics, his conclusion certainly represents his own continuing faithfulness to the teaching of Auguste Sabatier[14] and to that extent, his own brand of confessionalism. When describing his methods to the members of 'L'Union de libres penseurs et de libres croyants pour la culture morale', he states that, once the materials for the enquiry have been analysed, the historian's task of 'organising the facts and reconstructing the history' requires:

> ... une méthode souple et variée qui cherche à saisir les relations internes des faits ... en pénétrant la psychologie des personnages qui en ont été les acteurs[15].

Religious history in particular calls for 'psychology and intuition'. In the case of the gospels, for instance, it is possible to identify a body of authentic material which can then be reconstituted 'au triple point de vue de la chronologie, de la géographie et de la psychologie'.

This call for a psychological evaluation of the personalities and events of early Christianity, corresponding to his own belief in the priority of religious experience, is the Achilles' heel of Goguel's position. It is at this point that he is most vulnerable to his own forms of a priorism. These might pass undetected in the surroundings of the Faculté Protestante and the EPHE but his Liberal Protestant heritage was much more apparent to a critic like Loisy, just as his refusal to derive insights from comparative studies was no doubt a sign of his confessionalism to a critic like Guignebert. Psychological reconstructions are notoriously open to all the subjectivism which

---

13 *Ibid* p338.
14 For Sabatier's 'méthode de stricte observation psychologique et historique' v. the Preface to his *Esquisse d'une Philosophie de la Religion* (1897) and for details of his treatment of early Christianity, v.1.3. above.
15 *Op. cit.* p32.

writers of 'liberal' lives of Jesus had deployed in the nineteenth century. In his favour, however, it can be said that Goguel was well aware of the faults of a Renan and of the limits placed upon the history of early Christianity by the nature of the sources (cf. his own severe estimate of the Marcan outline and of Acts of the Apostles). He saw genuine difficulties of procedure in the case of the solutions being proposed by Form critics, as well as entertaining a not unjustified suspicion that their historical scepticism might be theologically motivated. His insistence on maintaining the literary-critical approach at a time when, from several quarters, it was looking outdated, was salutary if unexciting. Moreover, he was not merely advocating its use in the interests of conservative conclusions and this offered some guarantee of objectivity and of a check upon excessive psychological speculation.

It is however to be regretted that, as a self-proclaimed historian, he did not take more seriously the debate being initiated by the German critics on the nature of historiography: his brief comments on this score seem to indicate that history is a fairly straightforward task. But his own distinction between 'fact' and 'interpretation', which he applies both to the New Testament writers and to the work of the modern critic, is far too simplistic and does not do justice to the complexities in each case. Fact and interpretation, history and faith, are so intertwined in the documents themselves, that, whatever the standpoint of the modern historian, he cannot escape the methodological debate. We shall see that Goguel was aware of some of the issues, but that his desire at this stage in his career to embark upon the work of synthesis did not allow him to be sidetracked into theological and philosophical questions, which he was content to leave to others.

4.5 *RESURRECTION FAITH*

Goguel began his work of synthesis with *Au seuil de l'evangile: Jean-Baptiste* (1928) and *La Vie de Jésus* (1932). These do not fall directly within the scope of the present study, although it may be noted in passing that the former has sections on the disciples of John the Baptist and on the legendary developments in the story of the baptism of Jesus and that the latter considers once again the question of the growth of the Gospel tradition. Much more to our purpose is Goguel's work on the question of the resurrection. We have already seen that he presented a paper on this topic at the Congrès Renan of 1923 and that it provided a final section in his refutation of Couchoud of 1925. He chose to take it up again in a series of lectures at EPHE in the years 1929–31 and these were published in 1933. Articles in *RHPR* in 1930 and 1931 paved the way for the major work of 1933[1]. It is said that, like *La Vie de Jésus*, this work did not meet with much favour in Church circles[2] and this reaction corresponded to the secular circumstances of its composition and the non-confessional treatment of a subject where questions of faith are so crucial. But the work deserves close examination, precisely on account of the writer's intention to take a strictly historical view of resurrection faith in early Christianity.

In the Preface of *La Foi à la résurrection dans le christianisme primitif* Goguel rejects the opinion of Wehrung that the problem of the resurrection presents an indissoluble combination of historical judgements and judgements of faith[3] and states his own conviction that it is necessary to distinguish between history and religious thought and to establish a right relation between the two:

> La religion peut supposer des faits mais sa fonction est non de les énoncer, mais de les interpréter et de développer leur signification spirituelle ... Si la spéculation religieuse a ainsi le droit de dépasser les faits, elle n'a pas celui de les contredire. L'histoire, d'autre part, pour remplir toute sa tâche, ne doit pas se borner à dresser un inventaire de faits isolés les uns des autres, elle doit les réunir entre eux et s'efforcer de saisir leur enchaîne-ment. Pour cela elle ne peut pas négliger les sentiments et les émotions qui les ont accompagnés, que les faits ont fait naître, et qu'en même temps ils expriment par la manière même dont ils ont été présentés.[4]

A further basic distinction should be made between the resurrection as 'une affirmation de fait' and 'une affirmation de foi': strong priority, both chronological and religious, should be given to the latter[5].

Goguel proposes a threefold approach to his task: an analysis of the place of resurrection faith in the life and thought of the first Christians; a critical study of the narratives, intended to reconstitute the history of the tradition; and a psychological study of the con-

---

1 'Parousie et résurrection' *RHPR* X 1930 pp371–409; 'Le caractère de la foi à la résurrection dans le christianisme primitif' *RHPR* XI 1931 pp329–352.
2 Cf. P.–H. Menoud in *Verbum Caro* IX (1955) p5.
3 In *RGG*[2] Vol.I c.633 'Auferstehung Christi'.
4 *Op.cit.* pX.
5 The contention that resurrection faith was essentially 'une affirmation de foi' was strongly argued in the article 'Le caractère de la foi à la résurrection ...' cf. *art.cit.* p335.

version of Paul, in the light of similar phenomena from other cultures, which should then be related to the other New Testament Christophanies. In practice, much less space is devoted to this third approach; also, the first two sections overlap extensively, reflecting their origin as separate lecture courses.

Goguel's survey of the resurrection idea through the New Testament documents begins with the sermons in Acts, which though incorporated into a later document, can be taken to illustrate early beliefs. Their witness is to the glorification of Christ who in his resurrection has been made Messiah. They therefore attest a supernatural reality which is celebrated in 'le culte du Seigneur Jésus'[6] and significantly they do not appeal to any appearances of the Risen Christ. Paul systematizes this earlier thinking in his view of Christianity:

> Le paulinisme est une religion du "Seigneur", c'est-à-dire du Messie élevé au rang suprême et devenu le prince du monde futur par l'acte de Dieu qui l'a fait triompher de la mort.[7]

His more important contribution was, however, in the field of soteriology, where the justification, redemption and transfiguration of the sinner may all be seen as consequences of the resurrection of Christ. It is only in 'popular faith', of which evidence is to be found in the Synoptic Gospels and parts of Acts, that we find the need for appearance narratives. These are works of edification, and therefore care is needed in taking them at face value − for instance, the predictions of the Passion, including the references to the Resurrection, are all *vaticinia ex eventu* (elaborations in fact of an original logion in Luke 17,25). Even the appearance narratives say little of the resurrection event itself; their emphasis falls on the consequences of that event; and the idea in Luke-Acts that the Christophanies were limited in number shows that they were written at a time when such experiences had ceased and they were becoming materialised and codified into articles of faith.

If one examines the documents belonging to the phase of 'Deutero-paulinism' (Ephesians, Pastorals, I Peter, Hebrews, Revelation), we find that none of them refer to the appearances; for each writer the resurrection of Christ is subsumed in notions of exaltation, variously expressed as victory over death or evil powers, accession to heavenly life and all as a means of the be-

---

6 *Op. cit.* p26.
7 *Ibid* p40.

liever's salvation. Concerning the Fourth Gospel, Goguel repeats what he said in his article of 1930. The Farewell Discourses show that 'l'action du Christ glorifié se confond avec celle de l'Esprit'[8]. The emphasis is not so much upon the appearances as upon the resumed action of Christ and so the resurrection narratives may well be no more than 'l'expression symbolique d'une vérité d'ordre spirituel'[9]. Christ's victory begins with his incarnation and is concluded in his being raised to the Father through the Cross and the resurrection does not therefore have a separate role in Johannine soteriology. The Apostolic Fathers add little or nothing to ideas already found in the New Testament.

This first investigation reveals therefore an evolution in Christian doctrine, from the essential belief, which is 'la certitude de la vie céleste de Jésus' to 'un objet de croyance ... la preuve de la vérité de la doctrine chrétienne'[10]. There is also a development from the earlier idea of the resurrection as an act of God towards the opinion that Christ returned to life through his own power. Goguel concludes this survey with some reflections on the origins of the resurrection idea. In spite of certain resemblances, it is to be distinguished from the worship of dying and rising gods in the Ancient World, because it is based upon the personal adhesion of the disciples to Jesus which began before his death. Whatever the differences, it was their earthly Master who returned.

S'il y a, à certains égards, une différence et même une opposition entre les idées et la foi des disciples pendant le ministère de Jésus et celles du christianisme primitif, elles ont eu le même objet. C'est cet objet qui a pris des caractères nouveaux qu'il n'avait pas auparavant.[11]

The Gospels, written from the standpoint of Easter faith, tend to obscure this continuity, but in reality resurrection faith may be seen as the prolongation of the certainty in the mind of Jesus that the Kingdom of God would be realised in the face of all apparent setbacks.

The lengthy analysis of the accounts of the resurrection to which Goguel next turns is subdivided into four sections: The Tomb, The Appearances, The Ascension, The Descent into Hell. Within the

---

8 *Ibid* p89.
9 *Ibid* p91.
10 *Ibid* p105.
11 *Ibid* p110.

compass of this study, it will be impossible to summarise all the details of exegesis and criticism, occupying nearly 300 pages in the original. The best procedure is, therefore, to provide, under Goguel's own headings, the main conclusions, together with distinctive features of the argument.

The Burial of Jesus

There seems to have been an evolution in the tradition: at first Jesus was said to have been buried by Jews, for reasons of ritual purity, then later, to have been decently buried by a friend or friends, only given names at a later stage. This variety in the tradition leads Goguel to agree with Bultmann that there was a historical kernel for the story of the burial, against the view of Loisy that it is legendary.

The Burial and the Empty Tomb

Difficulties in the account of the women's visit to the tomb show that the story of its discovery empty was not organically linked in origin with that of the burial. Attempts made by Luke, by John and by the Gospel of Peter to attenuate the hiatus between the dispersal of the disciples and their reassembly on Easter Day are literary devices. This confirms that Jesus was buried by the Jews in a place not noted at the time by his followers.

The Third Day

A number of possibilities converge to explain why it was decided that Jesus rose on the morning of 'the third day': Old Testament phraseology, various cultic and mythological usages, (including possibly Christian observance of 'the Lord's Day'), the popular conception that the soul remained in the body for three days after death, the Talmudic idea that the general resurrection will take place three days after the end of the world. The fixing of a specific time may have marked the change from the 'passive' notion of God raising Jesus to the more 'active' idea that the body was reanimated by the Logos within.

The Empty Tomb

Goguel concludes that there were three stages in the development of the tradition:
(a) The fact of the empty tomb was in itself sufficient proof of

Christ's victory over death, conceived as his elevation to a heavenly life. There are no 'pure' examples of this type, although there was originally one such at the conclusion of Matthew.

(b) The significance of the empty tomb was made explicit by the intervention of angels, commenting on the event and asserting the resurrection. (In these first two stages, the empty tomb tradition was separate from that of the Christophanies).

(c) *Either* the discovery of the empty tomb is employed as an introduction to the appearance stories (as in Mark, and in an earlier stage of the composition of Matthew); *or* an appearance is introduced into the story of the discovery (John), or is directly juxtaposed to it (Matthew).

The impetus for this development came first, from the necessity to combine the Christophanies and the empty tomb stories, then from the need to supply precise information of a demonstrative kind to reinforce resurrection faith, and thirdly from the polemical intentions so apparent in Matthew 27 and 28. During the development no verification of the events was possible, because of distances in time and place and the uncertainty surrounding the burial. The most important general conclusion is that the empty tomb tradition must have preceded that of the appearances:

> La tradition sur le tombeau vide est certainement antérieure à la constitution de la tradition sur les apparitions, sans quoi il n'aurait jamais existé de récits parlant du tombeau vide sans parler en même temps des apparitions ... On pourrait supposer que les récits sur le tombeau vide sont nés en Galilée ... Le thème du tombeau vide n'aurait pas ... eu originairement le caractère de la constatation d'un fait, il aurait été déduit de la certitude que l'on avait de la vie céleste du Christ.[12]

The Meaning of the Empty Tomb and the Resurrection

One might have expected an early account of the body leaving the tomb but such materialism was excluded by the essentially spiritual conception which was held. Many texts in antiquity contain the motif of a disappearing corpse interpreted as a sign of assumption into heaven. This must have been the first 'message' of the empty tomb but it gave rise to problems in Christian thought and it became necessary to establish the resurrection and the exaltation of Jesus by other means. Fortunately there were those who had seen Jesus alive after his death and so the appearances tradition was developed. The

---

12 *Ibid* p201.

Old Testament examples of Enoch, Moses and Elijah can also be cited in favour of this earlier notion of an assumption into heaven, which is in striking harmony with the idea of Christ's heavenly glorified life in Pauline theology. Mt. 27,51–3 might be very old, signifying the immediate entry of Jesus into heaven. In the Gospel of Peter, the tomb opens but Jesus returns to heaven before the appearances.

Paul's Witness Concerning the Appearances

In I Corinthians 15,3–5 the burial of Jesus confirms his death and the appearances his resurrection. The lack of appearance narratives need not imply that Paul was ignorant of them, just as he may have been aware of the empty tomb tradition although 'son expérience personnelle ne lui permettait pas de concevoir une autre démonstration de la résurrection que celle qui résultait des apparitions'.[13] The 'five hundred brethren at once' cannot refer to the Day of Pentecost, because, although a connection between the Christophanies and the effusion of the Holy Spirit exists, Paul kept them separate. On the question of the appearance to Paul himself, Goguel claims that Paul did not include subsequent visions of the Lord which he received, because all the initial Christophanies listed had features in common, viz. they created resurrection faith (and in most cases included a call to the apostolate) and they were conveyed to men in a normal wakeful state, without ecstasy. However, 'la différence ... entre les christophanies et les visions reste de pure forme'.[14]

The Gospel Narratives

Mark knew of appearances in Galilee, to the disciples and to women of the company, with a special role for Peter. Matthew's appearance to the women is a late tradition; that to the disciples in Galilee includes some early elements, eg. the motif of doubt and the assurance of the spiritual presence of Christ. Luke's Emmaus Road story is a little masterpiece, whose absence of material features shows it to be 'archaïque' if not 'primitif'. It is not therefore an allegory of the Eucharist and is in marked contrast with the following appearance in the room in Jerusalem, which combines elements of doubt and certainty, material 'proofs' and the fulfilment of Scripture. In

---

13 *Ibid* p253.
14 *Ibid* p272.

John 20,19–23 the first greeting of Jesus and the display of his wounds are secondary features and therefore the original account was 'spiritual'; 20,26–29 is modelled on the former story but has an inbuilt contradiction. For the author 'une démonstration matérielle n'est pas nécessaire. La vraie foi peut s'en passer. Cependant la preuve matérielle déclarée superflue existe'.[15] John 21 contains independent traditions here combined by the editor: he may for instance have found the miraculous catch of fish in the Johannine signs source. The later ending to Mark takes its data from the Gospels, but is conceived somewhat in the manner of I Corinthians 15. In general, the diversity in the accounts is early and irreducible, reflecting spontaneous growth. Theological motifs abound: the theme of doubt is developed along apologetic lines, that of mission is central and authentic. The Galilee tradition is earlier than the Jerusalem tradition, the growth of the latter being explained by the importance of the Jerusalem community, the increasing stress upon the empty tomb tradition and the early decline of Christianity in Galilee.

Other Narratives

The Transfiguration is a transposed resurrection narrative which shows some affinities with Pauline theology; it suffered in the tendency to limit the number of Christophanies, perhaps being considered too 'spiritual'. The Gospel of Peter knows of the Galilee tradition and the Gospel of the Hebrews includes an appearance to James, which stems from ōphthē Iakōbō in I Corinthians 15. It is significant that orthodox writers of the second half of the third century were still appealing to non-canonical narratives.

The Ascension

The forty day period between resurrection and ascension is a comparatively late motif. For the author of Acts to have introduced this limited period and thus to have reduced the status of the Christophany to Paul, there must have been pressing reasons. It is probable that when visions and stories of visions multiplied in the early church they contained features which were Christologically dubious and open to polemic: it was therefore necessary to eliminate them. It was also necessary to explain why the visions had ceased and why the

---

15 *Ibid* p294.

tradition spoke of *physical* appearances of Christ on the one hand and, on the other, his heavenly assumption.

The Descent into Hell

In the early Christian centuries we find two traditions on this theme: a 'descensus-prédication' and a 'descensus-combat'. The first of these was current by the third quarter of the first century as evidenced by I Peter; but the second, mythical, idea is not necessarily linked with the general N.T. notion of Christ's victory over Satan and the supernatural powers and probably did not originate until the second half of the second century.

When introducing the third part of his work: La Psychologie des Christophanies, Goguel makes several general points, which are instructive for his position. Viewed psychologically, the rise of resurrection faith cannot have been sudden:

> *Natura non facit saltus*. Ce n'est pas au monde physique seulement que ce principe s'applique, c'est aussi au domaine psychologique et moral. La foi au triomphe de Jésus sur la mort ne s'est pas établie d'un seul coup. La femme porte de longs mois dans son sein l'enfant trop faible encore pour affronter la vie, il a fallu, de même, que la foi à la résurrection grandît lentement dans le coeur des disciples avant de pouvoir être publiquement proclamée.[16]

However, in this process one needs to distinguish between two types of Christophany: the first, most probably to Peter, which created a new faith and the more common type, of which Paul's experience is an example, which determined adhesion to a faith already constituted. Since there are no direct descriptions of the Petrine type, the psychology of the Christophanies must be studied from the case of Paul, considered in relation to parallel cases in the history of religions. An alternative to this psychological study would be the hypothesis that resurrection faith was produced by the influence of myths about dying and rising gods. Such an influence is discernible in the resurrection tradition, but if we ask whether it gave rise to the tradition, the answer must be no. Those who urge the parallels with the mystery religions as an explanation of the rise of Christianity commit the error of imagining that rites, myths and doctrines comprise the reality of religion, whereas they are only its

---

16 *Ibid* p394. For the *slow* awakening of resurrection faith according to Goguel cf. his review of Loisy, *La Naissance du christianisme*, RHPR XIV 1934 pp155–186, where he contests the idea that the disciples were persuaded of Jesus' imminent triumph immediately after his death.

expression. The true comparison is therefore on a psychological plane:

> ... il faut encore et il faut surtout comparer les sentiments et les émotions qui accompagnaient chez les chrétiens l'affirmation de la résurrection de Jésus à ceux que pouvaient éprouver les adeptes des mystères.[17]

Viewed in this light resurrection faith must be different in kind from the Mysteries, since it can be traced directly to the impression produced by the person of Jesus; the heroes of the mystery religions belong to a mythical antiquity. Thus Goguel reaffirms religious experience as the controlling category to be used in the analysis of early resurrection faith. On the one hand, this experience may be compared with that of other times, places and religions; but it is also to be regarded as *sui generis*, given the continuity of the historical Jesus and the glorified Christ in the experience of the first believers.

In providing some parallels for the resurrection stories, Goguel selects examples of visions from Christian history: those of Edmond Schérer, the Sadhu Sundar Singh, the Jew Ratisbonne and the recent report of visions of the Virgin at Ezquioga (1931). From a short examination of these, he concludes that they display two types of faith, that which produces the vision and inversely, that which is produced or at least reinforced by the vision. These are not identical.

> La première jaillit des profondeurs de la conscience dans laquelle elle s'est élaborée sous l'influence de causes qu'il n'est possible de discerner qu'en partie et dans lesquelles reste roujours un résidu, une inconnue rebelle à une analyse vraiment exhaustive. La foi qu'engendre ou fortifie la vision est, au contraire, consciente et s'accompagne d'une traduction intellectuelle, même quand, aux yeux du sujet, elle est une expérience de réalités sprituelles qui échappent aux moyens ordinaires de connaître.[18]

Here is no vicious circle but an ascending line, bringing faith from the unconscious into the conscious mind, although this ascent may not always be observed by the subject himself. If the conscious mind provides much resistance, there may be an explosion of the faith which has built up in the unconscious, whose shattering effect is eminently favourable to the production of visions. This was so with Paul, who had been subconsciously influenced by the new view of God preached by Jesus, a God who required personal and not legal morality. On this basis we may assume that even the first vision, that of Peter, was preceded by the conviction of the 'vie céleste du Christ'.

---

17 *Ibid* p400.
18 *Ibid* p419.

Thus the psychological chain of events can be reconstructed as follows: the disciples' Messianic beliefs during the lifetime of Jesus; the first vision; an epidemic of visions to those who had known Jesus; appearances to a wider circle (including perhaps the five hundred brethren); then rarification (Paul believed he had received the last); finally stabilisation, when resurrection faith was no longer the expression of a mystical experience, but became an affirmation of fact, shortly to become a dogma[19]. One may not speak of abnormal psychology in the first Christophanies; any mental disturbance was only accidental and of brief duration, natural indeed as an accompaniment to the emergence of a new religion[20].

Goguel's conclusions arc alrcady apparent from the body of his work. Resurrection faith is based on the conviction that Jesus was not finally overcome by death and, as the reaffirmation of hopes already placed in him during his lifetime, it is only new in its form, not in its religious substance or psychological origins[21]. This is a *saving* faith:

> ... c'est par sa vie céleste que le Christ sauve les pécheurs. Tout le reste, tombeau vide, apparitions, ascension, n'est que la manifestation et la démonstration de cette vie céleste.[22]

Because of the 'commonsense' anthropology of the early Christian milieu, this 'vie céleste' could not be purely spiritual, hence the tradition of the empty tomb. Such was the intensity of the new faith, that it was projected and materialised in ecstatic visions. But the alleged 'facts' are the expression of primary feelings and only necessary insofar as any feeling must be conceptualised in order to be expressed. The requirements of preaching and apologetic led to the elaboration of the full cycle of empty tomb-appearances-ascension, with the accompanying shift of emphasis from 'la manifestation d'un être céleste' to 'Jésus réanimé'[23]. The whole process was artless and

---

19 Goguel here quotes in support of his argument Bergson's distinction between dynamic and static religion in the latter's recently published *Les Deux Sources de la Morale et de la Religion* (1932). Bergson's idea of 'la fonction fabuleuse de la religion' found in the same work, is also used by Goguel, with regard to the rise of the resurrection narratives.

20 Goguel disagreed, for example with Loisy's use of the word 'illusions': 'Au lieu d'illusions, je parlerais plus volontiers d'expressions et de symboles et de leur adaptation à des situations qui se transforment' (*RHPR* 1934 p172).

21 Goguel asserts this contra Bultmann, 'Urchristentum und Religionsgeschichte' *ThR* NF IV 1932.

22 *Op.cit.* p440.

23 *Ibid* p448.

uncontrived. For instance, those who received the first visions 'unconsciously' reversed the real order of things and came themselves to believe that their faith was based on having seen Jesus alive after his death, rather than on their prior conviction that he was alive in ʻheaven. Having concluded that the tomb must have been empty, believers 'spontaneously' imagined the story of the women's visit. In all of this we see factors at work which are universal in religion. There is first 'la tendance à faire de l'histoire l'expression et la démonstration de la foi, à la constituer en histoire sainte'[24] Then there is the evolution from 'une conviction individuelle dérivant d'une expérience personnelle' to 'la reconnaissance d'un fait objectivement établi'. And finally there is the movement from 'des expériences et une foi qui sont celles d'individus ou de groupes fermés' to 'une doctrine et une foi qui puissent être celles d'une Eglise qui s'étend et tend à devenir universelle'. Thus the New Testament reveals how the character of resurrection faith changed: 'Elle n'a plus été l'aboutissement de la foi; elle en est devenu le point de départ'[25] .

Goguel's critics, in writing about *La Foi à la résurrection dans le christianisme primitif,* have naturally fastened upon his presuppositions, which so obviously control his presentation of the evidence[26]. His faithfulness to the symbolo-fideism of Sabatier and Ménégoz is reflected in his recurrent vocabulary. A key phrase to which he frequently returns is that of the 'vie céleste' of Christ as the object of the earliest Christian conviction. The conviction is 'intérieure, religieuse', it is 'une affirmation de foi' and hence 'une phénomène psychologique', a matter of 'des faits intérieurs et subjectifs'. In suggesting that true resurrection faith is the glorification or exaltation of Christ (found, for example in Paul and in the Fourth Gospel as originally conceived);in stating that this faith was 'materialised', 'concretised' and 'projected' in the 'popular faith' of the appearance narratives and in positing a trend away from the 'religious experience' of the individual or closed group towards 'dogma'

---

24 *Ibid* p454.
25 *Ibid* p455.
26 V. e.g. L. de Grandmaison, *Jésus-Christ* ([5]1931) Vol.II pp498–9 (with reference to Goguel's paper at the Congrès Renan); Lagrange in *RB* 1933 pp569–583; P. de Haes, *La Résurrection de Jésus dans l'apologétique des cinquante dernières années* (1953) Ch.5; H. Grass, *Ostergeschehen und Osterberichte* ([4]1970) *passim.*

and 'sacred history', Goguel was proposing a Liberal Protestant view, which saw a process of decline, or at least compromise, at work in early Christianity[27]. It is obvious that in this presentation he had to force some of the material into his mould. For instance, the idea that the earliest significance of the empty tomb was that of an assumption into heaven is very ill documented and the idea that 'spiritual' accounts of appearances (eg. the Emmaus walk) must have preceded more 'materialistic' accounts (eg. the upper room of Luke 24) is not easy to substantiate.

So Goguel's claim to operate as a historian is called into question. In spite of his attacks upon positivistic historiography and his advocacy of a sympathetic appreciation of 'religious' elements in early Christianity, he does not do full justice to the problems of faith and history in the resurrection material. His key is of course to be found in the 'psychological' reconstruction of the original chain of events: when he provides this outline in the final chapter, it is seen to be the controlling structure for all the previous exegesis and speculation. But, in spite of the parallels taken from other episodes in religious history, it is not at all clear that the structure is appropriate. For example, the evolutionary dictum of Leibniz: *Natura non facit saltus* inevitably clashes with the New Testament notion of the Christ-event inaugurating a new age, qualitatively different from the old. The comparatively smooth transition, in psychological terms, from the disciples' Messianic faith in Jesus during his lifetime to their subsequent resurrection faith runs counter to elements of bewilderment, doubt and surprise in the tradition. More generally, Goguel does not sufficiently acknowledge the paucity of psychological data in his sources upon which to base his reconstruction. Although he recognises the theological tendencies in the sources, he does not see that these are more determinative than psychological factors and that his speculations require a more solid foundation than the Lucan accounts of the conversion of Paul, upon which so much is made to depend. On the other hand, his excursions into the comparative study of religious psychology, although an appropriate

27 Cf. A. Sabatier, *Les religions d'autorité et la religion de l'esprit* (1903) pp514—5: 'Toute tendance à matérialiser et à localiser la religion, à supprimer la liberté de l'Esprit de Dieu, à en compromettre la transcendance par rapport à toutes les créations et institutions contingentes de l'historie, reste entachée de paganisme.'

line of enquiry before the lay audience of EPHE, were not entirely happy. A wider range of comparisons needed to be surveyed and having once admitted the comparative principle, he might have been more willing to use parallel material from Antiquity and not to have made such an absolute antithesis between the Mystery religions and his own reconstruction.

Nevertheless, this work remains an important individual achievement. Not only did Goguel maintain a comparative independence of current trends in New Testament scholarship[28] but he sustained his determinedly historical stance throughout an exhaustive enquiry. Even if his desire to avoid a theological treatment blinded him to theological elements in the documents themselves, his painstaking survey of all the relevant sources, in an area at once theologically sensitive and historically obscure, is a reminder of the need for contributions on this subject which are free of apologetics, whether Christian or anti-Christian.

4.6 PREPARATORY WORK FOR 'LA NAISSANCE DU CHRISTIANISME' AND 'L'EGLISE PRIMITIVE'.

During the years 1920–1939, apart from works already considered, Goguel wrote approximately 30 articles which can be compared to building-bricks for his historical edifice. Taken together they do not however comprise an architect's plan: many sections of the two large volumes on early Christianity are not represented among them, and a greater proportion of them deal with Paul and his theology than is allotted to the apostle in the final construction. But the resulting pile of separate studies was an impressive sign of work in progress on the series 'Jésus et les origines du Christianisme' which had been inaugurated by La Vie de Jésus of 1932. Moreover they reveal trends and underlying assumptions, as well as historical judgements, which were to be taken up into the final synthesis. A brief account of this preparatory labour should therefore be included at this point.

Whereas for Loisy, Paul was anathema, he was Goguel's favourite subject and, perhaps because the final plan and proportions of La Naissance du christianisme and L'Eglise primitive did not allow for

---

28 As noted by the Catholic critic P. de Haes, who characterises Goguel's method as 'un éclecticisme raffiné et souple' (op.cit. p200).

a complete exposition of Paul's views, Goguel was to return to the apostle in a series of articles written in his final years[1]. In the articles of the 1930s he seized upon precisely those features which antagonised Loisy in Paul and his interpreters: religious experience and certain inconsistencies, which for Loisy meant multiple authorship, but which signified to Goguel a direct outpouring of experience, inevitably unsystematic[2]. In writing on 'Paulinisme et johannisme' (an article significantly subtitled 'deux théologies ou deux formes d'expérience religieuse?') Goguel suggests that in Paul's thought the movement is 'from the experience to the formula' while in the second Christian generation that order is reversed[3].

We have seen that Goguel differed from many Protestant exegetes in his view of Paul's conversion and this is expressed in an article of 1934 in the words: 'La conversion de Paul n'a pas été précédée par une crise morale, mais elle en a provoqué une'. It was Paul's Christian experience, originating in his conversion, which explains apparent inconsistencies between Philippians 3,6 and Romans 7. In particular, his experience of the sacrificial death of Christ removed the prop of the Jewish sacrificial system and his missionary experience removed the idea of a special indulgence of God for the Jewish people. Under that indulgence he would have been safe (cf. Philippians 3,6) but now as a Christian he feels keenly the moral dilemma expressed in Romans 7.[4]

Paul was the founder of the Christian sacraments. Prior to Paul, baptism and the Eucharist were purely eschatological, anticipatory of a future salvation; but Paul's experience led him to interpret them as the expression and the means of obtaining union with Christ and as the starting points of salvation in the present. Paul, as a man of his time, saw no dichotomy between the sacraments and faith, the

---

1 'Ce que l'Eglise doit à l'Apôtre Paul' *RHPR* XXVIII—XXIX 1948—9 pp1—29; 'Le paulinisme, théologie de liberté' *Revue de Théologie et de Philosophie* 1951 pp92—104, 175—183; 'Le caractère, à la fois actuel et futur, du salut dans la théologie paulinienne' in *Studies in honour of C.H. Dodd* (1956) pp322—341.

2 Cf. Goguel's reviews of Loisy, *Naissance du christianisme* in *RHPR* XIV 1934 pp155—86 and of *Remarques sur la littérature épistolaire du Nouveau Testament* in *RHPR* XVI 1936 pp508—17; for details v. below 5.1.

3 *RHPR* X 1930 pp504—526; XI 1931 pp129—156.

4 '*Kata dikaiosunēn tēn en nomō genomenos amemptos* (Phil.3,6) Remarques sur un aspect de la conversion de Paul' *Journal of Biblical Literature and Exegesis* LIII 1934 pp257—268.

symbol and the reality[5].

Paul's theology can be described as an 'apocalypse' because it presents a cosmic drama of salvation. But the Jewish framework has been adapted so that the centre of gravity falls in the past (the Cross) and in the present (the moral and religious experience of the individual who appropriates salvation). Thus apocalyptic is 'actualised', although the cosmic transformation is still awaited. Paul never quite co-ordinated these psychological and cosmic strands, and further apparent inconsistencies arise because he drew upon two types of dualism: Jewish, which was dynamic, temporal and collective; and Greek, which was static, spatial and individual. But by the 'actualisation' and 'spiritualisation' of apocalyptic Paul introduced into Christian thought a 'sense of the beyond' and avoided the extremes of millenarian fanaticism and Gnostic speculation[6].

The more general articles on early Christianity of this period betray similar preoccupations as in the case of Paul, because they centre upon the problem of unity and diversity[7]. Again, religious experience is invoked as a partial solution but a large place is also assigned to sociological explanations.

Loisy had said that Jesus preached the Kingdom but it was the Church which came. Goguel prefers to say that the Church was the necessary form assumed by the followers of Jesus in order to ensure the survival of his work[8]. The formation of a church can be explained by the burgeoning of individual religious experience into a collective experience by means of moral, spiritual and intellectual contagion and also by the sociological forces which bring believers together and create the requisite organisms for stability and autonomy[9]. These

---

5 'Le rôle de l'apôtre Paul dans la constitution des sacrements chrétiens' *RHR* CXVII 1938 pp171–204.

6 'Le caractère et le rôle de l'élément cosmologique dans la sotériologie paulinienne' *RHPR* XV 1935 pp335–359; 'L'apocalypse paulinienne' *Revue de théologie et de philosophie* N.S. XXVII 1939 pp33–47.

7 'Quelques remarques sur l'unité de l'Eglise dans le christianisme primitif' *Bulletin de la faculté libre de théologie protestante de Paris* Mai 1936 pp1–9; 'Tu es Petrus' *Ibid* Juillet 1938 pp1–13; 'Le problème de l'Eglise dans le christianisme primitif' *RHPR* XVIII 1938 pp293–320; 'Unité et diversité dans le christianisme primitif' *Ibid* XIX 1939 pp1–54; 'L'idée de l'Eglise dans le Nouveau Testament' in *Origine et nature de l'Eglise* (1939) pp51–80. The following paragraphs summarise the main conclusions of these articles.

8 *Origine et nature* ... p62.

9 *RHPR* 1938 p318; *Origine et nature* ... p59.

two types of explanation can be called the absolute and contingent, the divine and human, the supernatural and natural, the ideal and empirical; both must be kept in view to understand the origins of Christianity[10]. There was always the danger that formulae would replace experience but forms of organisation were required to define the new group as a separate entity, just as doctrine, discipline and ritual were required to keep alive the awareness of a 'new religious object'.[11]

Diversity was present from an early stage (cf. the 'Hebrews' and 'Hellenists' of the first community in Jerusalem). Walter Bauer in *Rechtgläubigkeit und Ketzerei im ältesten Christentum* (1934) showed to Goguel's satisfaction that the old myth of a pristine unity destroyed by ambitious men was forever shattered in favour of a historical development from diversity to unity[12]. There were two main types of early Christianity[13]. One was represented by Jerusalem and was apostolic, dynastic, non-charismatic, non-democratic and provisional, since thoughts of Christ were confined to the past and to the future. The other, represented by Antioch, was prophetic, eschatological rather than provisional, 'Christocratic', with a concept of *ecclesia* both local and universal, corresponding to the distinction between empirical and ideal. Other evidence of diversity is provided by the coexistence of Hellenistic 'mystical' Christianity and the moralising Christianity of the Didache and James and also by the various 'heresies' envisaged in the New Testament writings. These latter may be categorised into two types: those which, if successful, would have radically changed Christianity, such as the gnosis attacked in Colossians and Ephesians, and those which were the survival of archaic forms, such as the Ebionites castigated in I John[14] and the Nicolaitans in Revelation[15].

Historically, however, the most important single development was the combination of the Jerusalem and Antioch types to form a 'précatholicisme' which is evidenced by such writings as I Clement

---

10 *Origine et nature* ... pp55—6; *RHPR* 1938 p319.
11 *Origine et nature* ... pp59—61.
12 *Bulletin* ... 1936 pp3ff; *RHPR* 1939 p15.
13 *Origine et nature* ... pp66ff; *RHPR* 1938 pp293ff; *ibid* 1939 pp6ff.
14 Goguel claimed that I John 2, 18—27 is aimed at a group which had a different conception of the Messiahship of Jesus than the writer's and which he therefore considered a negation of Messiahship; cf. *La Naissance du Christianisme* p400.
15 *RHPR* 1939 p12.

and the Pastoral Epistles[16]. One significant event leading to this synthesis was the expulsion of Peter by James from Jerusalem in 44 A.D. The Church of Jerusalem became hardened in its attitudes, and did not, for instance, offer any support to Paul, in spite of the collection he organised and his desire, during his final visit, to have the recognition of his Gentile mission renewed. His personal faith could not withstand the sociological pressure of the Jerusalem Christians but his universalism and anti-ritualism triumphed after the destruction of Jerusalem in 70 A.D.[17] It should not be thought however, according to Goguel, that the whole of early Christianity was dominated by the rift between Paul and Jerusalem, as the Tübingen school had supposed.[18] Other factors were involved in the making of *précatholicisme*. For example, the geographical centre of gravity shifted; Judaism itself became a 'church', so that Christianity had to develop distinctive forms of organisation[19]; Christology played a sociological role in providing sharp definition of the specific and transcendent nature of the 'new religious object';[20] there was a sense of tradition, bolstered by appeals to the Old Testament and by the ritual practices of Christians and a sense of unity, which Paul had helped to foster with his concept of the 'body of Christ'[21]

From the Jerusalem type of Christianity, *précatholicisme* took the idea of an apostolic foundation (a 'fiction' but not a 'fraud') and this was personified in Peter, who over against Paul provided a link between the Church and Jesus[22]. From the Antioch type, as further defined by Paul, it took the idea of a religious society both human and divine, which was better able to account for the delay of the Parousia. Moreover, Hellenistic Christianity had developed critiques of legalism (cf. in their different ways I Corinthians and I John) and ontological thinking in the realm of Christology which were further powerful factors in the triumph of universalism[23].

---

16 *Bulletin* ... 1936 p8; *Origine et nature* ... p74; *RHPR* 1938 pp293ff.
17 *RHPR* 1939 p31.
18 *Ibid* p28.
19 *Ibid* pp33ff.
20 *Ibid* pp46–7.
21 *Ibid* p50.
22 Goguel notes however that the *Tu es Petrus* pericope in Matt. 16 has notable affinities with Ephesians and thus represents a confluence of Petrine and Pauline traditions (*Bulletin* ... 1938 p13).
23 *RHPR* 1939 p38.

We have already noted how, on the question of the resurrection, Goguel showed too great a confidence in the ability of his sources to yield up psychological data and this confidence is similarly misplaced in the case of Paul and certain other areas of the early Church. Even if there are more psychological data for Paul than for the resurrection tradition, we have seen from Goguel's own treatment of Paul's 'moral crisis' how widely these data can be interpreted. But Goguel was surely right to maintain that the Pauline literature does not offer a complete systematic theology and his explanations for inconsistencies in Paul, where they do not lean too heavily upon 'religious experience' constitute a useful midway position between, on the one hand, Loisy's counsel of despair and on the other hand, the philosophical schemata to be employed by Bultmann in his *Theologie des Neuen Testaments* of a few years later[24]. Goguel's own schemata are more apparent in his overview of the early Church. He correctly identifies the diversity of opinions held and the variety of forces operative in early Christianity but he too readily associates these with some of his own preconceived antitheses. For example, it is very doubtful if the distinction between the local and the universal ecclésia is correctly described as that between the empirical and the ideal; or that the conflict between Paul and the church of Jerusalem is best explained as individual religious experience versus sociological forces. Goguel is ambiguous concerning whatever is formulated, collective and sociological because on the one hand these are, by observation, necessary features of any religious movement, but they seem to be synonymous in his mind for whatever is contingent, human and natural. This category confusion is clearly seen in Goguel's preference for the Christianity of Antioch over that of Jerusalem, not only because the former was to triumph but also because it provided a matrix for the individual, prophetic faith of Paul. Paulinism provided Goguel with a norm and most nearly approximated in his view to the absolute, the divine, the supernatural and the ideal[25]. But when he came to write his final volumes, this Protestant conviction was sufficiently tempered by his historical grasp of

---

24 Bultmann's existentialist categories were already apparent in, for example, his article on 'Romans VII and the Anthropology of Paul' of 1932 (ET in *Existence and Faith*, Fontana edition (1964) pp173—185).

25 We are here deliberately leaving out of consideration Goguel's estimate of Jesus himself, to whom such a statement might *a fortiori* apply, in order to confine our attention to the early Church.

ideas and events for gross distortion to be avoided and for the real complexities of the history of early Christianity to be exhaustively investigated.

4.7 CONCLUSIONS

Goguel's vast output during this twenty-year period is comparable to that of Loisy. But whereas Loisy had personal motives to establish his independence in the face of all contenders by means of his immense labours, Goguel's concerns were more general and more disinterested. Like Guignebert, he wished to contribute to the enlightenment of the educated French public, especially when he thought the public was being led astray, as in the case of Couchoud's activities. He doubtless also wished to maintain the tradition of French Protestant scholarship, which could be traced back to the *Revue de Strasbourg* group, which had always made a strong contribution to EPHE and which had produced its most eminent representative in his own teacher Auguste Sabatier[1]. This tradition was out of all proportion to the numbers of French Protestants and it was possibly to compensate for the lack of fellow workers that Goguel published so copiously. Unfortunately this also led to a certain prolixity of style which at times obscured his basic ability to make clear and incisive distinctions in dealing with New Testament problems.

We have already observed the confessionalism which is apparent in much of Goguel's work and which Loisy was quick to seize upon in reviewing successive volumes as they appeared. It was not of course any kind of ecclesiastical orthodoxy, nor even for that matter a particular brand of Christianity that transpired out of Goguel's work. One must always remember that he placed 'religion' above 'Christianity'. Rather, it was a set of assumptions inherited from Liberal Protestantism concerning the primacy of experience over dogma, of individual personality over the collectivity, of 'reality' over 'symbol'. These assumptions provided Goguel with criteria in his estimate of early Christianity, but, accepting that every historian

---

1 In his inaugural lecture at EPHE Goguel mentioned that Renan's *Vie de Jésus* did not help French Biblical scholarship; it had the effect: 'de compromettre ou, en tout cas, de retarder l'éducation critique de l'opinion que l'école de Strasbourg commençait à faire'. *RHR* XCVI 1927 p318.

in that field needs working criteria, one could wish that Goguel's had been more consciously chosen and more adequately justified.

It is certain that Goguel wished to avoid appearing to be a confessional writer. His works were published by 'scientific' presses and even when he was writing for his own Protestant Faculty he took historical subjects and seldom ventured into the hortatory style. At the most, in his contribution to the series *Origine et nature de l'Eglise*, he stated that the ideal of the Church was betrayed when the Church on earth arrogates to itself the place of the Kingdom of God; that the Church can be a means of grace provided this is to the glory of God; and that the balance between the ideal and the empirical etc. has to be achieved in practice rather than by theory.[2] These are hardly more than anodyne Protestant sentiments. He also saw himself as a fellow worker with Loisy and Guignebert. In his review of Loisy's *Naissance du christianisme* he lists agreements and disagreements between himself and the other two critics to show that there is considerably more overlap between all three than might commonly be supposed[3].

More difficult to assess is his refusal to be associated with either the *religionsgeschichtliche Schule* or the *formgeschichtliche Methode*. We have seen how in the case of the latter he was repelled by confessional elements in the writers, as well as by their techniques and conclusions. His rejection of comparative studies may however owe something to his own confessionalism, revealed in his insistence upon the specificity of early Christianity. This of course could simply be a matter of historical judgement and of his commitment to the historical method, but it is also reflected in his life-time pre-occupation with the New Testament documents. His historical work took him into the Apostolic Fathers and other second-century Christian literature, but his abiding devotion was to the historico-literary exegesis of the canonical documents and this marks him out as a *Neutestamentler,* rather than a historian of antiquity or a historian of religions. So his refusal to align himself with any school of criticism, or on the other hand with any kind of Protestant orthodoxy (whether it were the older fundamentalism or the neo-orthodoxy of the Barthians) attest both his independence and his rootedness in a long academic tradition. If there is an important distinction to be observed

---

2 *Op.cit.* pp62, 79.
3 *RHPR* XIV 1934 pp156, 170. For details v. below 5.1.

between 'Church historians' and 'historians of Christianity', then Goguel, by contrast with Loisy and Guignebert, veers towards the former category. But it has to be added immediately that, even if he hoped that his historical work would be of use to systematic theologians, he genuinely tried to write without apologetical intent. Germany had long provided examples of radical solutions to problems of Christian origins being propounded from within the academico-ecclesiastical 'establishment'. It was Goguel's achievement to continue this tradition but in a French setting where, in the Catholic estimate, he belonged to the independents and where, in the independents' estimate, he was too confessional. In that situation we do best to leave him with his own preferred title of 'historian', but a historian who might well have reflected more profoundly upon the problems of historiography and upon the conditioned nature of his own historical judgements.

5. *THE RESULTS*

5.1 *THREE CRITICS:INTERACTION*

It has been possible to review the work of our three critics separately, because personal and institutional factors prevented them from forming a close academic grouping or 'school'. Even their close physical proximity on the Left Bank in Paris did not encourage any regular collaboration. Loisy at the Collège de France was separated from Guignebert at the Sorbonne by the mere width of the rue St. Jacques. This same street becomes the rue du Faubourg St. Jacques and issues onto the Boulevard Arago, opposite the Protestant Faculty, where Goguel taught. Goguel also taught at the Sorbonne, both at EPHE and in the Faculté des Lettres; Loisy had two brief periods of tenure at EPHE. But they were only professional colleagues in the general sense of working in the same field, reading and reviewing each other's publications and occasionally speaking at the same gatherings[1]. It is true that Guignebert had social connections with Loisy. The two men were in frequent communication over the Congrès Loisy of 1927 and Loisy's diary of 1930–32 records numerous visits by Guignebert and Mlle. Brunot[2]. But Loisy's monastic existence in the centre of Paris from each November to May and his absence at Ceffonds for the rest of the year did not encourage a partnership[3]. Loisy, although senior to Guignebert by ten years, survived to write his obituary. Goguel was in any case the junior of Loisy by twenty-three years and that of Guignebert by thirteen years and outlived them both, so that he was able to assess their total output. Here we shall provide some brief indications of the responses

---

1 All three participated in the Congrès Renan of 1923 and the Congrès Loisy of 1927. Goguel and Guignebert shared the platform of the 'Union de libres penseurs et de libres croyants pour la culture morale' in 1926: cf. *Jésus et la conscience moderne* (1928).
2 BN n.a.f. 15663.
3 For descriptions of his austere life in Paris, v. Couchoud, *Le Dieu Jésus* (1955) pp43–6; M. Dell'Isola, *Alfred Loisy* (1957) *passim;* R. de Boyer de Sainte-Suzanne, *Alfred Loisy: entre la foi et l'incroyance* (1968) pp19–21.

to each other's work which are to be found in reviews, correspondence, speeches and obituaries.

We have already noted the welcome which Loisy extended to the *Manuel* of Guignebert[4] and also how he later took issue with Goguel for practising an over-literary analysis of the New Testament documents[5]. He could not of course accuse Goguel of confessional motivation when the latter refused to accept his own analysis of Acts and his theory of a 'style rythmé'; but, always quick to sniff out Protestant presuppositions, he was harsh in his rejection of Goguel's reply to the *mythologues*[6]. Loisy had given up his work as a reviewer before the final major volumes of Guignebert and Goguel began to appear in the 1930s but he spoke appreciatively of the achievement of Guignebert in an obituary:

> Déterminer aussi exactement que possible l'état moyen de la science historique touchant le christanisme, et principalement les origines chrétiennes, et présenter cette description avec toute la clarté désirable, former aussi des disciples capables de s'associer à cette grande oeuvre et de la continuer après lui, tel a été l'objet de la mission que Guignebert a voulu se donner.[7]

Guignebert always greeted the publications of Loisy with great respect and appreciation, including the non-scientific 'little red books': *La Religion* of 1917 is 'un beau livre et une belle action'[8]. He correctly read the *Mémoires* to conclude that Loisy had never been a rationalist and had always remained a religious man[9]. He agreed with 'Sylvain Leblanc' (Henri Bremond) that Loisy was 'un clerc qui n'a pas trahi'[10]. He had the highest praise for *Les Mystères païens et le Mystère chrétien* and commented, on the appearance of the second edition: 'J'ai éprouvé qu'il est admirablement propre à éveiller les curiosités et à les orienter'[11]. He differed slightly from Loisy on the latter's interpretation of Paul in *Les Mystères* ... and in the commentary on Galatians, wishing to place more emphasis on Paul's

---

4 Cf. above 2.1, n.10.
5 Cf. above 2.4, n.57; *Mém* III pp409—10.
6 Cf. above 2.5.2, n.38; *Mém* III pp456—7.
7 *RH* 1940 p179. Loisy's private opinion of Guignebert is expressed in a letter to Maria Dell'Isola of 2.12.35: 'M. Guignebert est en effet un savant très consciencieux, et pour moi un ami dévoué. Le malheur est que, laïque, il suit volontiers en exégèse les protestants libéraux qui n'entendent pas lâcher saint Paul.' (BN n.a.f. 16317).
8 *RH* 133 (1920) p335.
9 *RH* 169 (1932) p110.
10 *RH* 171 (1933) p589.
11 *RH* 171 (1933) p333.

background in Tarsus and Antioch[12], and he was surprised by the extremely literal translation and the strophic arrangement in *Les Livres du Nouveau Testament*[13]. He thought that Loisy's second commentary on the Fourth Gospel demonstrated soundly the essential connection between Paul and John[14]. He praised the 'doctrine si pleine, si ferme et si sage' of *La Naissance du Christianisme* and its associated volumes, dissenting only from Loisy's view that there was anti-Christian legislation as such before the third century and, more importantly, from the new treatment of the epistles. Guignebert concedes that it may be his 'long symbiosis' with the Pauline literature which prevents him from accepting Loisy's theories, but reserves the right to decide for himself. One is bound to be hesitant in the face of 'une restitution circonspecte, assurément, mais hardie, neuve et, pour tout dire, au regard du paulinisme, révolutionnaire'.[15] In his eulogy of Loisy at the 1927 Congrès, Guignebert said that he had been chosen to deliver it because 'je combats coude à coude avec vous, dans la même tranchée, pour la même cause'; Loisy has fulfilled Nature's expectations that he would be a ploughman: 'Vous avez longuement, profondément, mené la charrue aux champs du passé chrétien; vous y avez semé à pleine main le bon grain'[16].

Guignebert was more reserved in his estimate of Goguel but never less than friendly. He greeted *L'Evangile de Marc* ... (1909), on the Synoptic Problem, as 'solide, méthodique, nuancée, parfaitement claire'[17] but regretted that in *L'Eucharistie* (1910) Goguel relegated the pagan parallels to an appendix[18]. He considered that the *Introduction au Nouveau Testament* was 'indispensable', while dissenting from the degree of historicity which Goguel allowed to the Fourth Gospel, and expressing minor divergences of opinion about St. Paul. Goguel's treatment of Acts, if compared with that of Loisy, shows that the problems of its composition are still not resolved; it is however Loisy's treatment which will have prepared for the final solution[19].

---

12 *RH* 134 (1920) pp90, 96.
13 *RH* 153 (1926) pp75–6.
14 *RH* 153 (1926) p76.
15 *RH* 181 (1937) pp283–6.
16 *Congrès d'histoire du christianisme* t.1 (1928) pp9, 24.
17 *RH* 103 (1910) p353.
18 *RH* 107 (1911) p114.
19 *RH* 153 (1926) pp74–5.

Goguel is most strongly criticised for his over confidence in redis-
covering the historical Jesus. 'J'ai peur que la foi ne vienne au secours
de l'histoire en ses trop probables défaillances'.[20] In the *Vie de Jésus,*
Guignebert cannot even accept Goguel's proposed minimum of
information, and the use of 'psychology' and 'religious experience'
to eke out the meagre historical content reintroduces a subjective
element into criticism.

> M. Goguel estime que Loisy et moi-même minimisons à l'extrême, c'est-à-dire à l'excès.
> Nous estimons, nous, qu'il *conserve* jusqu'à la limite critique, c'est-à-dire au-delà ... Nul
> doute que de deux efforts également sincères, comme on été le sien et le mien, et de leur
> comparaison, il ne reste, en somme, un certain profit pour la science.[21]

Similar considerations apply to *La foi à la résurrection* ... : the
reconstruction relies too much on mysticism and metaphysics which,
however valuable, can only connect up with history in infinity,
beyond our reach. However, Guignebert did subscribe to Goguel's
conclusions in general, if not in detail, and he stressed this fundamental accord against confessional critics who seek to exploit the inevitable and desirable differences of opinion among independent critics.[22]

In direct reply to the reservations of Guignebert, Goguel, in reviewing *Jésus*[23], thinks that his fellow critic is too quick to suspect
confessional influences in works whose conclusions do not agree with
his own. He underestimates the role of individuals and he fails to see
that Hellenistic elements in early Christianity concerned the form
rather than the dynamism of the new religion: all Christology was
present in germ in the earliest resurrection faith, and the dynamism
goes back therefore to Jesus himself. The two critics have a different
outlook on religion itself:

> Il ne s'agit pas de *Werturteile* portés sur le christianisme mais de *Seinsurteile* non seule-
> ment sur le christianisme, mais sur la religion en général. Je conçois l'histoire du chris-
> tianisme comme l'histoire psychologique d'un sentiment religieux, de son extension, de
> ses transformations, de son expression et, si je puis dire, de son incarnation dans les
> doctrines, le culte, les institutions d'une Eglise. M. Guignebert y voit l'histoire de la
> formation d'une Eglise. Il est donc amené à attacher une importance décisive aux doc-
> trines.[24]

Guignebert treats Jesus and Christianity with respect but without

---

20 *RH* 161 (1929) p141.
21 *RH* 171 (1933) p560.
22 *RH* 181 (1937) p278.
23 *RHPR* 13 (1933) pp409–447.
24 *Art.cit.* p420.

the sympathy which is required in the study of religion. Goguel made similar points in his obituary of Guignebert[25]. While admiring much in his work, he feels bound to conclude that Guignebert's anti-theological positivism in the analysis and criticism of the texts almost amounted to 'une théologie négative', making him unnecessarily wary of some historically valid reconstructions. His distrust of psychological interpretations limited his attention to the exterior aspect of religious phenomena, at the expense of their 'dynamisme spirituel'.

Goguel's view of Loisy's Commentary on Acts has already been noted, in connection with his own *Introduction*[26] In a long review of Loisy's *La Naissance du Christianisme*[27] Goguel begins with a comparison between himself, Loisy and Guignebert, stressing the overlap of opinion. All agree that the problems of the Gospel narrative and of early Christianity are coinherent and that each can only be dealt with as a function of the other. Loisy and Guignebert see the Passion Narrative as a liturgical creation, while Goguel believes it to contain some historical elements. Guignebert denies any Messianic consciousness to Jesus and designates him a moral teacher whereas Loisy and Goguel think that he saw himself as an eschatological envoy with a divinely appointed role in the establishment of the Kingdom of God. Goguel and Guignebert cannot share Loisy's view of Paulinism being constituted by a series of additions to the Apostle's original letters. Of the many points of interpretation upon which Goguel disagrees with *La naissance du christianisme,* we may select the following. Loisy's use of 'myth', 'legend' and 'catechesis' should not of themselves exclude the possibility of historical information in the Gospels and Acts. Cultic explanations are aprioristic, deriving from sociological theory and lacking direct evidence of Christian worship in the first century. The depreciation of Paul is partly to be explained by Loisy's aversion towards both the apostle and his modern Protestant interpreters. It is unlikely that Paul was completely dependent upon the church of Antioch for his ideas; if he was a virtually unknown figure by the second century, as Loisy assumes, why were his letters so carefully preserved and interpolated to form such an imposing corpus? Loisy is wrong to suspect

---

25 *RHR* 120 (1939) pp212–5.
26 Cf. above 4.2, n.28.
27 *RHPR* 14 (1934) pp155–186.

everything in the epistles which doesn't follow logically and to imagine that a 'mystery of redemption' which was the doctrinal counterpoise of Christian worship could have developed so rapidly. Both
cult and doctrine are the products of *faith* and Paul's letters are the
direct religious expression of this faith, before doctrinal formulae
were codified: hence their illogicalities. These remarks on Paul are
further taken up and expanded in Goguel's review of *Remarques sur
la littérature epistolaire du Nouveau Testament*[28].

In his obituary of Loisy, Goguel pays tribute to his breadth of
interests and to the moral and intellectual unity of his life[29]. The
surprising critical conclusions of his final years do not disturb that
unity; rather, his 'souplesse d'esprit' was able to operate radical
transformations while remaining faithful to his critical principles
and methods. Deissmann had described the theory of Fr. Blass on the
rhythmic style of Hebrews as an 'honourable error'; so too with
Loisy, whose conjectures compel his fellow workers to re-examine
their own picture of Christian origins, to see if it is well founded.

By now the relationship between the three critics should be clear.
For reasons of temperament, Loisy did not seek any association with
the other two, while they were more mild and restrained in their
criticism of him and of each other. Goguel, with his teaching responsibilities at the Sorbonne as well as the Faculté Protestante,
did not wish to be labelled a confessional critic, while Guignebert
shared certain assumptions with Liberal Protestants (although
differing on a number of basic issues) and was happy to include
Goguel among the independents, over against Catholic confessionalism. Concerning their actual interpretations of early Christianity,
two major differences have emerged. First, as Professor Simon
remarks, Goguel 'showed greater confidence in the texts than either
of his two colleagues, who were consciously hypercritical and he
continued to be a Christian while he produced his studies'[30] (This
does not, of course, necessarily imply a straightforward correlation
between Christian belief and greater confidence in the texts).
Secondly, Goguel and Guignebert found it impossible to follow
Loisy 'dernière manière', on the 'style rythmé' and the compilation
theory of the epistles. But even if they did not form a 'school',

---

28 *RHPR* 16 (1936) pp508–17.
29 *RHR* 122 (1940) pp180–6.
30 Goguel, *The Primitive Church* ET (1963) p7.

their close awareness of each other's work and varying degrees of mutual acknowledgement, justify an attempt to compare their findings.

5.2 *CRITICAL CONCLUSIONS*

In our examination of 'critics at work', our study stopped short in each case of the final statements by which each of them would have wished to be remembered. It is now proposed to use these final works for an assessment of the historical achievement and presuppositions of the three critics, by examining the treatment accorded to several selected themes. Before taking these in turn, however, the nature of the material has to be reviewed and the circumstances of its production.

The work pattern of Loisy is clear. Having published a series of major commentaries in the 1920s, much of his effort in the years 1928—1931 was devoted to the writing of the *Mémoires*. But, as we have seen, it was his intention to return, if his health allowed, to a general treatment of Christian origins. This was all the more necessary because of his evolving theories described in detail above, which themselves, however, made the task more difficult.[1] Evidence for the continuity of his thought and writing between the 1920s and the 1930s is provided, for example, by the unpublished manuscript of a second edition of *Les Livres du Nouveau Testament*, with long introductions, considerably rewritten, for each book[2]; and by his ongoing work on Jewish apocalyptic[3], which is reflected in the final chapters of a revised edition of *La Religion d'Israël* (1933). This volume was intended to herald his final statement on Christian origins and the same year saw the publication of *La Naissance du christianisme*. This was supplemented by three further volumes, two on specific themes, *Le Mandéisme... et les origines chrétiennes* (1934) and *Remarques sur la littérature épistolaire du Nouveau Testament* (1935) and by a more general survey, *Les Origines du Nouveau Testament* (1936). Here then are 1500 pages of (almost) final thoughts on early Christianity[4]. Overall, they create an uneven impression, be-

---

1 Cf. above 2.6, n.2.
2 BN n.a.f. 15639—40; cf. above 2.5.1, n.22.
3 Cf. above 2.5, n.8.
4 Three occasional volumes of 1938—9, all polemical (directed at Couchoud, Dujardin,

cause of the repetition of material and the combative nature of the writing: *Le Mandéisme* ... is an attack upon the pan-Mandeism of Reitzenstein and its application to the Fourth Gospel by Bultmann; *Remarques* ... is the presentation of an extreme theory concerning which Loisy is also at pains to dissociate himself from Turmel[5] . Due to his advancing years, Loisy was in no position to plan a magisterial multi-volume work on the scale of Renan's *Histoire des origines du christianisme* and, in any case, his evaluation of the documents prevented him from writing a continuous narrative, just as his polemical inclinations ruled out a tone of Olympian detachment. However, in spite of these possibly unsatisfactory features, there is no lack of evidence for the final phase of Loisy's thought.

Guignebert contributed two volumes, *Jésus* (1933) and *Le Monde juif vers le temps de Jesus* (1935) to the important series 'L'Evolution de l'Humanité' edited by Henri Berr[6]. He had promised two further contributions, to be called *Le Christ* and *L'Eglise,* but at his death in 1939 he had only written part of *Le Christ*. From his manuscripts Mlle. Brunot edited a posthumous volume which was published in 1943[7].

Some account is here required of 'L'Evolution de l'Humanité' since it can be presumed that in contributing to the series, Guignebert was in general sympathy with the enterprise. Henri Berr, the general editor, devoted his long life to 'scientific history' and 'historical synthesis'.[8] In 1900 he founded the *Revue de Synthèse Historique* and in 1911 he wrote a programmatic work *La Synthèse en histoire* which sought to establish historical causality on a 'scienti-

---

'Saintyves', Guy-Grand and Guitton) also deal with aspects of early Christianity but do not introduce any profound change of standpoint.

5 Cf. above 2.5.3.

6 Guignebert was personally known to Berr. For example, they both took part in a discussion at the Congrès Renan in 1923 on 'L'enseignement de l'histoire des religions dans les Facultés des Lettres', when a motion was formulated urging an increase in the representation of the subject in French universities. (*Actes du Congrès* Vol.I (1925) p305).

7 It contains only two of the intended four sections planned by Guignebert: 'Jérusalem' and 'La naissance du christianisme'; he only left the first chapter of his third section on 'Le paulinisme' which is supplemented in the published volume by a lecture of 1933 on 'Le mystère paulinien'. There was to have been a final section on post-Pauline developments.

8 On Berr (1863–1954) see his own *La Montée de l'Esprit — Bilan d'une vie et d'une oeuvre* (1955); 'Hommage à Henri Berr' (*Revue de Synthèse* t.LXXXV (1964); H. Stuart Hughes, *The Obstructed Path — French Social Thought in the Years of Desperation 1930–1960* (1966) Ch.2.

fic' basis and which also took a positive view, not widely shared among historians, of the contribution of sociology. In 1920 he launched 'L'Evolution de l'Humanité' to be completed in a hundred volumes. The *Introduction Générale* lays down the basic principles[9]. What is needed is a French alternative to German *Weltgeschichte*, which hovers uneasily between 'micrography' and metaphysics. There will be an overall unity provided by the plan, but each volume will have its autonomous unity, as supplied by the author's expertise. The whole enterprise will be marked by 'science et vie': building on 'erudition', the 'laws' of causality and synthesis will help discover the inner logic of history[10] but the authors will also bring to life the 'progressive movement' to be found in societies, cultures and civilisations. The interaction of the individual and society (the 'human' and the 'social') is a prime concern and is exemplified by religion: 'Elle est d'essence humaine, – mais elle est fortement socialisée'[11]. World history should not be rigidly overclassified according to chronological, geographical, ethnic or philosophical principles and so Berr proposes four major divisions: 1. Introduction (Préhistoire, Protohistoire); Antiquité; 2. Origines du christianisme et Moyen Âge; 3. Le Monde Moderne; 4. Vers le temps présent. The titles within each division are sometimes on international topics and sometimes on a single race, nation, civilisation or aspect of a particular culture. The series enlisted a number of eminent historians, such as Lucien Fèbvre and Marc Bloch, while Berr himself wrote complementary volumes under the title *En marge de l'histoire universelle*, as well as providing a Foreword to each contribution.

Logic might have demanded that the Old Testament be considered in the first division, on the Ancient World, but in fact the second division began with two volumes on Israel and Judaism by Adolphe Lods, who taught at the Protestant Faculty and at the Sorbonne.

---

9 Vol.I. ppV–XXVII.

10 Hughes, *op.cit.* p25 points out that these 'laws' of causality are not conceived as universal eternal laws, but rather in the nature of generalities, similarities and uniformities.

11 *Op.cit.* pXI. On the treatment of religion in 'L'Evolution de l'Humanité', v. P. Honigsheim, 'The influence of Durkheim and his school on the study of Religion' in *Emile Durkheim 1858–1917* (1960) ed. K.H. Wolff, reprinted as: *Essays on Sociology and Philosophy* (1964). This article shows that Berr and his collaborators, although taking up and illustrating some of Durkheim's concepts, paid more attention than he did to the role of the individual and to the insights of psychology. In any case, it should be remembered that Guignebert shared something of Loisy's suspicion of the sociologists' theorising.

These were to be followed by the four titles assigned to Guignebert, who took up the story from the time of the Maccabean revolt, where it had been left by Lods. The significance of the appearance of the final volumes of Guignebert in this series lies not so much in any close adherence to the principles of 'synthesis', as in the opportunity to write about early Christianity in the context of universal human history. Berr's arrangement of events is obviously not confessional in an ecclesiastical sense, although his European standpoint is seen in the placing of Christian origins in a pivotal place in his scheme. It was all the more regrettable that Guignebert did not live to execute his assignment fully; and the state of his publications places certain limits on the exercise to be attempted below.

Whereas Loisy wrote on the religion of Israel and Guignebert on the Jewish *Umwelt* as 'background' to their final versions of early Christianity, Goguel produced a volume on John the Baptist[12]. This was a curtain-raiser for 'Jésus et les origines du christianisme' of which the first volume *La Vie de Jésus*, appeared in 1932[13]. It was published by the secular house of Payot in their 'Bibliothèque historique', although it should be noted that this series has always contained a high proportion of titles on comparative religion and on Christianity. We have seen how Goguel was occupied during the 1930s with articles preparatory for the next two volumes.[14] It is possible that they would have been published earlier but for the War, but *La Naissance du christianisme* and *L'Eglise primitive* appeared in 1946 and 1947 respectively. The separation of 'Christianity' and 'Church' corresponded of course to some of Goguel's preconceptions and he has been criticised for the duplication of material which his arrangement involved.[15] But as an exhaustive treatment of many of the problems of Christian origins in a recognisable historico-critical tradition, the work has won a place in the history of scholarship denied to those of Loisy (eccentric) and Guignebert (incomplete)[16].

---

12 *Au seuil de l'Evangile: Jean Baptiste* (1928).

13 A revised second edition, entitled *Jésis*, was published in 1950.

14 Cf. above 4.6.

15 Eg. M. Simon in 'Les origines chrétiennes d'après l'oeuvre de Maurice Goguel' *RH* 202 (1949) pp221–231. After suggesting some improvements, Simon writes, 'On souhaiterait que l'auteur eût parfois fait lui-même ces regroupements: l'exposé y aurait gagné en netteté et en vigueur'. (p225)

16 It was greeted by W.G. Kümmel as 'äusserst wertvolle und unentbehrliche Gesamtdarstellung des Urchristentums'. (*ThR* 18 (1950) p11).

In 1949 Goguel brought his findings together in a single work *Les Premiers Temps de l'Eglise* in the Protestant series 'Manuels et Précis de Théologie'[17]. Of the three critics Goguel was therefore the only one to complete at some leisure and without too much special pleading, a rounded account of early Christianity. So for Goguel and Loisy there is no lack of evidence; in the case of Guignebert we have noted the limitations.

Since much exegetical detail has already been provided for each separate critic, the following sections will only present general conclusions. Several other topics of comparison might also have been included, but the five selected allow for an adequate sampling of the evidence and sufficient indication of agreement and differences of opinion.[18]

5.2.1. The rise of resurrection faith

All three critics agree that the historical Jesus did not envisage the

---

17 The Preface differentiates this work from its predecessors as follows: '... nous plaçant à un point de vue non plus dynamique mais statique, nous essayerions de dire, non plus comment le Christianisme primitif s'est formé, mais ce qu'il a été, de le décrire et non plus de l'expliquer'. (*op.cit.* p7).

18 It is convenient to note at this point the English translations of these writers' major works, here under discussion:

		English translation (and translator)
(a)	Loisy	
	La Naissance du christianisme (1933)	*The Birth of the Christian Religion* (1948) (L.P. Jacks)
	Les Origines du nouveau testament (1936)	*The Origins of the New Testament* (1950) (L.P. Jacks)
(b)	Guignebert	
	Jésus (1933)	*Jesus* (1935) (S.H. Hooke)§
	Le Monde juif vers le temps de Jésus (1935)	*The Jewish World at the time of Jesus* (1939) (S.H. Hooke)§
	Le Christ (1943)	*The Christ* (1968) (P. Ouzts and P. Cooperman)

§ These appeared in the series 'The History of Civilisation', edited by C.K. Ogden, which incorporated many volumes from 'L'Evolution de l'humanité'.

(c)	Goguel	
	La Naissance du christianisme (1946; [2]1955)	*The Birth of Christianity* (1958) (H.C. Snape)
	L'Eglise primitive (1947)	*The Primitive Church* (1963) (H.C. Snape)

References below will be to the French originals, indicated as follows:
Loisy, *Naissance* ...
Guignebert, *Jésus; Le Christ*
Goguel, *Naissance* ...; *L'Eglise primitive*

founding of a Church and that the origins of Christianity as a religion are to be sought in the new assessment of Jesus resulting from faith in his resurrection. As a Catholic apologist, Loisy had claimed that the resurrection belonged to the realm of faith, not of history[1] and in his final phase; he insists once again on the power of faith:

> La foi religieuse n'est pas, de soi, autre chose qu'un effort de l'esprit, imagination, intelligence et volonté, pour rompre le cadre naturel, apparemment mécanique et fatal, de l'existence.[2]

Faith raised Jesus into glory; unconsciously and spontaneously, faith procured the visions and the proofs which it required. The disciples believed in the immortality of Jesus and this belief triumphed over the collapse of their hopes with the crucifixion which had come as a violent shock[3]. Guignebert and Goguel believe that there was more continuity than Loisy might suggest between the devotion of the disciples to Jesus during his lifetime and their subsequent resurrection faith, although for Guignebert Jesus had not been accepted as Messiah during his ministry and the Messianic faith was a consequence of resurrection faith[4]. Goguel insists: *natura non facit saltus*; the place of Jesus in the disciples' hearts ensured his resurrection[5]. Even if Guignebert cannot follow Goguel in all the psychological reconstruction which the latter proposes, he is happy to accept the idea of a basic 'foi-confiance' from which everything else flowed[6].

As well as this general agreement about the creative role of faith, the three critics concur broadly on the most probable sequence of events[7]. After the crucifixion, the disciples left Jerusalem in despair, not knowing where Jesus had been buried. Resurrection faith asserted itself in Galilee, and Peter was probably the first recipient of

---

1 Cf. eg. *L'Evangile et L'Eglise* (1902) pp117ff; *Autour d'un petit livre* (1903) p169.

2 *Naissance* ... p122. Despite his changing views on various aspects of the New Testament, Loisy remained very consistent in his interpretation of the resurrection, both as Catholic and as 'independent'.

3 *Ibid* p123.

4 *Jésus* pp641–2.

5 *Naissance* ... p91. In his section 'La création d'un objet religieux nouveau' Goguel offers little more than a summary of his views of 1933, reviewed above in 4.5.

6 *Jésus* pp664.

7 Loisy, *Naissance* ... pp130–2; Guignebert, *Jésus* pp650–2; *Le Christ* pp60–4; Goguel, *Naissance* ... p103 appears to point to Galilee as the place of origin of resurrection faith, although not necessarily of the first vision; in the second edition (1955) pp607–9, this doubt is maintained even though the Galilee appearances — tradition is said to be earlier than that of Jerusalem. For Peter as the *probable* recipient of the first Christophany cf *Naissance* ... p92.

a vision; collective visionary experiences followed. The apostolic group returned to Jerusalem, in all likelihood to await the Parousia there. The course of events outlined by Luke at the end of his Gospel and at the beginning of Acts is a tendentious and misleading account[8]. There is of course a difference of language among the critics: Loisy speaks of 'visions' and 'illusions' (although the work of faith is not necessarily illusory)[9]; Guignebert of 'contagious hallucinations', for which there are many parallels in the history of religions[10]; Goguel of 'Christophanies' and 'visions', the former of which are decisive for resurrection faith, being terrestrial, non-ecstatic and unexpected[11]. Here something of their presuppositions may be seen. But there is further agreement about the elaboration of the traditions concerning the empty tomb and the appearances. This was in the nature of an 'externalisation', a 'materialisation', a 'justification' of pre-existing faith, the 'symbol' of the glorification of Jesus.[12] The Bergsonian notion of a 'fonction fabulatrice' is invoked to account for the growth and fixation of a legendary cycle: this was taken retrospectively as objective 'sacred history', and wrongly assumed to have been the basis rather than the expression of faith[13]. The resulting collection of narratives is bound to be contradictory and irreconcilable[14].

Goguel, taking up the arguments of *La foi à la résurrection dans le christianisme primitif,* has a very precise account of how the resurrection cycle evolved[15], but he parts company from the other two, not only in his stress upon a psychological reconstruction but also in his assertion that the empty tomb tradition preceded the appearances tradition[16]. Loisy and Guignebert conclude, more convincingly, that the appearances were the earliest form of apologia on behalf of the resurrection[17], but Goguel speculatively posits an earlier empty

---

8 Loisy, *Naissance* ... p118; Guignebert, *Le Christ* p61; Goguel, *Naissance* ... pp75–76.

9 Loisy, *Naissance* ... pp120, 123; on pp130–1 he rejects modern theories which speak of 'quelques très lourdes hallucinations'.

10 *Jésus* pp637–8.

11 Goguel, *Naissance* ... pp59–60 distinguishes more precisely than in his previous work between 'Christophanies' and 'visions'.

12 Cf. e.g. Loisy, *Naissance* ... p122; Guignebert, *Jésus* pp652–61 Goguel, *Naissance* ... p53.

13 Goguel, *Naissance* ... p80; Guignebert, *Jésus* pp652ff.

14 Loisy *Naissance* ... p119; Guignebert, *Jésus* p652; Goguel, *Naissance* ... p73.

15 Goguel, *Naissance* ... pp76–81.

16 Cf. above 4.5, n.12.

17 Guignebert, *Jésus* p656; Loisy, *Naissance* ... p120.

tomb tradition which spoke of the direct assumption of Jesus into heaven[18]. He agrees with the other two that the 'third day' idea is an apologetical motif but again stands apart in not accepting any decisive influence from the Mystery religions in the development of the resurrection cycle.[19] Guignebert holds that in the Hellenistic world, the Mysteries favoured the acceptance of the resurrection idea[20] and although Loisy is not as explicit on this point, he shares with Guignebert the general idea of the importance of Hellenistic influence, especially in the setting of the cultus, upon the developing Christian tradition[21]. Against such collective ritual theories, Goguel always returns to the religious experience of the individual or the small group, clothing itself in a variety of symbols.

But as historians, our critics are unable to take the Gospel resurrection narratives, or the other early Christian texts, as anything more than the vivid, unselfconscious response of faith to the life and death of Jesus. The stories cannot be the direct transcripts of historical events, unless this is taken to mean mental or spiritual experiences. whose reconstruction is problematical. We have seen how Goguel's willingness to speculate in this direction reflects his own views of religion and of Christian origins in particular[22]. Guignebert's systematic doubt is not, he claims, rationalist prejudice: it is simply that the texts give the impression of faith rather than facts and one must avoid 'fideistic' prejudice as well as the hazardous reconstructions of some rationalists.[23] Loisy's presentation also has an anti-theological aspect when he comments that the first Christians did not have the sort of interest in 'scientific' proof which dominates the work of modern apologists[24].

Problems of faith and history are here at their most delicate: they are present in the texts as well as in the minds of modern critics and our three writers, in their desire to avoid distortion, probably do not make sufficient allowance for the theological seriousness of the documents. But their attempts, variously conceived, to evoke

---

18 For details, cf. above 4.5.
19 *Naissance* ... p81, n.1 allows for a minimal influence from that quarter upon 'accessory' features of the cycle.
20 *Jésus* p652.
21 Cf. his treatment of 'the Lord's Day', *Naissance* ... pp280–5.
22 Cf. above 4.5.
23 *Jésus* pp631–2.
24 *Naissance* ... p122. Loisy does of course stress the role of early Christian apologetic in the formation of the traditions about both the appearances and the empty tomb.

the religious convictions and environment of early Christianity and to trace possible stages of development through the texts, drawing upon comparative material where they thought it appropriate, together form a valuable antidote to writers on the resurrection whose main interest is in the realm of Christian apologetics.

5.2.2. Stephen and the Hellenists

The historian who wishes to write about the time between Jesus and Paul must give some attention to the 'Hellenists' of Acts 6ff and their spokesman Stephen, including not only the group's activities in Jerusalem but also its dispersion and consequent missionary work. The documentation in Acts has often been called into question and our critics agree that the Hellenists were a group (or 'synagogue') of Greek-speaking Jewish Christians, with a measure of separate organisation ('the Seven'), whose role and significance has been purposely diminished by the editor of Acts to the advantage of 'the Twelve'.[1] They disagree on the authenticity of Stephen's speech: Loisy ascribes the bulk of it to the redactor[2] but Goguel believes that, even if from a separate source than that of the trial of Stephen, it can be taken as a reliable guide to Stephen's highly original outlook[3]; Guignebert thinks that Stephen was a personification of the Seven[4], just as Peter represented the Twelve, and therefore minimises his individual role, but is prepared to make some very cautious use of the speech for an indication of the Hellenist position[5].

But however obscure the information, each critic gives the Hellenists a key role in the development of Christianity, particularly in providing the link between Jerusalem and Antioch, which was 'le vrai berceau' of the new religion[6]. The antithesis between Jerusalem and Antioch gives Goguel the basic structure of his *Naissance* ... : they stand for Jewish and Hellenistic Christianity respectively, the former

---

1 Loisy, *Naissance* ... pp140–2; Guignebert, *Le Christ* pp76–81; Goguel, *Naissance* ... pp191–3.
2 *Naissance* ... p145.
3 *Naissance* ... p197.
4 *Le Christ* p126.
5 *Ibid* pp127–8.
6 The phrase is that of Guignebert (*Le Christ* p200). In *Les Actes des Apôtres* (1921) Loisy had described Antioch as 'la seconde patrie du christianisme – à certains égards, c'en serait presque première'. (p461).

doomed to failure, the latter destined for success. Loisy and Guignebert insist that this expansion and development was uncalculated
and spontaneous. The separate organisation of the Hellenists, the
persecution of this group (and not the apostles), their dispersal and
their notable success in preaching to Gentiles in Antioch were the
result of circumstances rather than of any preconceived apostolic
plan[7]. But it was by such a means that the faith of the earliest community, still in many ways legalistic, nationalistic and Messianic,
began to be transformed into a universal religion of salvation. Goguel
assents to this general picture but allows for the possibility of some
conscious planning in the missionary outreach.[8]

Loisy, although he had previously speculated that the Hellenists
might have originated the worship of Jesus as Kyrios while still in
Jerusalem, merely points in his final phase to the critique of the Law
and the Temple which Stephen proclaimed and mentions that a
similar abrogation of the cult was advocated by contemporary
baptist sects and by the Essenes.[9] Both Loisy and Guignebert emphasise the links which joined the Hellenists to the moral liberal Judaism
of the Diaspora, but Guignebert goes on to credit them with the first
christological 'speculation', animated by the Greek spirit, and the
first impulse towards expansion[10]. They can be said to have preached
a kind of pre-Paulinism, involving faith in the name of Jesus Christ
with the minimum of cultic and legal requirements[11]. Goguel, however, will not allow that Stephen was a pre-Paulinist, nor a precursor
of the writer to the Hebrews. He derived his ideas directly from
Jesus: he shared with Jesus the view that the 'Son of Man' would
abolish Temple worship and legal requirements, and admit the
Gentiles. But his ideas were too radical for his time and milieu and
so he perished. He did however pose the two questions, one of fact
and one of principle, which were to receive their solution on the
terrain of Hellenistic Christianity: the problem of the pagan world
and the relation of the new religion to the faith of the Old Testament.[12]

For Loisy then, Stephen and his group are a bridge from Judaism

---

7   Loisy, *Naissance* ... pp176–7; Guignebert, *Le Christ* p200 (cf. the italicized phrase
'sans le savoir').

8   *Naissance* ... p200.

9   *Naissance* ... p144; for the suggestion about their use of Kyrios v. *RHLR* 1914 p392 n.1.

10 *Le Christ* pp129–30.

12 *Naissance* ... pp200–1.

to the Hellenistic world where Christianity was to come into its own. Guignebert goes further and celebrates in them the triumph of Greek ideas, without which Christianity had no future; he refers to the unconscious syncretism which the Hellenists operated in Antioch, replacing the eschatological hope with the cultic experience of a present 'Lord'.[13] 'Goguel turns Stephen into something of a Protestant hero and finds a golden thread linking Jesus to Stephen and Stephen, via his followers who evangelised Antioch, to Paul. All three therefore place the Hellenists in a series which led from Jesus to Paul, but for Loisy and Guignebert the figure of Jesus is far more obscure than for Goguel; according to them, the Hellenists, having placed their faith in a heavenly Christ, i.e. the object of resurrection faith, gave the impetus for a radical re-evaluation of Jesus. Goguel agrees that the Christianity of Antioch was very different from that of Jerusalem but he sees more. continuity and more individual influence. In terms of historical reconstruction we can therefore register a substantial measure of agreement and variations in accordance with the general tendencies already observed. This convergence of views is not however maintained in the case of Paul.

5.2.3. Paul

'Paul remains the pole star for him who would navigate the waters of early Christianity'[1]. The state of the documentation has helped to produce a general consensus on this point, and histories of the early church not only recount the career and theology of the apostle in detail, but make extensive use of the epistles for reconstructing the beliefs and practices of nascent Christianity. But we have seen how Loisy thought his way through this common prejudice, as he believed it to be, first by a consistent scepticism applied to the historical evidence, equally in the epistles and in Acts, and then by his theories of the composite nature of the epistles[2]. *La Naissance du christianisme* presents his previously formed conclusions on Paul, 'ce patron plus ou moins authentique de l'individualisme religieux'[3], and *Les Origines du nouveau testament* and *Remarques sur la littéra-*

---

13 *Le Christ* pp199—200.

1 C.K. Barrett, *From First Adam to Last* (1962) p3.
2 Cf. above 2.3 and 4; 2.5.3.
3 *Naissance* ... p188.

ture épistolaire ... continue the work of analysing the epistles into their component sections. Paul 'a été seulement un des plus grands missionaires des premiers temps',[4] and his career was only a sample of missionary work, by no means typical[5]. The inner process of his conversion cannot be known either from epistles or Acts[6]. He was 'for long years' the assistant of Barnabas. He played a part in negotiations between Antioch and Jerusalem but after his petulant break with Antioch occasioned by his quarrel with Peter, he developed an exaggerated sense of his own destiny and importance and became increasingly isolated, with only a handful of supporters[7]. Much of Loisy's chapter on Paul repeats his analysis of Acts and he readily admits that, on account of the redactor's intervention, he can only present the reader with 'probable hypotheses'[8]. It was partly because Loisy felt unable to follow most of his fellow-writers in the field in using Paul as the centrepiece of his presentation that he had such problems in the overall organisation of *La Naissance du christianisme*.

In this matter Guignebert and Goguel were more conventional. Out of four planned sections of *Le Christ*, the second and third were to be largely devoted to Paul. Guignebert accepts the authenticity of Romans, I and II Corinthians, Galatians, Philippians, Colossians and I Thessalonians[9]. He sees Paul as a 'religious worker' of exceptional interest to the historian and the psychologist. His thought is indissolubly linked to the subsequent evolution of Christian theology. His career, however restricted the information, gives us one aspect at least of the installation of Christianity in the Mediterranean world and its transformation into an autonomous religion of salvation; it illuminates the wider question of 'how a religion is born'[10]. Guignebert writes extensively on Paul's background, stressing the syncretism of Tarsus, and analyses his conversion in great detail, concluding that the Hellenistic Christianity established at Antioch and Damascus corresponded to deep aspirations in this ardent and mystical personality[11]. He provides a general introduction to Paul's

---

4 *Ibid* p159.
5 *Ibid* p229.
6 *Ibid* p160–1.
7 *Ibid* p185.
8 *Ibid* p188.
9 *Le Christ* pp132–44.
10 *Ibid* p202–3.
11 *Ibid* Deuxième Partie Ch.V.

'apostolic activity', which describes his motivation and field of activity, the religious and social milieux, the forms of his activity and the obstacles he encountered[12]. Guignebert shares nearly all of Loisy's reservations about the trustworthiness of Acts, and his account of Paul's career, based on that source, is deliberately hypothetical, but he does not join in Loisy's apparent delight in belittling Paul on the basis of the shortage of information.

Even if Paul was Goguel's hero, he does not allow his adulation to run beyond bounds and the chapter of *La Naissance du christianisme* on the subject of Paul and Paulinism forms one part only of a major section on the 'realization of Christianity on the basis of Hellenism'[13]. Paul's interpretation of the Gospel makes him the outstanding figure of the first Christian generation, but he saw himself and the historian sees him, as one of a number of missionaries. He cannot be called the founder of Christianity, for a religion comes to birth with the awareness of a 'new religious object', which was furnished by the person of Jesus, but without Paul's powerful expression of this awareness, Christianity would have been different and might even have failed[14]. Goguel stresses Paul's background in Diaspora Judaism, rather than Hellenism proper, but acknowledges his literary talents in Greek and even states that Paul may have been nearer to Greek polytheism than he himself would have admitted[15]. We are already familiar with Goguel's somewhat anti-Protestant view of Paul's conversion. He takes a more generous view than Loisy and Guignebert of the missionary narratives in Acts, although recognising their deficiencies[16]. He considers that Paul's missionary methods were a curious mixture of planning and improvisation[17]. He agrees with Loisy and Guignebert that after the quarrel with Peter at Antioch, Paul became isolated for the rest of his life[18]. Goguel does not however confine his treatment of Paul to the narrative sections of his work; he makes ample use of the epistles in his discussion of early heresies, of the doctrine and organisation of the church, of worship and of morality[19].

---

12 *Ibid* Ch.VI.
13 *Op.cit.* Troisième Partie, Ch.VI.
14 *Ibid* p223.
15 *Ibid* pp235—6.
16 *Ibid* p245.
17 *Ibid* p249.
18 *Ibid* p330.
19 Much of this discussion is found in *L'Eglise primitive.*

If certain historical details of Paul's career are hard to determine and if his precise contribution to the spread of Christianity can be variously estimated, this still leaves the intellectual or theological achievement of the epistles as his monument. But Loisy's demolition methods completely undermine the edifice of Paulinism, leaving anonymous blocks of material of indeterminate date (but not of the first generation), which, even if they were greatly influential in the history of dogma, cannot be reckoned as an individual accomplishment. However, Guignebert and Goguel, in accepting the authenticity of the major epistles are at pains to stress, for reasons we have noted, that Paul was not a systematic theologian and that inconsistencies abound, either on account of Oriental pre-logicality (Guignebert)[20], or because an intense experience was always finding new modes of expression (Goguel)[21]. Both critics recall that the epistles are works of circumstance, far from dispassionate, in which many things known to Paul and his readers, although lost to us, could be assumed.

Guignebert sums up his impressions of the Apostle thus:

> Il bataille, il morigène, il édifie, il exhorte, il s'indigne, il vaticine, parfois pêle-même, et dans une confusion que la maladresse de son style et la fragilité de sa logique rendent pour nous presque inextricable.[22]

But one can speak of the 'great Pauline themes' — God in his relations with mankind, the Lord Jesus and the 'Christian mystery', faith, the sacraments and the Church — which together comprise a 'gnosis'[23]. These doctrines are never purely speculative, although they can only find their justification in the realm of 'la mystique', beyond human reason. In introducing the exposition of Paulinism which he did not live to write, Guignebert points out that Paulinism was not and is not the whole of Christianity; he hopes however to indicate the more permanent elements of this all-pervasive thinking.[24]

As evidence of Paul's inconsistencies, Goguel cites his views on the death of Christ and on eschatology, his failure to harmonise ideas on individual and collective salvation and apparently different estimates of the Law.[25] But at the basis of his thought there is the idea of a

---

20 Cf. above 3.4.4.
21 Cf. above 4.6.
22 *Le Christ* p329.
23 *Ibid* pp330—4.
24 *Ibid* p335.
25 *Naissance ...* pp223—31.

divine drama of salvation encompassing creation and redemption[26].
His doctrine of redemption is a theological outworking of his personal experience of forgiveness and salvation, mediated through the
earliest community, but ideas of a 'double' creation and of the
transformation of humanity, previously not known in the Christian tradition, came from Hellenistic Judaism[27]. Paul's doctrine of
the Spirit is a psychological description of the life of the believer,[28],
but it is not possible to trace Paul's own Christian development, as
Sabatier had attempted. The most that can be said about the Hellenistic Mysteries is that they provided a few ideas and some terminology for the expression of more fundamental notions deriving from
Paul's Christian experience[29]. Controversies with Judaizers in Galatia,
paganising 'enthusiasts' in Corinth and Jewish gnostics in Colossae
anticipated many future debates in Christian theology and in particular the last named encouraged the development of a Christian
philosophy or cosmology, so that Paulinism acted upon Christian
thought not only as *fides qua creditur* but as *fides quae creditur*[30].

It is not necessary to reproduce the more detailed conclusions of
these critics about Paul's life and teaching in order to catch the
significance they attach to him in their account of Christian origins.
Loisy's version is the most determined counterblast to earlier standard
Protestant accounts, which gave such a preponderant place to the
Apostle. But even if his prejudice has produced a distorted picture,
it is important to note that Guignebert and (much more surprisingly)
Goguel are also anxious not to overestimate the place of Paul. Making
allowance for the anti-confessional strain in Guignebert, we may see
their restraint as a genuine historical concern, dictated by the nature
of the sources. In the first place, full measure is given to the 'tendencies' of Acts, the partisan nature of the epistles and the accidental
lack of information about other early Christian leaders. Then, there
is the recognition of sociological factors, which counterbalance the
influence of outstanding personalities. Again rather surprisingly it is
the Protestant Goguel who is more explicit about these factors, and
even if he overschematizes the contrasts between Jerusalem and

---

26 *Ibid* p251.
27 *Ibid* p253.
28 *Ibid* p259.
29 *Ibid* p275.
30 *Ibid* pp275–9.

Antioch, this antithesis provides a more convincing framework for Paul's activity than the overlengthy descriptions of Hellenistic religion whereby Guignebert compensates for the paucity of the sources. But of all three critics it may be said that in drawing attention to collective factors they were seeking to strike a balance, and that in this process Paul, the most obvious candidate for a personality cult in the New Testament, was likely to be somewhat diminished. Loisy in his insistence upon cultic and catechetical influences went too far, although it should be noted that, apart from his sustained anti-Protestantism, he was not attempting to strait-jacket the evidence in the interests of a pre-conceived theory. We have observed in Guignebert's exegesis of the epistles that he overplayed the parallels with the Mystery religions and that this was, in part, a historian's response to the documents in seeking to place them in the religious cross-currents of the age. Goguel might, on the other hand, have made more of the comparative material (not only in Hellenism but also in Judaism) but was inhibited from doing so because he regarded the early Christian experience as *sui generis*, even if subsequently moulded by environmental factors. But these accounts claim our attention as examples of what happens when Paul is released not only from hagiography, but also from the status of normative theologian in his own age and for the ages to come.

5.2.4. Early Christian Worship

We have seen how both Loisy and Guignebert maximised the ritual aspects of early Christianity, partly because of their insistence on the comparative material, partly because of the importance they attached to (often unrecorded) collective developments and also, in all probability, on account of Catholic preoccupations in that quarter. Loisy is clear that the heart of Christianity was a Mystery of salvation, cultivated by an intense group life in the worship of the Lord Jesus Christ:[1] only later did this Mystery crystallise into a system of doctrines[2]. Guignebert speaks of a religious sentiment which, in accordance with contemporary usage had to be expressed in a ritual

---

1 Cf. his statement in the Avant-propos of *Naissance* ... about the tradition concerning Jesus: 'ce fut dès l'abord une tradition de foi et presque aussitôt de culte ... le souvenir s'est transfiguré dans la foi et dans l'adoration'. (p8).

2 *Naissance* ... p275.

'demonstration', including the 'rite de passage' of baptism[3]. This view is midway between those of Loisy and Goguel, but the latter places his treatment of early Christian worship in his volume on the 'Church' rather than 'Christianity'; by means of worship, 'la religion s'affirme, se réalise, s'étend et se maintient' and thus, however important, worship is not of the essence. It acts as a force of conservation, with three functions: mystical, didactic and symbolic; and two elements: word and sacrament.[4] Goguel also has some valuable comments on research procedures in this area. By contrast with the other two and their liberal citation of parallels from the Mysteries, he successively calls into question the *formgeschichtliche Methode*[5]; the regressive method (eg. Lietzmann on the eucharist: it cannot guarantee a return to the origins); and the investigation of Jewish synagogue worship (Hellenistic Christianity must have diverged considerably from this). These are all expedients in the face of a dearth of evidence; it is however important to remember that a Palestinian tradition was the point of departure for all eucharistic developments and that Aramaic expressions were preserved in the worship of Hellenistic Christianity.[6]

According to Loisy, the earliest community practised baptism, as an act of purification and a sign of belonging to Christ, and common meals, when bread was broken in memory of Jesus and in lively expectation of his coming.[7] Thus in the 'Jesus-sect' a mystical bond was created which was the seed of an independent religion. The earliest creed was 'Maranatha', although the title 'Lord' was to acquire new significance in the Greek world[8]. Loisy does not entirely rule out the possibility of charismatic activity in Jerusalem but Goguel is adamant that the Jewish Christianity of the Jerusalem type was essentially non-charismatic[9]. Guignebert draws attention to the focus of devotion upon the person and the *name* of Jesus the Messiah. He is unable to pronounce on the precise origins of baptism, but he thinks it was practised in Jerusalem, accompanied by laying-on of

---

3   *Le Christ* pp83—4.
4   *L'Eglise primitive* p266.
5   Cf. his stricture upon Bertram quoted above 4.4, n.5.
6   *L'Eglise primitive* pp269—72.
7   *Naissance* ... pp134, 286.
8   *Naissance* ... pp275—8.
9   *Naissance* ... pp 112—5.

hands: 'c'est lui qui fait le saint'[10]. The Didache has probably preserved the spirit, if not the letter of the Jerusalem eucharist; Guignebert believes that even if Goguel is strictly correct in denying any
link between the earliest 'breaking of bread' and a memorial of
Jesus, nevertheless Loisy rightly posits a close relationship between
resurrection faith and the community meals and so these meals were
the visible sign of the communion of the faithful with each other and
with Christ[11]. Goguel emphasises the cultic links with Judaism,
which were to persist in Jerusalem and Jewish Christianity, long after
Hellenistic Christianity had diverged from earlier practice[12].

He believes that in the case of both baptism and eucharist an
evolution took place corresponding to his overall picture of Christian
origins. Just as Jewish Christianity faded away and Hellenistic Christianity was transformed into 'early catholicism', so, in the case of
baptism, the three stages were: the Jerusalem type, social in essence
and eschatological in its effects; the Pauline type, mystical and sacramental, which could not last because of the problem of post-baptis-
mal sin; and finally an 'institution of salvation', conveying the work
of Christ and employing the Trinitarian formula.[13] Similarly with the
eucharist: the primitive community emphasised the common meal,
with its joyful anticipation of the Parousia; Paul reinterpreted this
ritual in a sacramental direction; the post-Pauline developments led
to the Ignatian 'medecine of immortality', incorporating ideas of
'sacrifice' and 'mystery'.[14]

These views of Goguel have taken us into the Hellenistic milieu,
which is where Loisy and Guignebert place their emphasis although
we are limited in the case of Guignebert to his lecture on the Pauline
Mystery.

Loisy's chapter on the 'Birth of the Christian Mystery and of its
Rites' deals mainly with the Hellenistic sphere and, like Goguel, he
traces developments into the second century, but chronological
indications are extremely vague. For instance, in a discussion of 'the
Lord's Day', Loisy remarks that it arose 'de bonne heure' under the
impulse of solar myths[15] and that the festival of Easter developed

---

10 *Le Christ* p90.
11 *Le Christ* pp93–4.
12 *L'Eglise primitive* pp272–3.
13 *Ibid* pp337–9.
14 *Ibid* pp389–91.
15 *Naissance ...* p280.

'simultaneously', although the only direct evidence quoted is from Revelation and the second-century sources. Here there is an element of special pleading in favour of the conclusion that the resurrection narratives became 'le mythe d'institution de la Pâque chrétienne comme du dimanche chrétien'[16]. Here too becomes apparent Loisy's adherence to 'myth and ritual' theories which justify the priority he gives to cultic activity. In the Hellenistic cult, the use of the title 'Lord' enhanced the divine status of Jesus, because of its use for the saviour figures in the mystery cults and also because it was used for the name of God in the Septuagint[17]. The sense of Christ's presence at the eucharist, with the early emphasis on thanksgiving and communion, is reflected in the 'myths' of the multiplication of loaves and the resurrection narratives of Emmaus and at the lakeside. From an early stage the eucharist was a 'mystery', but a further, clearly sacramental stage is reached in I Corinthians, the Synoptic narratives of the Last Supper and the Johannine discourses (Loisy considers that the double series of instructions in John 13–14 and 15–17 is conceived 'dans une atmosphère tout eucharistique'[19]). By the identification of the elements with the body and blood of Christ, a religious rite is superimposed upon a common meal[20]. Sacrificial parallels from Israel and the pagan rites assisted this process[21]. An analysis of the Last Supper narratives supports this interpretation and also helps to show that both types of eucharist were known in Hellenistic Christianity[22]. It was a similar story with baptism. The earlier rite became 'un sacrement chargé d'efficacité mystique, un baptême d'esprit', and such a development was the more likely in the excitable atmosphere of the Hellenistic churches[23]. The 'mystical gnosis' of Romans 6 in which water symbolizes death, contrasts with the Johannine theory in which water is used as a principle and symbol of life.[24] To complete the process, an institution-myth was required and this was found in the water-baptism of Jesus by

---

16 *Ibid* p284.
17 *Ibid* p278.
18 *Ibid* p293.
19 *Ibid* p302.
20 *Ibid* p305.
21 *Ibid* pp309–10.
22 *Ibid* pp313–4.
23 *Ibid* p287.
24 *Ibid* p296.

John, to which the command of Matthew 28,19 was later added.[25]

According to Guignebert, the sacramental realism of Paul takes us to the heart of Paulinism[26]. The epistles inform us of four activities which establish and maintain Christian *koinōnia*: baptism, the eucharist, prayer and experiences of vision and ecstasy[27]. Baptism is the mystical means whereby the initiate is associated with the dying and rising Saviour, exactly as in the Mysteries. Guignebert refers to Orphic and Hermetic writings to show the closeness of thought. Like the Mysteries, Pauline mysticism depends on a 'jeu' of associations which nevertheless creates *koinōnia*. Pauline baptism includes a corporate dimension, as well as the salvation of the individual[28]. So too with the means of establishing communion with the Lord and among believers. Such ideas cannot come from Jewish worship or from the earlier 'breaking of bread'[29] and have their closest affinities with the sacred meals of pagan antiquity. Paul's eucharistic ideas were dominated, not by a historical reminiscence, but by the symbolism of blood. These were not conscious borrowings, but the natural adoption of the most readily understood 'means of grace' in the atmosphere in which Paul worked[30]. The apostle has nothing extraordinary to say about prayer, but his references to vision and ecstasy again echo extensively the pagan mystical literature[31].

Worship is therefore a reliable indicator of the respective positions of our critics. All admit an evolution of rituals originating in Judaism towards 'sacraments' which were gradually institutionalised. Loisy and Guignebert posit the copious assimilation of pagan elements, whereas for Goguel the development was more from within: he suggests that many so-called 'borrowings' can be explained by the limited number of appropriate symbols and images[32] and that the different stages of development corresponded to different concep-

---

25 *Ibid* p288. It should be recalled that in Loisy's view the Gospels encompass two 'cycles': that of Galilee can be called the baptismal catechesis (instruction of catechumens) and that of Jerusalem the eucharistic catechesis (revelation of a mystery) *(ibid* pp48–9).

26 *Le Christ* p333.

27 *Ibid* p361.

28 *Ibid* pp361–6.

29 There is some conflict of thought here with the analysis of the Jerusalem cult already described; it cannot be known how Guignebert would have resolved it.

30 *Ibid* pp366–75.

31 *Ibid* pp375–6.

32 *L'Eglise primitive* p295.

tions of the Church[33]. There is much agreement upon the exegesis of the relevant texts and upon the types of worship observed in the successive phases of early Christianity. But whereas for Loisy, worship is the very matrix of Christianity, so that Gospels and epistles present us with mystical reflections or cult-legends, for Goguel, it can only be the external expression of an inward faith, even though the early Christians themselves did not distinguish between 'spiritual' faith and sacramental 'realism'[34]. Guignebert takes a midway position; in the case of Paul for instance, worship is the 'form' of the Pauline mystery whose 'content' is the revelation of Christ in his cosmological and soteriological roles[35], but against Goguel he argues that Paul's Christ-mysticism was derived from his cultic experience in the Hellenistic communities. Therefore, within a common concern for the historical reconstruction of the growth and development of liturgical forms in early Christianity, we find the expected differences of emphasis, Loisy taking an extreme 'myth-and-ritual' position and Goguel maintaining a markedly Liberal Protestant outlook.

5.2.5. Doctrinal Diversity and Conformity

It is a sign of their 'independence' that each of these critics rejects the concept of a 'faith delivered once for all to the saints' and accepts the diversity of early Christian belief. Goguel, writing specifically on this point, posits a movement from diversity to unity, against the traditional view of a degeneration of pristine unity of faith into various heresies[1]. He agrees with W. Bauer that there was even more diversity in the first two generations than the sources allow us to perceive[2]. When writing about early 'heresies', he adopts a very relative definition of this term[3]. Loisy and Guignebert do not address themselves specifically to the question, since it is a theological rather than a historical 'problem' (which Goguel solves by recourse to the idea of a unity of religious experience). It is evident to them that there were major readaptations of Christian faith in the

---

33 *Ibid* pp390—1.
34 *Ibid* pp392—3.
35 *Le Christ* p356.

1 *Naissance* ... p14.
2 *Ibid* p18.
3 *Ibid* pp428—30.

first hundred years or so of its existence and that older versions continued to coexist with the new. In the case of Guignebert, the final
phase of his thought only considers the first of these readaptations,
the radical transformation of Christianity achieved in the Hellenistic
milieu. His earlier work on the heresies tends to be undertaken from
a second century perspective.[4] Loisy's chapter on the 'Les premières
théories du mystère' differs however from the more strictly evolutionary analysis of Guignebert by presenting side by side various doctrinal interpretations of Christ and the Church. The 'theories' in
Romans, Hebrews, Colossians, Philippians and the Fourth Gospel
are in the nature of mystical 'gnoses', mostly to be dated in the early
second century and themselves directed in part against other theories[5]. Loisy's further work on the epistles led him to discover even
more separate 'gnoses' of different tendencies and since he is in many
cases unable to suggest a precise date or place of origin, here is diversity at its wildest.[6]

However this same chapter of Loisy concludes with sections on
the 'mystery of the Church' and of the consciousness of the Church
(the latter devoted to Ignatius). Loisy believes that it was in acquiring a mystic consciousness of itself, against 'le débordement de la
gnose' that 'le christianisme commun' became the Catholic Church[7].
It was therefore the gnostic crisis which encouraged conformity,
although it should be remembered that orthodox Christianity is
itself 'une gnose disciplinée, sortie du mouvement qui a produit les
gnoses dites hérétiques, et qui s'est définie elle-même en les condam-
nant'[8]. In particular, it was Marcion who brought the crisis to a head
and precipitated the formation of normative and authoritative Christianity[9]. It should be noted that Loisy arrives at this viewpoint by
his late dating not only of the canonical epistles, but also of I Clement
and the Ignatian epistles.

Goguel on the other hand accepts a much more usual chronology
and authorship of the documents. He would agree with Loisy that
collectively they enshrine 'un mythe d'institution et de justification'

---

4 Cf. eg. GP VIE XII; *Le Christianisme antique* Ch.IX.
5 *Naissance ...* Ch.VIII.
6 Cf. the summary of *Remarques ...* in 2.5.3 Diagram 'B' above.
7 *Naissance ...* p367.
8 *Ibid* p369.
9 *Ibid* pp391ff.

of a religious group[10], although he allows for much more genuine historical reminiscence. The basic fact to be studied is the emergence of the 'ancienne Eglise catholique', i.e. the formation, stabilisation and organisation of a Christian religious society, a process in which sociological principles are operative and where the critic also has to take account of certain forms and groups which failed to stabilise.[11] The plan of Goguel's work, based upon the 'success' of Hellenistic Christianity over against the 'failure' of Jewish Christianity corresponds not only to his placing of the documents, but also to his opinion that the decisive moment in the formation of the Christian Church was c.70 A.D. This 'crisis of growth and adaptation' was occasioned by the disappearance of the first generation of eyewitnesses and apostles and the consequent intervention of 'tradition' and 'authority'; by the recession of charismatic activity; by the 'delay of the Parousia'; by the destruction of Jerusalem and the virtual removal of the Judaising party; by the shift of the Church's centre of gravity from East to West; and by the realisation on the part of the Roman authorities that Christianity was a separate religion[12]. Goguel does not suggest that these factors of themselves produced doctrinal conformity, as is made clear by his treatment of contemporaneous yet distinctive documents of the last part of the first century: Ephesians, the Pastorals, I Peter, Hebrews, the Fourth Gospel, James, the Didache, I Clement[13]. But the 'précatholicisme' of I Clement denotes another decisive break c.100 A.D. Although what 'Clement' writes is theoretical, his ecclesiasticism and reintroduction of a strongly Jewish tone prefigure the fully developed early Catholicism of the late second century A.D.[14] Moreover the writings of this period and of the first half of the second century are nearly all conscious of 'heresies' to be combated and they therefore represent the slow and in many ways pre-theological, assertion of a collective mind ('sound doctrine') against trends of thought, which may in themselves have been more vigorous and more original.[15]

All three critics had a similar view of the consolidation of doctrine

---

10 *Naissance* ... p17.
11 *Ibid* pp22—3.
12 *Ibid* pp32—3.
13 *Ibid* Pt IV.
14 *Ibid* p34; for details v. pp416—26.
15 *Ibid* p470.

in the second century A.D. Reference has already been made to the second century perspective of Guignebert, who, in common with Catholic writers, but for historical rather than theological reasons, stressed the emergence of a fully-constituted ecclesiastical system. It is probable that his account, if written, would have said more about institutional and political factors.[16] Not that these are ignored by Loisy and Goguel. In his chapter on 'L'Eglise catholique' Loisy writes of the decline of the prophets and the rise of the administrators, and moves on to the establishment of a rule of faith, the canon, the creed and the episcopate[17]. Goguel mainly attends to these matters in his second volume: they should be consigned to the 'period of organisation and consolidation' rather than the 'period of creation'[18] and they are therefore fully explored in *l'Eglise primitive* which deals in turn and exhaustively, with the doctrine and organisation of the church, worship, the Christian life and the formation of a Christian literature. None of our writers would therefore separate doctrinal conformity from ecclesiastical conformity.

Loisy and Goguel agree with Renan that it is at the end of the second century that early Catholicism is established and that this is therefore the *terminus ad quem* of their enquiries. Loisy's final page is very reminiscent of Renan in referring to the 'la préhistoire du christianisme' which he has conjecturally tried to reconstruct from 'la légende mystique de son institution', and after which there is abundant documentation[19].

It is true that Goguel makes one or two excursions into the third and fourth centuries (for intance, on the question of the Paschal controversy)[20] but his own grounding in the New Testament and his well-known lack of interest in events post-150 A.D. keep him firmly within bounds. Guignebert, from the evidence of his teaching and previous writing, would not have made such a significant break at this point and his volume *L'Eglise* would have been much more in the nature of a 'history of the early Church' than a 'history of Christian origins' as understood by Renan and his fellow-critics.

---

16 There was abundant material for him to draw upon in, for example, GP ESE, GP VIE 2–3, GP ER, GP PRR, GP VRER; cf. *Le Christianisme antique* Ch.VIII.

17 *Naissance* ... Ch.X.

18 *Naissance* ... p33.

19 *Naissance* ... p443; cf. Renan quoted above in 1.1.1, n.28–30.

20 *L'Eglise Primitive,* Troisième Partie, Ch.V.

5.2.6. Conclusion

This selective and comparative survey of the final thoughts of each critic has demonstrated decisively that they did not together form a 'school'. We have already seen how they were conscious of differences among themselves and they did not relinquish their distinctive positions. Loisy pursued his relentless dissection of the Epistles; he and Guignebert remained faithful to the principles of the *religionsgeschichtliche Schule* long after it had been replaced or transmuted in German scholarship; Goguel continued to operate his distinctions between 'Christianity' and 'the Church', 'experience' and 'dogma' etc. under distant theological influence.

Nevertheless there is a substantial measure of agreement among them concerning both findings and method. Their historical scepticism about the resurrection narratives, their awareness of the crucial importance of pre-Pauline Hellenistic Christianity and the decisive shift away from Jewish Christianity; their ready acceptance of inconsistencies of thought in the Pauline epistles (even if very differently explained) and their view (held in varying degrees) that Paul may not have been as central a figure historically as he is made to appear by the state of the documentation; their close attention to forms of worship as formative and stabilizing elements within the development of Christianity (even if the significance of the cultic dimension is very differently assessed); their recognition that diversity in Christian faith and practice was early and extensive, followed by the unifying, conformist trends of the second century. Such are broadly, the judgements to which their investigations lead them and their concurrence may indeed offer some assurance about the validity of their findings[1].

The three critics stand together in their commitment to a historical method, over against theological interpretation. The method is flexibly conceived and allows the consideration of ritual, psychological and social factors, even if the handling of such elements sometimes reveals a lack of expertise in the relevant disciplines. Flexibility is particularly apparent in the final statements of Loisy and Goguel. Loisy's scepticism about the documents led to an experimental

---

1 Cf. M. Simon. 'The Birth of Christianity. A comparative assessment of Loisy, Guignebert and Goguel'. *FF* 1948 pp135–9. 'Their agreement on essential points suffices to justify our confidence in the method that is common to them both (*sic*): that of historical research independent of doctrinal preconceptions' (p139).

presentation which, however tendentious and unsatisfactory (for instance, in virtually blotting out the first century A.D.) did make the valuable point that early Christian literature, especially as canonised in the New Testament, is the legitimation of early Christian religion. Goguel agreed with this but, taking a less hypercritical view of the texts, he made a leisurely inspection of early Christianity at different stages of development and on different topics, allowing for individual and collective influences and therefore doing greater justice to the complexities of this subject. What we have of the last writings of Guignebert comprise by contrast a more straight-line, evolutionary account, but accompanied by the very ample if not always judicious use of the Jewish and Hellenistic comparative material.

All three critics were therefore concerned with the birth of a religion, to be viewed dynamically as it developed internally and in relation to its environment; they were also preoccupied with the processes whereby this religion acquired self-consciousness, cohesion and stability sufficient for it to take its place in world history. But in order to make a balanced assessment of their contribution to historiography, their work needs to be set in the wider perspective of the history of interpretation.

5.3 THE FRENCH CRITICS IN THE HISTORY OF INTERPRETATION

In order to introduce the work of Loisy, Guignebert and Goguel it was necessary to consider the work of Ernest Renan and the state of religion in France during the turbulent decades 1890–1910. The ecclesiastical, ideological and institutional framework was seen to have some bearing upon their academic careers and critical orientation. But during the period following the First World War, religious debate lost something of its former intensity. Questions concerning Christian origins were not as near to the centre of intellectual life as had been the case, for example, at the time of the Modernist crisis.[1] Catholic contributions were inevitably muted[2]. Couchoud and his

---

1 For example, a composite volume *La Renaissance religieuse* ed. G. Guy-Grand (1928), with contributions by Catholics, Protestants, Jews and humanists, has very little on New Testament interpretation, except for a short piece by Couchoud.

2 For example, in his survey *Un Demi-siècle de pensée catholique* (1937), E. Magnin only

associates aroused a certain amount of public interest in the late 1920s, but this did not persist. Therefore, the critical work whose results have been examined has to be viewed in the seemingly narrower context of the history of Biblical interpretation. It is however an international context and one to which our critics were conscious of belonging, whatever their differences of opinion and approach by comparison with more traditional contributions.

The history of the study of Christian origins is naturally of great interest to Christian theology and to modern religious thought generally. For that reason it is well documented, although there has been a greater concentration of interest upon the question of the historical Jesus than upon that of the early Church. However, in the latter field, there are a number of useful *Forschungsberichte* and it is not necessary to repeat work already carried out.[3] Most such surveys, even those written by Catholics, concentrate upon developments in German Protestant scholarship and draw attention to successive phases: the Tübingen school; Ritschl and his followers (including Harnack); the *religionsgeschichtliche Schule*; Form-criticism; the perspective of 'salvation-history'.

Some of those who survey the field from an ecclesiastical standpoint are highly critical of students of early Christian history who exhibit 'positivism', 'historicism', 'rationalism' or 'evolutionism' in excluding from their accounts the possibility of the supernatural and

---

devotes 3 pages to exegesis out of 90 on the period 1918–37. It should however be noted that the contribution of M.–J. Lagrange and his colleagues of the Ecole Biblique de Jérusalem was massive by comparison with their numbers; cf. *L'Oeuvre exégétique et historique du R.P. Lagrange* (several writers, 1935).

3 V. eg. R. Bultmann, 'Urchristliche Religion (1915–1925)' *ARW* 24 pp83–164; L. Salvatorelli 'From Locke to Reitzenstein. The historical interpretation of the origins of Christianity' *HTR* XXII (1929) pp263–367; E. von Dobschütz, 'Die Kirche im Urchristentum' *ZNTW* 28, 1929, pp107–118; O. Linton, *Das Problem der Urkirche* (1932); F.–M. Braun, *Aspects nouveaux du problème de l'Eglise* (1941); S.J. Johnson, 'The Emergence of the Christian Church in the Pre-Catholic Period' in *The Study of the Bible Today and Tomorrow* ed. H.R. Willoughby (1947) pp345–65; L. Goppelt, *Die apostolische und nachapostolische Zeit* (1962, ET 1970), Introduction; articles on 'Urchristentum' in *ThR* 5 (1933) pp186–200, 239–258, 289–301, 319–334(Windisch); 14 (1942) pp81–95, 155–173; 17 (1948–9) pp3–50, 103–142; 18 (1950) pp1–53 (Kümmel). Cf. also surveys of work on the Acts of the Apostles, eg. A.C. McGiffert and J.W. Hunkin in *The Beginnings of Christianity* Vol.II Part III (1920) pp363–433; J. Dupont, *Les Problèmes du livre des Actes d'après les travaux récents* (1950) and *Les Sources du livre des Actes* (1960); W.W. Gasque, *A History of the Criticism of the Acts of the Apostles* (1975).

of divine intervention in history[4]. But this may be to assume that the study of early Christianity is *ipso facto* a 'godly discipline' and it does not reckon with the possibility that contemporary confessional concerns, especially in the areas of doctrine and church order, may distort historical judgement. The French critics were thoroughly acquainted with the debates of their day and were consistently critical of confessional motivation. They absorbed much, of course, from the German standard works — commentaries, histories, monographs, articles — and their debt was all the more inevitable by reason of their comparatively small numbers. But it is not only underinvestment which sets the French critics apart. Their 'historical' stance raised them above the ebb and flow of theological opinion.[5] Even Goguel, in whose work Protestant concerns are at times apparent, resisted changes in theological fashion in order to remain faithful to the search for historical truth inspired in him by Wilhelm Herrmann; the debt of Loisy and Guignebert to the *religionsgeschichtliche Schule* never extended to the theological synthesis of Ernst Troeltsch, the theologian of the school. One might characterise this position by saying that whereas confessional critics have been preoccupied with 'the Church', especially in its beliefs and its structures, the more independent writers have addressed themselves to 'Christianity' as a religion.

It would of course be unfair to suggest that the confessional writer is oblivious to the claims of historical objectivity. Many standard German Protestant works of the later nineteenth and early twentieth centuries are relatively free from any dominant theological or philosophical argument[6]. There was indeed among some scholars of Protestant allegiance a consciously articulated desire to turn away

---

4   Eg. F.V. Filson in 'The central problem concerning Christian origins' *The Study of the Bible Today and Tomorrow* ed. H.R. Willoughby (1947) pp329–44; one must either 'exclude divine working and work with tangible data' or accept 'the fact of God and the New Testament explanation of his workings'; 'this is one of those life issues on which there is no valid neutrality'. (p344).

5   Cf. eg. Loisy on the Harnack-Sohm controversy (v. above 2.2, n.69); Goguel's reservations about the Form critics (v. above 4.4); generally, their indifference to the growing 'consensus' between Protestants and Catholics in recognising corporate elements in early Christian life and thought (cf. F.–M. Braun, *op.cit.* Ch.III)

6   Eg. C. Weizsäcker, *Das apostolische Zeitalter der christlichen Kirche* ([2]1886); A. Harnack, *Die Mission und Ausbreitung des Christentums in den ersten drei Jahrhunderten;* ([2]1905); J. Weiss, *Das Urchristentum* (1914–17); H. Lietzmann, *Geschichte der alten Kirche I Die Anfänge* (1932).

from 'the theology of the New Testament' to 'the history of the early Christian religion'[7]. Seminal works emerging from the world of Protestant scholarship appeared to pose grave challenges to an orthodox understanding of Christian origins[8]. But the writers of these works occupied chairs of New Testament exegesis in faculties of theology, where there was an endemic tradition of dialectics between history and theology. By contrast, Loisy, Guignebert and Goguel felt no constraint to pursue what might be called the 'relevance' factor and had no immediate concern for any theological use to which their writings might be put. It was this attitude which differentiated them from much contemporary scholarship and which, in the history of interpretation, marks them out as a minority group.

The preponderance of confessional writing in this field may be gauged from the fact that many works fall into the categories of either 'History of New Testament Times' or 'History of the Early Church'. Standard terminology, such as 'apostolic age' or 'Urchristentum' suggest a quest for what is early and therefore normative. Even when no special distinction is made between the canonical and non-canonical literature, there is inevitably the impression of being on holy ground. Certain differences are of course to be found between Catholics and Protestants. The latter have inherited from the Reformation the idea of a 'Fall' somewhere in the early Church, whereby pristine purity and unity of doctrine were lost, until their rediscovery by the Reformers. Protestant writers have stressed antitheses such as Scripture and Tradition, or Spirit and Institution, and have located the 'Fall' at various points in the first and second centuries A.D.[9] In reaction against the decline into 'early Catholicism', Protes-

---

7   Cf. W. Wrede, *Über Aufgabe und Methode der sogenannten neutestamentlichen Theologie* (1897), translated with a substantial Introduction by R. Morgan in *The Nature of New Testament Theology* (1973). In *Ehrfurcht vor dem Leben* (A. Schweitzer Festschrift 1954) J. Héring writing on 'De H.J. Holtzmann à Albert Schweitzer' (pp21–9) draws attention to Schweitzer's sympathy with Wrede on this issue (p26).

8   Eg. W. Bousset, *Kyrios Christos* (1913); R. Bultmann, *Geschichte der synoptischen Tradition* (1921); W. Bauer, *Rechtgläubigkeit und Ketzerei im ältesten Christentum* (1934).

9   As examples of the perennial Protestant interest in this question cf. eg. O. Cullmann, 'The Tradition' ET in *The Early Church* (1956) pp55–99, for a theological defence of the fixing of the Canon in the second century; at the other extreme, E. Käsemann, 'Paul and Early Catholicism' ET in *New Testament Questions of Today* (1969) pp236–251 for 'early Catholicism' as a falling away from the doctrine of the authentic Pauline epistles.

tants have also stressed doctrine over ritual, charismatic over institutional elements, diversity of organisational forms over unilateral or monolithic tendencies, individual experience over collective representations, democracy over authority.[10]

Such distinctions have however often been disregarded by the Catholic writer because what he has wished to find above all in the early church is continuity. Catholic doctrines, institutions and rituals are to be traced back as far as possible and preferably to Jesus himself. The main distinction to be observed is between the 'deposit of faith' and the divinely appointed institutions on the one hand and the heresies and schisms by which they were threatened on the other[11]. Catholic resistance to Biblical criticism was of course in no small part due to the apparent undermining of the traditionally conceived continuity by such critical views as the non-historicity of the Fourth Gospel and the non-Pauline authorship of the Pastoral Epistles. It was however possible for Catholics in response to the new situation to make increasing use of the notion of 'development' and to point to certain phases in the early church (eg. the proto-Catholicism represented by I Clement and Ignatius) as bringing to fruition what had previously been in germ.[12]

These very brief remarks on the nature of confessional involvement in the question of the early church may serve as a reminder of factors which, consciously or not, have shaped much writing on the subject. Some of the sharper Protestant-Catholic controversy has of course been ironed out by a number of factors in twentieth century church life and scholarship: recognition of the eschatological dimension in early Christian thought; a more scientific approach to questions of text, language and concepts; the 'quest for the early Church' produced by kerygmatic theology, by 'Biblical theology' of the salvation-history variety and by the ecumenical movement itself[13]. Scholarly differences, for example as between 'radicals' and 'con-

---

10 Cf. the comments of S. Neill, *The Interpretation of the New Testament 1861—1961* (1964) pp186—9 on the confessional motivation behind the concept of 'early Catholicism'.

11 Cf. eg. Batiffol, *L'Eglise naissante et le catholicisme* (1909) described above in 1.2.

12 This type of argument is developed by the contributors on Christian origins to the two Catholic symposia produced in reply to Reinach's *Orpheus*: L. Venard and P. Batiffol in *Où en est l'histoire des religions?* (1912) Ch.XII and XIII; P. Rousselot and J. Huby in *Christus* (1913) Ch.XVI Section I. Cf. above 1.4, n.33 for the continuing influence of these accounts.

13 On this 'quest' v. G. Downing, *The Church and Jesus* (1968) Ch.1.

servatives' on the question of the historicity of the Acts of the Apostles, can cut right across confessional boundaries. But whether Catholic or Protestant, most Christian writers exhibit characteristics which are not simply dictated by the nature of the materials. For example, chapters on Judaism and on Greco-Roman religion are often conceived as 'background' evidence, rather than to illustrate the ongoing dialectic between Christianity and its environment. There is an understandable concentration of interest upon the doctrinal and ecclesiastical dimensions, at the expense of sociological analysis[14]. Protestant treatments may devote an inordinate amount of space to St. Paul, which, because he is particularly well documented, is understandable, although historically he may not have been as prominent as the records suggest.[15] Catholic accounts may over-indulge themselves in hagiography and martyrology, because the early Church must appear as the 'age of faith' *par excellence*[16].

It is not being suggested that the French critics were immune from their own brands of apriorism, which by now have been sufficiently demonstrated,[17] or that writers with a confessional allegiance have always allowed their view of early Christianity to be shaped merely by apologetics. But it can be said that in the work of Renan, Albert and Jean Réville, Loisy, Guignebert and Goguel, there was a French speaking tradition of historical research which provided an antidote to some of the covert theologising which may be found in Catholic and Protestant scholarship.[18] It may well be that for this very reason, the French tradition has received comparatively little attention in the history of interpretation. Renan is still read, of course, for his literary achievement, but his successors have not been widely noticed.

Even in France itself, the reception of the works of Loisy, Guignebert and Goguel was restricted, but this was not altogether surprising. Beyond the pages of the *Revue Critique,* the *Revue de l'Histoire des*

---

14 On this point v. John G. Gager, *Kingdom and Community: the Social World of Early Christianity* (1975) Ch.1.

15 Eg. in both C. Weizsäcker, *Das apostolische Zeitalter* ... and in J. Weiss, *Das Urchristentum*, Paul occupies 2 books out of 5, as well as cropping up elsewhere.

16 Eg. in J. Lebreton and J. Zeiller, *L'Eglise primitive* (1934) successive chapters are entitled 'Les Missions de Saint Paul', 'Saint Pierre et les débuts de l'Eglise romaine', 'Saint Jacques et Saint Jean'. Cf. the strictures of Guignebert upon this work in *RH* 180 (1937) pp308–319.

17 Cf. above, esp. 2.6, 3.7, 4.7.

18 On this point, v. M. Simon, 'Histoire des religions, histoire du christianisme, histoire de

Religions and the *Revue d'Histoire et de Philosophie Religieuses*, they could not expect much dispassionate comment. The Catholic journals were bound to be hostile to both Loisy and Guignebert and also, if not to quite the same extent, to Goguel. The most notable Catholic Biblical scholar, M.–J. Lagrange, never ceased his attacks upon Loisy, as his riposte to Loisy's *Mémoires, M. Loisy et le modernisme* (1932) sufficiently indicates[19]. The Catholic religious revival, literary and philosophical, had always been intransigently opposed to progressive trends in exegesis. Catholic novelists poured discredit upon 'progressives' within the Church and without, and a notable instance of this was *Augustin, ou le Maître est là* (1933) by Joseph Malègue, in which a young intellectual loses his faith through over-exposure to modern Biblical criticism[20]. It was only in the last few years before Loisy's death that the Catholic philosopher Jean Guitton began a cautious reassessment of Loisy's work (bringing down Loisy's wrath about his ears in the process)[21]. We have noted the reasons which excluded the independent historians of early Christianity from making common cause with the sociological school of religious studies in France associated with the name of Durkheim: there was a fundamental difference of mentality between the painstaking historico-literary approach of the exegetes and the more speculative theorising of the sociologists[22].

An interesting if idiosyncratic reaction to our critics was expressed by the Protestant economist André Siegfried during his speech at the reception of the Catholic historian Daniel-Rops into the Aca-

l'Eglise: réflexions méthodologiques' in *Liber Amicorum* (Bleeker Festschrift) (1969) p196.

19 Lagrange had already expressed his opposition to Protestant and 'rationalist' exegesis in *Le sens du christianisme d'après l'exégèse allemande* (1918) as well as in his numerous commentaries and articles; but his quarrel with Loisy was more personal, especially after the attacks made upon him in the latter's *Mémoires*. For his earlier differences with Loisy v. above 1.2.

20 On the author and his work v. Elizabeth Michael, *Joseph Malègue, Sa Vie – Son Oeuvre* (1957).

21 J. Guitton, *La Pensée de M. Loisy* (1936); cf. also the important references to Loisy in *Portrait de M. Pouget* (1941) and *Dialogues avec M. Pouget* (1954). For Loisy's reply to Guitton v. *Un mythe apologétique* (1939). It was not of course generally known that *Un Clerc qui n'a pas trahi: Alfred Loisy d'après ses Mémoires* (1931) by 'Sylvain Leblanc' was in fact by Henri Bremond, Catholic priest and academician; for details of its composition v. E. Poulat, *Une Oeuvre clandestine d'Henri Bremond* (Rome 1972).

22 Cf. above 2.5.2, n.23; 3.5,n.17. On the Durkheimian tradition in French religious studies, there is much information to be gleaned from *Introduction aux sciences humaines des religions*, ed. H. Desroche and J. Séguy (1970).

démie Française in 1956. It does however illustrate the traditional polarisation of opinion in France. Siegfried believed there to be a fundamental contradiction between the religiously committed writer who produced 'sacred history' and the necessarily agnostic view of the historian; the two attitudes could not expect to be found in a single author.

> Après avoir lu le Père de Grandmaison ou le doyen Maurice Goguel, chrétiens rompus aux méthodes critiques, je ne suis pas fâché de me referer à M. Guignebert, religieusement aveugle, mais scientifiquement compétent, me disant qu'ainsi la vérité est au moins cerné.[23]

But such close attention to the problems is probably to be explained by Siegfried's Protestant background. The more common attitude among the educated public was to consider that the study of Christian origins was an affair for the 'curés' and the 'anticurés'. Educated public opinion was only too easily distracted from a serious attention to real issues by the activities of Houtin, Couchoud and Turmel[24]. It was never easy in France to find acceptance for an 'independent' position on religious issues which was not at the same time fiercely rationalist and anticlerical.

Abroad, the French critics were not much noticed. In Germany, Loisy's and Goguel's earlier writings were extensively and sympathetically considered by Albert Schweitzer in the second edition of his *Geschichte der Leben-Jesu-Forschung* (1913)[25]. The later works of Goguel received regular and respectful attention in, for example, the pages of the *Theologische Rundschau*, but Loisy had to await a posthumous attempted rehabilitation of his reputation as both religious thinker and exegete in Friedrich Heiler, *Der Vater des katholischen Modernismus Alfred Loisy* (1947). England was somewhat more receptive, if only because most English scholars could read French, even when they were ignorant of German. Liberal Christians of several denominations had taken a close interest in French religious life at the time of the Modernist crisis and in particular it was the *Hibbert Journal* whose pages were hospitable to French contributors and commentators on the French religious scene. It will be recalled that Loisy himself wrote for this Journal[26] and interest in his post-

---

23 *Edouard Le Roy et son fauteuil* (1956) Part II (no pagination).
24 V. eg. references to Houtin and Turmel in André Gide, *Journal*, for 24.12.1931 and 23.7.1932. (Pléiade edition of *Journal 1899–1939* pp1097–8; 1141–2).
25 Ch.XXIV.
26 Cf. above 2.1, n.26 and 2.2, n.9; his contributions are to be found in *HJ* 8 (1909–10)

modernist writings was sustained by a number of contributors, including Miss M.D. Petre[27] and by the editor himself, L.P. Jacks. Jacks wrote a strong defence of Loisy in 1924—5, under the title 'A Creed in Harmony with Modern Thought' and continued to champion Loisy's writings[28], although allowing the opposite point of view to be put by Vincent Taylor[29]. It was Jacks who translated into into English Loisy's *La Naissance du christianisme* and *Les origines du Nouveau Testament*. The radical conclusions of Guignebert and Loisy aroused a mixed reception in England having some influence upon e.g. E.W. Barnes[30] and S.G.F. Brandon[31], while being strongly rejected by e.g. H.G. Wood[32] and T.F. Glasson[33].

Thus, whereas Goguel's writings, in a well established Liberal Protestant tradition, won themselves a recognised place in the history of interpretation, Loisy and Guignebert had but few followers.[34] But all three suffered an eclipse produced by a variety of circumstances: the second world war, the fresh impetus given to the study of Christian origins by discoveries at Qumran and Nag Hammadi and, perhaps most importantly, by the interpretations of early Christianity in the categories of existentialism (Bultmann) or of salvation-history (e.g. Cullmann, Daniélou). Such interpretations could not but have been suspect to scholars who had devoted their lives to historical objectivity, shorn of all theological perspectives.

5.4 *FINAL ASSESSMENT*

A final assessment of the critical work described above does not consist so much in saying wherein these critics were right or wrong,

---

pp473—97; 10 (1911—12) pp45—64; 26 (1927—8) pp249—51; 33 (1934—5) pp10—21, 219—21; 34 (1935—6) pp378—87; 36 (1937—8) pp380—94; 509—29).

27 She reviewed a number of Loisy's books, including the *Mémoires* (*HJ* 29 (1930—31) pp655—66); N.B. also her posthumous tribute *Alfred Loisy — His Religious Significance* (1944).

28 *HJ* 32 (1933—4) pp321—41; 495—513; 49(1950—51) pp22—31.

29 *HJ* 24 (1925—6) pp563—72; 33 (1934—5) pp22—36; 48 (1949—50) pp339—47.

30 *The Rise of Christianity* (1947).

31 *The Fall of Jerusalem and the Christian Church* (1951).

32 'The Radical French Critics Loisy and Guignebert' *HJ* 52 (1953—4) pp144—55, reprinted in *Jesus in the Twentieth Century* (1960) pp96—110.

33 'Loisy on New Testament Origins' *Modern Churchman* 41 (1951) pp317—23.

34 One should mention a continuing interest in the works of Loisy in Italy, upon which v. M. Guasco, *Alfred Loisy in Italia* (1975).

but in assigning to them a significance within the story of ongoing attempts by Biblical scholars and historians — ecclesiastical and secular — to rediscover the physiognomy of early Christianity. The attempts are never-ceasing for two reasons: the nature of the documents (which are partisan, of uncertain provenance and far from providing total coverage); and the stance of the modern critic. The documents can be interpreted, arranged and inter-related in endless permutations and our study has indicated that the ways of doing so are in part determined by the critic's general view of Christianity and religion. There may well never be a final definitive version. In the light of ongoing research, some ideas may fall by the wayside as no longer tenable. A consensus does not of course constitute a proof, but nevertheless one may say, for instance, in the light of ongoing historical work upon the texts, that Loisy and Guignebert overstressed the parallels with the Mystery religions at the expense of Jewish influences, that Loisy's theories of a 'style rythmé' and of the composition of Pauline epistles are highly unlikely and that Goguel was over-emphatic about differences between Jerusalem and Antioch. But in order to consider any lasting value in this phase of criticism it seems appropriate to ask two questions, which would have been taken by the critics themselves as significant and which could well help to 'place' them satisfactorily. The first question is, to what extent is their contribution a specifically *French* contribution? And secondly, can their work be fairly seen as an 'independent' contribution to their field of study?

5.4.1 A French contribution?

There seems little doubt that the work of the three critics was affected by the religious and intellectual climate prevalent in France. It is not irrelevant in this connection to mention the language and style employed by these writers, for unlike Germany and, to a lesser extent England, most writing about early Christianity in the French language was in the ecclesiastical sector and therefore reverential in tone. Renan had of course forged a literary style of some subtlety and amplitude which established a more independent tradition of writing, but whose 'imaginative' qualities precluded that sobriety which a more 'scientific' generation sought. It was part of Loisy's achievement, modelling himself upon Fénelon, to devise a prose style whose clarity and irony caused both offense and delight. Guignebert brought the language of the professional historian to bear upon the sacred texts and the sacred period of origins. Goguel was not a stylist, but helped to familiarise the French reading public with the increasingly international language of Biblical scholarship[1]. The insertion of this literary and linguistic activity into a French milieu is of some importance in making a final assessment.

Religiously, the milieu was predominantly Catholic. The deep-rooted and extensive presence of Catholicism meant that non-Catholics, whether apostate, rationalist or Protestant, could not but to some extent define themselves over against that presence when writing about what was traditionally an ecclesiastical preserve. Renan had delivered an unforgettable blow upon the Catholic system when, in the *Vie de Jésus*, he had described Jesus as an 'incomparable man'[2] and his successors were to continue to scandalise orthodox opinion in their treatment of the Gospels. But even more than Renan, they emphasised, in differing degrees, factors in early Christianity which ran counter to the Catholic version. Foremost among these was radical discontinuity (especially emphasised by Guignebert): between Jesus and the apostles, between the Palestinian and Hellenistic communities, between earlier spontaneous 'faith' and later orthodox 'belief'. Connected with this was the phenomenon of irreconcilable diversity, most ably demonstrated by Goguel, less successfully by Loisy in his analysis of the epistles. Thirdly, the importance given to comparative studies by Loisy and Guignebert contained an element of anti-Catholic diatribe: if Christianity was but one of several 'mysteries' of salvation in the Mediterranean world whose success was due to contingent as well as intrinsic factors, then its uniqueness and universality were called into question.

However, even apologists for the Church could not claim that France was the totally Catholic land of their desires. Several references have been made to the ideological polarisation of France under

---

1 Cf. M. Simon in *The Primitive Church* (ET 1964): 'His works are written without any regard for literary style' (p9). It should be recalled that the works of eg. Holtzmann, Harnack, Jülicher, J. Weiss, Bousset, Lietzmann, von Dobschütz and Bultmann were not available in French translation.

2 *OC* IV p96: 'l'homme incomparable auquel la conscience universelle a décerné le titre de Fils de Dieu, et cela en toute justice ...'; Henriette Psichari in *Renan d'après lui-même* (1937) claims that Renan's original draft of this passage better represents his 'integral thought': ' ... auquel la conscience de l'humanité a accordé le titre de Dieu et de fils de Dieu, le premier avec une exagération fâcheuse, le second avec justice' (p219).

the Third Republic and this meant that for most Frenchmen the only obvious alternative to the Catholic Church was rationalistic anti-clericalism. It is all the more to their credit therefore that in this situation our three critics steered a mid-way course. Guignebert was certainly closest to the republican ideology; but however alien he personally found religious belief — whether first-century Christianity or contemporary Catholicism— he believed as an academic duty that it deserved his sympathetic investigation. So he could not write as disparagingly as Salomon Reinach did in *Orpheus*, nor could he join the *mythologues*. Both he and Loisy kept their distance from the theories of Durkheim who was often regarded as the embodiment of the French secular University. Loisy's opposition to Reinach and Couchoud was unwavering and so too, to the surprise of many, was his anti-rationalism, which in the 1920s became something of a crusade for him[3]. The Protestantism of Goguel obviously predisposed him to take up the mid-way critical stance. All were united in their opposition to Catholic views of dogma; but their historical researches into early Christianity would not permit them to embrace the dogmas of rationalism.

This critical position, radical vis-à-vis Catholicism, but cautious of creating a 'system' of counter-orthodoxy, may also be connected with their academic status. Apart from Goguel's work at the Faculté Protestante, their employment was in secular institutions. By contrast with the theological faculties of Germany and England, with their strong ecclesiastical links, the Separation of Church and State in France had made final the distinction between the confessional and 'independent' sectors. It was in their desire to maintain a genuinely independent tradition that they eschewed the extremes.

A common desire among the three critics, even if variously expressed, was to view the origins of Christianity in the context of the history of religions, and, even more broadly, of the history of mankind. Goguel was no exception to this[4], and in considering the birth of Christianity he starts from general considerations about the birth of a 'new religious object'. In this common desire the French background is particularly apparent. Renan had formulated similar ambi-

---

3 Cf. esp. his collection *Religion et humanité* (1926).
4 Cf. his comment, quoted fully in 4.1, n.26 to the effect that he was 'more religious than Christian'.

tions[5]. The setting-up of the Section des Sciences Religieuses at
EPHE had supplied an institutional framework for such an ambition
to be realised, unparalleled in other countries, and the work of the
Liberal Protestants Albert and Jean Réville and Auguste Sabatier
had provided an impetus and an example. The commitment of Loisy
and Guignebert to this tradition has been noted in some of their
declarations of intent[6]. Goguel was an obvious successor to the
Réville-Sabatier heritage. However, one must record a wide gap
between our critics' aspirations and achievements in this quarter.
They saw themselves as historians of religion, but they were unfortunate in that the history of religions was a comparatively young
and underdeveloped field of study. If they had been able to draw
upon a well-established body of writing in such fields as the psychology, sociology and phenomenology of religion, they might have
made more striking contributions to the study of Christian origins.
In the circumstances, they were probably correct to continue to
tread the familiar ways of historical exegesis. By carrying out this
work in the spirit of Renan and other predecessors, they kept alive a
native tradition without any strict parallels in other countries and
susceptible of further development in the sphere of the history of
religions[7].

   In summary of much of the above, one may refer again to the
deliberately non-theological stance adopted by each critic. France as
the home of positivism may have been peculiarly suited to the
cultivation of such a stance, although these critics only exhibit
'positivism' in the very general sense of seeking to establish facts and
causality with a minimum of interpretation. But in the fields of New
Testament studies and church history, their approach represents a

---

5   Cf. above 1.1.2 n.27.
6   Cf. above 2.1, n.11—12; 3.1, n.9.
7   The so-called 'Chicago School' in the United States might appear to offer parallels, all
    the more because of the separation of Church and State in America, as in France, by
    contrast with Germany and England; cf. esp. the sociological perspectives of one of its
    more radical representatives, S.J. Case, who wrote *The Evolution of Early Christianity:
    a genetic study of first-century Christianity in relation to its religious environment*
    (1914); *The Social Origins of Christianity* (1923); *The Social Triumph of the Ancient
    Church* (1934). But R.W. Funk reports that although scholars of the Chicago School
    were critical of theological imperialism in Biblical studies, they retained strong con-
    fessional interests and did not achieve the transformation to a secular academic context:
    'The Watershed of the American Biblical Tradition: the Chicago School, First Phase,
    1892—1920' *JBL* 95 (1976) pp4—22.

conscious reaction against the preponderance of metaphysics in the German tradition. Already as a Catholic apologist, Loisy had sought to establish the claims of the historian over against theological control and as an independent critic he believed that he represented a French non-speculative tradition which he had learned from Renan[8]. The anti-theological bias of Guignebert has been fully documented above[9]. Goguel was always faithful to the cause of *Wahrhaftigkeit*, which he interpreted as historical research without dogmatic presuppositions[10]. The dangers of this critical stance were twofold: the introduction of unconscious preconceptions of the author's own, and the failure to do full justice to the theological content of the early Christian documents themselves. Our authors did not entirely avoid these dangers, but at the time of their writing they may be seen as entirely justified in pursuing their historical ideals. The French milieux to which they belonged and their personal biographies and allegiances encouraged and in part formed those ideals. The phase of criticism which they comprise has its home in what we have called the 'independent sector' of French religious thought, if that sector is enlarged to include the Liberal Protestants, and it is to the question of independence in their criticism to which we must finally return.

5.4.2 An 'independent' contribution?

The concept of 'independence' in the study of religion is open to much debate: it properly requires to be considered in relation to other issues, such as secularisation, the rise and development of historico-critical methods, the academic and institutional status of the 'history of religions', the possibility of historical objectivity, hermeneutics etc. In the particularly sensitive field of Christian origins the problem is intensified by the strong confessional interests at stake. The preceding remarks have shown that the issues emerged with special clarity in France because of ecclesiastical fixity on the one hand and the institutionalisation of a secular counter-culture in the State educational system on the other. It might of course be objected that this very confrontation of opinion led to an over-

---

8 V. above 1.1.2, n.12 and 14.
9 V. above 3.7.
10 V. above 4.1, n.9.

simplification of the issues, but since the critics in question endea-
voured, as we have seen, to occupy middle ground, they can be taken
to have contributed something of value to the elucidation of the
problem, if not its final solution.

An adequate treatment of the theoretical questions cannot be
attempted within the space of this study. Rather, in terms of the
French situation, it is proposed to survey a range of factors from
which these critics might have claimed independence, or from which
they may be deemed independent by the outside observer. Then,
more positively, it is proposed to mention the uses to which they
wished to put this independence and to estimate how far it was
mitigated or encouraged by their personal outlook or 'philosophy'.
Much of what is said under these headings will be by way of
summary of the more detailed examination of their views already
attempted.

It is possible to suggest a scale of factors which might carry
weight in the minds of European writers who, from a twentieth-
century standpoint, address themselves to the period of early Christianity:

(a) ecclesiastical control
(b) conscious theological interests
(c) general Christian assumptions
(d) general religious assumptions
(e) 'European cultural parochialism'

By the last phrase is meant the European outlook which, however
secular, regards the emergence of Christianity as a pivotal point in
human history, even though such a view might be by no means as
evident to, let us say, an Indian historian.

It is obvious that, on this scale, all three critics are independent
of factors (a) and (b). The assumptions which run through the work
of Goguel, deriving as they do from his Liberal Protestant background, are to be described as 'Christian' rather than simply 'religious'; whereas the general writings of Loisy show him to have left
behind a specifically Christian viewpoint in favour of a mystical
'religion of humanity', thus retaining significant religious assumptions. Guignebert, on the other hand, can be said to have abandoned
factors (c) and (d), except insofar as the Christian religion and religions in general, are for him a proper and worthwhile object of
study. In none of the critics is there positive evidence of a rejection
of factor (e); Loisy and Guignebert certainly envisage the historical

eclipse of Christianity; but neither of them appears seriously to question European cultural hegemony. There is therefore a sense in which Guignebert is the most independent and Goguel the least independent of the three critics; but it can only be in a limited sense, for to operate such a scale is to give the impression that the factors listed are all inhibiting factors. It could be argued for instance that even if ecclesiastical control is undesirable, a positive religious orientation can actively assist the objective study of religion. Nevertheless, insofar as the critics wished their historical work to be free of presuppositions, the scale provides some indication of how they stand in relation to certain major preconceptions in the European tradition.

In order to remedy some of the deficiencies of this analysis, it is useful to enquire how far the critics were free of negative attitudes towards their subject matter. Such attitudes are certainly to be found in Loisy and Guignebert. In the case of each critic there is a discernible tendency to project back upon early Christianity the hostility which each critic felt towards institutional Catholicism. With Loisy, this happens very notably in the Commentary on the Acts of the Apostles; with Guignebert we may allude to his constant preoccupation to demonstrate that central Catholic dogmas and institutions were secondary developments in the nascent religion. Each critic also uses language to describe early Christian literature and beliefs — eg. 'fiction', 'infantile', 'mediocre' — which would not normally issue from the pen of the confessional writer. These features indicate that Loisy and Guignebert brought to their task more value-judgements than they would admit to. Goguel on the other hand, while not afraid of making radical critical judgements — e.g. on the resurrection — which offended the orthodox, had as a Christian believer, a more positive attitude towards his materials. We may say therefore that, for anti-confessional reasons, there was some danger that Loisy and Guignebert presented distorted views and that, viewed in this light, Goguel had a more balanced outlook.

However, all the critics were united in excluding from their accounts the miraculous, the supernatural and ideas of a divine intervention in history. It is precisely at this point that the whole question of independence becomes most thorny. To many of their opponents, this position was the height of negativity since, questions of ecclesiastical conformity apart, it refused to take seriously the outlook of the early Christians themselves. But for the critics it was a real measure of their independence. They could justify their position by an appeal to the principles and working methods of modern historiography. It is of course possible to call these into question and to suggest that 'positivistic' assumptions are as dogmatic and distorting as those of the religious believer but in terms of the time and circumstances of their critical work, the critics' claim to independence on this point must be upheld[1]. It was essential, after the refining of historical methods throughout the nineteenth century, that these should be applied to the early church, discounting, as for other historical periods, the miraculous and the allegedly providential. Even if the methods were not fully adequate for the task, it was particularly important for them to be exploited in France, after the extensive work carried out in Germany.

Positively, therefore, it was in the name of history and of objectivity that they wrote. Guignebert appears as the most resolutely dedicated to these ideals. As a historian he happened to alight upon the early Christian period through his study of Tertullian. His existential motivation can in part be sought in the political and religious events which produced the Separation of Church and State and his commitment to secularism was never in doubt, but the historian always dominated the secular apologist, as his rejection of merely rationalist accounts shows. But perhaps such a dispassionate view of the events will not after all produce the most lively history-writing. In the cases of Loisy and Goguel, there was a more obvious element of personal involvement. This allowed for perspectives not solely dictated by history and these helped to nourish their wiritng without acting as a theological strait-jacket. The personal drama of Loisy, so minutely and publicly analysed by himself and others, lent a dimension of pugnacity to his writings as he dissociated himself from all available shades of opinion in what we have called his 'ferocious quest for independence'. At the same time, even though he kept strictly separate his historical writings and his general disquisitions on religion, the fact that he saw early Christianity as a great spiritual moment in the history of mankind gave him meta-historical vistas denied to the 'pure' historian. So his running battles with his contem-

---

1   On this issue cf. O. Chadwick, *The secularization of the European Mind in the Nineteenth century* (1975) Ch.8: 'History and the Secular'; discussing the interpretation of miracle by historians, Chadwick concludes 'all history was 'secular' by 1870' (p197).

poraries and his pan-mysticism are vitalising elements in his work. The case of Goguel is more straightforward. The obvious elements of confessionalism in his work, for example his life-long devotion to the historico-literary exegesis of the canonical documents, and his preference for certain aspects of early Christianity over against others, are counter-balanced by his allocation of space to all the aspects and by his quickness to detect excessive theological interests in other critics. His subdued confessionalism, therefore, provides a background for his writing which acts as an acceptable foil to his historical reconstruction.

It seems therefore that although the quest for absolute independence is illusory, more relative types of independence are worth pursuing. The perspectives of the individual historian and of the age in which he writes cannot but affect his selection and presentation of events. But this does not mean that the 'perspectivism' urged by certain Christian apologists, whether of the 'hard' or 'soft' variety[2], must inevitably dominate the academic study of Christian origins. The French experience described above may be seen as an argument in favour of continuing attempts, at different stages in the history of interpretation and in different cultural milieux, to renew the 'independent' tradition over against the ecclesiastical sector. This is not to deny the possibility of much valuable historical work being undertaken by critics of confessional allegiance. But a counterpoise seems desirable for reasons of academic objectivity, possibly located in the general history of religions, where the still lively questions of methodology might offer new perspectives.

Any academic study claiming to be 'independent' must of course, in the case of Christian origins, be scrutinised for possible distortion produced by anti-Christian sentiment. On this score, Marxist contributions might, for example, be more suspect than those of Liberal Jewish writers. But significant accounts of Christian origins by Hindu, Buddhist and Muslim writers are still awaited, as is a work by a major secular historian in his own right. Such activity, taken overall, might promote greater objectivity, even if there can be no final serenity. For, like absolute 'independence', absolute detachment is an unlikely ambition and probably not very desirable. The lack of serenity in French criticism was produced on the one hand by eccle-

---

2   Cf. Van A. Harvey, *The Historian and the Believer* (1966) Ch.VII

siastical sentiment clinging to the cherished 'myths' of its own origins and, on the other, by anti-ecclesiastical resentments. But the work described above, for all its occasional eccentricities, serves as a reminder of the ever-pressing need for the dispassionate analysis of texts which continue to be interpreted in widely differing ways.

As between 'confessionals' and 'independents' there may be no final agreement, especially concerning the wider significance of their investigations. Certainly, to be independent of Christian commitments and assumptions does not of itself guarantee historical objectivity. But in a field where the confessional concentration of interest is, most understandably, so high, the independent critic of proven historical competence will continue to occupy a significant place.

BIBLIOGRAPHY

(The place of publication is Paris, unless otherwise shown)

A. PRIMARY LITERATURE

(a) *Major published works for the purposes of this study*

1. Alfred Loisy

L'Evangile et l'Eglise (1902); *Autour d'un petit livre* (1903); *Le Quatrième Evangile* (1903); *Les Evangiles Synoptiques* (2 vols 1907–8); *La Religion d'Israël* (1906, revised edition 1933); *Leçon d'ouverture ... au Collège de France* (1909); *Jésus et la tradition évangélique* (1910); *A propos d'Histoire des religions* (1911); *L'Evangile selon Marc* (1912); *Guerre et Religion* (1915, revised edition same year); *Mors et Vita* (1916); *L'Epître aux Galates* (1916); *La Religion* (1917, revised edition 1924); *Les Mystères Païens et le Mystère Chrétien* (1919, revised edition 1930); *Les Actes des Apôtres* (1920); *Essai historique sur le sacrifice* (1920); *Le Quatrième Evangile. Les Epîtres dites de Jean* (1921); *Les Livres du Nouveau Testament* (1922); *L' Apocalypse de Jean* (1923); *L'Evangile selon Luc* (1924); *Les Actes des Apôtres* (abreviated edition 1925); *Mémoires pour servir à l'histoire religieuse de notre temps* (1930–1); *La Naissance du christianisme* (1933); *Le Mandéisme et les origines chrétiennes* (1934); *Remarques sur la littérature épistolaire du Nouveau Testament* (1935); *Les Origines du Nouveau Testament* (1936); *George Tyrrell et Henri Bremond* (1936); *Histoire et mythe à propos de Jésus-Christ* (1938); *Autres mythes à propos de la religion* (1938); *Un mythe apologétique* (1939).

2. Charles Guignebert

Tertullien (1901); *Manuel d'histoire ancienne du christianisme. Les origines* (1906); *Modernisme et tradition catholique en France* (1909); *La Primauté de Pierre et la venue de Pierre à Rome* (1909); *L'Evolution des dogmes* (1910); *Le Problème de Jésus* (1914); *Le Christianisme antique* (1912); *La vie cachée de Jésus* (1921); *Le Christianisme médiéval et moderne* (1922); *Le problème religieux dans la France d'aujourd'hui* (1922); *Jésus* (1933); *Le monde juif vers le temps de Jésus* (1935); *Le Christ* (posth. 1943).

3. Maurice Goguel

L'Apôtre Paul et Jésus-Christ (1904); *L'Eucharistie des origines à Justin Martyr* (1910); *Introduction au Nouveau Testament* (5 vols 1922–6); *Jésus de Nazareth, mythe ou histoire?* (1925); *Au seuil de l'Evangile: Jean Baptiste* (1928); *La Vie de Jésus* (1932, revised edition 1950); *La foi à la résurrection dans le christianisme primitif* (1933); *La Naissance du christianisme* (1946, revised edition 1955); *L'Eglise primitive* (1947); *Les premiers temps de l'Eglise* (1949).

(b) *General information concerning literary output*

1. Alfred Loisy

A bibliography of the published works of Loisy is contained in *Alfred Loisy: Sa Vie – Son Oeuvre* publié par E. Poulat (1960) pp304–23 (263 items listed, including 60 'ouvrages'.)

Some unpublished works, and much correspondence, are to be found in the Départment des Manuscrits of the Bibliothèque Nationale, Paris (n.a.f. 15634–15666). Their contents are listed in *Nouvelles acquisitions latines et françaises du Départment des Manuscrits pendant les années 1965–1968)* (1969) pp110–2.

Further correspondence of Loisy is to be found in other collections at the Bibliothèque Nationale, including the papers of Albert Houtin (n.a.f. 15718), Maria dell'Isola (n.a.f. 16317) and Félix Klein (n.a.f. 14039).

The extracts from Loisy's papers and correspondence which have been published are listed below in Section A.(b)4.

2. Charles Guignebert

A bibliography of the published works of Guignebert is contained in M. Brunot 'Charles Guignebert (1867–1939) Sa Vie et Son Oeuvre' *AnnUnivP* (1939) pp365–80, supplemented by further information in *RH* (1940) pp181–2 (96 items listed, including 17 'ouvrages').

For the unpublished lecture notes, now in the possession of Professor Marcel Simon of Strasbourg, the following abbreviations have been used, with the general prefix GP ('Guignebert Papers'):

(a) *Cours Publics*

ESE	L'Eglise, la Société et l'Etat au IIe et au IIIe s. – Vie externe (1906–7)
VIE2–3	La vie intérieure de l'Eglise au IIe et au IIIe s. (1907–9)
ECC	L'Eglise, le clergé et le culte au IIe et au IIIe s. (1909–10)
CF	L'Union de l'Eglise et de l'Etat au IVe s. – Constantin et ses fils (1910–11).
JT	Julien – Théodose (1911–12).
VIE4	La Vie intérieure de l'Eglise au IVe s. (1912–16).
OMC	Les Origines du monachisme chrétien (1916–17).
GQD	Les grandes querelles doctrinales du Ve s. (1917–18).
RUC	La Rupture de l'unité catholique (1918–19).
IEAC	Introduction à l'étude de l'Antiquité chrétienne (1919–21).
OER	Les Origines de l'Eglise de Rome (1928–9).
EREM	L'Eglise de Rome du la fin du Ier s. à l'Edit de Milan (1929–30).
ER3–4	L'Eglise de Rome au IIIe et IVe s. (1930–31).
OSG	Les Origines du schisme grec (1931–32).
PRR	La Politique religieuse de Rome au Ier et au IIe s. (1932–3).
VRER	La Vie religieuse dans l'Empire romain de Néron à Commode (1933–34).

(b) *Conférences Ouvertes*

1Cor	La Première Epître aux Corinthiens (1915–17)
2Cor	La Seconde Epître aux Corinthiens (1917–18)
Phil	L'Epître aux Philippiens (1918–19)
Rom	L'Epître aux Romains (1919–22)
Col	L'Epître aux Colossiens (1921–22)
QE	Le Quatrième Evangile (1922–25)
Mt	L'Evangile selon Mathieu (1928–33)

3. Maurice Goguel

A bibliography of the published works of Goguel up to c.1941 is contained in *ConNT 10* (1946) pp5–12 (compiled by H. Riesenfeld) (118 items listed, including 16 'ouvrages').

The remaining works of Goguel are given below:

(a) *Books*
La Naissance du christianisme (1946 and 1955)
L'Eglise primitive (1947)
Les Premiers temps de l'Eglise (1949)

(b) *Contributions*
'Christianisme primitif', 'Les premières réalisations du christianisme', 'La stabilisation du christianisme' in *Histoire Générale des Religions*' ed. M. Gorce & R. Mortier t.III (1945) pp171–254.

'Témoignage d'un historien' in *Protestantisme français* ed. M. Boegner & A. Siegfried (1945) pp318—52.

'Introduction', 'Jésus et l'Eglise', 'Les origines de l'organisation de l'Eglise', 'Eglise et Royaume de Dieu' in *Le Problème de l'Eglise* ed. M. Goguel (1947) pp1—30, 45—67, 187—94.

'La critique et la foi' in *Le Problème biblique dans le protestantisme* ed. V. Boisset (1955) pp11—44.

'Le caractère, à la fois actuel et futur, du salut dans la théologie paulinienne' in *Studies in Honour of C.H. Dodd* ed. W.D. Davies & D. Daube (1956) pp322—41.

(c) *Articles*
(i) *Coniectanea Neotestamentica*
    'Observations sur la conception protestante de l'autorité du Nouveau Testament' XI (1947).

(ii) *Revue d'Histoire et de Philosophie Religieuses*
    'De Jésus à l'Apôtre Paul' XXVIII—XXIX (1948—9) pp1—29
    'Ce que l'Eglise doit à l'Apôtre Paul' XXXI (1951) pp157—80
    'Quelques observations sur l'oeuvre de Luc' XXXIII (1953) pp37—51
    'Le livre d'Oscar Cullmann sur Saint Pierre' XXXV (1955) pp199—209

(iii) *Revue de l'Histoire des Religions*
    'Pneumatisme et eschatologie dans le christianisme primitif' CXXXII (1948) pp124—69; CXXXIII (1948) pp103—61
    'La seconde génération chrétienne' CXXXVI (1949) pp31—57, 180—208

(iv) *Revue de Théologie et de Philosophie*
    'Le paulinisme, théologie de liberté' (1951) pp92—104, 175—83

(v) *Svensk Exegetisk Årsbok*
    'Den andra kristna generationens problem' XIV (1949) pp43—87

(vi) *Zeitschrift für Systematische Theologie*
    'Einige Bemerkungen über das Problem der Kirche im Neuen Testament' XV (1938) pp525—43.

4. Published Correspondence etc.

In recent years a considerable amount of correspondence between leading French religious figures of the earlier part of the present century has been published. Much of it centres upon the Modernist crisis; but this growing corpus of literature contains many insights into French religious life generally. Not all of it is strictly relevant to the present thesis, but it is convenient to indicate the range of this extremely valuable source material. Further extracts appear in other more general works, including some of those listed under 'Catholic Modernism' in B.3. below

(a) *Books*
Correspondence Blondel-Valensin ed. H.de Lubac 3 vols. (1957—65)
Correspondence Blondel-Laberthonnière ed. C. de Tresmontant (1961)
Correspondence Blondel-Teilhard de Chardin ed. H. de Lubac (1965)
Correspondence Blondel-Wehrlé ed. H. de Lubac 2 vols. (1969)
Correspondence Blondel-Bremond ed. A. Blanchet 3 vols. (1970—2)
Correspondence Bremond-Tyrrell ed. A. Louis-David (1971)
Laberthonnière et ses amis ed. M.—T. Perrin (1975)

The Centro Studi per la Storia del Modernismo of the Univeristy of Urbino is publishing successive volumes of *Fonti e Documenti*, mainly in the form of correspondence. Volume I (1972) includes correspondence of Houtin with Buonaiuti, Rossi and Turchi, and of Paul Sabatier with Buonaiuti, Rossi and Quadrotta (ed. L. Bedeschi); and correspondence of Loisy with Buonaiuti, Piastrelli and Cento (ed. M. Guasco). Volume II (1973) includes further correspondence of Paul Sabatier (various editors) and correspondence of Loisy with Modernist sympathisers in Lombardy (ed. M. Guasco). M. Guasco has gathered the Loisy material together in *Alfred Loisy in Italia* (1975)

(b) *Articles*

M. Bécamel, 'Lettres de Loisy à Mgr. Mignot' *BLE* 1966 pp3–44, 81–114, 170–94, 257–68; 1968 pp241–68.

H. Bernard-Maître, 'Lettres d'Henri Bremond à Alfred Loisy' *BLE* 1968 pp3–24, 161–84, 269–89; 1969 pp44–56.

H. Bernard-Maître, 'Un épisode significatif du modernisme' *RScR* 1969 pp49–74.

M. Delcor, 'A propos de la question biblique en France — une correspondence inédite de l'époque moderniste' *BLE* 1969 pp199–219.

B. Neveu, 'Lettres de Mgr. Duchesne, Directeur de l'Ecole Française de Rome, à Alfred Loisy (1896–1917) et à Friedrich von Hügel (1895–1920)' *MEFRM* 84 (1972) pp283–307, 559–99.

N. Provencher, 'Un inédit d'Alfred Loisy' *Egl Th* 1973 pp391–413

E. Goichot, 'En marge de la crise moderniste: la correspondence Bremond-Von Hügel' *RScR* 1974 pp209–34; 1975 pp202–33.

A.H. Jones, 'The Correspondence between Alfred Loisy and Nathan Söderblom, 1901–27' *DR* 1976 pp261–75.

B. *SECONDARY LITERATURE*

1. *Studies of Loisy, Guignebert and Goguel*

M. Bécamel, 'Monseigneur Mignot et Alfred Loisy' *BLE* 1969 pp267–86.

J. Bonsirven, 'Loisy' *DB (Suppl)* Vol.5 (1957) col.530–43.

R. de Boyer de Sainte-Suzanne, *Alfred Loisy entre la foi et l'incroyance* (1968)

M. Brunot, 'Charles Guignebert (1867–1939) Sa Vie et son oeuvre' *AnnUnivP* 1939 pp365–80.

M. Brunot, 'Alfred Loisy' *RHR* 153 (1958) pp142–6

O. Cullmann, 'Maurice Goguel 1880–1955' *AnnEPHE* 1955, reprinted in *Vorträge und Aufsätze 1925–1962* (Tübingen and Zürich 1966) pp667–74.

P. Desjardins, *Catholicisme et critique — Réflexions d'un profane sur l'affaire Loisy* (1905)

T.F. Glasson, 'Loisy on New Testament Origins' *ModCh* XLI (1951) pp317–23.

M. Goguel, 'Charles Guignebert' *RHR* CXX (1939) pp212–5.

M. Goguel, 'Alfred Loisy' *RHR* CXXII (1940) pp180–6.

P. Guérin, 'La pensée religieuse d'Alfred Loisy' *RHPR* XXXVII (1957) pp294–330.

J. Guitton, *La Pensée de M. Loisy* (1936), reprinted in *Oeuvres Complètes —Critique religieuse* (1968) pp187–268.

J. Guitton, 'Souvenirs sur les relations entre M. Loisy et M. Bergson' *Mémorial J. Chaine* (Lyon 1950) pp186–202.

M. Dell'Isola, *Alfred Loisy — Entretiens et souvenirs* (Parma 1957)

F. Heiler, *Der Vater des katholischen Modernismus — Alfred Loisy* (Munich 1947)

L.P. Jacks, 'A Creed in Harmony with Modern Thought' *HJ* 23 (1924–5) pp577–87.

E. Lacoste, *Les dernières semaines d'Alfred Loisy, suivi de quelques souvenirs* (Lille 1963)

M.–J. Lagrange, *M. Loisy et le modernisme* (1932)

"S. Leblanc" (II. Bremond), *Un clerc qui n'a pas trahi: Alfred Loisy d'après ses Mémoires* (1931), reprinted with variants and 'dossier historique' in E. Poulat, *Une Oeuvre clandestine d'Henri Bremond* (Rome 1972)

F. Lafèvre, *Une Heure avec ... Première série* (1924) pp193–201: 'Alfred Loisy'.

M. Lepin, *Les Théories de M. Loisy — Exposé et critique* (1908)

M. Lepin, *Le Problème de Jésus — en réponse à MM. A. Loisy et Ch. Guignebert* (1936)

A. Loisy and M. Simon, 'Nécrologie — Charles Guignebert' *RH* 1940 pp179–82.

P. Menoud, 'Maurice Goguel 1880–1955' *VerbC* IX (1955) pp1–7.

A. Omodeo, *Alfredo Loisy, Storico delle·Religioni* (Bari 1936)

M. Petre, *Alfred Loisy — His Religious Significance* (1944)

E. Poulat (ed), *Alfred Loisy: Sa Vie — son oeuvre par Albert Houtin et Félix Sartiaux* (1960)

M. Simon, 'The Birth of Christianity: Loisy, Guignebert, Goguel' *FF* 1948 pp135–9.

M. Simon, 'Les origines chrétiennes d'après l'oeuvre de Maurice Goguel' *RH* 1949 pp221–31.

V. Taylor, 'The Alleged Neglect of M. Alfred Loisy' *HJ* 24 (1926) pp563–72, reprinted in *New Testament Essays* (1970) pp72–82.

H.G. Wood, 'The Radical French Critics, Guignebert and Loisy' *HJ* 52 (1953–4) pp144–55, reprinted in *Jesus in the Twentieth Century* (1960) pp96–110.

2. *Catholicism in France*

P. Alfaric, *De la foi à la raison* (1955)

R. Aubert, *La Théologie catholique au milieu du XXe siècle* (1954)

G. Baron, *Marcel Jousse – Introduction à sa vie et à son oeuvre* (1965)

P. Batiffol, *Questions d'enseignement supérieur ecclésiastique* (1907)

A. Baudrillart, *Vie de Mgr. d'Hulst*, 2 vols. (1912–4)

M. Bécamel, 'Le P. Joseph Bonsirven et Mgr. Mignot' *BLE* 1970 pp262–73.

P. Beillevert, *Laberthonnière, l'homme et l'oeuvre* (1972)

A. Blanchet, *Henri Bremond 1865–1904* (1975)

J. Brugerette, *Le Prêtre français et la société contemporaine* 3 vols. (1933–8)

J. Calès, *Le Père F. Prat S.J.* (1942)

J. Calvet, *Visages d'un demi-siècle* (1958)

J. Calvet, *Mémoires* (1967)

(Colloque d'Aix) *Henri Bremond 1865–1933* (Aix-en-Provence 1967)

(Colloque de l'Ecole Française de Rome) *Monseigneur Duchesne et son temps* (1975)

(Comité catholique de propagande française à l'étranger) *La Vie catholique dans la France contemporaine* (1918)

J.M. Connolly, *The Voices of France: a Survey of Contemporary Theology in France* (New York 1961)

J. Dagens and M. Nédoncelle, *Entretiens sur Henri Bremond* (1967)

A. Dansette, *Histoire religieuse de la France contemporaine* 2 vols. (1948–51); abridged ET Freiburg 1961

A. Dansette, *Destin du catholicisme français 1926–1956* (1957)

P. d'Espezel, 'Duchesne (Louis-Marie-Oliver)' *DHGE* (1959) col.965–84.

P. Fernessole, *Témoins de la pensée catholique en France sous la IIIe république* (1940)

C. Guignebert, 'Louis Duchesne' *RH* 141 (1922) pp307–14.

H. Hemmer, *Monsieur Portal* (1947); ET (adapted) London 1961

E. Hocedez, *Histoire de la théologie au XIXe siècle*, vol.3 'Le règne de Léon XIII 1878–1903' (1952)

A. Houtin, *Un prêtre symboliste: Marcel Hébert (1851–1916)* (1925)

A. Houtin, *Une vie de prêtre: mon expérience (1967–1912)* (1926); ET London 1927

A. Houtin, *Mon expérience II: ma vie laïque (1912–1926)* (1928)

F. Klein, *La Route du petit Morvandiau* 7 vols. (1946–52)

R. Ladous, *L'Abbé Portal et la campagne anglo-romaine* (Lyon 1973)

J. Lebreton, *Le Père Léonce de Grandmaison* (1935)

E. Lecanuet, *La Vie de l'Eglise sous Léon XIII* (1930)

E. Magnin, *Un demi-siècle de pensée catholique* (1937)

J. McManners, *Church and State in France 1870–1914* (1972)

E.–I. Mignot, *Lettres sur les études ecclésiastiques* (1908)

E.–I. Mignot, *L'Eglise et la critique* (1910)

H.W. Paul, 'In Quest of Kerygma: Catholic Intellectual Life in Nineteenth Century France' *AmHistR* LXXV (1969) pp387–423.

P.–L. Péchenard, *L'Institut catholique de Paris 1875–1901* (1902)

E. Poulat, 'Un problème: catholicisme et libéralisme en France sous Pie X' *Les Catholiques libéraux au XIXe siècle* (Colloque de Grenoble 1974)

B.M.G. Reardon, *Liberalism and Tradition: Aspects of Catholic Thought in Nineteenth Century France* (Cambridge 1975)

F. Sartiaux, *Joseph Turmel – prêtre, historien des dogmes* (1931)

A. Siegfried, *L'Abbé Frémont* 2 vols. (1932)

W.J. Sparrow-Simpson, *French Catholics in the Nineteenth Century* (London 1918)

J. Turmel, *Comment j'ai donné congé aux dogmes* (1935)

J. Turmel, *Comment l'église romaine m'a donné congé* (1937)

G. Weill, *Histoire du catholicisme libéral en France 1828–1908* (1909)

J. Wilbois, 'La pensée catholique en France au commencement du XXe siècle' *RMM* 1907 pp377–400, 526–58.

3. Catholic Modernism

Anon., *Il Programma dei modernisti* (Rome 1908); ET London 1908

L. Barmann, *Baron Friedrich von Hügel and the Modernist Crisis in England* (Cambridge 1972)

M. Blondel, *Letter on Apologetics and History and Dogma* ed. A. Dru & I. Trethowan (London 1964)

J. Brucker, *Les 'Etudes' contre le modernisme de 1888 à 1907* (1914)

E. Buonaiuti, *Le modernisme catholique* (1927)

L. da Veiga Coutinho, *Tradition et histoire dans la controverse moderniste (1898–1910)* (Rome 1954)

A. Fawkes, *Studies in Modernism* (London 1913)

H. Gouhier, 'Tradition et développement à l'époque du modernisme', *Ermeneutica e Tradizione* ed. E. Castelli (Rome 1963)

M. Guasco, 'Per la storia del modernismo: al di là dei documenti' *Humanitas* 1974 pp209–15.

J.J. Heaney, *The Modernist Crisis: Von Hügel* (London 1969)

K. Holl, *Modernismus* (Tübingen 1908)

A. Houtin, *Histoire du modernisme catholique* (1913)

F. von Hügel, *Essays and Addresses* 2 vols. (London and New York 1921–8)

F. von Hügel, *Selected Letters 1896–1924* ed. B. Holland (London & New York 1927)

E. Le Roy, *Dogme et critique* (1906)

H. de Lavallette, 'La fin du dogmatisme' *RScR* 58 (1971) pp179–208.

A.L. Lilley, *Modernism, A Record and a Review* (London 1908)

T.M. Loome, 'The Enigma of Baron Friedrich von Hügel III — As Modernist' *DR* 91 (1973) pp204–30.

R. Marlé, *Au coeur de la crise moderniste; le dossier d'un controverse* (1960)

M. Nédoncelle, *La pensée religieuse de Friedrich von Hügel* (1935); ET London 1937

M.D. Petre, *Autobiography and Life of George Tyrrell* 2 vols. (London 1912)

M.D. Petre, *Modernism: its Failure and its Fruits* (1918)

E. Poulat, *Histoire, dogme et critique dans la crise moderniste* (1962)

E. Poulat, 'Néochristianisme et modernisme autour de Paul Desjardins' *Paul Desjardins et le décades de Pontigny* ed. A. Heurgon-Desjardins (1964)

E. Poulat, 'Critique historique et théologie dans la crise moderniste' *RScR* 58 (1970) pp535–550.

E. Poulat, 'Panorama internazionale della crisi modernista' *Storia Contemporanea* 1971 pp673–83.

E. Poulat, 'Le modernisme, d'hier à aujourd'hui' *RScR* 1971 pp161–78.

M. Ranchetti, *The Catholic Modernists* (Oxford 1969)

J. Ratté, *Three Modernists* (New York 1968)

A.E.J. Rawlinson, *Dogma, Fact, and Experience* (London 1915)

B.M.G. Reardon, *Catholic Modernism* (London 1970)

B.M.G. Reardon, 'Newman and the Catholic Modernist Movement' *CQ* 1971 pp50–60.

J. Rivière, 'Modernisme' *DTC* Vol.X (1928) col. 2009–2047.

J. Rivière, *Le Modernisme dans l'Eglise* (1929)

F. Rodé, *Le Miracle dans la controverse moderniste* (1965)

P. Sabatier, *Modernism* (London 1908)

N. Söderblom, *Religionsproblemet inom Katolicism och Protestantism I Första Boken — Modernismen* (Stockholm 1910)

A. Vidler, *The Modernist Movement in the Roman Church* (Cambridge 1934)

A. Vidler, *A Variety of Catholic Modernists* (Cambridge 1970)

4. *Protestantism in France*

J.R. Beard (ed) *The Progress of Religious Thought as Illustrated in the Protestant Churches of France* (1861)

M. Boegner and A. Siegfried (ed), *Protestantisme français* (1945)

M. Boegner, *L'Exigence oecuménique* (1968); ET London 1970

H. Cordey, *Edmond de Pressensé et son temps (1824—1891)* (Lausanne 1916)

(Faculté de Théologie Protestante de Paris) *Etudes de Théologie et d'Histoire* (1901)

C.T. Gérold, *La Faculté de théologie et le séminaire protestant de Strasbourg 1803—1872* (Strasbourg 1923)

O. Gréard, *Edmond Schérer* (1890)

"Ignotus", 'Protestantisme et modernisme' *RChr* 1909 pp425—33.

E.G. Léonard, *Histoire générale du protestantisme* Vol.III 'Déclin et renouveau' (1964)

E.G. Léonard, *Le Protestant français* (1953)

J. Marty, *Albert Réville: Sa vie — son oeuvre* (1912)

G. Maugain and H. Lemaire, *Paul Sabatier 1858—1928* (1931)

F. Ménégoz, 'La Théologie d'Auguste Sabatier' *RChr* XIV (1901) pp422—30.

F. Ménégoz, 'Symbolo-Fideism' *ERE* Vol.12 (1921) pp151—2.

B.M.G. Reardon, *Liberal Protestantism* (1968)

J. Réville, *Paroles d'un libre croyant* (1898)

J. Réville, *Le Protestantisme libéral, ses origines, sa nature, sa mission* (1903); ET London 1903

J.E. Roberty, 'Notes sur le protestantisme libéral' *RChr* 1910 pp391—407.

E. Rochat, *La Revue de Strasbourg et son influence sur la théologie moderne* (Geneva 1904)

A. Sabatier, *De la vie intime des dogmes* (1890)

A. Sabatier, *Esquisse d'une philosophie de la religion* (1897); ET London 1897

A. Sabatier, *Les Religions d'autorité et la religion de l'esprit* (1903); ET London 1904; new edition with Introduction by G. Marchal: 1956

A. Sabatier, *The Doctrine of the Atonement; Religion in Modern Culture* (London 1904)

T. Silkstone, *Religion, Symbolism and Meaning: a Critical Study of the views of Auguste Sabatier* (Oxford 1968)

J. Viénot et al., *Auguste Sabatier: sa vie, sa pensée et ses travaux* (1903)

J. Viénot, *Auguste Sabatier I La jeunesse 1839—1879* (1927)

G. Weill, 'Le protestantisme français au XIXe siècle' *Revue de Synthèse Historique* XXIII (1911) pp210—39.

5. *Religious Thought and Religious Studies in France*

A. Albalat, *La Vie de Jésus d'Ernest Renan* (1933)

P. Alfaric, *A l'école de la raison* (n.d.)

J. Baruzi, *Problèmes d'histoire des religions* (1935)

H. Berr, *La Synthèse en histoire* (1953)

H. Berr, *La Montée de l'esprit* (1955)

Dom J.—M. Besse, *Les Religions laïques — un romantisme religieux* (1913)

R. Bessède, *La Crise de la conscience catholique dans la littérature et la pensée française à la fin du XIXe siècle* (1975)

G. Bloch (ed), *Lettres inédites d'Anatole France à Paul-Louis Couchoud et à sa femme* (Nos. 99—104 of *Le Lys Rouge* 1968)

J. Boulenger, *Renan et ses critiques* (1925)

J. Bricout, *L'Histoire des religions et la foi chrétienne* (1910)

J. Bricout (ed), *Où en est l'histoire des religions?* 2 vols. (1912)

J.—M. Carré, *Les Ecrivains français et le mirage allemand* (1947)

D.G. Charlton, *Positivist Thought in France during the Second Empire 1852—1870* (Oxford 1959)

D.G. Charlton, *Secular Religions in France 1815—1870* (Oxford 1963)

F. Charpin (ed), *La Question religieuse — Enquête internationale* (1908)

T.N. Clark, *Prophets and Patrons: the French University and the Emergence of the Social Sciences* (Harvard 1973)

(Congrès d'Histoire du christianisme) *Jubilé Alfred Loisy* 3 vols. (1928)

(Congrès International de l'Histoire des Religions) *Actes du premier congrès* 2 vols. (1901); *Centenaire Renan* 2 vols. (1925)

F. Copleston, *A History of Philosophy Vol.IX: Maine de Biran to Sartre* (London 1975)

A. Coutrot and F.—G. Dreyfus, *Les Forces religieuses dans la société française* (1965)

P.—L. Couchoud, *Théophile, ou l'étudiant des religions* (1928)

G. Crespy, *Contemporary Currents of French Theological Thought* (Richmond, Virginia 1965)

H. Daniel-Rops and A. Siegfried, *Edmond Le Roy et son fauteuil* (1956)

H. Delacroix, *La Religion et la foi* (1922)

H. Desroche and J. Séguy (ed) *Introduction aux sciences humaines des religions* (1970)

C. Digeon, *La crise allemande de la pensée française* (1959)

E. Durkheim, 'Le sentiment religieux à l'heure actuelle' *ASR* 27 (1969) pp73—7.

R. Dussaud, *L'Oeuvre scientifique d'Ernest Renan* (1951)

(Ecole Pratique des Hautes Etudes — Section des Sciences Religieuses)
Etudes de critique et d'histoire (1889)
Etudes de critique et d'histoire (deuxième série) (1896)
Problèmes et méthodes d'histoire des religions (1968)

G. Fonsegrive, *De Taine à Péguy: l'évolution des idées dans la France contemporaine* (1920)

R. Griffiths, *The Reactionary Revolution: The Catholic Revival in French Literature 1870—1914* (London 1966)

J. Guitton, *Portrait de M. Pouget* (1941)

J. Guitton, *Dialogues avec M. Pouget* (1954)

J. Guitton, *Ecrire comme on se souvient* (1974)

M. Guyau, *L'Irréligion de l'avenir* (1887)

G. Guy-Grand (ed), *La Renaissance religieuse* (1928)

L. Halphen, *L'Histoire en France depuis cent ans* (1914)

T. Hanna (ed), *The Bergsonian Heritage* (Columbia 1962)

J. Huby (ed), *Christus: Manuel d'Histoire des religions* (1913)

H.S. Hughes, *The Obstructed Path: French Social Thought in the Years of Desperation 1930—1960* (New York 1966)

A.H. Jones, 'The Publication of Salomon Reinach's *Orpheus* and the Question of Christian Origins', *Religion*, Spring 1977 pp46—65.

M.—J. Lagrange, *Quelques remarques sur l'Orpheus de M. Salomon Reinach* (1910); ET 1910

M. Larkin, *Church and State after the Dreyfus Affair: the Separation Issue in France* (London 1974)

S. Lukes, *Emile Durkheim* (Harmondsworth 1973)

J.—M. Mayeur, *L'Histoire religieuse de la France 19e—20e siècle: problèmes et méthodes* (1975)

F. McKenzie, R.C. Knight, J.M. Milner (ed), *Studies in French Language and Literature presented to R.L. Graeme Ritchie* (Cambridge 1949)

A. Mellor, *Histoire de l'anticléricalisme français* (1966)

B. Neveu, 'Louis Canet et le service du conseiller technique pour les affaires religieuses au Ministère des Affaires Etrangères' *RHD* 1968 pp134—80.

H.W. Paul, 'The Debate over the Bankruptcy of Science in 1895' *FrHistS* 5 (1968) pp299—327.

W.S.F. Pickering, *Durkheim on Religion* (London 1975)

J. Pommier, *La Pensée religieuse de Renan* (1925)

E. and O. Poulat, 'Le développement institutionnel des sciences religieuses' *ASR* XXI (1966) pp23—36; reprinted in Desroche and Séguy (ed), *Introduction aux sciences humaines des religions* (1970) pp79—98.

H. Psichari, *Renan d'après lui-même* (1937)

H. Psichari, *Les Convertis de la belle époque* (1971)

P. Sabatier, *L'Orientation religieuse de la France actuelle* (1911)

G.C. Rawlinson, *Recent French Tendencies from Renan to Claudel: a Study in French Religion* (1917)

S. Reinach, *Orpheus* (1909)
S. Reinach, 'De Bello Orphico' *Cultes, mythes, religions* vol.4 (1912) pp438–83.
J. Réville, *Les Phases successives de l'histoire des religions* (1909)
W.J. Sparrow-Simpson, *Religious Thought in France in the Nineteenth Century* (London 1935)
L.S. Stebbing, *Pragmatism and French Voluntarism* (Cambridge 1914)
(Union de libres penseurs et de libres croyants pour la culture morale)
   Dieux et religions (1926)
   •*Jésus et la conscience moderne* (1928)
H.W. Wardman, *Ernest Renan: a Critical Biography* (London 1964)
K.H. Wolff (ed), *Emile Durkheim 1858–1917* (Ohio 1960); reprinted as *Essays on Sociology and Philosophy* (New York 1964)

6. Studies of Early Christianity

E.W. Barnes, *The Rise of Christianity* (London 1947)
P. Batiffol, *Etudes d'histoire et de théologie positve* (1902)
P. Batiffol, *Etudes d'histoire et de théologie positive: deuxième série* (1905)
P. Batiffol, *L'Eglise naissante et le catholicisme* (1909); ET London 1912; new edition with Preface by J. Daniélou: 1971
P. Batiffol, *Orpheus et l'évangile* (1910)
W. Bousset, *Kyrios Christos* (Göttingen 1913); ET 1970
S.G.F. Brandon, *The Fall of Jerusalem and the Christian Church* (London 1951)
R. Bultmann, *Die Geschichte der synoptischen Tradition* (Göttingen 1921); ET 1963
R. Bultmann, *Das Urchristentum im Rahmen der antiken Religionen* (Zürich 1949); ET 1956
P.–L. Couchoud, *Le Mystere de Jésus* (1924); ET 1924
P.–L. Couchoud, *Jésus le dieu fait homme* (1937); ET 1939
P.–L. Couchoud, *Le dieu Jésus* (1951)
"H. Delafosse" (J. Turmel), *Les Ecrits de saint Paul* 4 vols. (1926–8)
E. von Dobschütz, *Problem des apostolischen Zeitalters* (1904)
G. Downing, *The Church and Jesus* (1968)
E. Dujardin, *Le dieu Jésus* (1927)
E. Dujardin, *La première génération chrétienne* (1935)
L. Duchesne, *Les Origines chrétiennes* (n.d., c.1892)
L. Duchesne, *Histoire ancienne de l'église* I (1905)
E. de Faye, *Etude sur les origines des églises de l'âge apostolique* (1909)
L. Goppelt, *Das apostolische und nachapostolische Zeit* (Tübingen 1962); ET London 1970
L. de Grandmaison, *Jésus-Christ* 2 vols. (1931)
H. Grass, *Ostergeschehen und Osterberichte* (Göttingen 4 1970)
A. von Harnack, *Die Mission und Ausbreitung des Christentums in den ersten drei Jahrhunderten* (1902); ET London 1904
A. von Harnack, *Marcion: das Evangelium vom fremden Gott* (Leipzig 1921)
A. von Harnack, *Entstehung und Entwicklung der Kirchenverfassung* (Leipzig 1910); ET London 1910
E.–A.–E. Havet, *Le Christianisme et ses origines* 4 vols. (1878–84)
J. Lebreton and J. Zeiller, *L'Eglise primitive* (1934)
H. Lietzmann, *Geschichte der alten Kirche* 4 vols. (Berlin 1932–44); ET 1938–50
E. Meyer *Ursprung und Anfänge des Christentums* 3 vols. (Berlin 1921–3)
E. Renan, *Les Origines du christianisme* (*La Vie de Jésus* (1863); *Les Apôtres* (1866); *Saint Paul* (1869); *L'Antéchrist* (1873); *Les Evangiles* (1877); *L'Eglise chrétienne* (1879); *Marc-Aurèle* (1882); reprinted in H. Psichari (ed), *Oeuvres Complètes* vols.IV–V)
A. Réville, *Histoire du dogme de la divinité de Jésus-Christ* (1869)
A. Réville, *Jésus de Nazareth* (1897)
J. Réville, *Les Origines de l'épiscopat* (1894)
M. Simon, 'Le christianisme: naissance d'une catégorie historique' *R UnivB* XVIII (1965–6) pp397ff.
M. Simon and A. Benoit, *Le Judaïsme et le christianisme antique* (1968)

G.–A. Van den Bergh van Eysinga, P.–L. Couchoud, R. Stahl, *Les premiers écrits du christianisme* (1930)

J. Weiss, *Das Urchristentum* (1917); ET 1937

C. Weizsäcker, *Das apostolische Zeitalter der christlichen Kirche* (Freiburg 1886); ET London 1894–5

7. History of Interpretation

P. Batiffol, 'The French School of Early Church History' *ConstQ* 1913 pp240–59.

J. Boisset et al., *Le Problème biblique dans le protestantisme* (1955)

F.–M. Braun, *Aspects nouveaux du problème de l'Eglise* (Fribourg 1941)

F.–M. Braun, *L'Oeuvre du Père Lagrange: étude et bibliographie* (Fribourg 1943); ET (adapted) Milwaukee 1963

R. Bultmann, 'Urchistliche Religion (1915–1925)', *ARW* 24 (1926) pp83–164.

J.T. Burtchaell, *Catholic Theories of Biblical Inspiration Since 1810* (Cambridge 1969)

F. Cabrol, 'Mgr. L. Duchesne: son oeuvre historique' *JTS* 24 (1922–3) pp253–81.

E. von Dobschütz, 'Die Kirche im Urchristentum' *ZNW* 28 (1929) pp107–18.

L. Duchesne, 'Lettre à un ami' *RMI* III (1912) pp24–32, 64–76.

E. Dujardin, *Grandeur et décadence de la critique* (1931)

J. Dupont, *Les Problèmes du livre des Actes d'après les travaux récents* (Louvain 1950)

J. Dupont, *Les Sources du livre des Actes* (Bruges 1960); ET (revised) London 1964

C.W. Emmett, *The Eschatological Question in the Gospels and other Studies in Recent New Testament Criticism* (Edinburgh 1911)

W.W. Gasque, *A History of the Criticism of the Acts of the Apostles* (Tübingen 1975)

K.P. Gertz, *Joseph Turmel (1859–1943): ein theologiegeschichtlicher Beitrag zum Problem der Geschichtlichkeit der Dogmen* (Bern & Franfkurt 1975)

P. de Haes, *La Résurrection de Jésus dans l'apologétique des cinquante dernières années* (Rome 1953)

J. Héring, 'De H.J. Holtzmann à Albert Schweitzer' in *Ehrfurcht vor dem Leben* (Schweitzer Festschrift, Bonn 1954) pp21–9.

A. Houtin, *La Question biblique chez les catholiques au XIXe siècle* (1902)

A. Houtin, *La Question biblique au XXe siècle* (1906)

J. Huby, *Les Mythomanes de l'Union Rationaliste: MM. Alfaric, Couchoud, Bayet* (1933)

S.J. Johnson, 'The Emergence of the Christian Church in the Catholic Period' in *The Study of the Bible Today and Tomorrow* (Chicago 1947) pp345–65.

W. Klatt, *Hermann Gunkel* (Göttingen 1969)

W.G. Kümmel, 'Urchristentum' *ThR* 14 (1942) pp81–95, 155–73; 17 (1948–9) pp3–50, 103–42; 18 (1950) pp1–53.

W.G. Kümmel, *Das Neue Testament: Geschichte der Erforschung seiner Probleme* (Munich 1970); ET London 1973

M.–J. Lagrange, *La Méthode historique* (1903); ET London 1906

M.–J. Lagrange, *Le Sens du christianisme d'après l'exégèse allemande* (1918); ET London, 1920

(M.–J. Lagrange) *L'Oeuvre exégétique et historique du Père Lagrange* (1935) *Le Père Lagrange au service de la Bible* (1967)

Dom H. Leclercq, 'Historiens du christianisme' *DACL* IV (1925) col.2533–2735.

O. Linton, *Das Problem der Urkirche* (Uppsala 1932)

A.C. McGiffert and J.W. Hunkin, 'The History of Criticism' in *The Beginnings of Christianity* Vol.II Part III (1920) pp363–433.

C. Maignial, 'Brèves notations sur le mythisme dans l'histoire des religions et devant la foi' *Cahiers du Cercle Ernest Renan* No.82 (1973)

B.M. Metzger, 'Considerations of Methodology in the Study of the Mystery Religions and Early Christianity' *HTR* XLVIII (1955) pp1–20.

R. Murphy (ed), *Lagrange and Biblical Renewal* (Chicago 1966)

R. Morgan, *The Nature of New Testament Theology* (London 1973)

J. Pommier, *Renan et Strasbourg* (1926)

L. Saltet, *La Question Herzog-Dupin* (1908)

L. Salvatorelli, 'From Locke to Reitzenstein: The Historical Investigation of the Origins of

Christianity' *HTR* XXII (1929) pp263—367.

A. Schweitzer, *Von Reimarus zu Wrede* (1906); ET London 1910; 2nd edn: *Geschichte der Leben-Jesu-Forschung* (1913)

A. Schweitzer, *Die Geschichte der paulinischen Forschung* (1911); ET London 1912

B.B. Scott, *Adolf von Harnack and Alfred Loisy: a Debate on the Historical Methodology of Christian Origins* (unpublished Ph.D. dissertation, Vanderbilt University, Nashville, Tennessee 1971)

J. Steinmann, *Richard Simon et les origines de l'exégèse biblique* (1960)

H. Windisch, 'Urchristentum' *ThR* 5 (1933) pp186—200, 239—58, 289—301, 319—34.

INDEX OF NAMES